Friends for Keeps

Dorothy Eaton Watts

REVIEW AND HERALD® PUBLISHING ASSOCIATION
HAGERSTOWN, MD 21740

All Bible quotations are from the King James Version unless otherwise credited.

Bible texts credited to Amplified are from *The Amplified Bible*. Copyright © 1965 by Zondervan Publishing House. Used by permission.

Scriptures credited to ICB are quoted from the *International Children's Bible, New Century Version*, copyright © 1983, 1986, 1988 by Word Publishing, Dallas, Texas 75039. Used by permission.

Bible texts credited to Moffatt are from: *The Bible: A New Translation*, by James Moffatt. Copyright by James Moffatt 1954. Used by permission of Harper & Row, Publishers, Incorporated.

Scripture quotations marked NASB are from the *New American Standard Bible*, © The Lockman Foundation 1960, 1962, 1963, 1968, 1971, 1972, 1973, 1975, 1977.

Texts credited to NIV are from the *Holy Bible, New International Version*. Copyright © 1973, 1978, 1984, International Bible Society. Used by permission of Zondervan Bible Publishers.

Texts credited to NKJV are from The New King James Version. Copyright © 1979, 1980, 1982, Thomas Nelson, Inc., Publishers.

Bible texts credited to NRSV are from the New Revised Standard Version of the Bible, copyright © 1989 by the Division of Christian Education of the National Council of the Churches of Christ in the U.S.A. Used by permission.

Bible texts credited to Phillips are from J. B. Phillips: *The New Testament in Modern English*, Revised Edition. © J. B. Phillips 1958, 1960, 1972. Used by permission of Macmillan Publishing Co., Inc.

Bible texts credited to RSV are from the Revised Standard Version of the Bible, copyright © 1946, 1952, 1971, by the Division of Christian Education of the National Council of the Churches of Christ in the U.S.A. Used by permission.

Verses marked TLB are taken from *The Living Bible*, copyright © by Tyndale House Publishers, Wheaton, Ill. Used by permission.

This book was
Edited by Richard W. Coffen
Designed by DeLaine Mayden
Typeset: Optima 9.5/10.5

PRINTED IN U.S.A.

98 97 96 95   5 4 3 2 1

Library of Congress Cataloging in Publication Data
Watts, Dorothy Eaton, 1937-
        Friends for keeps / Dorothy Eaton Watts.
            p.   cm.

        1. Friendship—Prayer-books and devotions—English.   I. Title.
BV4647.F7W36   1995
242'.2—dc20   95-37640
                                                  CIP

ISBN 0-8280-0923-6

Meet Dorothy Eaton Watts

The author of this year's daily devotional enjoys birding, hiking, and gardening as leisure-time activities. Her companion on outdoor adventures is Matanuska Gold Nugget, a golden retriever. A lover of animals, Mrs. Watts has had a variety of pets, including a python and three monkeys. She collects antiques, biographies, and stories for children.

The Watts have three grown children: David, Esther, and Stephen. They have five grandchildren. At the time this book was written, Mrs. Watts lived in British Columbia, where her husband was the conference president.

Mrs. Watts grew up in the hills of southern Ohio and attended Mount Vernon Academy, Columbia Union College, and Andrews University. Married to a pastor, she has lived in British Columbia, Manitoba, Saskatchewan, and Ontario in Canada; as well as Oregon, Michigan, Maryland, and Alaska in the United States. She spent 16 years as a missionary in India.

Mrs. Watts trained as an elementary teacher and is presently a freelance author, editor, and speaker. She has edited both the children's and junior editions of *Mission*. This is her twelfth book and her third junior devotional. The other two were *This Is the Day* (1983) and *Stepping Stones* (1988).

This book grew out of her church school Week of Prayer seminar called "Making Friends" and an adult seminar entitled "Building Better Relationships." She has presented her relationships seminars at churches, schools, camp meetings, and women's retreats.

MAKING FRIENDS

Kent's New Friend

MAKING FRIENDS

Be friendly to others, and they'll be friendly to you. Be interested in others, and they'll be interested in you.

Kent sat staring out the window while his friend Craig studied nearby. His eye moved to the parking lot, where someone had just gotten out of a car. "Oh, no!" Kent frowned. "I don't want to run into *him!*"

Craig looked out the window to see one of Kent's teachers from the year before crossing the parking lot. "Why not?" he asked.

"He doesn't like me. Last spring he got mad at something I said in class."

"Oh?" Craig chuckled. "He probably thinks you don't like him, so he's not being friendly to you. People usually like people who like them. Why don't you go down there and talk to him?"

"Are you kidding?"

"Of course not! Go try it!"

Maybe Craig knows what he's talking about, Kent thought. *After all, he's one of the most popular guys in school.*

"I'll give it a try!" Kent said, a grin spreading across his face. "Let's see if you're right!"

Kent felt a little strange walking across the parking lot to catch up with his professor. What if the teacher ignored him or made some comment about his behavior the year before?

"Hi!" Kent said. "How was your summer?"

"Kent! Good to see you!" his teacher said with a smile. "It was great! Tell me about yours."

Kent adjusted his stride to his teacher's as they walked across the sun-dappled campus. Kent felt warm inside. He was accepted. He'd just made a new friend!

"It really works!" Kent later confessed to Craig.

"Sure it does!" Craig nodded. "People aren't judging you when you meet, they're too busy worrying about how you may be judging them! People need to be connected. They want friends. If we take the initiative, they'll almost always respond to our friendliness. Be interested in people, and they'll be interested in you. What you give is what you get."

"Cool!" Kent said. "No wonder you have so many friends!"

Tony's Invitation

"Did you invite Tony to your birthday party?" Mother asked Patty at breakfast one morning.

"Oh, Mom, I don't want to invite Tony! He's Italian, and he's not even friendly! He's weird!"

"He's just shy," Mother countered. "You'd be shy too if you moved to a new country where you didn't know anyone. It's no sin to be shy!"

"Mom, do I *have* to?"

"No, you don't *have* to, but I think you should give him a chance. You might make a new friend!"

Patty thought about it all day. At last she made out an invitation to Tony. *He probably won't come anyway,* she thought.

But Tony was one of the first to arrive at Patty's party. He smiled as he handed her a gift tied with a big red bow. Later he beamed as she opened it and exclaimed over the delicate white lace collar inside.

"My mother made it!" Tony said.

The card that came with the gift said *"Buon campleano!"*

"That means 'Happy Birthday' in Italian," Tony explained.

"How do you say 'Thank you' in your language?" Patty asked.

"Grazie."

"Grazie!" Patty repeated, holding up her new collar. *"Grazie!"*

"Teach us some more words!" one of the girls said. "How do you say 'Hello'?"

"Buon giorno," Tony replied.

"Buon giorno," the children repeated.

"Can anyone think of another game to play?" Patty asked when the refreshments were finished.

"I know some games we play in Italy," Tony suggested.

"Yes! Yes!" Patty's friends gathered around. "That would be fun! Tony, teach us some Italian games."

That night as Patty helped her mother clean up after the party, she confided, "I'm really glad I asked Tony to my party. He may be shy, but he's lots of fun! In fact, I think he was even more fun because he's from another country!"

DO NOT FORGET TO ENTERTAIN STRANGERS. HEBREWS 13:2, NIV.

MAKING FRIENDS

Shy people are waiting for someone else to make the first move of friendship. Is there anyone new in your neighborhood?

Rosalynn's Fear

"I WAS AFRAID BECAUSE I WAS NAKED; SO I HID." GENESIS 3:10, NIV.

MAKING FRIENDS

Fear of rejection can keep us from making friends with God and with each other. Friends will accept us, so what's there to fear?

Why is making friends often difficult?

We can find the answer in the story of Adam and Eve. God came looking for them, wanting to be their friend. But they ran away and hid because they were embarrassed and afraid of what He would say.

People have been hiding ever since. We hide not only from God, but also from each other. We're afraid of rejection. We think, *What if he doesn't like me? What if she doesn't want to be my friend?* It hurts to be rejected, so we hide to keep from getting hurt.

Rosalynn Smith was like most of us. She wanted to be liked. She did her best to make sure she was the kind of girl others would choose as a friend.

Her house in Plains, Georgia, was only a couple blocks from school. Every day she walked past her father's garage to eat lunch at home.

One day as she walked past the garage, her dad called out, "Rosalynn, where are you going?"

"Home for lunch," Rosalynn replied.

Mr. Smith began to chuckle. He dropped his tools and laughed harder.

"What's so funny?" she asked.

"It's not lunchtime yet," he said, looking at his watch. "It's recess!"

Rosalynn burst into tears. "I'm so stupid! Now everyone will laugh at me! I'm so embarrassed! I can't go back. I'm going home."

"Now, that's silly!" Mr. Smith said. "So what if they laugh? You're going right back to school where you belong."

"Please, Daddy, no!"

But Mr. Smith was firm, and Rosalynn went back to school, where everyone laughed at her all over again. Rosalynn felt humiliated and was sure she'd never have a friend again as long as she lived!

Now that Rosalynn is grown up and has become Rosalynn Carter, the wife of former United States president Jimmy Carter, she knows her fears were unfounded. Her friends enjoyed the joke, but they were still her friends.

George's Patience

"Go back to Africa!"

George Haley pretended not to hear. He walked quickly through the halls crowded with White students. He could feel their hate, and it hurt bad.

George, one of the first Black students to be admitted to the White school, had been accepted by the teachers but not by the students! They sent him ugly notes. They harassed him. They refused to sit beside him.

One day at an intersection a carload of students tried to run him down. He scrambled out of the way, falling on his face in the gutter. Above the spin of wheels, he heard, "Hey, missing link, why don't you walk on your hind legs?"

It was 1949, and George had chosen to attend that school because he wanted to help break down the wall of prejudice between Whites and Blacks. He wanted to be friends with the White students, but they wouldn't let him. Finally he wrote to his father, sharing his frustrations.

His dad responded, "They act the way they do out of fear. Be patient with them. Give them a chance to know you."

It was hard to be patient, but George kept trying. Things got better the second year. However, it wasn't until his third year that he got up courage to go to the cafeteria.

As he approached a table, someone jostled him, sending his tray flying. It seemed everyone was laughing as he retrieved his lunch.

But there was one who didn't laugh. Miller Williams came to his side. "I'd like to eat with you," he said, smiling. "What's happening here isn't right, and I'm taking my stand with you."

That was the turning point for George Haley (brother of Alex Haley, author of *Roots*). Miller introduced his friends to George. They began to see that prejudice had kept them from knowing a really neat guy. He soon was surrounded by friends. During his senior year they chose him to edit their school paper.

WHEN THE WAY IS ROUGH, YOUR PATIENCE HAS A CHANCE TO GROW. JAMES 1:3, TLB.

MAKING FRIENDS:

Be patient with people. Give them a chance to know you. Is there someone of another race who might become your friend if you give him or her half a chance?

9

Friends Are Not Afraid

BUT PERFECT LOVE DRIVES OUT FEAR. 1 JOHN 4:18, NIV.

MAKING FRIENDS

A friend isn't afraid to take us in when the whole world has shut us out.

Don Bartlett couldn't help it that people were afraid of him. He was born with only half a nose, no upper lip, and a cleft palate. No one could understand him when he tried to speak. Further, he was born to a Native American family who had no money to help him.

His classmates showed their fear by refusing to play with him at recess. They tried to chase him away with insults: "Flat nose, flat nose, you can't talk!" or "Smelly Injun" or "Donald Duck, say quack, quack."

Teachers seemed afraid of him too. He overheard one teacher say, "Why did the principal put him in *my* room?"

Another responded, "I don't want him in my room either!"

"I was aching for someone to be my friend, to accept me, to love me, to help me learn to talk!" Don says about his childhood.

Then one day a well-educated lady who lived in a beautiful home sent for him. "I want you to wash my car," she said smiling her acceptance.

Don stood there speechless, not knowing what to do. "I had never done that," he says. "I didn't even know water came out of a faucet."

The lady understood. She took Don gently by the hand and led him to the faucet, showing him how to turn it on. Again she put her hand over his and demonstrated how to wash the car.

"I cannot very well describe that feeling I had when she touched my hand," Don says. "She accepted me. She came into my lonely life."

Don's new friend continued to help him. She taught him to talk. When necessary, she put her fingers into his mouth to show him how to move his tongue. Through her encouragement, he continued school. He finished university with a Doctor of Philosophy degree. Eventually he became a well-known speaker on the needs of those with disabilities.

And wherever Don Bartlett speaks, he tells of the lady who wasn't afraid to accept him despite his handicap.

Jesus Accepts Us

Wendy sat in the London stadium as she listened to Billy Graham tell about his Best Friend, Jesus.

"Jesus will never drive you away, no matter what you have done," Pastor Graham said. "He's a Friend who will never reject you. He accepts you just as you are. Won't you come to Him today?"

Wendy had a hard time believing that Jesus really would accept her after all the bad things she'd done. Ruth Graham, the evangelist's wife, tried to help her. One evening before the meeting, Ruth told Wendy, "One day you'll come to something difficult in your life. And then you'll either go back on drugs or go on with Christ."

Several days later Ruth was sitting in the stadium when someone handed her a note from Wendy. "I'm on drugs again," the note said. "Come help me."

Ruth left her seat and went in search of Wendy. She found her with another girl near the stadium entrance.

"Wendy's best friend died this afternoon from an overdose," the girl explained. "She's really upset."

"Wendy! Wendy!" Ruth put her arm around the dazed girl, but there was no response. Then she opened her purse to look for some paper on which to write a note. All she could find was a package of Kleenex tissues. She took out the cardboard and quickly wrote: "God loves me. Jesus died for me. No matter what I've done, if I confess to Him He will forgive me."

She tucked the cardboard into Wendy's pocket and asked one of the crusade staff members to take the girl home.

A year later Ruth Graham was again in London. A smiling young woman greeted her. "I'm Wendy," the girl said. "Remember that note you put in my pocket? I read it again and again. It became my lifeline to God. I accepted Jesus as my friend, and He has made all the difference!"

WHOEVER COMES TO ME I WILL NEVER DRIVE AWAY. JOHN 6:37, NIV.

MAKING FRIENDS

Jesus wants to be your friend. He'll never reject you. He accepts you just as you are and loves you more than any other friend could ever love you.

Jeanne Was Different

FOR THERE IS NO DIFFERENCE BETWEEN JEW AND GENTILE— THE SAME LORD IS LORD OF ALL. ROMANS 10:12, NIV.

MAKING FRIENDS

Friends accept us as a total package. The wrappings of race, nationality, and culture don't make a difference between real friends. It's what's inside the package that counts!

Everyone stared as Jeanne Wakatsuki walked into the sixth-grade classroom. Jeanne smiled. *I hope they like me,* she thought as she shyly glanced around the room.

No one smiled back. No one spoke to her during recess. She stood alone waiting for someone to ask her to join their group. No one did. *I wonder why no one speaks to me?* she thought. That afternoon she discovered why.

It happened during reading period. "Please read the next page, Jeanne," the teacher said.

Everyone turned to stare as she began to read. She read clearly, making no mistakes.

Radine, the girl who sat in front of Jeanne, turned around and whispered, "I didn't know you could speak English!"

Jeanne smiled back, but inside she began to understand what it was going to be like to be the only Japanese girl in her class. She felt unaccepted, shut out. It didn't feel good to be seen as someone foreign, someone different, someone who didn't belong.

Jeanne decided to try that much harder to be accepted. She became a good student and a star athlete. She worked on the school newspaper and yearbook. She was kind, helpful, and friendly to all. She tried hard to make people forget she was Japanese.

Radine, her best friend, belonged to the Girl Scouts. *I wish Radine would ask me to join,* Jeanne thought. But Radine never did. So Jeanne decided to bring up the subject. "I want to join Girl Scouts," she said. "Can I belong?"

Radine's friendly face turned to a frown. "I don't know. But we can sure find out. My mom's the assistant troop leader."

The next day she reported, "Jeanne, Mom says no. I'm sorry."

"That's OK," Jeanne replied with a smile. But inside she felt angry and hurt. She had thought Radine was her friend. Why did people have to shut her out because she was of a different race, nationality, and culture?

Maya's Lavender Dress

Maya watched her grandma stitch ruffles on the hem of the lavender taffeta dress. She loved the look of the shiny material and the rustling sound it made.

"I wish it were new," Grandma sighed. "I've cut up one of my old dresses to make it."

"It's beautiful!" Maya exclaimed. "I'm going to look like a movie star on Sunday!"

"Clothes aren't everything!" Grandma cautioned. "You'd better be learning your part for the program!"

All Maya could think about for days was her wonderful lavender dress with the ruffles. *The other girls will want to be my friends when they see my new dress,* she thought.

She imagined people crowding around her after the program to say, "Maya, how lovely you are!"

However, when Sunday came, the dress didn't work the magic that Maya had planned. The girls giggled at the noise her dress made as she squeezed past them to say her part. She felt a churchful of eyes staring at her skinny legs and cut-down old-lady dress. Her knees shook, and her hands felt cold and wet.

"What are you looking at me for?

"I didn't come to stay . . . to stay . . . to stay . . ."

Maya's mind went blank. Her face felt hot, and she couldn't remember the rest of the verse. Her eyes sought out the minister's wife. She wasn't laughing. "I just came to tell you, it's Easter Day," the minister's wife prompted.

Maya repeated the words, just above a whisper, and then she bolted from the platform and past the rows of giggling girls. Embarrassed, she didn't stop until she was all the way home.

Like Maya, many of us are hung up on clothes. We know better, but we still envy people who look like they walked out of a fashion magazine. However, we might miss knowing some really terrific people just because they look like something that tumbled out of the Dorcas cupboard.

JAN. 8

"MAN LOOKS AT THE OUTWARD APPEARANCE, BUT THE LORD LOOKS AT THE HEART." 1 SAMUEL 16:7, NIV.

MAKING FRIENDS

The brand of athletic shoes has nothing to do with whether or not the person will make a good friend. Jesus doesn't judge people by their designer jeans, and neither should we.

13

Ted's Artificial Leg

"GOD HAS SHOWN ME THAT I SHOULD NOT CALL ANY MAN IMPURE OR UNCLEAN." ACTS 10:28, NIV.

MAKING FRIENDS

People with cancer and other disabilities want to be accepted and treated as normal people. Make a list of the people you know who have cancer or a physical handicap. Choose one to be your friend.

What's it like to be a teenager with one leg? How does it feel to have cancer, lose all your hair during chemotherapy, and have to go back to school bald?

Ted Kennedy, Jr., knows it isn't much fun. People stare at you, whisper behind your back, and act as if cancer were contagious and your artificial leg dangerous to their health.

"People are taught that we should look perfect," Ted told an interviewer. "We see all kinds of ads on television. I didn't think I'd get a date in the world. I thought, *What girl would want to go out with some kid with one leg?*"

Ted is lucky that he had family and friends who accepted him just as he was—one leg missing, but still someone who could be lots of fun to have around.

Once Ted was riding on the back of a friend's bicycle when the front wheel hit a bump, toppling the bicycle, sending both boys flying. When Ted got up, his artificial foot was pointing backward.

He reached down, twisted it around the right way, and walked off. People stared in disbelief. He and his friend had a good laugh about that!

Ted's family and friends wouldn't allow him to feel sorry for himself. They included him in everything from ski trips to football games. His cousins threw the ball to him just as hard as they would to anybody else. They never allowed him to feel different, shut out of things because of his disability.

Sure, Ted lost some friends because he had cancer. Some people whispered behind his back and called him names. Others went out of their way to avoid him in the halls. Some no longer invited him to their parties.

About the loss of friends Ted says, "People who act like that were never really your friends to begin with. Real friends accept you."

Accepting Feelings

Sharon had lost her best friend and needed to tell someone about it. She chose Jim Conway, her pastor, because she knew he would accept her feelings without criticizing her. They sat across the room from each other in Jim's comfortable living room.

"Tell me about losing your friend," Jim said.

Sharon began to cry. Her whole body shook, and she found it hard to talk.

Jim crossed the room and sat down on the floor at her feet. "It's OK," he said. "Cry all you want."

After she had finished her story, Jim said, "You must feel that no one will ever be your friend again. You probably feel it's all your fault, and you just don't know how to be friends. You're no doubt wondering if you'll always have to be alone in the world without friendship."

"Yes! Yes!" Sharon nodded. "That's exactly how I feel. I feel that no one will ever want me for a friend." She stopped crying and sighed. "Thanks for understanding how I feel," she said, smiling at last.

"I know a friend who loves you very much," Jim continued. "Jesus loves you just as you are, and He wants to be your friend. He understands how you feel, and He can help you find another friend."

Again Sharon nodded and smiled. "I know. Will you pray for me, Jim, please?" And so he did. Sharon went away feeling lots better because someone had accepted her feelings without judging or criticizing. That's what friends do for each other.

As Jim Conway writes in his book *Friendship:* "Being a friend is not sitting as a judge behind a high desk looking down as your friend pathetically exposes his or her inner feelings to you. Friendship is sitting cross-legged on the floor on the same level as your friend, seeing through your friend's eyes, and understanding what your friend feels."

DON'T JUDGE OTHER PEOPLE. MATTHEW 7:1, ICB.

MAKING FRIENDS

A friend gives you freedom to express your feelings without fear that you will be judged. A friend is someone who knows all about you, warts and all, and loves you just the same.

Accepting Temperaments

GOD CREATED MAN IN HIS OWN IMAGE. GENESIS 1:27, NIV.

MAKING FRIENDS

God created each of us as unique individuals, with unique personalities and temperaments. I don't have to conform to someone else's image, but neither should I expect that person to conform to mine.

I stood on the platform of the train station in Bangalore, India, waiting for my husband, Ron. The train was late, and I paced up and down the sidewalk, getting more upset by the minute. At last the train puffed into the station. By the time he jumped off the train my patience had run out.

"I thought you'd never get here!" I said, frowning.

"Why? What's wrong?"

"Everything!" I complained. "But mostly the kids." I recited my complaints as we rode home, as he took his shower, and as he ate breakfast.

"Do you know what your problem is, Dorothy?" he asked.

"What? *My* problem?" I looked at him in disbelief.

"Yes, Dorothy, *your* problem!" Ron chuckled. "You're trying to play God to our children. You're trying to make them over into your own image. There's no way our children are going to turn into the serious, hardworking, get-things-accomplished-now sort of person you are. They aren't made that way. So why don't you stop trying to change them?"

"Humph!" I grunted. "Maybe you're right."

I hated to admit it, but that's exactly what I'd been trying to do—remake the children into my own image. How ridiculous when they were all so different!

Things went a lot better when I stopped trying to change my children and began instead to appreciate them for the special people they were.

I had to learn that other people may be different, but that doesn't make them wrong. The way we each approach life, our particular temperaments and personalities, has a lot to do with our genetic makeup—the way our DNA is lined up. In other words, that's the way God made us.

Look up the following words in the dictionary: "sanguine," "choleric," "melancholy," and "phlegmatic." Do the descriptions make you think of some people you know? Try to find out more about the temperaments.

Puppies in the Bed

As Dottie May lay in bed trying to sleep she got a marvelous idea. She threw back the covers, tiptoed across the room, and carefully opened the door to the hall. She could hear the radio. Her dad would be sitting in his big chair while listening to the news. She could hear her mother talking on the phone in the kitchen.

Slowly she tiptoed down the stairs to the basement, where her pet cocker spaniel, Frisky, was tending six puppies in a wooden box. Dottie May lifted out two puppies. Holding them close, she tiptoed back up the stairs to her bedroom, closed the door quietly, and jumped into bed with the puppies. What fun! Their tiny paws tickled as they climbed over her body. Dottie May giggled softly.

Just then she heard the thud of footsteps on the stairs. *Oh, no!* she thought. *That's Mother coming upstairs to say good night. What will I do?* She pushed the puppies to the foot of the bed, pulled the cover tight about her chin, and pretended to be asleep.

Mother opened the door and turned on the light. "What are you doing, Dottie May?" she asked.

"Sleeping, Mom!" Just then the puppies started to squirm.

"What's going on down there?" Mother sounded suspicious.

"Nothing! It's just my toes," Dottie May said, wiggling them furiously under the covers.

Mother threw back the blankets, picked up two puppies, and laughed. "Funny looking toes," she said.

Now I'm really going to get it! Dottie May thought. *I've been bad, and Mom will punish me for sure.*

Her mother reached down and kissed Dottie May. "I love you, Dottie May. Good night. Go to sleep; and no more tricks!"

When Mom was gone, Dottie May felt good. Her mother loved her even though she'd done something wrong. *Mom is my best friend!* she thought as she drifted off to sleep.

"I HAVE LOVED YOU WITH AN EVERLASTING LOVE." JEREMIAH 31:3, NIV.

MAKING FRIENDS

God is like Dottie May's mom. No matter what we do wrong, He's still our best Friend. His love will last forever. Nothing we can do will stop Him from loving us. Friends are like that.

A Happy Religion

The year was 1757. Thirteen-year-old Francis Asbury was curious as to why Methodists were so happy. He found church very boring. It didn't make him feel happy to hear about sinners being destroyed. Religion was no fun at all!

His friend George challenged him to spy on the Methodists to discover their secret. After several weeks Francis reported, "I've learned why the Methodists are happy."

"Tell me," urged George.

"It's because they know for sure they are children of God. They're certain they'll go to heaven!"

"Nobody can be sure of that!" exclaimed George. "Not even if you went to church every week!"

Francis thought a moment, then replied, "When King George I died, it became the duty of the prime minister to inform the prince of Wales that he was the new king.

"When he reached the lodge where the prince was staying, His Royal Highness and his wife had gone to bed. So the prime minister went to his bedroom to wake him. Kneeling, he announced, 'Your Majesty, you are now King George II!'

"The new king yawned and replied, 'That's one big lie!' The prime minister had to repeat the message."

"What's that got to do with the Methodists being happy?" George asked.

"The Bible tells us that all we have to do is to trust Christ, and we'll be saved. The moment we accept Him we can be sure of going to heaven. Most of us go around saying, 'That's one big lie.' However, the Methodists believe it, and they're happy!"

When Francis was 15 years old he heard Alexander Mather preach about God's wonderful grace that accepts us no matter what we've done. That evening he went forward to accept Christ as his Saviour. For the first time in his life he felt truly happy!

Francis felt as though he were soaring on wings of love. Inside he felt warm, happy, and accepted. He knew now that God was His friend.

TO ALL WHO RECEIVED HIM, HE GAVE THE RIGHT TO BECOME CHILDREN OF GOD. ALL THEY NEEDED TO DO WAS TO TRUST HIM TO SAVE THEM. JOHN 1:12, TLB.

MAKING FRIENDS

God wants you to be His friend. All you need do is believe His word and accept the friendship He offers.

Friendship Takes Time

I wish they'd go away, Edith Hugoniot thought as she tidied up after breakfast. *I'm tired of 30 pairs of eyes watching everything I do.*

The eyes belonged to the Tharu people of Santpur, India, where Edith lived in a two-room mud house with a thatched roof. She and her husband were Wycliff Bible translators and had come there to share the good news of God's love.

"Look at all their pots," commented one of the children looking in the open doorway.

"Yes," another agreed. "Look at all the things they have!"

Edith tried not to show how much she resented their comments. *We don't have more things,* she thought. *We just have different things.*

When the house was clean Edith called her two young sons, Kenny and David, to go for a walk. But, of course, the eyes had feet that followed them, forming a parade behind Kenny.

Kenny stopped. "Mom, do those kids have to follow us *everywhere?*" he asked.

Edith prayed as she tried to think what to say. She didn't want to pass on her own critical feelings to the boys. "You know, Kenny," she said at last, "when Jesus lived on earth, He always had a crowd following Him. Never once did He tell them to go away. He just loved them."

Satisfied, the boys continued their walk, but Edith was still bothered by the situation. Later, alone in the bedroom, she drew the curtain tight so that no one could see. Then she lay on the bed and cried.

"Lord," she prayed, "I just don't love these people. In fact, I can hardly tolerate the way they stare at us. I know You want me to bring Your love to them, but I just can't."

Then in a "still small voice" God spoke to her. "'The fruit of the Spirit is love.' Fruit takes time to grow."

Because Edith was willing, in time love for the Tharu people did grow in her heart.

BUT THE FRUIT OF THE SPIRIT IS LOVE. GALATIANS 5:22, NIV.

MAKING FRIENDS

Some people are hard to like. If we're willing, Jesus can help us learn to like them. Don't be in a hurry. Friendship takes time to grow.

Blessing Auntie

LOVE YOUR ENEMIES. PRAY FOR THOSE WHO DO BAD THINGS TO YOU. MATTHEW 5:44, ICB.

MAKING FRIENDS

We can get rid of our enemies by turning them into our friends. The transformation from enemy to friend begins when we ask God to bless them and make them happy.

"Auntie is impossible!" Ellen confided to her friend Catherine Marshall. "She finds fault with the children and nags at me all the time. I can't stand having her around!"

"Have you prayed about it?" Catherine asked.

"Of course. I pray every day that God will change Auntie and make her easy to live with," Ellen replied. "However, it doesn't work. She's worse than ever!"

"Why not forget about trying to change Auntie?" Catherine suggested. "Why not just ask God to bless her, to make her happy?"

"But she doesn't deserve it!" Ellen exploded.

Catherine just smiled as Ellen mulled over the new idea of blessing mean old Auntie who didn't deserve it. Suddenly a smile crossed Ellen's face. "I guess none of us *deserves* anything from God, do we?"

"Nothing we could ever do would be good enough to earn a scrap from His hands," Catherine said. "I certainly don't deserve His constant goodness and love."

"I'm willing to try your idea," Ellen said. "Can we pray about it now?"

Together the two friends knelt and prayed for faultfinding Auntie. Ellen's prayer went something like this: "Lord, please bless Auntie. Give her whatever she needs. Make her happy. Help the children love her. Help me be kinder to her, too. I wish for Auntie joy and happiness and all good things."

A few days later Ellen phoned Catherine. "You won't believe how different Auntie is acting! This blessing business is dynamite! I've never seen Auntie so happy, and we actually enjoy having her around!"

We all have people who annoy us. Some people seem born for the purpose of making our lives miserable. We don't like being around people who do bad things to us. Yet it is these very people whom God wants to turn into our friends! We can do our part by wishing them joy and asking God to make them happy.

Stranger on the Dock

Julie and Janet Hedstrom raced to the dock. They stopped when they saw the bearded man sitting there as he had been every day. The stranger didn't swim, fish, or go boating. He never spoke or read. He just sat there all day, doing nothing.

"I wish he'd go away!" Julie complained. "Just once I'd like to go to the dock and not find him there!"

The day was a scorcher, and the girls wanted to go swimming, but not with that strange man sitting there. Finally their mother persuaded them to sit on the beach and read while she went in the water. The day got hotter, and Janet and Julie ran back to the house to change into their swimsuits.

While they were gone, the man spoke. "I think your daughters are afraid of me," he said. "I won't hurt them."

"Their dad died two years ago," Mother answered. "They aren't used to being around men."

"Five months ago a drunk driver killed my wife, my son, and my daughter," he said quietly.

"I'm so sorry!" Mrs. Hedstrom responded, feeling suddenly guilty for all the harsh things she and the girls had said about him during the past few days. They had decided he was rich, lazy, and up to no good. "I can't imagine the pain you must be feeling," she added. "Losing my husband was hard enough."

The man wiped away some tears, then continued, his voice breaking, "Last Monday my doctor told me I have cancer and only three months to live."

Oh, God, this is too much pain for any person to bear! Mrs. Hedstrom thought. She groped for words that might help. "I've found peace with God in the Bible," she said. "I hope you will too."

She swam away from the dock to hide the tears that were now falling fast. *To think that we made fun of a person who was hurting so badly!* she thought.

LOVE YE THEREFORE THE STRANGER. DEUTERONOMY 10:19.

MAKING FRIENDS

Loving people we don't know means reserving our judgment until we find out what they are really like. Our opinions of people change as we take time to know them.

Peggy's Plan

"Do good to them that hate you, and pray for them which despitefully use you, and persecute you."
Matthew 5:44.

Making Friends

We can't force anyone to be a friend. Peggy's formula for dealing with enemies is one that works: prayer, patience, and time.

Peggy Winters was Black, and some of her classmates found that reason enough to be mean to her. One day as the class came in from recess, they noticed that someone had written a bad word across Peggy's drawing on the bulletin board.

Her teacher removed the drawing and looked to see how Peggy was reacting. Peggy had her face bent over her desk and was reading a little book.

After school the teacher inspected desks and discovered Peggy's book, a New Testament. Written on the inside cover was a note that said: "Remember Matthew 5:44. Love, Dad."

Her teacher found the text and read: "Love your enemies, bless them that curse you, do good to them that hate you, and pray for them which despitefully use you."

The next morning Peggy was all smiles. "I've got surprises for everyone," she told her teacher. "May I give them out now?"

Her teacher nodded. Peggy reached into the box and brought out a ballpoint pen for everyone. At the top of each was a bubble of liquid with a tiny plastic boat floating inside.

After school one day, Peggy approached the teacher's desk. "I need to talk to you."

Her teacher closed the book she was grading and looked at Peggy standing there twisting her braid around her finger. "You can't make them like me," she said.

"I know," her teacher nodded. "But I can try. They shouldn't be mean to you."

"I have a plan," Peggy said. "It's the PPT plan. Dad told me about it. Do you know what I'm talking about?"

"No," her teacher admitted.

"Prayer, patience, and time. I want them to like me, but I'll just have to be patient and give it time. Meanwhile, I can pray for them."

"Right," her teacher agreed.

Peggy started to leave, but she had one more thing she wanted to tell her teacher. "When we love our enemies like the Bible says, then sometimes they aren't enemies anymore."

Shaneen's Miracle

Eight-year-old Tim, 6-year-old Claire, and 4-year-old Laurie understood how it felt not to belong anywhere. When their mother was hurt in an accident, they were put in foster homes before Don and Sharon Dykhouse decided to adopt them. Tim, Claire, and Laurie would be together. They would become Don and Sharon's children. They would belong to someone.

But the children didn't understand. They'd been pushed around to many homes and didn't believe that this was for real. They wouldn't let Don and Sharon love them.

Then the Dykhouses decided to adopt Shaneen, a large silky-haired black dog that needed a home. He wasn't in the house very long before he decided to be friends with the children.

When Laurie cried, Shaneen licked her face and teased her into playing tug-of-war with him. Soon she'd be laughing as she chased the dog around the house. Shaneen taught Tim how to play catch, and every day they had a lot of fun together. Whenever Claire felt really sad, she went to Shaneen, and the dog would lie there and let her hug him and cry.

Little by little Shaneen worked a miracle of love with the three children. He played with them, followed them around, and accepted them just as they were. It didn't matter if they laughed or cried; he was there to be with them. The children began to feel as if they belonged, that they were part of the Dykhouse family.

One day Laurie asked her new mother, "Is Shaneen a foster dog or an adopted dog?"

"Adopted," her mother answered. "That means we're not just looking after him. He belongs to us. He's family."

"What if he's bad? Will you send him away?" Laurie asked.

"Never!"

"We're adopted too," Tim said.

"You sure are!" Sharon said with a smile. "You're our children. We'll never ever send you away. This is where you belong."

HIS PURPOSE WAS TO MAKE US HIS CHILDREN. GALATIANS 4:5, ICB.

MAKING FRIENDS

God accepts you as His child. He's adopted you into His family. He'll never send you away. You belong to Him forever. Will you accept His love?

23

Lass's New Friend

"I WILL ACCEPT YOU," SAYS THE LORD GOD. EZEKIEL 43:27, NKJV.

MAKING FRIENDS

Jesus accepts you. He sees wonderful possibilities in your life. He wants to be your Friend. Will you accept His offer of friendship?

Phillip Keller found Lass chained from her collar to a steel post and hobbled with another chain from her neck to her back leg. The dog crouched in the dirt. Her ears were laid back, and she was snarling and snapping.

"I can't do a thing with her!" the owner said. "She jumps fences, chases cars, and terrorizes the neighborhood."

Phillip studied the sad-looking border collie. She was 2 years old, possibly beyond hope. Phillip looked into her eyes and thought, *You're an intelligent dog. I feel sorry for the way you've been treated. You could make a wonderful sheep dog. I think I'll try to help you.*

Lass didn't show gratitude. All the way home she lay behind the seat of the car and growled, baring her teeth when Phillip tried to touch her.

At home on his ranch he provided a fine kennel, good food, sparkling water, and a long chain so that she could exercise. However, Lass refused to enter the kennel. She refused to eat or drink or to allow Phillip to pet her. She began to lose weight.

Understanding Lass's longing, Phillip set her free. She bolted into the woods. For several days she remained hidden. Then one evening she appeared on top of a large rock, behind the house.

Phillip called her name, but she ran. He took food and water to the rock. The next morning it was gone. For several weeks he left food and water for her. Each night it disappeared.

I wish she'd come to me, Phillip thought. *I wish she'd get to know me, to trust me, to learn to love me, to work with me, to be my friend.*

Then one evening Phillip stood outside his house while watching his sheep graze in the golden sunset. It was a beautiful scene, and Phillip was entranced, his hands clasped behind his back.

Suddenly he felt a soft warm nose touch his hands. Lass had come home. She'd accepted him as her friend.

The Green Cord

'm not ready for Jesus to come, 15-year-old Ellen Harmon thought. *Oh, how awful to be lost!*

For three weeks Ellen was depressed, feeling that God had rejected her. Then a dream gave her hope.

She seemed to be sitting with her face in her hands, thinking, *If Jesus were upon earth, I'd go to Him, throw myself at His feet, and tell Him all my troubles. He'd have mercy on me.*

Then a door opened, and an angel spoke to her. "Do you want to see Jesus? Take everything you possess, and follow me."

Gladly Ellen gathered up her treasures and followed the guide. He led her up a steep stairway. "Keep your eyes fixed upward," he said, "lest you grow dizzy and fall."

At the top the angel said, "You must leave everything here." Ellen laid down her treasures and followed her guide through an open door. There stood Jesus, more glorious than she had imagined. About this experience she later wrote: "I knew at once that He was acquainted with every circumstance of my life and all my inner thoughts and feelings.

"I tried to shield myself from His gaze, feeling unable to endure His searching eyes, but He drew near with a smile, and, laying His hand upon my head, said, 'Fear not.' The sound of his voice thrilled my heart with a happiness it had never before experienced" *(Early Writings,* p. 80).

Her guide opened the door and told her to pick up her treasures again. He gave her a green cord, coiled tightly, and said, "Keep this close to your heart, and when you wish to see Jesus, take it out and stretch it as far as you can."

The dream gave Ellen hope. She knew now that God loved her. The green cord represented faith to her mind, and she saw how easy it was to trust God.

GOD IS BEING PATIENT WITH YOU. HE DOES NOT WANT ANYONE TO BE LOST. 2 PETER 3:9, ICB.

MAKING FRIENDS

Prayer, like Ellen's green cord, is ours to use anytime we want to contact our Friend Jesus. He knows everything about us, loves us anyway, and wants us to be saved.

Love in a Look

THE LORD TURNED AND LOOKED STRAIGHT AT PETER. LUKE 22:61, NIV.

MAKING FRIENDS

We can communicate either acceptance or rejection with our eyes.

It was bitterly cold in northern Virginia. An old man, clutching his coat, stood on the riverbank. On the other side, the warmth of a hearth awaited him, but he had no boat and no bridge spanned the river.

"I think I hear horses," the old man spoke into the wind. "Perhaps one of the riders will give me a lift across the river."

Sure enough, a group of five riders galloped into sight then slowed to a walk as they neared the river.

The first horseman plunged his horse into the icy river without so much as a nod, and the old man said nothing. He let the second rider pass as well, then the third, and the fourth.

As the fifth rider came near, the old man called out, "Sir, could you please give me a ride across the river?"

"Of course!" The stranger stopped and gave a hand to the old man as he climbed up behind him. In no time they had crossed the river, and the old man slid to the ground.

"Excuse me, sir," the fifth rider said. "Why didn't you ask the other horsemen for a ride?"

The old man replied, "I simply looked into the other riders' eyes, and I saw no love there. I knew it would be useless to ask them for a ride. When I looked into your eyes, I saw a willingness to help. I knew that you wouldn't refuse my request."

"Interesting," the gentleman said. "I'm grateful to you for sharing that with me." With a lift of his hat, President Thomas Jefferson rode off to the White House.

Communication experts agree that the face is the most important source of information about emotions. Especially the eyes speak clearly of what's in a person's heart.

Peter experienced this truth the night he denied that he knew Jesus. Jesus looked at him just as the cock crowed the third time. In that look Peter saw love and acceptance. Realizing that Jesus still loved him after what he'd done made Peter feel ashamed. That one look of love changed Peter's life.

Body Language

his verse describes the body language of the prodigal son's father. It's the body language of love. Open arms communicate acceptance.

Can you imagine what the body language of the older brother looked like? I can picture him standing before his father, his arms crossed, frowning his disapproval.

Closely crossed arms or legs communicate unacceptance and dislike. People with crossed arms are giving a message that they want you to stay away. It's their way of protecting themselves from your getting close. Closed arms communicate rejection.

Melissa was married to an evangelist who traveled a lot. Almost every Sabbath they visited a different church. Since her husband was usually preaching, Melissa sat alone in the audience.

I wonder why no one will sit beside me? she thought as week after week she sat in an empty pew. *People seem to be avoiding me for some reason.*

Then one day she took notice of her body language. She was sitting at the end of the pew, her arms and legs crossed tightly. By her choice of the end position and her crossed arms and legs she was unconsciously turning people away.

Her body language was saying to everyone, "Stay away! I don't want you to sit with me! This row is for me alone."

The next week Melissa did an experiment in communication. She sat near the center of the pew. She unfolded her arms and legs, letting them rest in a relaxed manner. She smiled and nodded slightly to people who looked her way. The pew filled up with people on each side of her.

Her body language was now saying, "Please join me! I'd love to have you share my pew! I'd like to be your friend!"

If someone with arms crossed is standing against the building, it's probably not a good time to ask that person to join your game. If a girl is sitting in the closed position, she'll probably say no if a guy asks her for a date.

HE RAN TO HIS SON, THREW HIS ARMS AROUND HIM AND KISSED HIM. LUKE 15:20, NIV.

MAKING FRIENDS

We communicate rejection by tightly closed arms and legs. We communicate acceptance by an open body position.

Eye Messages

COME, LET US LOOK ONE ANOTHER IN THE FACE. 2 KINGS 14:8.

MAKING FRIENDS

Want to be my friend? Come, let's look each other in the face. Eye contact is important; so is eye level.

Our golden retriever, Matt, is one smart dog! He knows that eye contact is important for communication. The other day I watched him trying to get the attention of my husband, who was reading the newspaper.

Matt sat in front of Ron and whined the soft, pathetic sort of whine he gives when he wants to go outside.

"Hi, Matt!" Ron said as he continued reading the paper.

Matt got up and ran to the door, whining a little louder.

No response from his master!

Matt went back and sat in front of Ron, staring at the paper for a moment, that paper that was preventing him from getting his message through. So he reached up one paw and knocked the paper out of Ron's hands!

"Matt!" Ron scolded.

"Arf! Arf!" Matt answered, running toward the door.

"Oh! Do you want out?" Ron asked, getting up at last.

Matt rolled his eyes at Ron as if to say, "Boy, are you slow! What do you think I've been trying to tell you for the past three minutes!"

Eye level is also important. If you want to give a friendly, accepting message, you need to be on the same eye level as your friend. If you stand above your friend, looking down at him or her, you're giving a message of superiority, of wanting to be in control.

Even our dog Matt knows that much about friendship! We often take him walking on a bike trail along a river near our home. Usually we meet a number of people out walking their dogs. When Matt sees another dog approaching, he immediately lies down with his chin on the ground, making himself as low as possible. This gives a message of friendliness and acceptance to the other dog.

Want to get a message across to a small child? Don't tower over him or her like a menacing giant. Squat down until you are eye level and give your message. Guaranteed the kid will think you're tops!

28

A Posture of Acceptance

The psalmist is asking God to take on a posture of acceptance. The letters SOLER can be used to describe a friendly posture.

Squarely face. If you want to show you're interested in someone, shoulder to shoulder, face to face, squarely face the person who is speaking. "He gave me the cold shoulder" is an expression we use to say someone has rejected us.

Open position. A friendly person keeps his or her arms and legs uncrossed.

Imagine for a moment a baseball game. An umpire makes a call that the manager disputes. Waving his arms, he runs toward the umpire. The umpire stands there with his arms tightly crossed. What is his message? "I won't budge an inch from my position. No use to argue with me!"

Lean forward. You can communicate interest and acceptance by inclining your body slightly toward the person who is talking. Think again about a baseball game. When the game gets exciting, what's the posture of the fans? They're sitting on the edge of their seats, leaning forward expectantly.

Leaning away from a person says "I don't agree with you" or "I'm rather bored with what you have to say" or "I don't want to get close to you."

Eye contact. Many of us have a hard time establishing eye contact. We look all around the room, at the floor, or at something else that's happening. When we don't look at someone in the face, we're saying, "I'm not much interested in what you have to say. I'd like to get out of here as soon as possible."

We subconsciously interpret the lack of eye contact as unfriendliness. We don't stay around people who refuse to look us in the eye.

Relaxed muscles. Tense muscles tell people that we're afraid of them, that we don't trust them. A relaxed posture communicates that we're at ease with the person, happy to be with him or her, that we trust him or her.

DO NOT HIDE YOUR FACE FROM ME. . . . INCLINE YOUR EAR TO ME.
PSALM 102:2, NKJV.

MAKING FRIENDS

Practice using the posture of acceptance: squarely face, open position, lean forward, eye contact, relaxed muscles.

The Touch of Love

JESUS REACHED OUT HIS HAND AND TOUCHED THE MAN. MATTHEW 8:3, NIV.

When Jesus touched the man with leprosy, he was healed. When Jesus touched the blind man, he could see. When Jesus touched the dead girl, she came back to life. There's miracle-working power in the touch of love.

Once Helen Colton, a reporter for the New York *Times*, interviewed Marilyn Monroe, a popular movie star about 40 years ago. Marilyn had shared about her childhood, being shunted from foster home to foster home, never really feeling that she belonged to anyone.

"Did you ever feel loved by any of the foster families with whom you lived?" Helen asked.

"Once," Marilyn answered, "when I was about 8 years old. The woman I was living with was putting on makeup, and I was watching her. She reached over and patted my cheeks with her powder puff. For that moment I felt loved by her."

Marilyn picked up a powder puff from her dressing table and dabbed her cheeks as she remembered. Tears filled her eyes. The memory of that touch of love was powerful.

A gentle touch communicates love and acceptance. A light touch on the arm, a pat on the back, an arm around the shoulder, or a gentle squeeze of the hand says "I care about you. I want to be your friend."

Try to think of at least three people you could make happy by a touch of love. Here are some ideas:

1. Your parents. How long since you've hugged your dad or given a back rub to your mom? A quick squeeze of the hand before you rush off in the morning could do wonders for family relations!

2. Senior citizens. Can you think of an elderly person on your block, in a nursing home, or at your church? Find an opportunity to give that person a hug this week. Don't be surprised if he or she starts to cry!

3. Persons with disabilities. We often avoid touching people in wheelchairs. They have the same needs as the rest of us. You could make a difference by a shoulder squeeze as you say "Hi!"

MAKING FRIENDS

Touch is a powerful way to communicate acceptance.

Kinds of Hugs

I wonder what kind of hug Laban gave Jacob. Here are some possibilities:

1. A-frame Hug. The two people lean toward each other, only the top part of their bodies touching.

2. Baby Burp Hug. A person pats you rapidly on the back as though you were a baby needing to burp. This hug feels as though the person is doing something because it is required.

3. Drumbeat Hug. A person nervously beats a rat-a-tat-tat on your back with his or her fingers. It feels as though he or she wants to get this over with as soon as possible.

4. Chimpanzee Hug. The person alternately flaps his or her left and right hands from the wrists, lightly slapping you on the back. It feels as though the person is uncomfortable with you and wants out as soon as possible.

5. Full-bodied, Full-Palm Hug. The hugger presses his or her palms with fingers closed on your back, or rubs his or her hands gently up and down your back. This caressing feels good. It says "I am your friend. I like being close to you." When we want to feel close to our families, such as in a time of emotional crisis or a funeral, we always give full-bodied hugs.

Try this: Give a hug test to family members. Treat it like a game. Exaggerate your body, finger, and hand movements. Try each of the five hug styles. Ask them to guess which type of hug you are giving. How do they feel about each kind of hug? Which kind did you prefer?

Virginia Cason, daughter of the late H.M.S. Richards, Voice of Prophecy speaker, treasures the memory of her father's hugs. She remembers many times when he would put his arm around her shoulders, give her a loving squeeze, and say, "Honey, Mother and I love you very much. God loves you too. And we're asking the good Lord to help you make the right decisions."

AS SOON AS LABAN HEARD THE NEWS ABOUT JACOB, HIS SISTER'S SON, HE HURRIED TO MEET HIM. HE EMBRACED HIM AND KISSED HIM AND BROUGHT HIM TO HIS HOME. GENESIS 29:13, NIV.

MAKING FRIENDS:

A good hug makes us feel accepted, loved, cared about. A good hug has the power to take away hurt, to ease tension, and to give strength to face a difficult task.

Martin's Fear

THE LORD IS COMPASSIONATE AND GRACIOUS, SLOW TO ANGER, ABOUNDING IN LOVE. . . . HE DOES NOT TREAT US AS OUR SINS DESERVE OR REPAY US ACCORDING TO OUR INIQUITIES. PSALM 103:8, 10, NIV.

MAKING FRIENDS

God doesn't get angry at us when we're bad. He treats us with love, tenderness, and patience.

Martin, come here!" Mrs. Luther was frowning, and she held a leather strap in her hand.

"Yes, Mama." Martin trembled as he approached the angry woman.

"You took a nut from the kitchen. That's stealing! No boy of mine is going to be a thief!" Mrs. Luther shouted, laying the strap to Martin's legs and back.

"I'm sorry, Mama! I won't do it again!" Martin cried loudly, but she kept up her beating until the blood began to flow.

"That should teach you a good lesson, young man!" she said, putting away the strap. "Your father will hear about this!"

All day Martin worried about what would happen when his father came home. *He'll probably give me another whipping,* Martin thought. *I can't take another one. I'll run far away from this town. I'll go so far they'll never find me again.*

Martin slipped quietly out of the house and ran through the narrow streets. He ran past the mines and the smelting furnaces on the far side of town. He could see trees and fields in the distance, but it was getting dark and he was tired.

I'll find a place to sleep now, he thought. *Tomorrow morning I'll head for the country.* Looking around, he found an old house. It seemed no one lived there. Martin curled up beside the house and tried to sleep.

It was dark already by the time his parents discovered he was missing. They looked for him everywhere, thinking he was hiding inside the house. When they couldn't find him, they got the neighbors to help them search the town. At last they found him—cold, hungry, and miserable—near the old house.

He went home with them, and after that he tried hard to be good so that he wouldn't be punished. He was afraid of them, and he was afraid of God. He thought God was like his parents, mean and cruel. When he grew up, Martin Luther discovered that God is not like that at all!

The Boy Who Lost His Name

"I don't want to say my prayers," 3-year-old Daniel complained at bedtime.

"Come on," his mom coaxed.

"Nope!" Daniel jumped into bed, crossed his little arms, and frowned. "Don't want to!"

Mother sat down on his bed. "Do you know why we picked the name Daniel for you?" she asked.

Daniel shook his head.

"Because Daniel was a man who always said his prayers. Remember how he was thrown into the lions' den because he wanted to say his prayers? God delivered him because he prayed."

"Don't care!" Daniel pouted. "Don't want to pray."

"OK," Mother said, getting up. "I guess we can't call you Daniel anymore. You'll just have to be a boy without a name."

The next morning when Daniel came to breakfast, he was greeted with, "Hi, boy! Sit down and have your breakfast."

"My name's not boy; it's Daniel," he said.

"Want some toast, boy?" she asked.

All day long no one said his name. Finally he decided to say his prayers, and he got his name back.

It's not just 3-year-olds who want to be called by their name.

Our name sets us apart from everyone else. Being called by name makes us each feel acknowledged and recognized, someone who is important.

We feel good toward people who remember our name. It just shows they care.

Here are some ways to remember names:

1. Make sure you understand the name the first time you hear it. Don't hesitate to ask for the person to repeat the name.

2. Use the name immediately in conversation.

3. Write down the name.

4. At the end of the day, try to match names and faces.

5. Use a person's name each time you greet him or her.

JAN. 28

I HAVE CALLED YOU BY NAME; YOU ARE MINE. ISAIAH 43:1, TLB.

MAKING FRIENDS

We like people who remember our names. Use people's names often in conversation. It makes them feel good.

Archie Gives In

**DO NOT
FOLLOW THE
CROWD IN
DOING WRONG.
EXODUS 23:2,
NIV.**

MAKING
FRIENDS

Peer pressure, the
desire to be
accepted by
others, is a power-
ful influence. It
takes a lot of
strength to hold to
your convictions
in front of
a crowd.

Archie Shipowick knew something of the sorrow that alcohol can bring. His father had wasted much of his hard-earned money on liquor. At the age of 14 Archie determined that he'd never drink.

But things can change in two years. One night his friends invited him to join them for a celebration at the village tavern.

I don't have to drink anything, Archie told himself. *I'll just go along for the fun.*

Once inside, drinks were passed around. Someone thrust a glass into Archie's hand. For a moment he hesitated. He remembered his resolve never to drink. Then he noticed his friends staring at him, waiting for him to respond.

Everyone is drinking, Archie thought. *They're expecting me to be full of fun, to drink and laugh with the rest.* He accepted the glass and drained it, holding it out for a refill.

The warmth of the liquor reaching up into his brain stilled any misgivings he had. If this was what it took to be accepted, then this is what he'd do.

The rest of the night was a bit blurred. He awoke the next morning with a sick stomach, a foul-tasting mouth, and a splitting headache.

"I've made a pot of black coffee for you," his mother said. "Drink some. I know it will help."

"Oh, Mama! I got drunk last night, didn't I? I'm sorry." Archie looked into her sad, dark eyes. "I just couldn't help myself. They all wanted me to drink with them and . . . and . . . well, I wanted so much to be a part of . . ."

"I know," Mrs. Shipowick said, running her hand through his dark-brown hair. "You wanted to be part of the group, and when they kept offering you drinks, you couldn't refuse."

Archie looked at his mother in amazement. "That's exactly how it was! I sure wish I'd had the guts to say no!"

Robert's Decision

Robert was in Hong Kong for the first time. A ship's captain, he hoped to arrange for some trading partners.

If I can just meet the right people, he thought, *I'll be on my way to success!* Looking around the hotel lobby, he noticed a prosperous-looking middle-aged businessman. *Might as well start with him!* Robert walked over and introduced himself.

"So you've come here to trade?" the man asked.

Robert nodded. "That's why I'm here! I hope to do a good business hauling goods between here and San Francisco."

"Let's have a drink while you tell me about your plans," the businessman said, motioning toward the bar.

"Sorry, sir," Robert said. "That's very kind of you, but I don't drink."

The businessman raised his eyebrows. "You can't be serious! That's how business is done here! A lot of deals are made over a bottle of whiskey."

"Yes, sir, I *am* serious," Robert smiled. "I'd be glad to talk with you, though, about my plans. Could we sit down here?"

They found a seat, and the older man continued, "Let me give you some advice, young man. You're new to this business. If you want to be accepted, you've got to have a friendly drink now and again with business acquaintances. It will be expected of you. No need to drink a lot; just a sip or two will show that you want to be friends."

"I can't do that, sir," Robert insisted. "That would go against my beliefs. I'll find some other way to be friendly without sacrificing my principles."

"And your business? Don't you want to succeed?"

"Of course," Robert replied. "God will help me."

"If that's your plan, God will need to help you!" the businessman laughed.

And God did help Robert. Captain Robert Dollar became the owner of a large fleet of freighters with offices overlooking San Francisco Bay. He did business throughout the Pacific, making friends wherever he went.

JAN. 30

"THOSE WHO HONOR ME I WILL HONOR."
1 SAMUEL 2:30, NIV.

MAKING FRIENDS

It isn't necessary to sacrifice principle in order to make friends. Acceptance by God and your own conscience is more important than acceptance by people.

35

Acceptance Checkup

**I CAN DO
EVERYTHING
THROUGH HIM
WHO GIVES ME
STRENGTH.
PHILIPPIANS
4:13, NIV.**

ate yourself on the following skills for making friends. In which areas do you need God to help?

1. I make the first move toward friendship with new people.

Never   Sometimes   Usually   Always

2. I accept people of all races, cultures, and nationalities.

Never   Sometimes   Usually   Always

3. I make friends with people with disabilities.

Never   Sometimes   Usually   Always

4. I accept people just as they are, without expecting them to make any changes.

Never   Sometimes   Usually   Always

5. I give my friends freedom to express their feelings without the fear that I'll criticize them.

Never   Sometimes   Usually   Always

6. I don't try to conform to someone else's temperament, and I don't expect others to conform to mine.

Never   Sometimes   Usually   Always

7. I pray for the people I don't like and those who do bad things to me.

Never   Sometimes   Usually   Always

8. I reserve judgment on strangers until I find out what they're really like.

Never   Sometimes   Usually   Always

9. I use the body language of acceptance: squarely face, open position, lean forward, eye contact, and relaxed muscles.

Never   Sometimes   Usually   Always

10. I use touch to communicate acceptance.

Never   Sometimes   Usually   Always

11. I learn people's names and use them in conversation.

Never   Sometimes   Usually   Always

12. Acceptance of my friends isn't as important to me as acceptance by God. I can hold to my convictions against the crowd.

Never   Sometimes   Usually   Always

13. I believe that God accepts me just as I am. I believe He loves me no matter what I've done.

Never   Sometimes   Usually   Always

Friends Listen

Four-year-old Kelly could hardly wait until the blessing was finished so that she could tell Daddy what a good girl she'd been while he was away.

After the amen she started in. "Daddy, guess what I did while you were gone."

"Pass the butter," said Daddy.

"Daddy," Kelly tried again, "I was a very good girl."

"This is absolutely delicious," Daddy said. "Nothing like good home cooking after you've been on the road."

"Ding-dong, Daddy, ding-dong." Kelly pretended to ring a bell as she often did when she wanted his attention.

"Yeah," Daddy chuckled. "I'm sure glad to be home."

Kelly sighed and started to eat.

Josh McDowell, well-known Christian author and representative for Campus Crusade for Christ, hadn't yet learned that friends listen.

"Honey, you're not communicating with your family," she told him.

"Yes, I am."

"No, you don't listen. We start to share something with you, and you cut us off."

"Dottie was right," Josh now admits. "I'd usually hear what was being said, but my mind would be going a mile a minute. I'd look like I was listening, but my family could see right through me."

He wrote himself notes: "Listen to your children. Pay attention to them."

He started a nighttime ritual of listening. Every night at 7:00, even when there was company, Josh excused himself for an hour to play and talk with and listen to his children.

Every morning at breakfast he reserved 45 minutes to listen to his family. He began setting up listening dates with his wife, Dottie. Josh learned that you can't really be friends with your family or with anyone else unless you learn to listen.

Josh isn't the only one who has trouble listening. How well do you listen to your friends? to your brothers and sisters? to your parents?

> **EVERYONE SHOULD BE QUICK TO LISTEN. JAMES 1:19, NIV.**

MAKING FRIENDS

God gave us two ears and one mouth so that we might listen twice as much as we talk. Friends listen.

Look at Me!

Peter and John understood the importance of eye contact in communication. So did Kendra.

Kendra sat on the kitchen floor, building a house with her set of Lego blocks while her mother fixed supper. "Mommy, look what I've made!" she said.

"Honey, that's nice," her mother replied, as she continued to peel potatoes.

"See how big I've made it!" Kendra tried again.

"Uh-huh," Mother said as she set the pot of potatoes on the stove, then rummaged through a drawer for the right lid.

Kendra got up, went to her mother, and pulled on her skirt. "Mommy!" she said. "Look at me with your eyes!"

Focusing your eyes on someone is an important way to communicate that you're interested. Eye contact indicates that you're tuned in to them.

Only 30 percent of our understanding of what someone says comes to us through our ears. Most of a person's message enters our brain by way of our eyes: body position, facial expressions, gestures, and the look in one's eyes.

"Eyes are the windows of the soul," said one wise man. This is true. Our eyes reveal what we really think and feel.

Did you know that when you agree with your friend, your pupils grow larger? If you disagree, your pupils grow smaller.

Did you know that you can tell when a person is telling the truth by watching his or her eye movements? When we lie, our eye movements are about 12 times faster than the usual rate. Rapid blinking of the eyelids can tell us that a person is upset or may be hiding something.

Eyes that dart about the room while we're talking tell us that the person wants to escape. He or she isn't interested in what we have to say.

Eyes that twinkle with laughter and have a special sparkle to them when we're talking tell us that our friend finds it fun to be with us. He or she is interested in what we have to say.

PETER LOOKED STRAIGHT AT HIM, AS DID JOHN. THEN PETER SAID, "LOOK AT US!"
ACTS 3:4, NIV.

MAKING FRIENDS

Eye contact is vital to understanding what our friends are thinking and feeling.

Leonard Listened

Nineteen-year-old Leonard Lee was tired of people telling him what to do. He decided to run away from home and from God. He headed for Alaska, where he figured he could do as he pleased.

He set out walking from Calgary, Alberta. By February he'd gone 1,000 miles. Then the blizzard came—a howling, blowing, fierce storm that made walking almost impossible. The wind tore through him like knives.

I'm not going to make it, Leonard thought.

Just then he heard a voice say, "Turn to the left!"

"I must be hearing things!" Leonard mumbled.

"Turn to the left!" the voice repeated.

Leonard felt that God was speaking to him. He turned to the left into the storm and struggled on for several miles until he came to a frozen creek. He decided to follow it to the right. As he turned, again the voice urged, "Turn to the left!"

Leonard obeyed. A few steps to the left he discovered a cabin, half buried in the snow. He dug his way to the door and pushed it open.

A low moan came from somewhere in the inky blackness. Leonard lit a match and saw the form of an old man lying on a bunk bed. Ice had formed on his eyebrows and beard.

Quickly Leonard gathered wood for a fire. Soon the cabin was warm, and the old man began to talk. He'd been there for a week with a broken leg. In desperation he had cried to God for help, and God had used Leonard to answer that prayer.

"If I'd continued the way I was going," Leonard later said, "I would have died in the storm. The old man gave me directions to the nearest trading post, and I was able to get help."

After that experience, Leonard's thoughts went something like this: *What if I hadn't listened when God spoke to me in the blizzard? He must have a plan for my life. I think I should be listening to Him every day.*

LISTEN TO THE WORDS OF GOD.
JEREMIAH 9:20, TLB.

MAKING FRIENDS

God invites you today, "Be My friend. Please listen to Me."

When God Listens

NOW HEAR MY PRAYERS; OH, LISTEN TO MY CRY. PSALM 88:2, TLB.

MAKING FRIENDS

God is our Friend—He listens to us.

I know that God is a friend who listens. Let me share a story of one time when God listened to my cry.

We had just moved to Lansing, Michigan, where my husband was working in the conference office. His job took him away from home every weekend. Usually I went along, but this particular weekend I couldn't go because he wouldn't be back in time for me to teach on Monday.

I felt very lonely that Friday evening. The house seemed so big without him. My children were far away, and I had made no friends yet in Michigan. I'd met a lot of nice people, but they were just acquaintances. What I needed was a friend!

I sat down at the piano to play some hymns. Music often makes me feel better, but that night it just made me feel more lonely and sorry for myself. I came to hymn number 505 in the *Seventh-day Adventist Hymnal*, "I Need the Prayers of Those I Love."

Tears filled my eyes as I sang, "I want my friends to pray for me . . ." *What friends?* I thought. *I don't have even one friend in Lansing I can call.* My eyes blurred, and I couldn't see to play the notes.

I remember looking out the window, tears streaming down my face, and saying aloud, "God, please! I need a friend!"

The next day I got a note from Muriel. I'd met her only once. My husband and I had spent a Sabbath afternoon with her and her family after he'd preached in their church.

The letter said "Dear Dorothy, I just thought I'd let you know that I'm praying for you. I'd like to be your friend."

Wow! God had heard my cry! He'd cared enough to answer my prayer!

Did you know that "His heart of love is touched by our sorrows and even by our utterances of them. . . . Nothing that in any way concerns our peace is too small for Him to notice" (Ellen G. White, *Steps to Christ,* p. 100)?

Giving Attention

his text describes the crippled beggar at the Temple gate. He'd just asked Peter and John for money. And now you can be sure he wasn't cracking his knuckles, watching pigeons on the roof, or cleaning his fingernails!

That beggar was looking straight at Peter and John. He was leaning toward them, listening with his whole body. He wanted nothing to distract him from getting their reply!

The crippled man was on the right track. We don't get much from a conversation unless we give our attention to the other person. Paying attention works wonders in human relations.

Allen Ivey and John Hinkle set up an experiment to prove the importance of paying attention. They trained six college students in the SOLER method of attending to a speaker: squarely face, open position, lean forward, eye contact, and relaxed muscles.

Then they videotaped a class with the six students listening to a guest speaker. He knew nothing about their secret plan. He started by reading from his notes. He spoke in a monotone, used no gestures, and paid little attention to the students. He was boring!

At a given signal, the six students uncrossed their arms and legs, leaned forward in their chairs, fixed their eyes on the speaker, and focused their whole body on paying attention. Within 30 seconds the teacher made his first hand movement. His voice became vibrant, more alive. He looked at the students, talking from his heart. He became alive and interesting! The transformation was accomplished by simply giving attention.

Several minutes later, again on cue, the six leaned back, crossed their arms and legs, and yawned. They looked around the room and out the windows. They picked up pens and drew doodles on their pads. They fiddled with change in their pockets.

The teacher seemed embarrassed. He tried to get them interested again. When he didn't succeed, he went back to reading his notes. He was as boring as before!

SO THE MAN GAVE THEM HIS ATTENTION, EXPECTING TO GET SOMETHING FROM THEM.
ACTS 3:5, NIV.

MAKING FRIENDS

If we want to get the most out of a conversation (or a speaker), we need to listen with our whole body.

Body Truth

Greg slouched down in his chair, his legs stretched out in front of him. He stared at the ceiling and wished the evening would come to an end. *I wish I'd never come here,* he thought. *These games are boring; these people are dull.*

"Having a good time, Greg?" Danny shouted across the room.

Startled, Greg responded, "Yea! Sure! This is a great party!"

Everyone laughed. "You sure had me fooled!" Danny said, and they all laughed again.

Greg was embarrassed. He'd said he liked the party, but his body language told the real truth.

Tom, a university student, wanted to have friends, but he wasn't doing very well. After a seminar on friendship, he approached the teacher and asked, "Why don't people like me? I try to get close to people, but I just don't connect."

"Oh?" the teacher asked. "So you're finding it difficult to make friends?"

"Yea! It's always been like this. Nothing works for me." As he spoke, Tom turned sideways, looked down at the floor, and fidgeted with his pencil.

"I think I see your problem," the professor continued. "Do you realize that your body language is turning people off?"

"How's that?"

"You don't make eye contact with people when they're speaking. You turn your body away, and you do distracting things with your hands. Everything about your body language since you began talking with me has said 'I want out of here. I'm afraid of you.' That sort of body language makes people nervous."

"No kidding?" Tom asked, looking up and smiling. "That's weird! Why do I do that?"

"I think you do it because you're focusing on yourself," the teacher smiled. "You're thinking *I wonder if he'll like me.* Try focusing on the other person. Show your interest by your body language. Look at the person. Smile. Turn your body toward him or her. Relax."

Tom did what the teacher had suggested. It made a big difference. Today Tom has lots of friends.

**WHO WINKS WITH HIS EYE, SIGNALS WITH HIS FEET AND MOTIONS WITH HIS FINGERS.
PROVERBS 6:13, NIV.**

MAKING FRIENDS

Watch your body language. It tells the truth about your feelings.

Ruth's Visitor

Five-year-old Sarah skipped down the street. At Ruth's house she stopped to watch her neighbor sweep the sidewalk. After a moment she said, "Lady, I know a song I can sing."

Ruth stopped sweeping and smiled at the golden-haired girl. "So, you know a song that you can sing! I'd like to hear it."

Sarah sang a song, her yellow curls bobbing up and down.

"Thank you," Ruth said, clapping her hands. "I liked that. Do you know any more songs?"

Sarah jumped a square closer to Ruth and confided, "I know lots of songs. I'm going to be a singer when I get big and sing on TV. I'll make lots of money for my mother."

"Very good," Ruth said, leaning forward on the broom handle. "I'm listening!"

Each time Sarah finished a song, Ruth clapped and said, "Thank you. I liked that."

When at last Sarah had finished all the songs she knew, she stepped up close to Ruth and said, "Lady, I guess I don't really sing so good. They don't like to hear me much at home. But I sure like to sing—and *you* listened!"

"Of course, I listened," Ruth replied. "Wasn't it lucky that I came outside just when you wanted to sing?"

Sarah took another step closer and put one hand on the broom and the other on Ruth's dress. She looked up at Ruth intently and whispered, "I want to tell you a secret."

Ruth squatted down so that she was the same level as Sarah. "What's your secret?" she asked. "Tell me!"

"Lady, you listen sweet!" Sarah whispered. With that she ran off.

Ruth stood up and watched the little girl go. *Now, I think that's the nicest thing anyone has said about me in a long time,* she thought. *"Lady, you listen sweet!"*

Can you find six things Ruth did that made Sarah think she was a good listener? All six things have to do with her body language.

I GAVE YOU MY FULL ATTENTION. JOB 32:12, NIV.

MAKING FRIENDS

Listening involves more than just being quiet while your friend speaks. It means giving your full attention.

Closed Questions

MAKING FRIENDS

Use closed questions sparingly. Closed questions are conversation stoppers.

This question that the Lord asked Moses is a closed question. Closed questions deal with facts. There's only one correct answer. They can be answered with one or two words.

Closed questions are like true-false questions or multiple-choice test questions. The person asking closed questions, like a teacher giving a test, wants to control the agenda of the conversation.

Closed questions are conversation stoppers. Ask too many of them, and you begin to sound like a trial lawyer. People begin to feel that you're prying, and they'll resent it. Closed questions will get you information. But they won't get a conversation going.

The following dialogue uses closed questions.

It's the morning after Cindy's big party. At breakfast Mother asks, "Did you have a good time last night, Cindy?"

"No."

"What did you do?"

"Oh, nothing much."

"Who was there?"

"Everybody."

"Who's everybody?"

"You know. The gang." Cindy sighs and gets up from the table.

"What did you eat?"

"Pizza."

At this point Cindy is on the way out of the kitchen. "Got to go, Mom. I've got some homework to finish."

Mom sure is nosy these days! Cindy thinks. *I don't think she trusts me at all. You'd think I'd committed a crime or something! I wish she wouldn't be like that!*

Meanwhile, Mother is finishing her breakfast and thinking, *Now, what's with Cindy these days? She never wants to talk to me! I wonder what she's trying to hide. I think I need to watch her more closely.*

Asking one question after another puts the person on the defensive. It makes it appear that you're trying to catch them making a mistake. It pushes their panic button, and they try to escape.

Open Questions

ere Jesus used an open question. Open questions ask for a person's opinion. There's no correct answer. Any answer the person gives is acceptable because that's how he or she feels about it. An open question is like an essay question on a test. Ask 10 different people, and you could get 10 different answers.

Open questions keep the conversation going. They don't restrict the other persons, but let them carry the conversation wherever they like. Open questions deal with feelings, opinions, and explanations.

The following dialogue is another version of the morning after Cindy's big party. It uses open questions. Notice the difference.

Mother asks, "Hi, Honey! How do you feel the morning after Heather's party?"

"Rotten. I hate Heather's dumb parties. I'm not going to any more of them. Never!"

"Why not?"

"Because they're boring and stupid."

"It sounds really bad."

"Bad isn't the word. It was awful! We didn't do anything but sit around and drink 7-Up soft drink and eat pizza and watch TV. Bob told his stupid jokes we've all heard a million times before. It was so boring! It was no fun at all!"

"What might have made it more fun?"

"Well, it should have been planned. You know, like the parties you help me give. There should have been some games, contests, prizes, and all that stuff. Something should have been happening!"

"Want to plan one of your parties for next month?" Mom asked, smiling. "I'd be glad to help."

"Great! We'll show them how to have a really good time!"

Cindy goes to her room thinking, *I sure have a neat mom. She's interested in me and wants to help me have a good time. I'm glad she's someone I can talk to so easily.*

And back in the kitchen Mom is thinking, *What a special daughter Cindy is, always so open and willing to share about her life. I'm sure lucky to have such a daughter!*

"WHAT DO YOU THINK, SIMON?" HE ASKED. MATTHEW 17:25, NIV.

MAKING FRIENDS

Open questions show that you're interested in your friend's opinions, feelings, and ideas. They make the person feel important. They keep a conversation going.

45

God's Way

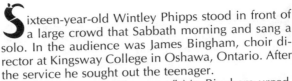

TEACH ME YOUR WAY, O LORD. PSALM 27:11, NIV.

MAKING FRIENDS

Friendship with God is a two-way street. He listens to you, but then He wants you to listen to Him, too.

Sixteen-year-old Wintley Phipps stood in front of a large crowd that Sabbath morning and sang a solo. In the audience was James Bingham, choir director at Kingsway College in Oshawa, Ontario. After the service he sought out the teenager.

"Please come to Kingsway," Mr. Bingham urged. "We need your voice in the choir."

"That sounds great!" Wintley agreed. He began to sing with the choir even before he enrolled as a student.

However, boarding school life irritated him. *I don't have to put up with this,* he thought. *I'm quitting, going back to public school.*

He marched into the dean's office. "I've had it!" he said. "You can't do this and you can't do that. Lights have to be out at a certain time. There's just too many rules. I'm leaving."

"Do you really want to go?" the dean asked.

"Yes, I do!" Wintley was emphatic.

The dean's next words surprised him. "For once why don't you do what *God* wants you to do, instead of what you want to do?"

Wintley returned to his room, got on his knees, and prayed: "God, whatever You want me to do, I'll do. If You want me to be a garbage collector, I'll do it. And if the only music I'll know in my life is singing hymns while I ride on the truck, that's fine too. But Lord, You know that I'd like to travel and use my talents for You. If that's Your will for me, open the doors and somehow let me sing."

The next day Wintley had proof enough that God listens when we pour out our heart to Him as to a friend. Someone from the Heritage Singers asked if he'd join their group for the summer. He was on his way to finding God's plan for his life.

Today Wintley Phipps is a pastor of a large Seventh-day Adventist church. He has given concerts around the world, sharing the joy he's found in Jesus, his best friend.

The Strange Soldier

Years ago Poland became involved in a bitter war. The enemy advanced through the land, killing people and burning their homes. Men, women, and children fled in terror. One whole Adventist congregation of 33 members decided to flee together.

They left in an open wagon pulled by two strong horses. It was winter and very, very cold. At the end of one day it was so cold that they knew they must find shelter or they'd freeze.

Ahead they saw a village where they hoped to find food and shelter. To their surprise, it was full of Polish soldiers.

Mr. Hann, the leader of the group, went to the captain and asked, "Please, sir, give us a place to stay and some food."

"No! We have enough only for ourselves."

"Please, sir, we'll freeze to death unless we find some shelter," Mr. Hann begged.

"No!" the captain insisted. "I can't help what happens to you. I'm responsible only for my men."

Back in the wagon the 33 Adventists knelt to pray. Suddenly a strange soldier approached them. "Are you the family that needs help?"

"Yes," Mr. Hann replied.

"Follow me."

The leader followed him to the captain's house. The strange soldier said to the captain, "I order you to give food and shelter to these people."

"Yes, sir!" the captain said, and saluted. The next morning the strange soldier showed the Adventists where to get more food for their journey.

"What's your name?" someone asked.

He smiled and replied, "When the need is the greatest, God is nearest."

They were surprised to hear a soldier talk about God. They looked in wonder at each other. One of them turned to ask why he spoke of God—but he was gone!

They inquired, but no one knew where the soldier had come from or where he'd gone. Even the captain had never seen him before. Who was that strange soldier who helped those 33 Adventists?

THEREFORE HE WILL LISTEN TO ME AND ANSWER WHEN I CALL TO HIM. PSALM 4:3, TLB.

MAKING FRIENDS

God is a friend who not only listens but also does something about our problems.

Fraidy Cat

Job's problem was similar to Fraidy Cat's problem. No one seemed to understand what either of them was trying to say.

Fraidy Cat was a gray-and-white kitten adopted by Arthur and Pam Gordon. For the first few days she hid under their bed and cried, so they called her Fraidy Cat.

Then one day Fraidy got pregnant. Before long she developed a cough. Pam and Arthur didn't worry, though, because she still had a good appetite. She wasn't as active as usual, but the Gordons thought that was natural for a cat that would soon have kittens.

Early one morning Fraidy jumped on the bed, curled up on Arthur's lap, and cried a weak, sad little cry.

"Something's wrong with Fraidy Cat," Arthur said. "Fraidy Cat, what are you trying to tell me?"

Fraidy Cat just lay there and gave another faint, plaintive meow. Then another.

I do wish I could understand cat language! I know something's wrong, but I can't understand what she's trying to say.

That day Fraidy Cat didn't eat, so Arthur took her to the vet.

"I think she has a little cold," the vet said after examining her. "She doesn't have a fever. She'll be OK."

The next morning Fraidy was too weak to jump on the bed. Her eyes were glazed, and she just lay on the floor panting. So Arthur took her to a different vet.

"She has a serious infection," the vet told him. "The kittens are dead. She'll die soon too. I think you should have her put to sleep."

How sad! Arthur thought. *How I wish I could have understood what she was trying to tell me. Maybe I could have helped.*

Just like Fraidy Cat, our friends want to give us messages. They use words instead of meows to send their messages. But those words might have different meanings for us. We think we understand, but we may be wrong. In the next few readings, we'll learn how to decode our friends' messages.

OH, THAT THERE WERE SOMEONE WHO WOULD LISTEN TO ME AND TRY TO SEE MY SIDE OF THIS ARGUMENT. JOB 31:35, TLB.

MAKING FRIENDS

The purpose of listening is to not just hear the words, but to understand the message, the thought, the feeling behind the words.

Are You a Mind Reader?

Job said to his three friends, "I know full well what you are thinking." Could he read minds? Probably not. Job was making a mistake that most of us make. We *think* we can read minds. This mistake can get us into all sorts of misunderstandings. For example:

One evening Ted wanted to find out if his father was going to watch him play basketball. He asked, "What are you doing tonight, Dad?" Ted knew he was talking about the basketball game, and supposed that his dad knew that, too.

"You can have it!" Mr. Baxter replied. He was thinking, *Ted wants the car. I'm not busy, so he can have it. No problem.*

Ted heard the words "You can have it!" and thought, *He's saying "You can have your old basketball game. I'm not interested."*

Ted answered, "I don't want it now." He was thinking, *I did want you to come and see me play. Now I don't want you there.*

Mr. Baxter was really irritated by that reply. He said, "Then why did you ask?" To him it seemed dumb to think his son would ask for the car, have his dad agree, then say he didn't want it.

Ted was getting really upset with his father. He thought, *How can he be so dense? He doesn't want to come see me play basketball, and then he wonders why I'm upset!* Just before slamming the door, he yelled, "What's the use?"

Both Mr. Baxter and Ted thought they could read each other's mind. All the time neither one understood what the other was talking about. This sort of thing happens often among family members and friends.

A lot of relationship problems would never happen if we'd stop trying to read minds. It just doesn't work. You do *not* always know what I mean, even if we are the best of friends.

The solution? Stop trying to read minds!

I KNOW FULL WELL WHAT YOU ARE THINKING. JOB 21:27, NIV.

MAKING FRIENDS

We should try to say exactly what we're talking about, not expect our friend to know what we mean. Then instead of trying to read our friend's mind, we should check to see if we got the right message.

49

Check It Out!

My thoughts are not your thoughts. Isaiah 55:8, NIV.

Making Friends

Checking out the message we got lets our friends know that we really do want to listen. We want to get their intended meaning, not what we think their meaning is.

Isaiah evidently thought he could read God's mind. God had to remind him that "my thoughts are not your thoughts." And what is true between us and God is also true between friends.

Friends who want to understand will learn to check with the person speaking to make sure they understand the message. They care enough to make sure they get it correct. Here's how it worked for Dave and Sue.

Sue was cleaning out her dresser drawers, not a job she particularly enjoyed. To make it more fun, she put her favorite cassette in the player and turned up the volume.

Her brother, Dave, stuck his head in the door and said, "Turn down your music, please!"

Sue thought, *I know what he's thinking. He's just annoyed at me because Mom made him do the dishes last night so that I could go to my music lesson. He's trying to pick a fight. And besides, he probably doesn't like my choice of music.*

Then Sue remembered that Dave hadn't really said any of those things. Maybe she'd better check to make sure she'd read his mind correctly!

"So what's wrong? Don't you like my music, or are you just mad because Mom made you do dishes for me last night?"

Dave laughed. "I'll never understand girls! No, I'm not mad because I had to do the dishes. And actually, I think that's a neat recording. My problem is that I'm trying to study for my chemistry exam, and I can't concentrate. So would you mind turning it down low?"

"No problem!" Sue said, lowering the volume. "You can even shut my door if that will help."

After the door was closed, Sue thought, *I'm sure glad I checked that one out!*

We can check out the messages we receive by telling the other person what we heard. Sometimes we might be right. Sometimes we'll be wrong.

Changing Shoes

In a cartoon Nipper comes to his friend Wellington and says, "I've got this problem in math. Help me figure it out."

His friend replies, "No, I can't figure it out, Nipper." Then his face lights up, and he says, "I know! Let me put your shoes on!"

Nipper goes to get his shoes. "OK," he says, "but what has that got to do with the math problem, Wellington?"

Wellington replies, while slipping into Nipper's sneakers and tying the laces, "My mom says if I was in your shoes I could understand your problems better."

Wellington had the right idea. Communication is all about getting inside another's skin, walking in that person's shoes, understanding what life is really like for him or her.

Why did Jesus leave heaven to be born as a human being? He did it so that He could be our friend. He came to walk in our shoes and to make it possible for us to walk in His. He came to live our lives, to get inside our skin, to bring understanding between us and God.

How do we climb inside someone's skin? How can we walk in someone else's shoes? We do it by listening to the other person's story, checking to make sure we understand what he or she is saying.

We don't try to read the person's mind. We really pay attention to what is being said and try to reflect back the correct meaning to the speaker.

It means a lot to a person just to know a friend is making the effort to put himself or herself in the other's place, to try and understand what he or she is thinking.

Good listening requires us to really care about what the other person is trying to say. We aren't thinking about what story we'll tell next, but we're trying to draw out our friend so that we really hear what's being said and understand what the other person feels.

HE GAVE UP HIS PLACE WITH GOD AND MADE HIMSELF NOTHING. HE WAS BORN TO BE A MAN AND BECAME LIKE A SERVANT. PHILIPPIANS 2:7, ICB.

MAKING FRIENDS

Listening requires us to try and put ourselves in the other person's shoes. We let our friend know what we understood so that he or she can tell us if we're correct.

Face Messages

FEB. 16

**THE VERY LOOK
ON THEIR FACES
GIVES THEM
AWAY. ISAIAH
3:9, TLB.**

MAKING
FRIENDS

We communicate
by our facial
expressions. We
need to make sure
our face says what
we want it to say
to our friends. We
also need to
check with our
friends to make
sure we're reading
their faces
correctly.

Even 2-year-olds get a message from the look on a person's face! A smile tells them that all is well, and a frown can speak of anger.

Two-year-old Jackie was riding in the front seat with her mother, Irene Kassorla. Usually Irene talked to her little daughter as she rode along, but this morning she was unusually quiet.

Jackie looked up at her mother's face. Her forehead was wrinkled. She was frowning. Her lips were tightly closed.

A troubled look came over the little girl's face. *Uh-oh!* Jackie thought. *I'm in trouble. Mommy thinks I've been naughty. She's unhappy about something I did. She's angry with me!*

Jackie reached over and touched her mother's arm. "Mommy, are you angry?" she asked.

"Angry?" Irene sounded surprised. "No, honey. I was just thinking about what to have for supper tonight. What made you think I was angry?"

"Your face didn't look happy, Mommy," Jackie said.

"Was I frowning?" Irene asked as she stopped at a traffic light.

"Uh-huh."

"Sorry!" Mother said smiling. "That was just my thinking face."

As she drove on, Irene thought, *I'm glad Jackie checked out her impression. If she hadn't given me a chance to explain, we might have had a very unhappy shopping trip!*

Irene began to notice that she did frown whenever she was thinking. She tried to be much more careful after that so that people didn't think she was angry when she was only planning what to have for supper!

Ginger Church once shared Irene's problem. One day her 6-year-old son asked, "Mama, don't you ever smile?"

Startled, Ginger realized it was true! She looked in the mirror and saw more frown lines than laugh lines. She took her problem to God, asking Him to change her face! And He did! Now her face has lots more laugh lines!

The Inner Voice

Ejnar Lundby was scheduled to preach in a church in Oslo, Norway. He decided to spend the evening praying for Kristian, a friend who was scheduled to be executed the next morning for a murder he hadn't committed. Pastor Lundby reached for the phone to cancel out.

As his hand touched the phone, an inner voice said, "No! You must go to the meeting!"

I don't want to go to that meeting, but I believe God is speaking to me. I must listen to Him!

He dressed and went to the meeting, still wondering what God had in mind.

"Something is urging me to ask you to pray for a man who is to be executed tomorrow for murder," Pastor Lundby told the audience. "Let me tell you the story about this man whom I believe is innocent."

As he talked, Mr. Lundby noticed a man leave his seat, hurry down the aisle, and out the door. After the meeting, the man was waiting for the pastor. "I was at the scene on the night of the murder. I saw who did it; it was not Kristian!"

"Will you testify in court?" Pastor Lundby asked.

"Yes, I'll be glad to do it," the stranger replied. "My conscience has been bothering me for many weeks about this."

Pastor Lundby got the stranger to write down what he saw. That night he took it to the home of the state prosecutor.

The next morning the state prosecutor ordered a postponement of Kristian's execution. The stranger was brought to court to testify. Kristian was released, a free man!

"Every day I take time to pray and then quietly wait for God to speak to me," Pastor Lundby says. "Whenever I hear that silent, inner voice asking me to do something, I try to obey immediately. In this way God has led me to some really exciting adventures for Him!"

YOUR EARS WILL HEAR A VOICE BEHIND YOU, SAYING, "THIS IS THE WAY; WALK IN IT." ISAIAH 30:21, NIV.

MAKING FRIENDS

If we make a practice of quietly listening for God's voice each day, God *will* speak to us. He may not speak out loud, but He'll speak to our minds, telling us what He wants us to do.

Dot's Skates

I KNOW THAT YOU ALWAYS HEAR ME. JOHN 11:42, ICB.

"Dear Lord, I want a pair of roller skates." Dot knelt beside her bed at Mount Vernon Academy and told her Friend all about her problem. "I not only *want* skates, I *need* skates! I feel so lonely sitting on the sidelines watching everyone else skate on gym night."

"I can't write home for money since I know Mom and Dad are having a rough time paying the bills," Dot continued, "so I'm asking You for some roller skates. I know You can do anything." Dot thought of all the miracles she'd heard about, really big things God had done for people. "This seems like a very small thing to ask. The skates don't even have to be new."

Dot crawled into bed, wondering if God had been listening. Did He care about something so small as roller skates? She didn't have long to wait. Three days later she discovered a letter in her mailbox. The postmark was Oak Hill, Ohio. It was from Elizabeth Morris, a family friend who attended her church back home in Jackson, Ohio.

Dot ripped open the envelope, and two crisp bills fell out, a $10 bill and a $5 bill. *Wow!* Dot thought. *That's just how much the pair of used skates costs that I saw advertised on the bulletin board!*

"I felt impressed to send you this money," the letter said. "I'm sure you could use a little spending money for something you need just now." Dot raced downstairs to the bulletin board. The notice was still there! And the skates were just her size! Within an hour she had her skates and was on her way to join her friends in the gym.

As she glided around the gym with her friends, Dot was beaming. *God, You really did hear my prayer!* she thought. *Thank You for my skates! What would I do without a Friend like You!*

MAKING FRIENDS

"Prayer is the opening of the heart to God as to a friend" (*Steps to Christ*, p. 93). Take to God all the desires and needs of your heart. He'll listen to you.

Alexander's Secret

sn't that a strange verse? Shouldn't it read, "I will *listen* to hear what he will say to me?"

Twelve-year-old Alexander of Macedonia understood that indeed we do have to *look* in order to understand the message a person—or even an animal—is trying to give.

The year was 344 B.C. There was excitement in Pella, the capital of Macedonia. Important men had gathered on an open plain outside the city. King Philip himself was there with his son, Alexander.

The crowd had come to see the horses brought by a dealer from Thessaly. Alexander gasped in surprise when a groom led out the most magnificent horse he'd ever seen. "What's his name?" Alexander asked.

"Ox-blaze," the man replied.

"Demonstrate what he can do," the king commanded.

One after another the best riders in the kingdom tried to ride Ox-blaze. He bucked, kicked, and threw them all.

"Take him away!" King Philip demanded.

"No, Father!" Alexander protested. "Let me try!"

The king shook his head.

"Please, Father! Give me a chance," Alexander begged.

"Very well!" the king said with a frown. "It will teach you a good lesson! If you fail, you must pay for the horse yourself."

Alexander took the bridle from the groom and turned the horse around so that he faced the sun. The prince had noticed that Ox-blaze had been frightened by his own shadow dancing on the ground in front of him. With his shadow behind him, the horse stopped trembling. Alexander swung himself onto his back.

Ox-blaze was off like an arrow across the plane, while King Philip and the others watched with concern. At last Alexander turned the tired horse, returned to the group, and dismounted.

"The horse is yours!" King Philip said. "What was your secret?"

Do you know the answer?

I WILL LOOK TO SEE WHAT HE WILL SAY TO ME. HABAKKUK 2:1, NIV.

MAKING FRIENDS

We need to open our eyes to understand the message our friends give by their body language.

Body Language Quiz

Below are seven body language descriptions. Do you understand what each person is saying?

1. Jake shuffles slowly down the hall, hands in his pockets. His shoulders are slumped over, his head down, eyes on floor. Jake is telling you that he's:
   (a) angry   (b) dejected   (c) mischievous

2. Michael stands beside you, arms crossed, hands closed into the fist position. He's frowning. Michael is telling you that he's:
   (a) cold   (b) comfortable   (c) defensive

3. Tiffany sits, her legs crossed. One foot is jiggling up and down in a slight kicking position. She's twiddling her thumbs. Tiffany is telling you that she's:
   (a) bored   (b) angry   (c) relaxed

4. Josh is sitting at the table, having a good-natured debate with his friends. He has his elbows on the table, his arms up, the fingertips of one hand touching the fingertips of another, making a pyramid. What is Josh feeling?
   (a) boredom   (b) confidence   (c) anger

5. Ken sits on a sofa in the student lounge. His two hands are clasp behind his head. His left knee is bent, the left foot resting on his right leg. Ken is feeling:
   (a) superior   (b) inferior   (c) confused

6. Cathy is sitting with you at a table for two. She has her right elbow on the table, her hand covering her mouth, as she leans forward to talk to you. She is being:
   (a) honest and open   (b) closed and cautious

7. The principal has Steve in his office. He rubs his neck, then gets up, walks to the window, and looks out. His hands are clasped tightly behind him. The principal is trying to:
   (a) think   (b) get self-control   (c) relax

I UNDERSTAND WHAT YOU ARE SAYING. JOB 13:1, TLB.

MAKING FRIENDS

Learning to read people's body language helps us understand what they're trying to say to us.

Answers: 1. b. 2. c. 3. a. 4. b. 5. a. 6. b. 7. b.

Train Talkers

FEB. 21

Tania was sitting alone on one of the big tires in the playground. Chantel ran over to join her. "Hi, Tania," Chantel said as she plopped down on the tire. "Want to play with Amy and me?"

"I got a new dress for my birthday," Tania said. "It's blue with white ruffles around the collar and cuffs. It's the prettiest dress you ever did see. I'm going to wear it to church next Sabbath. You'll see how beautiful it is."

"Want to play a game of hopscotch with us?" Chantel repeated her request.

"And that's not all I got for my birthday," Tania continued. "I got a new pair of black patent-leather shoes with bow-shaped buckles. They're so shiny you can see your face in them."

"Recess will be over soon," Chantel insisted. "Come play a game with Amy and me."

"I'll wear my new shoes to church this week, and you can see what I mean." Tania paid no attention to what Chantel said. "I'm going to get a new purse to match the shoes. Won't that be neat?"

"I don't know," Chantel said, jumping off the tire. "See you later. I'm going to go play hopscotch with Amy."

Tania sighed. *Now why did she go away just when I was enjoying talking to her? I guess she just doesn't like me. Nothing I can do about that!*

There *is* something Tania can do to make friends. She can stop being a train talker! She can learn to listen to what other people are saying.

Train talkers go nonstop. No matter what you say, they just keep going down their own track at high speed, paying no attention to your comments or suggestions.

Two doctors did a research project on train talkers. They discovered that people who speak 80 percent of the time and listen only 20 percent of the time aren't well liked. The people with the most friends are those who listen more than they talk!

[THERE IS] A TIME TO BE SILENT AND A TIME TO SPEAK. ECCLESIASTES 3:7, NIV.

MAKING FRIENDS

An interesting conversation is one that moves back and forth between friends. Are you a train talker with friends? With God?

57

The Value of Silence

A good friend knows the value of silence. There are three times when silence aids friendship.

1. *In ordinary conversation.* Just as a number is increased 10 times by adding a zero to the end of it, so conversation is made more valuable with the addition of silence.

Too often we're listening for a chance to interrupt to tell our story, instead of listening to what the other person is saying. We should keep silent when our friends are speaking so that we may learn what they're thinking and feeling.

2. *When you're angry.* It's very easy to make a cutting remark when you're angry. There's a lot of wisdom in counting to 10 (or 100 if necessary!) before you say something you'll later regret.

If you find yourself wanting to interrupt your friend because of anger, try taking a sip of water or fold your hands and smile. Just a moment of silence may save a friendship.

3. *When your friend is hurting badly.* There's something magic about a silent, attentive listener that calms a person who is upset. Having such a quiet listener in a time of stress actually slows the other person's heart rate and relaxes his or her muscles. After a period of having a friend listen, a hurting person invariably feels better, more able to cope.

Richard Lindaman worked hard for four years, studying when others were playing. Why? He wanted desperately to be a doctor. On his college graduation day he received notice that his application for medical school had been turned down. He felt as though his whole world had collapsed.

He says, "I knew that I needed to talk to someone. I needed to explode and get a lot of things off my chest. But most of all, I needed to be with someone who cared. I called up my roommate. We met, and I talked. He sat there for three hours listening. That's all he did—listen. And that's exactly what I needed."

EVEN A FOOL IS THOUGHT WISE IF HE KEEPS SILENT. PROVERBS 17:28, NIV.

MAKING FRIENDS

Friends wisely use silence to understand friends, to help them cope with pain, and to control themselves in times of anger.

Silent Love

About everything that could go wrong in Job's life had gone wrong. Outlaws had stolen his camels and donkeys and killed his hired hands, and lightning had struck and killed his sheep and servants. His 10 children died in one night.

His three friends heard about his tragedy and came to visit. When they saw his terrible pain, they did nothing but sit with him in his sorrow, saying nothing. For seven days!

Most of us would have a hard time keeping silent for seven minutes, let alone seven days! Yet that's what Job's friends did for him. This was an example of "silent love"—just being there for a friend who hurts.

Keith Miller had that kind of friend. It happened when his dad died. After the funeral service many people came to his house to sit and talk to him, trying to take his mind off his pain.

But one man was different. Keith didn't even know the man's name, but he remembers that he was tall with leathery skin and white hair. He sat on one end of the sofa all evening holding his felt cowboy hat in his hands. He said not one word. People came and went, but the tall man sat there silently staring at the hat in his hands.

When all others had gone, the tall man got up, went over to Keith and said, "Son, I knew your daddy, and he was a fine man." He shook hands with Keith, turned around, and left.

"I've never forgotten the kindness of that man," says Keith. "The fact that he spent the whole evening with me, saying nothing, but just being there with me, had a tremendous effect upon me."

Before that Keith never liked to attend funerals or visit people when they were having trouble. Now he tries his best to show silent love to people when they're hurting.

THEN THEY SAT UPON THE GROUND WITH HIM SILENTLY FOR SEVEN DAYS AND NIGHTS, NO ONE SPEAKING A WORD. JOB 2:13, TLB.

MAKING FRIENDS

When we really hurt badly inside, having a friend show silent love means a lot. It helps to have a friend listen to our pain, to feel it with us. Just being there is often enough.

59

Grass Fire Miracle

FEB. 24

CALL UPON ME IN THE DAY OF TROUBLE; I WILL DELIVER YOU. PSALM 50:15, NIV.

MAKING FRIENDS

What a friend God is! He hears us when we cry for help. Sometimes He works miracles to care for His friends.

Young Reuben stared at his dad. Mr. Matiko's face was blackened, his shoes charred, his clothing burned.

"Dad! What happened?"

"I saw a miracle today," Mr. Matiko said. "God parted the fire just as He did the Red Sea. He saved our crop!"

Reuben listened wide-eyed as his dad told the story.

"I'd taken five loads of grain to the railroad terminal and was on my way back when I noticed smoke from a grass fire in the distance. It was in the direction of our land. I knew that our grain was in danger."

Reuben could picture the large granary on the farm about three miles away. Beside the granary sat a large pile of straw.

"As I approached the granary bin, I could see a great wall of fire about 500 yards wide heading for the granary and straw pile. I set the horses free, took off my jacket, and frantically began beating at the flames."

Reuben looked at his dad's mooseskin jacket, charred and blackened by the fire and smoke.

"I couldn't stop the fire, so I called out 'Lord, I can't save the grain. It's in Your hands.' I put my jacket over my head and ran forward into the flames, since I knew I couldn't outrun them. I broke through the wall of flame and struggled on until it was safe to breathe."

Reuben felt goose bumps down his spine. *What a scary thing it would be to run through flames!* he thought.

His dad continued, "I looked back and saw the wall of fire part as it reached the straw pile and wheat bin. It swept by on each side, leaving both untouched."

"I want to see!" Reuben said excitedly.

"All right," his father agreed. "After supper I'll take the whole family to see the miracle God performed today."

The news spread quickly, and soon people were coming from miles around to see the evidence that God does hear us when we pray!

Sunset Encounter

I t isn't easy to run away from God. Glenn Aufderhar knows by experience. He quit school during his eighth-grade year, left home, and tried to leave God. But the Holy Spirit followed Glenn to the sawmill where he got a job. One Friday night the Holy Spirit shadowed Glenn as he and his friends headed for a theater. He saw Glenn puffing on his Red Dot cigar, trying to act cool.

The Holy Spirit came near Glenn as he stopped in front of the theater to read the posters just at sunset. The silent speaking of the Holy Spirit caused Glenn to glance up at the setting sun. At that moment God's Spirit brought back to his memory a Friday evening worship when he was 5 years old.

The story that night was on the trial of Jesus. Little Glenn wished he could change the outcome of the story. He didn't want Jesus to suffer. He didn't want Jesus to be crucified on that cross. He ran to the cook-stove, grabbed a few sticks of kindling. "If I'd been there, things would have been different!" Glenn cried, holding the sticks as if they were spears. "I would have protected You, Jesus!"

Now standing in front of the theater, Glenn felt overcome with emotion. He threw his Red Dot cigar on the ground, and without a word he left his friends. He didn't even turn around to see how they reacted to his sudden departure.

That night Glenn heard God's Spirit speaking to his heart as he looked at the sunset. He knew God was calling him back to Himself and to His church. In his heart Glenn responded, *Yes, Lord, I am coming back to you. I'll do whatever You want me to do with my life.*

God led Glenn back into the church and back to school to become a minister, evangelist, conference president, and eventually president of the Adventist Media Center.

FEB. 25

WHERE CAN I FLEE FROM YOUR PRESENCE? PSALM 139:7, NIV.

MAKING FRIENDS

You can't run away from God's voice. Because He loves you so much, He's speaking to you today, "Please, be My friend." Are you listening? What's your answer?

Listening to Problems

GIVE ME AN UNDERSTANDING MIND. 1 KINGS 3:9, TLB.

MAKING FRIENDS

Good listeners don't need to have answers. In fact, having the answers stops the listening process. Forget answers. Forget advice. Just try to understand how your friend feels.

"I don't have any friends," Lisa complained to her teacher.

"You must be feeling lonely without any friends," Mrs. Grant said. "Want to tell me about it?"

"I don't get invited to their parties," Lisa began. "No one sits beside me during lunch."

Mrs. Grant studied Lisa as she talked. The girl wore a blouse with two safety pins where the buttons should be. Her greasy hair was pushed back behind her ears. She needed a bath. *She doesn't take very good care of herself,* Mrs. Grant thought. *She doesn't like herself, so how can she expect others to like her? I wonder if I should tell her straight out what's wrong?* "No, wait. Just listen," an inner voice prompted. So Mrs. Grant said nothing.

Lisa talked and cried, sharing how she felt left out of the group. Mrs. Grant handed her some tissues. At last Lisa smiled and said, "Thanks a lot, Mrs. Grant! I feel better now, and I think I know what to do."

"Oh? What's that?"

"I need to be neater," she ran her fingers through her stringy hair. "Since Mom got sick I've been too upset to take care of myself."

"I think you're on the right track," Mrs. Grant agreed.

The next few weeks saw a dramatic change in Lisa. She dressed in clothes that were mended and pressed. Her hair was squeaky clean. She smiled a lot more, and little by little she made friends. Lisa was able to solve her own problem. All she needed was someone to listen while she sorted out her feelings.

Too often we listen to our friends to discover their problem so that we can come up with the answers. Try listening to your friends without giving any solutions to their problems. You'll be surprised at how often a friend will say, "You really helped me!" Your listening made it possible for your friend to come up with his or her own solutions.

Making More Friends

I t was Week of Prayer at the academy. After chapel Pastor Wright was available to talk with students. Fifteen-year-old Tracy made an appointment.

"What did you want to talk about?" Pastor Wright asked when they were comfortably seated on the sofa.

"Is it wrong to want to be popular?" Tracy asked.

"Of course not!" Pastor Wright responded. "Jesus wants us to have friends, provided they're the right kind."

Tracy nodded. "I'm shy," she said. "It took a lot of courage for me to come here this morning, but I really do want to know how to make more friends."

"I can give you a few suggestions that have worked for me," the pastor said. "First of all, you need to be just as friendly to other people as you would like them to be to you. Give away a lot of smiles! They're free! Almost always the person will smile back.

"Next, greet people by name. As you walk down the halls or across campus between classes, speak to each person you meet. Say the person's name with your greeting.

"Third, you don't have to be a great talker to make friends. Just be interested in people. Get them to talk about themselves and their interests. Try it out in the dining room. Get the other kids at the table talking about their classes, work assignments, or hobbies. You won't have to say much at all.

"Fourth, look for something good in each person, and then tell him or her about it. Watch for opportunities to compliment people about a song they sang, an article they wrote, or something they're wearing. We all feel good toward someone who appreciates us."

"That sounds easy enough," Tracy said. "Smile. Say 'Hi.' Get them talking about themselves. And compliment others. I'll sure give it a try."

One year later shy Tracy was elected vice president of the sophomore class. Can you guess why?

FEB. 27

DO TO OTHERS WHAT YOU WOULD HAVE THEM DO TO YOU. MATTHEW 7:12, NIV.

MAKING FRIENDS

Be to others the friend you'd like them to be to you. Smile, greet them by name, encourage them to talk about themselves, and appreciate them.

Pleasing Our Friends

YOU ARE MY FRIENDS IF YOU DO WHAT I COMMAND. JOHN 15:14, NIV.

MAKING FRIENDS

We listen to our friends' wishes. If God is our Friend, we'll listen to His Word to find out His wishes.

"Come on, you guys!" Brandon called as he raced out the door at recess. "Let's play baseball!"

A dozen friends followed Brandon to the baseball diamond. Jon ran to catch up. "Anybody want to shoot baskets?" Jon asked.

"Nah! We're playing baseball," Brandon answered. "You can play too."

"I promised Ted I'd play basketball," he said. "Thanks anyway." Jon spent recess shooting baskets with his best friend.

Jon's response was normal. We want to please our friends by doing what they ask of us. It's easy to turn your back on the crowd if your best friend wants to do something different.

It's the same in our relationship with Jesus. If we accept Him as our best friend, then we'll want to listen closely to what He has to say so that we can do what He asks us to do.

How can we listen to God's voice? Sometimes His voice comes quietly to our hearts at an important time in our lives. More often, we hear God's voice through the words of the Bible.

One way you can hear God's voice is to rewrite a Bible verse, putting your own name in the verse. Try it now with John 3:16. Put your own name in the blanks.

"For God so loved _____ that he gave his one and only Son that [if] _____ believes in him _____ shall not perish but have eternal life" (NIV).

Try it again with 1 Peter 5:7. "_____, give all your worries to him, because he cares for you" (ICB).

What's really neat is to have a special notebook where you keep your messages from God. As you read the Bible, listen for God's voice speaking directly to you. Write the verse out in your prayer notebook. Put your own name in the verse. That makes it your message from God; it will seem more real. Then write out a short prayer as your response to that message. Let Him know you're listening and want to please Him.

Listening Checkup

In which areas do you need to improve?

1. I have good eye contact when I'm listening to people.

Never   Sometimes   Usually   Always

2. I give attention with my whole body when someone is speaking.

Never   Sometimes   Usually   Always

3. I'm careful not to ask too many closed questions.

Never   Sometimes   Usually   Always

4. I use open questions to show that I'm interested in a person's opinions, feelings, and ideas.

Never   Sometimes   Usually   Always

5. I listen to people not just to hear the words but to understand their thoughts and feelings.

Never   Sometimes   Usually   Always

6. I try not to be a mind reader, but check to see if I got the message my friend was trying to give.

Never   Sometimes   Usually   Always

7. I try to put myself in my friends' shoes when they're speaking, and then I check to see if I'm correct.

Never   Sometimes   Usually   Always

8. I watch the facial expression of people to get a better idea of what they're trying to tell me.

Never   Sometimes   Usually   Always

9. I'm alert to the body language of people.

Never   Sometimes   Usually   Always

10. I feel comfortable in being with a friend in silence or when he or she needs to talk.

Never   Sometimes   Usually   Always

11. I don't try to solve my friends' problems.

Never   Sometimes   Usually   Always

12. I smile at people I meet and greet them by name.

Never   Sometimes   Usually   Always

13. I encourage people to talk about themselves and their interests.

Never   Sometimes   Usually   Always

14. I'm listening for God's message to me in Scripture.

Never   Sometimes   Usually   Always

15. I know that God listens to me when I pray.

Never   Sometimes   Usually   Always

FEB. 29

LISTEN TO ME; PAY ATTENTION TO WHAT I SAY. PROVERBS 7:24, NIV.

FFK-3

65

Two Pieces of Cake

EVERYONE IS THE FRIEND OF A MAN WHO GIVES GIFTS. PROVERBS 19:6, NIV.

MAKING FRIENDS

We feel drawn to people who are willing to share themselves and their possessions. Want to make a friend? Find something to share.

Bill Stidger stood on a corner in Boston while waiting for a streetcar to Fenway Park. The Boston Red Sox were playing again. *I'm glad I'm going early. The bleachers will be crowded today after 14 straight wins,* he thought.

The streetcar stopped. Bill got on, paid his fare, and took a seat across from two boys with lunch bags on their laps. They seemed just as excited about their lunches as they were about the baseball game.

"Mom said I'd need a big lunch today. I've got two chicken sandwiches, two hot dogs, and two peanut-butter-and-jelly sandwiches. That should last about a week! What have you got?" the boy nearest Bill asked.

"I've got lots of sandwiches too. But guess what else I've got? Two big slices of chocolate cake!" the other boy boasted.

"Wow! Two slices of cake!" his friend sounded impressed. "I don't even have one slice. Wish Mom had sent me some cake."

"Whatcha think I brought *two* slices for?" his friend said with a grin and poked him with his elbow. "One's for you!"

"Really?"

"Yeah! Wanna see?"

The second boy opened his lunch sack. His friend licked his lips at what he saw. "Yum! Let's have it now!"

"No!" The boy with the cake closed his bag and moved it to his side. "You've gotta wait until we get to the ballpark!"

Bill smiled at the boys' exchange. *No doubt about it—they're friends!* he thought. *I like their spirit of sharing.*

Bill was right. Friends share. They're willing to share tangible things such as food, money, toys, and clothes. They're also willing to share more intangible things such as love, joy, and faith. Friends share interests and good times together, but they also share each other's burdens and heartaches. Friends take turns and share opportunities. Friends share themselves—their opinions, their thoughts, and their feelings.

The Miracle Chickens

"Hello," Mrs. Brown said. "Yes, it is. . . . Where? . . . When? . . . How did it happen? . . . Is he hurt badly? . . . I'll be right there!"

She hung up the phone and dashed across to the neighbor's house to ask her to care for the baby. Cheryl and Don could stay there too, when they came from school. Mrs. Brown rushed to the hospital to see her husband who had been badly hurt in an automobile accident.

That was the beginning of several months of really bad times for the Brown family. Father's last paycheck came to only $80, and that would never see them through the winter. The insurance would help, but no matter how she figured, Mother still needed $5 more each week.

I wonder if I should pay tithe? Mrs. Brown thought. *Does God expect me to share with Him when I don't have enough to feed my family?* She was tempted to spend the tithe money, but she remembered Malachi 3:8-11.

"I'll trust God," Mother said as she took the tithe envelope and put inside $8 plus an extra $1 for a thank offering.

Before long the windows of heaven began to open. Don came in from the barn and said, "Where shall I put the eggs? The fridge is full, and I've got half a bucketful left."

Mother brought out the old wooden crate that held 12 dozen eggs. By the end of the week it was almost full. Never before had they had more eggs than they could eat. Mrs. Brown sold them and got $4.90. Every week thereafter the hens laid enough eggs for Mother to earn the $5 she needed.

Then, very strangely, the week Father was able to go back to work, the hens again started laying only enough for the family to eat. *What a wonderful friend God has been to us!* Mrs. Brown thought. *We shared with God, and He kept His promise to share the blessings of heaven with us!*

MAR. 2

BRING ALL THE TITHES INTO THE STOREHOUSE . . . ; IF YOU DO, I WILL OPEN UP THE WINDOWS OF HEAVEN FOR YOU AND POUR OUT A BLESSING. MALACHI 3:10, TLB.

MAKING FRIENDS

Want to be a friend of God? Remember to share one tenth of everything with Him as He's requested. Then wait to see what blessings He'll share with you!

67

He Shared His Bed

MAR. 3

SHARE WITH GOD'S PEOPLE WHO NEED HELP. BRING STRANGERS IN NEED INTO YOUR HOMES. ROMANS 12:13, ICB.

MAKING FRIENDS

Hospitality, the sharing of one's home, is one way we can make friends. Is there someone new in your school whom you might invite to share the hospitality of your home for a meal or a night?

George Boldt stood behind the counter of a small hotel in Philadelphia. The hands on the lobby clock pointed to 1:00 a.m. The rooms were full. Outside it was raining hard. *I might as well lock the door and go to bed,* he thought.

Just then the door opened, and an elderly couple walked in. "All the hotels are filled up," the white-haired man said. "Can you possibly give us a room?"

"Sorry," George replied, "there are three conventions in town. There are no rooms anywhere."

The man looked at his wife and sighed.

"But I simply can't send a nice couple like you out into the rain at this time of night," George continued. "Would you perhaps be willing to sleep in my room?"

"We wouldn't want to put you out."

"Oh, I'll do just fine; don't worry about me. I insist you stay. Follow me."

The next morning as the old man paid his bill, he said to George, "You are the kind of manager who should be the boss of the best hotel in the United States. Maybe someday I'll build one for you!"

George laughed. He never expected to hear from the man again. What a surprise George got two years later when he received a letter from his rainy-night guest. Included with the letter was a round-trip ticket to New York. "Come see me," the letter said. "I have something to show you." It was signed by William Waldorf Astor.

Once in New York, a mystified George followed Mr. Astor to the corner of Fifth Avenue and Thirty-fourth Street. There he saw a palace of reddish stone. It looked like a castle against the New York sky.

"That's the hotel I've just built for you to manage!" the old man commented as he grinned at the flabbergasted young man. The sign on the building read "The Waldorf-Astoria Hotel."

Thomas Shares

Two hundred fifty years ago two 12-year-old boys, Peter and Thomas, met near the back door of a palace in Florence, Italy.

Thomas was working there as a kitchen boy, and Peter had just arrived from his hometown, Cortona.

"Peter! Good to see you! What are *you* doing here?" Thomas asked.

"I've come to learn how to paint," Peter said. "I have no money and no place to stay. Could you share your room? When I become a famous artist, I'll pay you back."

"That's a deal," Thomas agreed. "Follow me."

They climbed several flights of stairs to a small attic room among the chimney pots. Its only furniture was a straw mattress and two chairs. Later Thomas brought him some scraps of food discarded by the palace cook. He told no one about his friend who shared his room and his food.

"This is great!" Peter said. "Now I need paper, pencils, brushes, and paints."

"I wish I could help you," Thomas sighed, "but I won't get paid any money for three years. But I've got an idea. I'll bring charcoal from the kitchen, and you can draw pictures on the wall."

With the charcoal Peter drew figures of men, women, birds, trees, animals, and flowers all over the walls.

Then one day the owner of the palace asked, "Who lives in this room?"

"Thomas, the kitchen boy."

"Send for him," the rich man ordered. When the boy arrived the man asked, "Did you draw these pictures?"

"No, sir," Thomas said, hanging his head. "It's my friend Peter. He has no money and no place to stay. Please don't send him away."

"On the contrary," the rich man replied. "I would like to pay his way to the best painting school in Florence."

Fifty years later everyone knew about the famous artist Peter of Cortona. He lived in a fine house with his lifelong friend, Thomas.

CHEERFULLY SHARE YOUR HOME WITH THOSE WHO NEED A MEAL OR A PLACE TO STAY FOR THE NIGHT. 1 PETER 4:9, TLB.

MAKING FRIENDS

Friends cheerfully share whatever they have with those who are in need. Lifelong friendship often results from such unselfishness.

Vincent's Gift

**TO GIVE IS
HAPPIER THAN
TO GET.
ACTS 20:35,
MOFFATT.**

MAKING
FRIENDS

Can you think of
someone who
needs food or
clothes? What
could you do to
help? Discover for
yourself that it's
more fun to give
than to get.

Dressed in an old sheepskin coat, Vincent de
Paul led a small herd of sheep over the rough
ground near Pouy, France. He skipped along the
path, hardly thinking of the animals in his care. His
mind was on the 30 sous in his pocket. He put one
hand inside to make sure they were still there. How
rich he felt!

*I hope a peddler comes soon so that I can spend
it,* Vincent thought. *Maybe I'll buy a pretty comb for
Mother's hair. Then perhaps I can buy myself a whistle or a flute.*

Just then Vincent looked up to see a man hob-
bling toward him—slowly, painfully—across the un-
even ground.

He seems to be quite poor, Vincent thought. *He
looks cold and ill. I wonder what he wants.*

"Alms, for pity's sake," the old man croaked.
"Have you anything for a poor man who has had
nothing to eat for two days?"

Vincent put his hand into the pocket and brought
out his 30 sous. He placed the coins in the man's outstretched hand. "That's all I have. I hope it helps."

"*Merci beaucoup!*" the old man whispered his
thanks. "God bless you for your kindness."

Vincent called to the sheep and led them to the
next pasture. Down deep inside he felt warm and
happy. He smiled at the thought of the food the
money could buy the old man. *It really is more fun to
give than to get,* he mused.

After that Vincent looked for opportunities to give
something away. When he grew up he became
known as "the man who is everybody's friend." He
gathered money from the rich and gave it to the poor.

Today, nearly 400 years later, there are Saint
Vincent de Paul Centers in many cities. Poor people
can go there to get food, clothing, and a place to sleep.

Secret Admirer

Celia walked into a north Chicago restaurant and took a booth near a window. She couldn't help noticing the pretty young woman in the next booth who was sitting alone. The girl wore an excited expression on her face and a corsage on her dress.

A waitress came by with a menu and a glass of water. Celia noticed that she then went over to the girl with the corsage. She overheard the waitress say, "So, what's the big occasion? Who sent you the flowers?"

"I don't know, but I'm so thrilled! I couldn't believe it last night when the doorbell rang, and the delivery boy handed me the flowers," the girl replied.

"Well, wasn't there a card?" the waitress asked.

"Yes. It said 'Happy Birthday from your secret admirer,' and I have no idea who that could be!" the girl giggled.

"Well, that's exciting!" the waitress agreed. "I'd like to do something for your birthday too. I'll pay your check today," she said putting the bill in her pocket. "Happy birthday!" And the waitress was off to serve another customer.

The girl still wore a big smile as she left a few minutes later. Celia noticed that she was hunchbacked. When the waitress returned to her table, Celia asked about the girl.

"She lives alone and has no family or friends that I know about. She often comes in here to eat, so I've decided to be her friend. I sent the flowers to her, hoping to bring a little excitement into her life. I think I've enjoyed my secret gift to her even more than the one she knows about. Did you see the glow on her face! Making her happy has made my day!"

"And you've made my day!" Celia beamed at the waitress.

WHEN YOU DO A KINDNESS TO SOMEONE, DO IT SECRETLY. MATTHEW 6:3, TLB.

MAKING FRIENDS

If you really want to have fun giving something to someone, try doing it without him or her ever knowing it came from you. It will put a glow on your friend's face and a very special glow in your own heart as well.

Joe's Enemies

**LOVE YOUR
ENEMIES, DO
GOOD TO THOSE
WHO HATE YOU.
LUKE 6:27,
NIV.**

MAKING
FRIENDS

Christ's formula
for turning
enemies into
friends does work,
but sometimes it
takes longer than
it did with Joe.
Don't give up if it
doesn't happen
right away.

"It doesn't work to love your enemies," Joe confronted his teacher with before school started.

His teacher looked up from the papers she was grading. "Did you try it?"

"Yes. Last night on the way home some boys threw stones at me. I didn't do anything, like you said, but they didn't stop. They called me bad names and chased me home."

"It must work, because Jesus said it does," his teacher insisted.

"Then how long will I have to put up with this?" Joe asked, frowning.

"Let's pray about it at worship," she replied. "Jesus will show us what to do."

After prayer the children thought it would be fun to make some Sabbath school papers into a book. They made beautiful covers and tied them all together with blue yarn. They decided that Joe would give the book to the boys who threw the stones.

That evening after school Joe went looking for the boys who had thrown the stones. "Look what I brought you!" he shouted.

"Brought us?" The boys' mouths dropped open in astonishment.

"Yeah! Come see! It's a book full of stories, pictures, and puzzles. You'll like it."

One of the boys took the book. Joe opened his lunch box and brought out an apple. "I had this left over from lunch," he said. "I want you to have it. We have lots more at the farm."

Another boy took the apple. "Thanks," he said. The boys ran off with the apple and the book, and Joe smiled all the way home.

The next morning the boys were waiting for him beside the road. "Hi!" They waved and smiled. "We liked the book! Make another one for us sometime."

"OK!" Joe called back. "I will."

He ran all the rest of the way to school and burst into the classroom. "Teacher, it worked!" he said, catching his breath. "I think I've just made some new friends!"

The Two Brothers

According to a Hebrew legend, there were two brothers who were farmers. They lived in separate houses and had separate granaries. One was married, and the other was single. They shared the work equally and also shared the harvest equally.

It isn't fair to divide the grain equally, the single brother thought one evening. *After all, he has more mouths to feed than I do. Each evening I'll take a sack of grain from my granary and put it quietly into his.*

So that night when it was dark, the single brother carried the sack of grain and put it into the married brother's granary.

As the married brother sat enjoying his family, he thought to himself, *It really isn't fair that we get exactly the same amount. I have children to care for me when I get old, but my poor single brother has no one. I'll take a sack of grain from my granary and sneak it into his.*

The next morning each brother shook his head in bewilderment as he counted his bags of grain. Although they had each given one away, they still had the same number left. The same thing happened for many days.

Then one night the single brother was a little late, and the married brother was a little early. They met each other halfway between the two granaries. Then they understood why their bag count was always the same. They set down their sacks of grain, hugged each other, and laughed.

According to this Jewish folktale, God was so pleased when he saw how much the two brothers loved each other that He said, "This spot is holy ground." The legend says that is where Solomon built his temple.

This story has been passed on for many generations. I don't know how much of it is true, but it certainly illustrates the truth that we can't give without also receiving.

MAR. 8

WHATEVER MEASURE YOU USE TO GIVE— LARGE OR SMALL—WILL BE USED TO MEASURE WHAT IS GIVEN BACK TO YOU.
LUKE 6:38, TLB.

MAKING FRIENDS

God has His own way of making up to us all that we share with others. "The way you give to others is the way God will give to you" (Luke 6:38, ICB). What a special friend He is!

Money in a Bottle

EACH ONE SHOULD GIVE, THEN, WHAT HE HAS DECIDED IN HIS HEART TO GIVE. HE SHOULD NOT GIVE IF IT MAKES HIM SAD. . . . GOD LOVES THE PERSON WHO GIVES HAPPILY. 2 CORINTHIANS 9:7, ICB.

MAKING FRIENDS

Being a friend of God includes giving cheerfully for the needs of His church and His work in the world.

It was January 1990. Ryan Davis had decided in his heart that he wanted to do something to help build the new church in Hendersonville, Tennessee.

Ever since he was 3 years old, Ryan had heard people talking about it. He'd gone up front each Sabbath, taking dollar bills from outstretched hands. He'd stuffed other people's money into the little church sitting on the table at the front. Now he wanted to give his own money.

Ryan got a two-liter soda bottle and put it in a kitchen cabinet. *I'll fill it with coins,* Ryan decided. *When it is full, I'll give the money to the church building fund.* Ryan's Christmas money and birthday money went into the jar. He did chores to earn money and put it into the jar.

Then one day when Ryan was shopping with his mother, he was attracted to a display of Micro Machine automobiles (tiny cars, smaller than Hot Wheels). He already had 200 in his collection. He picked out one he didn't have. He longed to add it to his collection.

His mother saw how much he wanted the tiny car. "I'll split the cost with you," she offered.

Ryan shook his head. He put the car back on the shelf.

"Why don't you get it?" Mrs. Davis urged. "I know you have the money."

Then Ryan told his secret. "I can't, Mom. That money is for the church building."

When they got home, Ryan took out his bottle and shook the contents onto the living room carpet. He counted the coins and put them back in the bottle. Every month he counted his money. One day the total came to $101.50. "I think it's time to take it to church," he said.

The next week he was invited up front to present his soda pop bottle full of coins. As he handed it over to the church elder, he felt really happy inside. No doubt God was watching that Sabbath morning. I think He must have smiled as He accepted Ryan's gift of love.

The Bus Pass

It was the day Ed and Ray had been waiting for—the day the writer's club trophy would be awarded. Ed and Ray were both excellent students in their junior year of high school. One of them was bound to win the trophy. At 4:00 the judges would tally the points and announce the winner.

Most people expected Ed to win. His parents were well off, and they had given him books, music lessons, and travel. Ray's father was an unskilled laborer; he'd not had Ed's advantages.

"You're going to win the trophy, Ed!" his friends announced as they greeted him before school started. "You've got 108 points, and Ray has only 105 points."

Ed turned to his friend Ray. "I thought you had more points than I did. What happened?"

"My bad luck, I guess," he sighed. "I forgot a paper at home that's worth 10 points."

"But you have until after school to get everything turned in," Ed said. "Why don't you jump on the bus at noon and go get your missing paper? There'd be lots of time."

Ray just shook his head. The buzzer for first class sounded, and there was no more time to talk. Ed worried about his friend's predicament all day. At lunchtime he made a beeline for Ray. "Come on, man! Why don't you go get your paper? It's not too late! You deserve to win!"

"I don't have the bus fare," Ray admitted. "It can't be helped. It's my own fault I forgot the paper. Just forget it."

"No, I won't forget it," Ed responded, reaching into his pocket for his bus pass. "Here. Use my pass. Go home and get that paper."

"You sure you want me to do this?" Ray looked hard at his friend.

"Yes, I'm sure. Now, go for it!"

That evening the club secretary read off the points. Ed still had 108; Ray had 115. "The trophy goes to Ray!" he announced. Everyone cheered, and Ed cheered the loudest of all.

MAR.. 10

GIVE YOUR BROTHERS AND SISTERS MORE HONOR THAN YOU WANT FOR YOURSELVES. ROMANS 12:10, ICB.

MAKING FRIENDS

A real friend is willing to share opportunities and honors, wanting a friend to succeed even if it means his or her own failure.

You Go First

BE HUMBLE AND GIVE MORE HONOR TO OTHERS THAN TO YOURSELVES. PHILIPPIANS 2:3, ICB.

MAKING FRIENDS

Real friends are more interested in your happiness than they are in their own. Friends are willing to take turns, to give you the opportunity they'd like for themselves.

Bronya Sklodovska struggled to read a difficult story to her parents. Four-year-old Manya got impatient, snatched the book from Bronya's hands, and read the whole story without a mistake.

"How did you do that?" her mother asked.

"I don't know. It was easy," the little girl said as she shrugged.

Bronya didn't like the idea of her baby sister being more clever than she. Manya was not only more intelligent than her sister, but she was also smarter than most other children in Warsaw. She joined the Gymnasium, where only the cleverest children in Poland were allowed to attend. She finished with highest honors.

Meanwhile Manya's mother had died, and Bronya had to take care of the family. After graduation Manya got a job so that she could save money to go to Paris, France, to study in the university. She knew Bronya also longed to study in Paris, but money was scarce.

"I've got an idea!" Manya told Bronya. "If you and I keep on saving for ourselves, neither one of us will get to study. So, you go. I'll send money to help you. When you finish, it will be my turn to go to Paris. Then you can help me."

"No! It wouldn't be fair," her sister objected. "You're much smarter than I am. You go first."

"Don't be silly, Bronya. You're older. You've already waited a long time. You must go first."

So Bronya went to Paris, and Manya stayed in Warsaw. After several years Bronya became a doctor. She sent for Manya so that she could begin her studies in mathematics and physics. In Paris Manya was called Maria. She fell in love with a French scientist, Pierre Curie.

You've heard of the Curies. They won the Nobel Peace Prize in physics for their discovery of radium. Maria later received the Nobel Prize in chemistry. I think she deserved the Nobel Prize for friendship, too, don't you?

Tim, Baseball, and the Colonel

im sat on the back steps of his home and wiped away his tears with the back of his hand.

Next door the colonel sat on his porch in a rocking chair. Noticing that Tim seemed unhappy, the old man got up and walked over to see what was wrong. "Why aren't you over on the baseball sandlot?"

Tim didn't speak. He was afraid he'd start crying, so he just lowered his head and swallowed hard.

The colonel sat down beside him. "How many boys on your Eagles team?" he asked.

"Fourteen."

"Since only nine can play at once, that gives you a chance to share your playing positions, I suppose."

How does he know so much? Tim thought. *He never comes to the sandlot.* Aloud he said, "But I like to pitch. They won't let me."

"Then why not play outfield, or catcher, or second base?"

"No! I just like to pitch. I'm the best pitcher. We win when I pitch."

"Let me ask you a different question, Tim," the colonel continued. "Which part of your body is the most important?"

Tim frowned. He wasn't sure what this had to do with baseball. "The brain?" he asked.

"Probably so," the colonel said. "Then I guess it doesn't matter if we cut off your ears, nose, hands, and feet. They aren't so important, so they don't matter."

Tim laughed. "I think I see what you mean, Colonel. One position is just as necessary as another. Outfield is just as important as second base. A catcher is just as important as a pitcher. Every team member is just as important as every other team member."

That's it!" the colonel said, and his face brightened. "Never try to shove yourself into the number one spot. Help your team members succeed."

"I could teach Tony how to play. He's new, and we've never given him a chance."

"Now you're talking like a champ!" said the colonel.

LOVE IS . . . NEVER . . . SELFISH. . . . LOVE DOES NOT DEMAND ITS OWN WAY. 1 CORINTHIANS 13:4, 5, TLB.

MAKING FRIENDS

Friends don't try to have their own way all the time. They're willing to take turns, to share the honors.

Share Your Talents

GOD HAS GIVEN EACH OF YOU SOME SPECIAL ABILITIES; BE SURE TO USE THEM TO HELP EACH OTHER.
1 PETER 4:10, TLB.

MAKING FRIENDS

When we use our talents to help someone else, we're taking a step toward friendship.

It was a cold, blustery winter evening in Boston. An old man, playing on a battered violin, sat on the sidewalk in front of the Boston Public Library. The instrument squeaked and whined as he tried to play a tune with his nearly frozen fingers.

It was almost closing time, and crowds were pouring from the library. They cast disgusted looks in his direction and made a wide berth around him.

"There ought to be a law against beggars in the streets," someone complained.

"The sound is enough to kill a cat!" commented another.

Just then a student from the nearby Boston University School of Music stopped in front of the old man and listened for a moment at his feeble attempts to make music. *It could do with a tuning,* she mused.

"Please, may I see your violin for a moment?" the girl asked with a smile.

The man stopped playing, hesitated a moment, then handed over his violin and bow. She tightened some knobs and tested the strings. She worked a moment more, then smiled, satisfied that it was in tune.

"May I play it, sir?" she asked.

He shrugged his shoulders. "If you want to, miss."

She began to play a piece she had done for her recital, a familiar tune to many, "Ave Maria." The violin responded to her expert touch. The music soared, and people stopped to listen.

The girl smiled at the crowd that gathered, nodding her head toward the old man's cup. People reached into their pockets and purses and placed coins and bills into his empty cup. Someone stuck in a $5 bill.

Tears streamed down the old man's wrinkled face as he listened to music his gnarled fingers could never produce. His toothless smile of gratitude was all the thanks the girl needed.

The music finished, the girl handed back the violin and went on her way, content that by using her talent she had made a happier world for one old man.

Sharing Trouble

It happened in Oklahoma City several years ago. Streetcar brakes squealed, and a man screamed. Quickly a crowd gathered to see what had happened. They saw a man trapped underneath the streetcar. "Get me out! Get me out!" he begged. "It hurts! Please, help me!"

A police officer came and radioed for help. An emergency crew arrived.

"We can't do it," one of the men said, after they had tried for several minutes to lift the car. "We need heavy equipment that will take at least a half hour to reach here."

"No! No!" the man screamed. "I can't live with this pain for a half hour!"

"Just hold on!" an officer shouted to him.

"I can't! Somebody help me!" the man cried hysterically.

Sirens wailed and an ambulance arrived, but there was nothing they could do until the equipment came to set him free.

It was then that a very ordinary man from the crowd stepped forward, rolled under the car, and lay down beside the terrified man. He put an arm around him and began to talk quietly. "It's OK. I'm here to help you. More help is coming. I know it hurts terribly, but we'll get through this together."

The man stopped screaming. He opened his eyes and looked at the stranger lying beside him. "Thank you, friend," he said.

For 30 minutes the stranger lay beside the trapped man, talking to him softly. Then they heard a shout from the crowd: "It's come! The equipment is here!" Everyone clapped. Within moments the equipment lifted the streetcar that pinned the man down.

The very ordinary man who had lain beside him quietly disappeared into the crowd. Anybody could have shared the man's troubles and could have carried away the memory of the man's words, "Thank you, friend." The man may have been quite ordinary, but his act of friendship was most extraordinary.

SHARE EACH OTHER'S TROUBLES AND PROBLEMS. GALATIANS 6:2, TLB.

MAKING FRIENDS

If we want to be someone's friend, we need to be willing to share that person's troubles and problems. A friend shares the bad times as well as the good.

Khama, the Lion Killer

MAR. 15

NOT EVERYONE WHO SAYS TO ME, "LORD, LORD," WILL ENTER THE KINGDOM OF HEAVEN, BUT ONLY HE WHO DOES THE WILL OF MY FATHER WHO IS IN HEAVEN.
MATTHEW 7:21, NIV.

MAKING FRIENDS

Talk is cheap; it's the doing that counts. Friends do more than promise; they perform.

Khama wasn't much of a talker. He listened quietly to the instructions of the chief of the African Bamangwato tribe. "A lion has attacked my herds and killed an ox. I want it killed."

"No problem! We'll kill that old lion," the hunters promised. They went off into the jungle with their guns, making a big show of bravery. By dusk they came home, telling how hard they had tried, but the lion had somehow escaped them.

Every morning the hunters made a big show of going off to find the lion. They beat the grass and shouted, and they returned home every evening to tell how the beast was nowhere to be found. "But just wait until we find it!" the hunters boasted around the campfire. "We'll teach that lion a good lesson about attacking the chief's herd."

After listening to the promises of his warriors, the chief went to sleep worried. And sure enough, every morning there would be another ox gone.

Khama, a quiet young man in the village, got fed up hearing the hunters' boastful talk every evening of what they were going to do the next day. He watched until all the hunters were asleep, and then he slipped away into the tall grass.

When morning came the hunters stretched and slowly got up. "This is the day we will kill that old lion!" they began to boast. "Just wait until we find it! Then you'll see what we can do!"

Just then the tall grasses parted. Khama, with the dead lion, walked into the village.

Which one do you think was the real friend of the chief?

When the old chief died and the tribe had to elect a new chief, guess whom they chose? They passed by all the boasters who had so much to say about what they could accomplish. They chose Khama, a friend they knew they could count on!

A Friend in Need

It happened four days after my surgery. My incision was still red and painful, and I was feeling exceedingly sorry for myself.

"Come walk by the river with the dog and me," Ron said.

"But it hurts to walk," I whined.

"Then sit in the car while Matt and I walk. Enjoy the sunset," he suggested.

I went along to please him. It was a glorious sunset! The whole river appeared as liquid gold. I started to cry. My tears flowed unchecked, and my throat ached from the tension of wondering how long the pain would last.

I watched the gold change to softer shades of peach, apricot, and mauve. I thought of Ron and Matt walking off into the sunset of life without me. By this time my imagination was working overtime, and I was sure I'd never get well! Poor, poor me! Why must I feel so miserable? More tears.

Just then I heard the rapid beat of feet on the hard path. I looked up and saw Matt racing, tongue hanging out, straight toward the car. He came around to my side. I opened the door. He laid his head on my knee and looked up at me with those wonderful adoring eyes as if to say "Whatever is wrong with you?"

I forgot myself as I tried to get him to go back to Ron. He refused to go without me. Ordinarily he follows the one who moves the fastest. This was unlike him. No amount of coaxing would make him leave. Matt stayed by my side, refusing to enjoy the walk without me. Amazing! Somehow our dog sensed that something was wrong and wanted to help. I felt warmly cherished because Matt wouldn't leave my side.

And then it seemed as though I heard Jesus whisper to my fearful heart, "Dorothy, I'm here too. I'll never leave you or forsake you."

MAR. 16

I WILL NEVER LEAVE THEE, NOR FORSAKE THEE. HEBREWS 13:5.

MAKING FRIENDS

Jesus is a friend we can count on. He'll always be with us in times of trouble. He wants to share our problems and difficulties. What a wonderful friend He is!

81

Moving Day

**LOVE YOUR
NEIGHBOR AS
YOURSELF.
MATTHEW
19:19, NIV.**

MAKING
FRIENDS

Helping a neighbor on moving day is one way to make new friends. Are you friends with your neighbors? Can you think of some ways that you could share with those who aren't yet your friends?

82

The For Sale sign was gone, and some people were unhappy about it. It was an all-White neighborhood, and their new neighbors, the Clarks, were Black. When the Clarks made an inspection tour of their new house, no one spoke. The looks they received from people as they drove by were unfriendly.

"Our neighbors don't seem to want us," Mrs. Clark noted. "I hope we're not making a mistake."

Moving day came. The Clarks arrived before the van and began unloading their car. They were surprised when a teenager showed up to help.

"Hi, my name is Ted Davis," he said. "Welcome to our neighborhood. Here, let me help with those boxes." He picked up two and carried them into the house.

A few minutes later Mrs. Davis came with a hot drink, doughnuts, and a bouquet of red roses. "I'm Cora Davis, Ted's mom," she said. "I figured the utilities weren't turned on yet, so you could use a little something to start your day."

"Thank you!" Mrs. Clark beamed. "What a pleasant surprise! I'm sure we're going to enjoy living here."

A little later Ted's sister came over. "Hi, I'm Donna Davis. Mom said I should bring your children over to our house. Moving is bad enough without little kids under your feet."

"You don't know how much I appreciate your offer!" Mrs. Clark replied. "I was worried about keeping them out of the way while I'm telling the men where to put things. You're a lifesaver!"

By evening the van was unloaded, the beds were made, and enough kitchen stuff unpacked to fix supper. "Well, now how do you feel about our decision to move to this neighborhood?" Mr. Clark asked as they sat around the table, exhausted from their long day.

"Great!" Mrs. Clark answered. "What a difference friends can make!"

Sharing Hope

MAR.. 18

Watching the enormous shark that had been keeping pace with their ship for hours, Joseph Bates stood by the railing of the ship on which he was cabin boy. A hunk of meat fastened to a rope trailed in the water. The sailors hoped it would tempt the shark closer.

Joseph was not alone. Other sailors stood by ready to hook the shark should it come near enough. The wily animal kept its distance, but refused to leave.

"That shark could snap you in half with one bite and swallow you in two gulps!" one of Joseph's companions said. "Anyone for a swim?"

"Not me!" Joseph shuddered. "I think I'll climb the mast to see if there's anything else in sight."

Joseph climbed the main masthead to scan the horizon. There was nothing to see but water, sky, and the persistent shark. Joseph began his descent. When he reached 50 feet above the deck, he lost his hold and fell backward, striking a rope that propelled him into the ocean.

"Help!" he shouted as he went under the waves. He came back up splashing and panting for breath. He set out swimming, but his heavy clothing made movement difficult. *I'll never catch up with the ship!* Joseph panicked at the thought of being left alone with the shark. *If someone doesn't help me, I'm finished!*

Just then he noticed several crew members standing at the ship's stern. *Don't just stand there; do something!* Joseph's unspoken wish was a prayer for help.

The first mate hurled a coil of rope with all his might. Joseph grasped the end of the rope as it floated by.

"Hold on!" the sailor shouted.

There's no way I'll let go! Joseph thought. *This rope is my only hope!*

Joseph held on until he was pulled aboard the ship. The shark had missed its dinner!

How do you think Joseph felt about friends who were willing to help?

JESUS CHRIST OUR LORD— OUR ONLY HOPE. 1 TIMOTHY 1:1, TLB.

MAKING FRIENDS

Many people feel as if they're drowning in problems, troubles, and sorrows. They need a friend who'll offer hope. The Lord Jesus Christ is our hope. Shouldn't we be willing to share Him?

Sharing Good News

GO EVERYWHERE
IN THE WORLD.
TELL THE
GOOD NEWS
TO EVERYONE.
MARK 16:15,
ICB.

MAKING
FRIENDS

Friends want to
share good news
with each other.
Have you shared
the good news
about Jesus with
anyone lately?

Nine-year-old Juan lived in a small village in Central America. Every Sabbath he went to a small white church with a red-tiled roof. He sat on a wooden bench up front to listen to the preacher.

One Sabbath Juan heard the minister say, "God expects every one of you to be a witness for Jesus. No one is too old to tell someone about Jesus. No one is too young to share the Good News that Jesus died for us and is coming again soon to take us to heaven."

Juan sat up straighter. *That means me. I'm only 9 years old, but I'm not too young to talk to someone about Jesus. Wow! I wonder who I could tell?*

By the time he'd gotten home, Juan had made a decision. "Mom," he said, "I think I'll tell the store-keeper about Jesus. What should I say?"

"Take him one of these magazines," mother suggested. "If he likes it, you could take him another one next week."

Juan took the paper and skipped down the road to the little country store where his mother bought groceries.

"*Buenas días*, Juan!" the shopkeeper said. "May I help you?"

"I didn't come to buy anything today," Juan replied. "I just came to give you something. It's a surprise."

"What is it?" the storekeeper asked. "I like surprises."

"This paper," Juan answered. "It tells us that Jesus is coming soon. If you like it, I'll bring another next week."

"*Gracias,* Juan. I've been wanting something good to read."

Every Sabbath afternoon after that Juan took a magazine to the storekeeper. Then one day Juan invited his friend to church, and he accepted. Juan walked very tall as he escorted his visitor into church the next Sabbath. After church he introduced him to the pastor.

"I like your church," the storekeeper said. "I think I'll come again." He kept coming, and one Sabbath he was baptized. It all happened because one boy was willing to share the good news.

Jill Found It Hard

Jill had recently found Jesus as her friend. She wanted to spend time with Him each morning in Bible study and prayer. There was only one problem. Her roommate in the public university wasn't a Christian.

Jill shared her problem with Joan. "Could I come to your room every morning to read my Bible and pray?"

"Of course; come down anytime," Joan said.

Joan became a real friend, helping Jill hunt for God's promises. This continued for several weeks. Then one morning Joan didn't answer Jill's knock.

A faint light shone under the door. Joan was evidently there. *Why doesn't Joan unlock her door for me?* Jill wondered. She knocked one more time.

The door opened just a crack. "Jill, it's time you took a stand for Jesus," Joan said. "Sharon has to be told sometime, so go back to your own room and talk to God there. Don't be afraid to witness for Him. Go share your faith."

The door snapped shut. *How can she do this to me?* Jill blinked to hold back her tears. *I know I ought to share my faith, but I'm so scared.*

Back in her room Jill knelt by her bed. It was hard to concentrate on prayer. What would Sharon say when she walked in? Maybe she'd ask a question, and Jill could share her new faith. She determined to try.

Jill heard footsteps in the hall. She stayed on her knees, thinking in this way to confess her faith in Jesus. The door opened and shut. Sharon said nothing, just picked up her books and walked out. And that's how it was for the rest of the year. Sharon was no longer a friend.

Word got around. There were no more invitations to parties. It was hard to be cut off from old friends, but Jill felt glad that she had been true to her best friend, Jesus.

IF ANYONE PUBLICLY ACKNOWLEDGES ME AS HIS FRIEND, I WILL OPENLY ACKNOWLEDGE HIM AS MY FRIEND. MATTHEW 10:32, TLB.

MAKING FRIENDS

Have you been honest with your friends about your relationship with Jesus? He wants you to let others know openly that He is your friend, even though it's hard to do.

Sharing Yourself

[LOVE] IS
NEITHER ANXIOUS
TO IMPRESS NOR
DOES IT CHERISH
INFLATED IDEAS
OF ITS OWN
IMPORTANCE.
1 CORINTHIANS
13:4, PHILLIPS.

MAKING FRIENDS

If we want to
make friends, we
must stop acting
big and be open
and honest about
the person we
really are.

A famous psychiatrist boasts that he can get the most difficult person to talk within five minutes of entering his office. His secret? He simply shares something about himself, something that lets the patient know he's human and makes mistakes like everyone else.

The same principle worked for Brenda, the new third-grade teacher. Although she was new to the school, she wasn't new to teaching. She'd taught many years in other schools. The other teachers were polite, but none made any move to be her friend.

One time after a particularly difficult day, Brenda crossed the hall to Janelle's fourth-grade room. The children were all gone, and Janelle was pinning pictures on a bulletin board.

"Hi, Janelle!" Brenda began. "I hope your day wasn't as bad as mine. Nothing seemed to go right. The kids were restless and bored. I feel like I did one lousy job today!" She flopped down on one of the student desks and sighed.

Janelle stopped her work and stared at this woman she thought of as the perfect teacher, the one who had it all together all the time. "I love it!" she burst out. "How nice to know that you have bad days like the rest of us! I thought nothing ever went wrong for you."

She sat down on a desktop opposite Brenda and shared a funny story from her own day. They laughed, and Brenda shared something that had happened on the playground. They laughed some more. They shared about this and that. Then Janelle told Brenda about a difficult health problem she was facing.

"I needed to talk to someone about it," Janelle said, smiling through her tears. "It's neat to know you're my friend. Thanks for listening."

Janelle would never have shared if Brenda had cherished exaggerated ideas of her own importance. Because she wasn't anxious to impress, but honestly shared her feelings about the day, she made a new friend.

Popularity Isn't Everything

He was more popular than a rock band. He drew larger crowds than a movie star. A football stadium couldn't hold the multitudes that flocked to see Jesus, the miracle worker.

If popularity was what He wanted, He had it! The crowds were ready to crown Him king. But Jesus knew that popularity with the crowd isn't really that satisfying. Real satisfaction and happiness come from being with real friends.

Twelve good friends and three close friends, that's what Jesus had. Friends take time and energy to cultivate. Three is the maximum number of intimate friends most people can handle well.

Think of friendship as a set of four concentric circles, one circle inside another circle as on a target board. Draw one. Label each segment to represent a different level of friendship.

1. *Close Friends.* Usually we can handle from one to three people as close friends. With these people we share our true selves, our hopes, dreams, and deep thoughts and feelings.

2. *Good Friends.* These are people you enjoy being with. You do lots of things with these people: play games, go to parties, and work on special projects. You share some of your opinions and feelings with them, but not as deeply as level-one friends.

3. *Casual Friends.* This group might include up to 100 people. You see them at church, at camp, or at school. You share the same group experiences, but you don't share your lives in a special way as you do with those in levels one and two.

4. *Acquaintances.* Some people have 500 or more friends on this level. The older you get, the more people you know. You know their names, a little bit about them, but you don't do much together.

The neat thing is that you can use your friendship skills to move people from the outside of your friendship circle toward the inside of your friendship circle.

MAR. 22

AFTER SIX DAYS JESUS TOOK WITH HIM PETER, JAMES AND JOHN . . . AND LED THEM UP A HIGH MOUNTAIN BY THEMSELVES. MATTHEW 17:1, NIV.

MAKING FRIENDS

We share more of ourselves with those in the inner core than with those on the outer segments of our friendship circle. Sharing ourselves with someone moves them toward the inner circle.

Joseph's Sacrifice

MAR. 23

IN YOUR LIVES YOU MUST THINK AND ACT LIKE CHRIST JESUS. . . . HE GAVE UP HIS PLACE WITH GOD AND MADE HIMSELF NOTHING. PHILIPPIANS 2:5-7, ICB.

MAKING FRIENDS

Love strips away our feeling of superiority and makes us approachable. We become vulnerable, willing to let others know that we're no different than they are.

Few tourists visit the tropical paradise of Molokai, because it's a leper colony. One of the Hawaiian islands, it was made famous by the sacrifice of Joseph Damien.

Joseph Damien was a young man in Belgium when he heard about the miserable conditions of the lepers of Molokai. "I'd like to be a friend to those forgotten people," he said. "I feel that's what God wants me to do."

However, when Joseph first saw the ugliness of the lepers' disfigured faces and crippled limbs, he turned away. How could he be a friend to such grotesque people?

He chose to live apart in a little hut of his own, cooking his own meals and washing his own clothes. No leper was allowed in his home. As you can easily understand, he didn't make much progress in being their friend or in getting them to become friends of Jesus.

One day as Joseph walked the sandy beaches alone, he realized what he must do. Talking was not enough. *I must demonstrate Christ's love to them,* he thought. *I can't do that unless I can be their friend. And how can I be their friend if I'm always trying to avoid them?*

So Joseph began to mingle with the lepers. He helped them build better houses. He worked beside them, helping them dig wells. He sat in their houses and ate with them, sharing everything with them. He truly became one of them, because ultimately he caught the disease and finally died from leprosy himself.

However, before Joseph died, everyone on the island had become his friend, and everyone on the island had become a friend of God.

Joseph used an important key to making friends, vulnerability. It's the same key Jesus used. He gave up his high position to come and be as we are. He positioned himself among the poor so that He might reach the poor. He became approachable, but at the same time, He opened himself to attack. He could now be hurt and rejected.

Barbara Confesses

Barbara copied her term paper from an English magazine, then bragged about it to her friends. "Miss Judd will never know, and think of the time I've saved!"

Her friends laughed—all except Ellen. "That's cheating," she said. "I wish you wouldn't hand in that paper."

"Don't be a spoilsport," Barbara frowned. "No one will find out."

However, two days later in English class Miss Judd asked Barbara to stand. She ripped her copied term paper into several pieces, then said, "Go to my office, and stay there until you can write one of your own."

Barbara was furious. She put the word out that Ellen had tattled on her. Her classmates began ignoring Ellen, because no one likes an informer.

Ellen wondered what to do. Barbara wouldn't even speak to her. At last she decided to enlist the help of Miss Judd. She dropped by her office and explained her problem.

The next day in English class Miss Judd held up a magazine, then began to read an article. Barbara gasped. Ellen turned to see Barbara jump to her feet, her face pale.

"Where did you get that magazine?" Barbara blurted out.

"It's my own," the teacher said. "Why do you ask?"

"Do you get it all the time?"

"Yes, of course."

"Then Ellen didn't tell you!" Barbara exclaimed. "I thought she had told you that I copied my term paper. I've told everybody she did, and we've been so mean to her."

Then turning to Ellen, Barbara continued, "Oh, Ellen, can you forgive me? I want everyone to know right now that I've been a mean, little snob as well as a cheat. Ellen, you've been a true friend, and I'm sorry."

Ellen smiled at Barbara and nodded. After that Ellen and Barbara became close friends. Why? Because Barbara was willing to be open and honest. She was willing to admit her wrong and say that she was sorry.

CONFESS YOUR SINS TO EACH OTHER. JAMES 5:16, NIV.

MAKING FRIENDS

"I was wrong" may be the hardest words for anyone to speak. Yet honest confession of faults is necessary for a friendship to survive.

Windows

MAR. 25

DO THINGS IN SUCH A WAY THAT EVERYONE CAN SEE YOU ARE HONEST CLEAR THROUGH. ROMANS 12:17, TLB.

MAKING FRIENDS

Build windows instead of walls. Become transparent, allowing people to see the real you inside. If you want lasting friendships, cultivate transparency.

Imagine building a house with no windows! If you wanted privacy, you'd certainly have it, because no one could see inside and know if you were there or not. But neither could you see out to know what was going on in the world. You'd be completely isolated from others.

In a way, that's what many of us do with our inner self. We build walls around our hearts to protect ourselves from hurt. We pretend to be like James Bond, "Mr. Cool," completely detached from personal involvement. We build these walls because we're afraid that if people could look inside us and know what we're really like, the sight would repel them. We don't want to get hurt, so we build walls without windows.

Windows are transparent. People can see right through them to what is going on inside the house. If we want friends, we need to become transparent as glass so that people will see what we're really like on the inside.

Jesus was a very transparent person. That's why people were so drawn to Him. Remember the story of the Samaritan woman at the well?

"I'm tired and thirsty," Jesus said. "Please, help Me. Give Me a drink of water." Jesus shared a feeling and a need. He was opening a window to His humanity.

"The man you're living with isn't your husband," Jesus said. By this statement He was showing that He could see inside of her carefully built walls of prejudice and pretense. It also opened up another window into Himself, showing that He was more than human. He was also divine.

Jesus' transparency drew the woman to Him. It caused her to want to open up some of her windows and share the truth about her life. She ran into the city and told her friends, "Come meet a Man who told me everything about my life! I felt completely transparent in His presence. He's my friend."

Chuck Owns Up

huck Swindoll was under stress from too many things to do and not enough time to do them. He was irritable and short-tempered at the breakfast table.

One of the children answered back, and the angry words flew across the table from father to child and back again from child to father.

His wife, Cynthia, frowned. The direction of his angry missiles changed. This time Cynthia was the target.

The children stopped eating and watched wide-eyed as their dad scolded their mom. Curt, the oldest son, could stand it no longer. He threw down his napkin and walked out slamming the door behind him.

What's happening to me? Chuck thought. He looked around the room at his family. All were in tears. He began to shake from embarrassment and pressure. *Why am I doing this to them? I've just lost what I've spent years trying to gain, a respectful authority.*

Chuck left the table that morning with a plan. He canceled his appointments for the weekend and scheduled an afternoon powwow with his family. Only Curt couldn't make it, because he'd gone to work.

They sat on the floor in a circle, and Chuck confessed his sin of the morning. There were tears all around and other confessions as well. By the time they were finished, relationships had been restored, and hearts were happy again.

After the family conference Chuck took the whole family to the office building that Curt was cleaning.

"I've had such a hard day," Curt said. Chuck noticed the tears welling up in his son's eyes.

"I'm sorry, son," Chuck said, finding a catch in his own throat. "I'm sorry for my impatience this morning."

For the next hour the family talked, and then they all helped Curt finish his job. Later they went to a restaurant for supper to establish the restoration of friendship in their home.

MAR. 26

**HE WHO CONCEALS HIS SINS DOES NOT PROSPER, BUT WHOEVER CONFESSES AND RENOUNCES THEM FINDS MERCY.
PROVERBS 28:13, NIV.**

MAKING FRIENDS

On a scale of 1 to 10, how do you rate in being honest and open in your family? Family members need to be open and honest with each other if they want to be friends.

No Pets Allowed!

**BE SURE THAT
YOUR SIN WILL
FIND YOU OUT.
NUMBERS
32:23, NIV.**

MAKING FRIENDS

There's no
pretending with
friends. We aren't
afraid for them to
discover that we
aren't perfect.

Our family was enjoying a weekend holiday in the Nilgiri Hills of southern India. On Sunday morning we planned to eat out. We were about to leave our pet monkey, Bosco, in the room when 12-year-old Stephen noticed a broken window pane through which Bosco could escape. Bosco would have to go with us.

However, at the hotel where we went to eat, a sign said "No pets allowed."

"Lock Bosco in the car," my husband ordered.

"He'll get out!" 8-year-old David protested. "He knows how to roll down the windows." A leash wasn't the answer either, because Bosco knew how to untie knots and undo hooks.

"Mom, you'll have to baby-sit Bosco while we eat," 11-year-old Esther suggested.

"Hey, that's no fair!" I complained. "I know what we can do. I'll hide him inside my sweater."

I buttoned the bulky-knit red sweater down the front and stuffed Bosco inside. Crossing both arms over my middle, I said "Now there! Nobody will know he's here. Let's go! Act as though everything is normal."

Ron walked in first, followed by our three children. The only vacant table was on the far side of the room. Suddenly all talking stopped. Everybody was staring at me! I looked down. Two feet of monkey tail hung down the center of my skirt!

Just then Bosco popped a button and stuck his head out. Everyone burst out laughing! It was no use pretending any longer. I brought him out for all to see.

A waiter headed my way. My embarrassed family tried to act as if they'd never seen me before. Fortunately, he let Bosco stay with us. Afterward I wondered why I'd tried so hard to pretend he wasn't there.

Every once in a while I'm tempted to button up my sweater and hide my mistakes inside, hoping people won't discover what kind of person I really am. But sooner or later the tail of my sin slips out for everyone to see.

Marian's Big Moment

arian Anderson, world-renowned singer, sat on the stool before a large mirror in her dressing room. She'd just completed a magnificent performance to a packed theater of admirers. The applause had been thunderous. Now she sat relaxed while a newspaper reporter asked her questions.

"Marian, what would you say was the greatest moment in your life?"

Marian was silent for a while. She had many great moments to choose from.

She recalled the night that the great Toscanini told her, "A voice like yours comes to us but once in a century." *No, not that moment.*

She thought of the private concert she gave at the White House for President and Mrs. Roosevelt with the king and queen of England present. *That's not it either.*

Into her mind flashed the scene in Philadelphia, her hometown, when she'd received the $10,000 Bok Award for being the person who had done the most for the city. *That was a great moment, but not the greatest.*

She remembered the Easter Sunday in Washington, D.C., when she stood at the Lincoln Memorial and sang for a crowd of 75,000 people that included cabinet members, Supreme Court justices, and many members of the United States Congress. *An exhilarating moment, but not the greatest moment of my life.*

Miss Anderson smiled as she came to the scene that meant the most to her. She told the reporter, "The greatest moment of my life was the day I went home and told my mother she wouldn't have to take in washing anymore!"

Sol Hurok, a musician friend of Marian's, said about her, "Marian hasn't simply grown great, she has grown great simply."

Marian Anderson had dined with kings, queens, presidents, and prime ministers. She'd associated with many great and powerful men and women. She'd thrilled to the applause of millions, but her greatest thrill was connected with the glow of appreciation that she saw in her mother's eyes.

MAR. 28

DON'T TRY TO ACT BIG. DON'T TRY TO GET INTO THE GOOD GRACES OF IMPORTANT PEOPLE, BUT ENJOY THE COMPANY OF ORDINARY FOLKS. ROMANS 12:16, TLB.

MAKING FRIENDS

Some people go to great lengths to hide their humble origins when honesty about them would pave the way for true friendship.

93

Wasps in Your Shirt

MAR. 29

DON'T BE LIKE THE PLAY-ACTORS. MATTHEW 6:5, PHILLIPS.

MAKING FRIENDS

Play actors don't make good friends. Stop pretending; get real.

Bruce sped down the four-lane highway on his motorcycle. It was a hot day, and his shirt was open, the wind whipping his bare arms and face. It was rush hour. A car followed close behind him, a car led the way in front of him, and a panel truck was passing him on the left.

Just then a wasp flew into the opening of Bruce's shirt and sank its stinger into the tender flesh in Bruce's armpit. The wasp tried to get out, but the wind kept it inside. It stung again on Bruce's back, then his stomach. *I don't dare stop,* Bruce thought. *I'm so boxed in here I have to stay cool and keep my place in the traffic if I don't want to cause an accident.*

The wasp stung again! *Maybe I could steer the bike with one hand and swat it with the other.* Bruce tried to figure out what to do with that pesky wasp. *No, that won't work. I'd look ridiculous trying to catch a wasp inside my shirt. People would laugh, and I'd be embarrassed. No, I'd just better pretend nothing is wrong.*

So that's what Bruce did. He sped along the freeway smiling and acting as though he was having the time of his life, when in reality he was feeling miserable.

Finally Bruce was able to exit onto a side road. He pulled off his shirt, and the wasp flew away. He counted six welts on his chest and back. They still hurt later that night.

Philosophizing about that experience, Bruce says, "All around us there are people with wasps in their shirts who have chosen to look like Joe or Josephine Cool. They don't want to be embarrassed or to embarrass us, so they miss an opportunity for true community and belonging."

Do you have some wasps in your shirt? What are you trying to hide from others? A bad habit? Your family situation? Your grades? Your inability to read well? Something from your past? How you really feel about an issue?

Hiding From God

I remember the time I tried hiding something from God. It all started in Bible class. I was proud of the fact that I always had the top marks.

That was until Eileen McCartney joined Mount Vernon Academy. She was everything I was not: musical, blond, beautiful, and popular. And to top it all off, she was smart! It didn't seem fair for her to shine even in the area where I wanted to be the star. I was just plain jealous of Eileen.

Then came the first big Bible test. I knew all the answers but two. Glancing over to Eileen's paper I saw the answers I needed. I wrote them in quickly.

"That's cheating!" the Holy Spirit spoke to me.

But I rationalized it this way: *I did study well. I really knew those answers all along. I didn't need to see her paper. If I'd thought for a while the answers would have come.*

For days I kept trying to fool my conscience into believing I hadn't done wrong. Then I noticed something strange. When I tried to pray, I couldn't. I could hear the Holy Spirit whispering to me, "You sinned, Dorothy. That wasn't right." God didn't seem to be my friend anymore.

Then I noticed another strange thing. I was avoiding Eileen and the Bible teacher.

I decided it was no use playing games any longer. I surely wasn't deceiving God or myself. So I confessed my sin of cheating to God. And of course, He forgave me and accepted me.

Then I went to my teacher and confessed that I had cheated on the test. It made a difference in my grade, but that no longer mattered. It felt good to know that I was hiding nothing from anyone. Now I could face Eileen, my teacher, and my God. An added bonus was that Eileen and I became good friends and roommates.

MAR. 30

YOU KNOW MY FOLLY, O GOD; MY GUILT IS NOT HIDDEN FROM YOU. PSALM 69:5, NIV.

MAKING FRIENDS

Openness and honesty are the only way to go if you want to be a friend of God. Any attempt at hiding sins will shut the door to friendship with Him.

Sharing Checkup

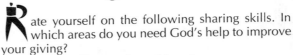

MAR. 31

A gift opens the way for the giver. Proverbs 18:16, NIV.

Rate yourself on the following sharing skills. In which areas do you need God's help to improve your giving?

1. I'm willing to share things I own.
   Never   Sometimes   Usually   Always
2. I'm willing to share my home, to offer hospitality even to people I may not know very well.
   Never   Sometimes   Usually   Always
3. I'm willing to share my money with people who are in need.
   Never   Sometimes   Usually   Always
4. I'm willing to give my tithes and offerings, sharing what I possess with God.
   Never   Sometimes   Usually   Always
5. I'm willing to share with my enemies.
   Never   Sometimes   Usually   Always
6. I'm willing to take turns, sharing opportunities with others.
   Never   Sometimes   Usually   Always
7. I don't insist on having my own way.
   Never   Sometimes   Usually   Always
8. I'm willing to share my talents to bless other people.
   Never   Sometimes   Usually   Always
9. I'm willing to share the troubles, problems, and pain of my friends.
   Never   Sometimes   Usually   Always
10. I do more than talk about what I'll do for people. I get busy and do something concrete to help.
    Never   Sometimes   Usually   Always
11. I'm willing to share my faith and to confess my love for Jesus openly.
    Never   Sometimes   Usually   Always
12. I'm willing to be vulnerable—open and honest—in my relationships, hiding nothing.
    Never   Sometimes   Usually   Always
13. I'm willing to share honestly my dreams, thoughts, opinions, and feelings with my friends.
    Never   Sometimes   Usually   Always
14. I'm open and honest with God and people, confessing my sins, saying I'm sorry.
    Never   Sometimes   Usually   Always

KEEPING FRIENDS

The Road to Friendship

**THE TONGUE
HAS THE POWER
OF LIFE
AND DEATH.
PROVERBS
18:21, NIV.**

KEEPING FRIENDS

We erect
roadblocks with
the words we
say. The tongue
has power to
bring life or death
to a friendship.

Imagine for a moment that friendship is a two-way street. I want to enjoy your friendship. You want to be my friend too. We both set out on this road called friendship, hoping to meet, but roadblocks bar the way. We try to communicate but turn around disappointed.

Have you ever had that frustrating experience? Have you tried to be friends, only to face a roadblock? Have you tried talking to a friend, only to find that the conversation suddenly stops, and he or she has other things to do?

Sue had that problem whenever she tried to be friends with Tanya. Within minutes of getting together, Tanya would start criticizing the way Sue had done her hair or the way she dressed. "That doesn't suit you at all! You should wear it back like this. Here let me show you." Or she might laugh and say, "Where did you get that sweater? It looks like something out of Noah's ark!"

Sue would respond, "I know why you said that. You're just trying to make me mad. You're jealous because Mike talked to me at the picnic."

And Tanya would come back with, "You're paranoid! No wonder you don't have any friends."

Sometimes Tanya was bossy. "Stop playing that dumb music! You know I can't stand it."

Once Sue was feeling discouraged and tried to tell Tanya how she felt. Tanya laughed and said, "Hey, Sue, cut it out! You shouldn't let yourself get down like that. It's not as bad as you think. Have some fun, and forget your troubles. You'll feel better tomorrow."

Sometimes Sue smiled and took it. Other times she'd get so angry that she'd say, "Shut up!" and walk out. Sue was facing roadblocks in her relationship with Tanya.

Roadblocks are expressions that we use to communicate unacceptance. There are four basic kinds of roadblocks: (1) judging, (2) sending solutions, (3) avoiding the other's concerns, and (4) unfair expectations. This month we'll learn about how to avoid erecting these four roadblocks.

Roadblocks

Roadblocks are words we use to communicate our desire for the other person to think, feel, or act differently. They communicate unfriendliness and unacceptance. Roadblocks are fighting words that bar the road to friendship.

Judging. The judging roadblocks are criticizing, name calling, diagnosing, labeling, blaming, and shaming.

"You shouldn't wear your hair that way." (Criticizing)

"It's your own fault!" (Blaming)

"Stupid! You're nothing but a skinhead!" (Naming, labeling)

"You're just jealous!" (Diagnosing)

Sending Solutions. The sending solutions roadblocks are ordering, commanding, demanding, threatening, preaching, moralizing, interrogating, and advising.

"Stop humming that song!" (Ordering)

"You do it, or I won't be your friend." (Threatening)

"You shouldn't talk like that. Christians should be more tolerant." (Preaching, moralizing)

"Why did you do that? Why couldn't you have been more careful?" (Interrogating)

"If I were you, I'd pay no attention to it." (Advising)

Avoiding the Other's Concerns. The roadblocks of avoidance are diverting, distracting, arguing, reassuring—all things we try to do to get people who are feeling bad to feel better.

"Let's talk about something more pleasant, like the ski trip next week." (Diverting, distracting)

"I hate to disagree with you, but the facts are that what you're suggesting won't work." (Arguing)

"You'll feel better after a good night's sleep." (Reassuring)

Unfair Expectations. Some indicators of unfair expectations are jealousy, possessiveness, selfishness, boasting, complaining, manipulation, and taking a person for granted.

A FOOL GETS INTO CONSTANT FIGHTS. HIS MOUTH IS HIS UNDOING! HIS WORDS ENDANGER HIM. PROVERBS 18:6, 7, TLB.

KEEPING FRIENDS

Roadblocks are a problem because they communicate unacceptance. Roadblocks give the idea that you know better than your friends how they should think, feel, or act.

Stolen Apples

DON'T GOSSIP. DON'T FALSELY ACCUSE YOUR NEIGHBOR OF SOME CRIME. LEVITICUS 19:16, TLB.

It was just before school when June told her friend Sue, "Someone stole a basket of red apples from our fruit stand last night."

"Really! Well, guess what I saw on the way home from school. That new boy, Phil, was carrying a basket of red apples! Do you suppose he's the thief?"

At recess June passed the story on to Mary, "I think maybe Phil is a thief. Someone stole a basket of red apples from our fruit stand, and last night Sue saw Phil with a basket of red apples."

Mary whispered the story to Kate, and Kate passed it on to Betty. By noon almost everyone had heard that Phil was the thief who had stolen a basket of red apples from the fruit stand at June's house. Everyone, that is, except Phil!

At noon he brought out a sack of red apples. He tossed one to Betty. She turned away without catching it.

"Hey! What's wrong?" Phil asked. "Don't you like apples?"

"I don't want any of your stolen apples, Mr. Thief!" she said.

"Thief? Stolen apples? What are you talking about?"

"Didn't you steal a basket of red apples from June's fruit stand?" she asked.

"No!" Phil was getting angry now. He didn't like being labeled a thief. "I worked for these apples. I helped Mr. Banks after school, and he gave me a basket of apples. So there! I'm not a thief!"

Phil's teacher overheard the exchange and called everyone into the classroom. "Now, how did this story get started?" she asked Betty. "Did you see Phil steal the apples?"

"No, I heard it from Kate, who heard it from Mary. June told Mary that Sue had seen him with the basket of apples."

June's face felt hot as all eyes turned her way. "I'm sorry, Phil. I guess I jumped to a false conclusion. I'll try to be more careful after this. Please forgive me for calling you a thief."

KEEPING FRIENDS

It's easy to label people when we know only a few facts. If you want to keep your friends, be careful of gossip and jumping to conclusions.

Marjorie's Mistake

It was a lovely summer day. Marjorie Neagle was out for a drive along the back country roads. The farms were run-down and overgrown with weeds. Piles of junk sat in the yards, and ragged children played around dilapidated houses.

Around one corner she came to what seemed to be the worst farm of all. The weeds were taking over. The unpainted shack looked like it was ready to fall down. A scraggly bearded old man in faded overalls sat on a rickety chair in the middle of his potato patch while he hoed.

What a lazy man! Marjorie thought. *He's got to be the laziest man I've ever seen. Imagine sitting down to hoe your potatoes! No wonder the place is grown up in weeds!*

After going down the road a couple miles, Marjorie turned around to drive by and get another look at the shiftless man sitting down to hoe his potatoes. As she drove slowly by she got a look at him from a different angle, and what she saw changed her opinion of the man.

In the *National Enquirer* Marjorie wrote about what she saw. "I saw something which stopped me cold in my tracks. From this side I observed, leaning against the chair, a pair of crutches, and I noticed an empty overall leg hanging limply to the ground. In that instant the lazy, shiftless character I had seen was transformed into a figure of dauntless courage."

After that experience Marjorie decided never to judge a person after only one look or one conversation.

"I thank God that I turned for a second look," Marjorie said.

Too often I've made a judgment on the basis of appearances, and in so doing I erected a roadblock to friendship.

C. L. Paddock writes: "In a court of justice the judge and jury hear both sides of a case before making any decision. We ought to be as fair as that."

STOP JUDGING BY MERE APPEARANCES. JOHN 7:24, NIV.

KEEPING FRIENDS

The judging roadblock shows our unacceptance of others. We must tear down the judging roadblock if we want to keep our friends.

Siegfried's Label

PEOPLE WILL SAY BAD THINGS ABOUT YOU AND HURT YOU. . . . REJOICE AND BE GLAD. . . . PEOPLE DID THE SAME EVIL THINGS TO THE PROPHETS WHO LIVED BEFORE YOU. MATTHEW 5:11, 12, ICB.

KEEPING FRIENDS

None of us likes to be called a name that labels us as different. However, a label doesn't change who we really are on the inside.

Siegfried Horn was the only Seventh-day Adventist in a Jewish school in Leipzig, Germany. His mother had enrolled him there so that he wouldn't have to go to school on Sabbath. Had he refused to attend classes on Sabbath in the government school, she would have been sent to jail.

Siegfried found it hard to be the only redheaded boy with a small turned-up nose among so many blackheaded boys with large straight noses. One day he came home crying.

"What's wrong? Are you hurt?" Mrs. Horn asked.

"No," Siegfried sobbed. "They called me a goy."

"Do you know what a goy is?" his mother asked leading him to a seat on the sofa.

"It's somebody who's different," Siegfried replied between sniffles.

"*Goy* is a Hebrew word that means somebody who is non-Jewish. You're a Christian. That makes you a Gentile, or a goy. Aren't you happy to be a Christian?"

"Yes, I guess so," Siegfried nodded. "But they laugh at me!"

"So what?" his mother said. "Are they unkind to you?"

"No," he admitted. "They aren't mean. They just laugh because I'm different. I guess I can't help that, can I?"

Mrs. Horn smiled at her young son and continued, "Siegfried, you're like Moses. He was the only Hebrew in a Gentile world. People respected him, and God honored him because he stood firm for what he believed. You're a Christian in a Jewish world. People will respect you, and God will honor you if you're proud to be what you are—a goy."

After that Siegfried didn't let it worry him. In fact, he came to like that name better because the boys said it with love and respect. He thought, *Goy is a badge that says I am myself and no one else. You can accept me or you can reject me, but you cannot change me.*

Criticizing God

ob wasn't the last person to criticize God. Catherine Marshall had her go at judging God, too.

Her granddaughter Amy had been born with severe genetic problems in her liver, kidneys, and brain. "She won't live more than a few weeks," the doctors told her parents.

However, her family wouldn't accept that verdict. "The doctors don't have all the answers," Amy's father said. "Our Lord God does. I claim a miracle for the healing of our daughter."

Church members and friends joined the family in a four-day all-out prayer meeting. At the end Catherine felt confident that God would heal her tiny granddaughter.

Six weeks later she held Amy as the nurse was pumping bile from the baby's stomach. Amy cried loudly in protest.

"Please, stop!" Catherine begged.

The nurse looked up at the heart monitor. "It's time to put her back in the heated crib," she said, taking her from Catherine's arms. The nurse ran from the room and in a moment was back with a doctor. He bent over the crib for a moment, then said, "I'm sorry. The baby has expired."

No, God, You can't let her die! Catherine silently begged as she stood looking at the lifeless form of baby Amy. *This isn't right, God! Bring this child back to life! You have the power.* But the baby never moved.

Catherine couldn't believe that God had refused to answer their prayers for healing. To let her grandchild die seemed so cruel, so unfair. For six months she felt miserable, cut off from God. He was no longer her friend.

"I can't even pray anymore. Why?" Catherine complained.

A friend suggested that the reason was that she had erected a roadblock by judging God to be unfair. Her critical attitude was blocking any communication with Him.

When she confessed her sin to God, she allowed Him to become her friend once again.

THE LORD WENT ON: "DO YOU STILL WANT TO ARGUE WITH THE ALMIGHTY? OR WILL YOU YIELD? DO YOU— GOD'S CRITIC— HAVE THE ANSWERS?" JOB 40:1, 2, TLB.

KEEPING FRIENDS

Want to be a friend of God? Tear down the judging roadblocks. Accept that He who sees the end from the beginning knows what's best for His children.

Albert's First Fight

KEEPING
FRIENDS

Keep quiet rather
than add another
roadblock to the
road of friend-
ship. Putting up
your own road-
block doesn't get
rid of the one the
other person
has built.

The boys in the village of Günsbach, Germany,
were having a wrestling match. To one side
stood a shy first grader, Albert Schweitzer.

I wish they'd ask me to play, Albert thought. But
no one did, and he couldn't help overhearing some of
their remarks.

"Watch out for the preacher's son," someone
sneered. "He wouldn't want you to get his fine
clothes dirty."

"Yeah! He thinks he's better than the rest of us,"
another commented.

Albert didn't like their remarks. Rather than cause
trouble, he usually said nothing as his father had
taught him. But this day it was more than he could
take. He walked up to George Nitschelm, one of the
toughest boys in the school, and said, "I'll wrestle
you, and I bet I win!"

"Oh, so you want to fight?" George spat on his
hands and rubbed them together. A circle formed
around the two. "Come on, my fine gentleman!"

Albert winced at the word "gentleman." It was a
term of contempt. It meant you weren't one of the
people, but a rich boy unable to do anything. *I'll
prove them wrong,* he thought. *I'll show them that
I'm no different from them.*

Albert flung himself at the big boy. In no time
George had slammed the boy into the mud, but
Albert was quick and slipped out of George's
clutches. George wasn't prepared for Albert's fury.
The crowd grew silent as they watched Albert knock
the wind out of their hero. Finally, Albert got George
pinned down, and he was declared the winner.

Now, surely they'll accept me as one of them, he
thought. Albert stood, waiting for their approval, his
face streaked with sweat and mud.

Instead George whined, "Well, if we had as much
to eat at home as you, I'd have licked you!"

The roadblocks were still up. It took Albert several
months of trying to be friends before the roadblocks
came down on his side as well as theirs.

Carole's Careless Words

arole Mayhall clenched her teeth as she scrubbed the barbecue grill. *This has got to be the dirtiest, greasiest, ugliest job there is! I could sure use some help!* she thought as she added more scouring powder and rubbed harder.

Sweat dripped from her nose. She stopped a moment to rest her tired shoulder muscles. *Company is coming tomorrow evening, and I've got to get this grease off the grill, or we'll have burned food or, worse yet, a fire. I sure wish Jack were helping me,* Carole thought. *Great! Now I'm out of paper towels. I hope there are some in the basement.*

Carole went inside to look for the paper towels. There sat Jack in the family room, his feet up on an ottoman, relaxing after a long walk. He'd been trying to get back onto a regular exercise program.

"Oh, you're home," she said.

"I'm sure tired!" he replied. "I've just walked five miles! Pretty good, huh?"

Thinking about how tired her shoulders were from scrubbing the barbecue grill, she answered, "Boy, just think of all you could have accomplished with that kind of energy!"

The smile disappeared from Jack's face.

Carole went down into the basement to look for the paper towels. While there she thought, *Well! I put my foot in my mouth again! Why can't I think before speaking! That was a real put-down. I took away all Jack's joy of accomplishment. I've made him feel bad. I wish I could take those words back, but it's too late for that.*

Back upstairs, Carole apologized, "Jack, forgive me for my careless words just now. I'm so sorry. I wasn't thinking. Five miles is terrific! Will you forgive me?"

"Sure, honey, I forgive you," Jack smiled.

Carole went back to cleaning the barbecue, determined that in the future she'd try harder to prevent careless words by thinking before speaking.

APR. 8

DON'T TALK SO MUCH. YOU KEEP PUTTING YOUR FOOT IN YOUR MOUTH. PROVERBS 10:19, TLB.

KEEPING FRIENDS

Put-downs are one of the judging roadblocks that we want to avoid. Thinking before speaking will keep your foot out of your mouth.

Getting Even

But I tell you, Do not resist an evil person. Matthew 5:39, NIV.

KEEPING FRIENDS

Jesus taught us how to handle insults. Don't fight. Don't get even. Ignoring it or trying to correct it are smart ways to go. The sooner we learn this principle of friendship, the smoother life will be.

A Charlie Brown cartoon illustrates how many of us go about handling insults.

Lucy says, "I wonder if I wouldn't be more popular if I had a new name. The wrong name can be a real hindrance to a person's functioning in society. I think a name consistent with a person's personality is important."

Lucy sits there pensively, head in her hands, thinking.

Charlie Brown tries to help, "How about Supermouth?"

The next frame shows Charlie Brown lying flat on his back, seeing stars. Lucy had gotten even!

A newspaper report tells of a man who killed two people with a shotgun. "Why did you do it?" the police asked.

"They called me names," he replied.

Is violence the way to deal with roadblocks? Actually, violence does no damage to roadblocks. It's aimed at the person who erected the roadblock. Wrong way to go!

Here are some steps to take in dealing with insults when they come your way. I found them in a book for teens called *Friends Forever,* by William L. Coleman. Give them a try the next time you're insulted.

1. *Divide the insults.* Some are meant to be friendly. They might hurt, but the person who said them didn't mean any harm. The person was probably trying to say "I like you."

2. *Don't let it get to you.* Chalk it up to something evil people do. Don't let it get under your skin and make you feel bitter and hurt. You can't help what people say, but you have a choice of how you react. You don't have to let it make you mad.

3. *Confront the person.* Sometimes friends insult us without realizing what they're doing. If it happens frequently, you may want to tell them in a nice way that it really bothers you a lot. Friends usually don't mean to hurt us. If they know we don't like it, they'll stop.

Controlling Others

What's the one personality trait that gets the prize for ruining more friendships than any other? According to Dr. Alan Loy McGinnis, author of *The Friendship Factor,* it's the tendency to control others. This trait is always destructive to relationships, because it pushes people away.

Roadblocks show that we're trying to get the other person to change so that he or she will be the way we want him or her to be. So we name, shame, criticize, command, and advise. When others don't like our attempts to control, we get upset.

Roadblocks are a way of our trying to manipulate others into being something different than they are. The minute we start trying to control, the other people get the message of unacceptance, and they turn away.

D. L. Moody, one of the most famous Christian evangelists of the past century, understood this principle of friendship. He was a tolerant, understanding man who refused to criticize people.

One of Moody's famous sayings was "Right now I'm having so much trouble with D. L. Moody that I don't have time to find fault with the other fellow."

Abraham Lincoln was another person who knew that criticizing doesn't win friends. Once when his wife spoke harshly about some individuals, he said, "Don't criticize them, Mary; they're just what we would be under similar circumstances."

John F. Kennedy was one of the most popular presidents of the twentieth century. He was always surrounded with friends. One of the reasons was his tolerance of others. During election night in 1960 Kennedy and his friends sat around the TV watching the returns come in. When Richard Nixon refused to concede the election even though it was obvious he'd lost, Kennedy's friends grew angry.

Kennedy himself was calm. He said simply, "If I were he, I would have done the same thing." No wonder people liked him. He refused to control others.

SELF-CONTROL MEANS CONTROLLING THE TONGUE! A QUICK RETORT CAN RUIN EVERYTHING. PROVERBS 13:3, TLB.

KEEPING FRIENDS

Roadblocks are an attempt to control. We avoid friends who try to control us. Not other-control but self-control is the key to keeping friends.

Good Advice

A FOOL FINDS NO PLEASURE IN UNDERSTANDING BUT DELIGHTS IN AIRING HIS OWN OPINIONS. PROVERBS 18:2, NIV.

KEEPING FRIENDS

Unsolicited good advice is bad for a relationship. An important principle for friendship is "Seek first to understand, then to be understood."

Stephen sat drawing doodles on his notebook page instead of writing the essay he'd been assigned. His mother, who was supervising his home-schooling, sat down at the table beside him. "What's wrong?" she asked. "Why aren't you doing your work?"

Stephen shrugged his shoulders and looked out the window.

"Come on, honey, tell me what's wrong. I know something's bothering you. Tell me. I'll try hard to understand."

"I don't know," Stephen hedged. "You'll think I'm stupid."

"No, I won't!" Mom declared. "Honey, I love you, and I care about what's bothering you. Why are you so unhappy?"

"Oh, I don't know."

"Yes, you do!" Mom insisted. "Now out with it!"

"I want to get a job," Stephen blurted out. "I'm tired of school. I don't want to study anymore."

"You what?" Mom exploded. "What do you mean you don't like school? You've got to do it whether you like it or not. You'll never make anything of yourself without an education. It's very important. If you'd settle down and study as hard as your sister does, you'd like it better. You have a good mind, but you just don't concentrate! You've got to try harder! Apply yourself!"

Stephen just sat there shaking his head and staring out the window. *I knew it! She won't listen to me! She doesn't understand what I'm saying to her at all! What's the use of trying?* he thought.

"Come on, Stephen," Mom spoke more softly, laying a hand on his arm. "Don't clam up like that. Talk to me. Tell me how you feel."

Yeah? Stephen thought. *It's better if I keep quiet, because when I talk you don't understand. You just get upset and try to tell me what to do.*

Mom was using several roadblocks of "sending solutions." She advised, preached, moralized, argued, and interrogated. These roadblocks caused all communication to stop. She was trying to change Steven, not to understand him.

The LDP Formula

wo-month-old Jenny Covey was one sick little girl. She'd been vomiting all morning. She had diarrhea and didn't want to eat. Her parents, Sandra and Stephen Covey, were worried.

"Honey, we've got to call the doctor," Stephen decided. "We just can't go on watching her suffer. I don't care if the doctor is at the football game. Jenny needs help."

"OK, I'll call the stadium and have him paged," Sandra said.

The doctor wasn't happy to be taken away when the game was at a crucial stage. "Yes?" he said briskly. "What is it?"

"This is Mrs. Covey," Sandra explained. "It's Jenny. She's so sick. We don't know what to do."

"Tell me more," the doctor said. "How is she acting?"

"She's been vomiting all morning, and we can't get her to stop. She won't eat, and she has diarrhea bad."

"Which is your pharmacy?" he asked. "I'll phone in a prescription."

After she hung up Sandra felt uneasy. He'd been in an awful hurry. She hadn't even told him the baby's age. He wasn't their regular doctor, but the one on call.

"I hope he knows she's only 2 months old," Sandra worried.

"What if he doesn't know that?" Stephen asked. "Is it safe to give the medicine?"

"We'd better call back. You do it."

So Stephen called and had the doctor paged again.

He wasn't any happier the second time until he heard what Stephen had to say about her age. "I had no idea she was a newborn!" he exclaimed. "Good thing you called. I'll change the prescription immediately."

The LDP formula for keeping friends is: **L**isten, **D**iagnose, then **P**rescribe. Too often we diagnose our friends' problems and tell them what to do when we haven't even taken time to listen so that we might understand the situation. Foolish for a doctor; just as foolish for a friendship.

WHAT A SHAME—YES, HOW STUPID!— TO DECIDE BEFORE KNOWING THE FACTS! PROVERBS 18:13, TLB.

KEEPING FRIENDS

Diagnosing and advising are things we often do without really understanding the problem. The more we listen for the facts, the less likely we are to erect sending solutions roadblocks.

Advising God

WOE TO THE MAN WHO FIGHTS WITH HIS CREATOR. DOES THE POT ARGUE WITH ITS MAKER? DOES THE CLAY DISPUTE WITH HIM WHO FORMS IT, SAYING, "STOP, YOU'RE DOING IT WRONG!" ISAIAH 45:9, TLB.

KEEPING FRIENDS

Want to stay a friend of God? Tear down the sending solutions roadblocks.

Too often I've argued with God, giving my advice about how He ought to do things. I've been really good about sending God solutions, as though He Himself weren't quite able to figure out what needed to be done.

While in India I rode a motor scooter. One day on a busy street crowded with cars, cycles, bullock carts, and donkeys, a man walked out in front of my scooter. I slammed on the brakes, but not in time to prevent an accident.

The badly injured man was rushed to a hospital, where he lay unconscious for eight days. I stormed heaven with my prayers, telling God what He should do. "God, You *have* to save that man's life. Please help the doctors do the right things so that he'll live!"

The man died. When God didn't answer my prayers, I became very angry. Now to the sending solutions roadblock I added the judging roadblock. "God," I said, "You're *so* cruel. You could have healed him, and You didn't. I'm mad at You, God. I'm not talking to You anymore." And I didn't—for two years.

I knelt at my bedside pretending to pray so that my husband wouldn't know how I felt. I went to church, but I had no relationship with God. The roadblocks were up. I wasn't talking.

Then one day a beggar came to our gate, and I turned her away with cruel, unkind words. My husband saw, and he asked, "Dorothy, what's wrong?"

"Nothing!" I snapped.

But I knew very well what was wrong. Ellen White says that "the darkness of the evil one encloses those who neglect to pray" *(Steps to Christ, p. 94)*. I knew I needed to get rid of the roadblocks. I needed Jesus to be my friend again.

"God," I prayed, "I know it was foolish to try to advise You! From now on I won't argue with You. I'll trust You to do what's right. Help me tear down the roadblocks. I want to be Your friend."

Training Frances

Human nature is much the same today as it was 2,500 years ago. Most of us don't like the advice of friends any more than King Zedekiah did.

When someone is quick to supply the answer to all our problems it's as though he or she were saying, "You're really dense if you haven't been able to figure out what to do!"

Frances McClure had such a friend when she was a young mother in Florida. Frances was doing everything she could to help Pastor McClure with the meetings and still take care of her newborn girl who had colic and cried continually.

Every evening they picked up an older woman to bring her to the meetings. That woman acted as if she were a child expert, even though she'd never had children.

"You really must do something about the baby's crying," the woman advised. "You aren't burping her correctly. I'll show you how it's done."

Another day she gave different advice. "Frances, you have too many clothes on the baby for such warm weather. It's no wonder she cries!"

"The formula isn't the right temperature," she commented on another occasion. "No wonder the poor thing cries!"

In commenting about her frustration, Frances said, "What was I to do? The child was mine, and she didn't come with a set of instructions. I was doing the best I could! Even when I tried to comply with the woman's counsel, she would often change her advice. She even continued her training program during the daytime hours by telephone."

No matter how hard Mrs. McClure tried, nothing she did was right. *I've had enough!* Frances decided. *This lady thinks she has all the answers, but her unsolicited advice brings me only confusion and discouragement.*

At last Frances talked to the woman. She said, "I'm the mother of my child, and I'll decide what's best for her." She would be the woman's friend, but without her advice.

EVEN IF I DID GIVE YOU COUNSEL, YOU WOULD NOT LISTEN TO ME. JEREMIAH 38:15, NIV.

KEEPING FRIENDS

It's hard to be friends with people who think they know all the answers. They discourage us. Unsolicited advice is a roadblock to friendship.

The Skating Party

LET US DISCERN FOR OURSELVES WHAT IS RIGHT. JOB 34:4, NIV.

KEEPING FRIENDS

Sending solutions—ordering, commanding, and preaching—make people feel rebellious. Avoid this roadblock if you want to have friends at home as well as at school.

Dottie stared at the invitation. "You are invited to a skating party at the Dickenson Street Rink from 7:00 to 10:00 Friday night."

Not another Friday night event I can't go to because of Sabbath! I wish I weren't so different, Dottie pouted.

"Well! Are you coming to my party?" Patty asked.

"I don't know," Dottie said, stalling for time. "I want to, but I'll have to ask Mom."

"Oh, please come!" Patty urged. "I know it's Friday night, but surely you can make an exception for my birthday."

"I'll try," Dottie replied. To herself she thought, *Mom will say "No" and I can blame her. Then Patty will be mad at Mom instead of me.*

But it didn't work that way. Mom didn't put up the expected roadblock. "You make up your own mind," Mom said. "You're old enough to know what's right and what's wrong. It's between you and God. If you decide to go, then I won't say another word."

Dottie stewed about her problem all evening. It was late that night before she finally made her decision.

The next day she told Patty, "I've decided not to come to your party. I don't want to make you feel bad, but that's my Sabbath. That's my time for God and my family."

After school Dottie ran all the way home to tell her mother about her decision. "You know, Mom, you sure were smart to make me decide for myself!" she said. "If you'd preached at me and ordered me to stay home, I'd have obeyed, but I'd have pouted about it for a week."

"I'm proud of you," Mom said. "I knew you'd be a lot happier if I didn't hand you a ready-made solution to your problem. You've got a good head on your shoulders, and you used it!"

"I've got the best mom in the world!" Dottie meant every word as she gave her mother a hug.

Lonely Greg

Joseph had a choleric personality. He was good at erecting the sending solutions roadblocks. He was bossy, acting as though he knew it all.

Greg had a similar personality. He tried to change people. The other kids in his youth class couldn't stand him because he said things such as:

"You shouldn't listen to that!"

"You'd better smarten up, or you'll get into trouble!"

"I know what we ought to do this afternoon. Listen to me."

He felt really baffled when he walked up to a group, and they sort of melted away, leaving him standing alone. He felt hurt when he learned on Monday that there had been a hayride, and he hadn't been invited. He felt disappointed when no one sat in his row during Sabbath school.

"Greg, got some time tomorrow?" Pastor Jack, the youth leader, asked one Sabbath morning.

"Sure thing!" Greg brightened. "What's up?"

"Oh, I just thought maybe we could have a game of tennis and talk for a while."

Sipping a cool drink after the game, Greg sat facing Pastor Jack across a restaurant table. For once Greg was silent. He had a feeling this talk was about him.

"Greg," the pastor began. "I've noticed that you don't have any friends. I think I know why."

"Why?" Greg leaned forward. "I've been wondering that myself. I sure try to be friendly!"

"That's the point," Pastor Jack continued. "You try too hard. You come across as very bossy and overbearing. People don't like someone who's always telling them what they should and shouldn't do."

"But I'm only doing it for their own good."

"I know, but it's not working. Every time you try to boss, it puts up a roadblock. Your behavior is pushing people away. Try easing up a bit. Stop giving out so much advice. OK?"

Greg resolved to change. It wasn't easy, and it took several months before anyone responded. Once people realized that the roadblocks were really gone, they no longer tried to ignore Greg.

"SO YOU WANT TO BE OUR KING, DO YOU?" HIS BROTHERS DERIDED. AND THEY HATED [JOSEPH] BOTH FOR THE DREAM AND FOR HIS COCKY ATTITUDE. GENESIS 37:8, TLB.

KEEPING FRIENDS

Bossiness drives people away from us. No one likes cocky people who think they know it all.

Hospital Visit

DO NOT BE INTERESTED ONLY IN YOUR OWN LIFE, BUT BE INTERESTED IN THE LIVES OF OTHERS. PHILIPPIANS 2:4, ICB.

KEEPING FRIENDS

Sending solutions is the roadblock that we use to try to make people feel, think, or act differently. When we do this we're communicating our unacceptance of them and their problems.

It's visiting hours at the local hospital. Miss Patient is recovering from an operation. The four Ing sisters have come by on Sabbath afternoon to visit. Their names are Divert Ing, Distract Ing, Argue Ing, and Reassure Ing.

Let's listen in on their conversation.

Miss Patient: "This was such a painful operation! I really didn't think I'd make it this time. It was just . . ."

Reassure Ing: "Now, my dear, it's not nearly as bad as you think. You'll feel better after a few days."

Argue Ing: "The facts are that yours is not a life-threatening illness. Other diseases are much worse! I know what I'm talking about, because I was a nurse, you know!"

Divert Ing: "She's right! I had my gallbladder out at Memorial Hospital 10 years ago. Now, *that* was a painful operation, and very dangerous. Your pain is nothing compared to what I went through."

Distract Ing: "That's the hospital my grandson was taken to when he broke his arm last month. Old Dr. Beyer set it. He did a horrible job. My daughter had to have it reset when it didn't heal straight."

Miss Patient: "Oh . . . oh . . . dear . . . I don't feel good at all."

Reassure Ing: "You're going to be as good as new before you know it!"

Divert Ing: "Speaking of Dr. Beyer, did you know he lives on my street? I hear he has an alcohol problem!"

Argue Ing: "Well, alcohol isn't nearly as bad as drugs! The son of our next door neighbor is on drugs. Imagine! And he's a member of the church, too!"

Whatever happened to the concerns of Miss Patient? All her visitors tried to avoid her pain. They argued, reassured, diverted, and distracted from the one thing that was uppermost on her mind. I expect that Miss Patient felt a lot better after the Ing sisters went home.

Saying the Right Thing

I came home from school one day and said to my husband, Ron, "I'm going to quit teaching. I had a terrible day. I'm an awful teacher."

Ron sat on the bed beside me and said, "Stop talking like that! [Ordering] You're a wonderful teacher and you know it!" [Arguing]

"No, I'm not. I did a lousy job! I just want to give up teaching. Nothing went right today!" I whined.

Ron replied, "You'll feel better after a good night's rest. It's not as bad as you think." [Reassuring]

More tears.

He tried again. "Listen to this joke I read in the paper today. It's good." [Distracting]

Louder sobbing.

Ron gave up then and went out to mow the lawn.

I curled up on the bed and started to cry. *Nobody loves me!* I thought. *No one understands how terrible today was!*

Of course, Ron was trying to communicate love and friendship, but he put up roadblocks and couldn't reach me.

While I cried, he was outside thinking, *I just erected a bunch of roadblocks. No wonder she's crying. I'd better go tear them down and start over.*

He came back inside. "Honey," he said above my sobs, "you really did have a terrible day. You feel like you did a lousy job. Nothing went right. You want to quit teaching. It must really have been an awful day, because I know how much you enjoy teaching."

I stopped crying and sat up. The roadblocks were gone! He understood! He really had listened! He cared! I had a friend who loved me, and I felt a whole lot better.

"Want to talk about it?" Ron asked.

"Maybe later," I answered. I was smiling now. I got off the bed and headed out the bedroom door. "Right now I'm going to fix supper."

It didn't matter now how awful my day had been, because the roadblocks were gone. We had connected. Friendship was restored.

APR. 18

HOW WONDERFUL IT IS TO BE ABLE TO SAY THE RIGHT THING AT THE RIGHT TIME!
PROVERBS 15:23, TLB.

KEEPING FRIENDS

It really is possible to learn how to say the right thing. We'll make a lot of progress on the road to friendship by tearing down the roadblocks that can come between us and others.

115

Cutting Remarks

SOME PEOPLE LIKE TO MAKE CUTTING REMARKS, BUT THE WORDS OF THE WISE SOOTHE AND HEAL. PROVERBS 12:18, TLB.

KEEPING FRIENDS

Words have tremendous power to hurt or heal. Words we use to ignore someone else's pain cut deep.

Carole Mayhall, author of the book *Words That Hurt, Words That Heal,* had just finished giving a lecture. A woman, we'll call her Vera, approached Carole shyly.

"May I talk to you for five minutes?" Vera asked.

Carole could tell that Vera was distressed. Behind her glasses tears glistened in her eyes. "Of course!" Carole responded, leading her to a quiet corner of the auditorium.

"I understood exactly what you were talking about," Vera began. "May I tell you my experience with words?"

Carole nodded.

"Two years ago I was on the verge of a nervous breakdown after some deep hurts in my life. It seemed the least little thing would start the tears flowing. I'd been active at church, but had to cut back because I couldn't handle the stress. Physically and mentally I just didn't have the strength to carry on."

"That sounds like a wise thing to do," Carole encouraged.

"Well, the pastor of my church didn't think so!" Vera responded. "He visited me after I quit my church offices to let me know how he felt about it."

"What did he say?"

Vera's lips began to tremble. "He said, 'Unless you pull yourself together and snap out of this, the people in the church are going to stop praying for you.'"

"You've got to be kidding!"

"No! Honestly! That's what he said." Vera's tears were flowing freely now as she remembered the hurt of that cutting remark. "I became so depressed that I had a complete breakdown. I've spent two years trying to recover from those hurtful words."

Tears were now spilling down Carole's face, too. "Tell me how God has used that experience in your life, Vera," she asked softly.

"The minister sure let me down, but Jesus didn't. He's used this experience to make me more understanding of the power of my words. I do a lot of hospital visitation. Just this week I led one patient to Jesus. Isn't that exciting?"

Blaming God

oger Bandy was a paramedic with the Los Angeles Fire Department. October 21, 1984, was a quiet day until a call came in that evening for help at the scene of an accident.

A drunken driver had been traveling at 90 miles an hour when he broadsided a car. The car had been folded nearly in half and dragged for 100 feet. The driver of the car was dead. Roger ran to the passenger side.

AN ENEMY DID THIS. MATTHEW 13:28, NIV.

"Oh, no! It's not you, Sherry!" he cried as he looked into the lifeless face of his only daughter. Frantically he applied his CPR skills until the ambulance arrived and rushed her to the hospital. She was dead on arrival.

"Why, God, why?" Roger prayed. "Why didn't You give her three more seconds to get out of the way of the car? It's Your fault, God. You could have done something, but You didn't!"

Roger wasn't the first person to ask that question when faced with tragedy. Tens of thousands of people ask it every day. Who is to be blamed for all the pain, suffering, and death in the world?

Our text says that we should blame the enemy, Satan. For the time being Satan is the ruler of this world. But God still controls the universe. For reasons that are hard for us to understand, He doesn't prevent most tragedies from happening.

Roger Bandy was like a lot of us when he thought God would always step in and save those who loved Him. He told his doctor, "I felt that if I lived a 'good' life and helped others, my family and I would somehow be insured against personal tragedy. I was furious when God didn't keep His side of the bargain."

Roger made a common mistake. He had unreal expectations of God. God hasn't promised us that skies would always be blue, that no rain would ever fall in our lives. But He has promised always to be with us in our trouble.

KEEPING FRIENDS

If we want to maintain friendships, we have to tear down the roadblock of unreal expectations.

Watch Me!

**PRIDE GOES
BEFORE DESTRUC-
TION, A
HAUGHTY SPIRIT
BEFORE A FALL.
PROVERBS
16:18, NIV.**

KEEPING FRIENDS

It's an unreal
expectation to
expect people to
praise us all the
time. No one
likes a person
who is forever
asking people to
watch how great
he or she is.

Ten-year-old Jerry was strong. He could hit a ball farther, run faster, and do a lot of things better than the other kids. The trouble was that he knew it and liked to tell everyone how wonderful he was. He expected people to praise him constantly for the terrific things he could do.

It happened one day that he was at the seaside for a vacation. He soon discovered that he could row a boat faster than anyone else at the beach. "I'm the best!" Jerry boasted. "Watch how fast I can go!"

Only one boy challenged him. Jerry couldn't allow that to happen, of course, so he rowed even harder to keep ahead. As he spurted forward, he shouted, "Watch me beat him! Just watch how fast I can go!"

Just then Jerry's right oar slipped out of the lock. This caused him to fall over backward, landing on the bottom of the boat, with his feet sticking straight up. In the confusion he let go of the oar, which the waves carried out of his reach.

But Jerry wasn't going to let a little thing like a lost oar cause him to lose. He stood up and continued using his one oar, paddling first on one side and then the other. The boat sped forward.

"Watch me!" he shouted again. "See what I can do!"

Just then the boat hit a large wave, knocking the oar out of Jerry's hands and flipping him right over the side of the boat into the sea!

Several boats came to rescue him and his lost oars. A man fished him out of the sea and brought him to the beach, where a crowd had gathered. As he walked out of the water, dripping wet, someone shouted, "Watch me!" Everyone laughed.

Jerry laughed with them, since there wasn't much else he could do. Do you suppose he learned his lesson about bragging?

Complaining Friends

A while back I had a friend, we'll call her Lizzy, who was going through some hard times. She had no family members to help out, so I decided to do what I could to make her happy.

On one visit to Lizzy's tiny cottage I discovered that her only sheet was full of holes. I went home to see what I could find to meet her need. I chose a set of sheets with soft pastel stripes. *She'll love these pretty sheets,* I imagined. *How pleased she'll be! I can't wait to see how her old eyes light up at the sight of them!*

I took them to her the same day, so eager was I to see her pleasure at my gift! Lizzy accepted the sheets without a smile or a thank-you. She fingered the soft cotton. Finally she looked up at me with disappointment showing in her eyes, "My dear, I was so hoping the sheets would be white!"

Inside I felt anger welling up. How dare she complain when I had given her the best that I had! *You don't look a gift horse in the mouth!* I thought to myself.

"Anything else I can do for you, Lizzy?" I queried.

"I've been longing for cheese," she sighed. "You know I can't afford cheese on my pension."

My heart went out to the old lady. It must be rough not being able to buy the things she wanted. "I'll bring you some the next time I come," I promised.

You guessed it! When I arrived with three tins of processed cheese, Lizzy again complained, "My dear, I was so hoping you'd bring fresh cheese!"

I'd purposely bought the canned cheese, because I knew that it would keep well in the hot climate. She had no fridge.

Both Lizzy and I put up roadblocks of unfair expectations. When our expectations weren't met, we complained and felt cheated.

I HAVE LEARNED TO BE SATISFIED WITH THE THINGS I HAVE AND WITH EVERYTHING THAT HAPPENS. PHILIPPIANS 4:11, ICB.

KEEPING FRIENDS

Complaining is the result of unreal expectations. We much prefer to associate with people who are content with what they get, not always wishing for something different.

119

Possessive Friends

IT IS POSSIBLE TO GIVE AWAY AND BECOME RICHER! IT IS ALSO POSSIBLE TO HOLD ON TOO TIGHTLY AND LOSE EVERYTHING. PROVERBS 11:24, TLB.

KEEPING FRIENDS

Possessiveness is based upon an unfair expectation of friends. Trying to hold on too tightly may push our friends away from us.

Mrs. Walters found Chelsea crying as she sat inside the big tire on the playground. "What's wrong, Chelsea?" the teacher asked. "Did someone hurt you?"

"It's Stephanie."

"But I thought Stephanie was your very best friend," the teacher remarked.

"Not anymore. I hate her!"

"Maybe you've misunderstood," Mrs. Walters suggested. "What did she do?"

"She's playing with Peggy!" Chelsea began sobbing all over again. "She doesn't like me anymore. Peggy's her friend now!"

"Oh, I see." Mrs. Walters had a flash of understanding. "You want Stephanie all for yourself, right?"

Chelsea nodded. "She's *my* friend! She shouldn't want to play with Peggy. I don't know why she doesn't like me."

"Let's go find out," the teacher said, tugging at the girl's hand.

Chelsea slowly crawled out of the old tire and went with Mrs. Walters to where Stephanie was jumping rope with Peggy. The girls stopped as the teacher and Chelsea came near.

"Stephanie, is it true that you don't like Chelsea any more?" Mrs. Walters asked.

"No! That's not true!" Stephanie shook her blond curls. "I really like Chelsea. She's my very best friend, but she wants me to have only her for a friend. I like everyone and want to play with the other girls sometimes."

"That seems fair to me," Mrs. Walters agreed. "Did you tell Chelsea you didn't want to play with her?"

"No! Peggy and I begged her to jump rope with us. Three is more fun than two, but she ran away and wouldn't play."

"Thank you, Stephanie," the teacher said, leading Chelsea to a quiet corner of the playground. "You know, Chelsea, being too possessive of friends pushes them away from us. It sounds to me like you've been holding on to Stephanie too tightly. Think maybe you could share your friendship?"

Chelsea smiled, nodded, and ran off to jump rope with the other two girls.

Wearing Out Your Welcome

Andrea moved into a new neighborhood and was delighted when Shannon, her next-door neighbor, welcomed her warmly. They had lots in common. They were about the same age and each had two small children. It was fun to spend a morning together listening to music, baking, and talking.

Then it happened that Shannon's husband got a new job in which he had to travel for several days every week. Shannon didn't like being alone, so she gathered up the children and went over to spend the morning with her friend, Andrea. At lunchtime she took her children home for their naps. After an hour or so she was back to spend the afternoon with Andrea.

After several weeks of this, Andrea complained to her husband, "I'm getting behind in everything! Shannon was here all day again today."

"Tell her how you feel," her husband, Jim, suggested.

"I've tried!" Andrea said. "I give her all kinds of hints, but she doesn't seem to take any of them."

"Tell her plainly," Jim insisted.

"I don't want to make her feel bad," Andrea countered, but she gave his suggestion a lot of thought. She prayed about her problem, too. At last she felt ready to talk.

"Shannon, you're my best friend, but it's gotten to the place I dread hearing my doorbell ring because I know it's probably you, and you'll be here for the day. To put it plainly, I need time alone in my home with my family. I have work to do. You need to build your own life and not depend on me for all your support. I'm sorry, but that's how I feel. Can you understand?" Andrea begged.

Shannon began to cry. "I didn't know you didn't want me."

"I do want you . . . sometimes, but not all the time," she replied.

"I guess I've been pretty selfish, haven't I?" Shannon asked. After a good talk, the two friends decided to have a more normal relationship.

APR. 24

DON'T VISIT YOUR NEIGHBOR TOO OFTEN, OR YOU WILL OUTWEAR YOUR WELCOME! PROVERBS 25:17, TLB.

KEEPING FRIENDS

We lose friends quickly if we selfishly put too many demands on their time. It doesn't pay to wear out your welcome.

King of the Castle

KEEPING FRIENDS

A quick way to lose friends is to inform them that you're better than they are. Praising yourself, boasting, and conceited actions are hefty roadblocks to friendship.

Charlie was the tallest boy in the little one-room church school. He was only in third grade, but he was bigger than David in fourth and Marcus in sixth. He was even stronger than Sammy in seventh.

Workers had left a large pile of dirt in one corner of the playground. At recess Charlie climbed on top. Waving both hands in the air, he shouted, "I'm the king of the castle. Nobody's strong enough to get me down! Ha! Ha! Ha! I'm the king of the castle!"

The other boys rushed to Charlie's self-proclaimed castle, and one by one they tried to pull him off.

"You think you're too smart," wiry Sammy said as he lunged for the king. Charlie easily jumped aside.

"Stop your bragging!" yelled Marcus as he grabbed Charlie's hand and pulled. Charlie jerked free.

"I'll show you who's king!" David called as he took a running jump and landed on top of the dirt pile beside Charlie. The two wrestled for a moment, and then Charlie pushed David backward off the pile. He landed on his back.

The others ran to his side. David sat up unhurt, but fighting mad. "Let's pull down that smart aleck!" he said.

"Yes, let's show him who's king!" the others agreed.

"I'll take on all of you!" Charlie smirked atop his little mountain of dirt.

David, Marcus, and Sammy stormed the castle from different angles. Together they pulled and pushed Charlie off his perch.

He was unhurt except for his pride. "No fair, three against one!" he began to whimper, and ran off to tell his teacher. "They called me a smart aleck. They picked on me," he complained.

After listening to the story from both sides, his teacher commented, "Charlie, it seems you asked them to take you on. Those who don't like the name smart aleck probably shouldn't act so conceited. Right?"

"I guess so," Charlie said, hanging his head.

Jealous Jerry

It was Donald's birthday. His friends had gathered in his driveway to see his birthday present, a brand-new bike. He beamed as he wheeled it out of the garage.

It was bright blue with shiny chrome that shone like real silver. It had a soft leather seat with springs and leather saddlebags fastened behind. Everyone thought it was great—everyone except Jerry, who up until then had been Donald's best friend.

"Wow!" Martin exclaimed. "What a beauty!"

"Red ones are prettier," Jerry said.

"Look at that chrome!" Brent ran his hand over the shiny handle bars.

"It will soon look dull and rusty," Jerry growled.

"Those saddlebags are neat!" said Craig.

"Wire baskets are much better," sneered Jerry.

"You can all have a turn riding it," Donald said. "But first turn goes to Jerry." The others nodded. They expected Jerry to go first, since he and Donald were best friends.

"No, thank you!" Jerry said in a very unfriendly way. "I don't care to ride your bike." He walked away, leaving Donald and the other boys wondering what had happened.

After that Jerry started hanging around with Mike. They became best friends until Mike got a pair of in-line skates, the very best. After that Jerry didn't want to play with Mike.

Jerry became best friends then with Peter. That lasted until Peter got a whole new football outfit for his birthday—knee pads, shoulder pads, helmet, and all. Jerry made fun of the outfit and after that had nothing more to do with Peter.

Brian was Jerry's next friend. Everything went just fine until Brian's dad took him on a fishing trip in the mountains. After that Jerry ignored Brian.

What was Jerry's problem? He was just plain jealous. He was jealous of Donald's new blue bike. He envied Mike's super in-line skates. He coveted Peter's football outfit. He resented the fact that Brian got to go on a fishing trip, and he didn't.

ANGER IS CRUEL AND FURY OVERWHELMING, BUT WHO CAN STAND BEFORE JEALOUSY? PROVERBS 27:4, NIV.

KEEPING FRIENDS

Envy is a sure way to ruin a relationship. Friendship can't last in a climate of jealousy. Envy destroys trust, affection, and freedom between friends.

Jesus and Roadblocks

**WHOEVER SAYS
THAT GOD LIVES
IN HIM MUST
LIVE AS
JESUS LIVED.
1 JOHN 2:6,
ICB.**

KEEPING FRIENDS

Jesus lived on this earth without judging or demanding. He lived without complaining, jealousy, and boasting. He can help us tear down the roadblocks in our relationships.

Can you imagine Jesus erecting roadblocks? Can you picture Him naming, shaming, blaming, and criticizing? Was He bossy, demanding, and self-centered? Did He ever make people feel that they were stupid or that He wasn't willing to share their pain?

What if Jesus had said to Mary Magdalene, "You should be ashamed of yourself! How disgusting! The Pharisees are right to stone you! You're getting what you deserve!" (naming, blaming, shaming, and moralizing)

What if Jesus had said to Nicodemus that night when he came with his questions about being born again, "Don't worry about it. Let's go have supper. You'll feel better in the morning." (ordering, distracting, and diverting)

What if that night when Peter denied his Lord, Jesus had yelled at him, "Stupid! Jerk! Is that any way for one of My disciples to talk? You should know better than that!" (naming, shaming, criticizing, and moralizing)

What if Jesus had said to Martha that day when she wanted her sister to help in the kitchen, "Honestly, Martha! Stop nagging your sister. You aren't thinking straight! You're just jealous!" (demanding, judging, and diagnosing)

What if Jesus had said to the woman at the well, "Liar! How dare you mention God when you're such a sinner!" (naming and shaming)

But Jesus didn't say any of those things. He loved people too much to erect roadblocks. He came to break the barriers we erect. He came to tear down our roadblocks. He came to restore relationships, not destroy them.

Roadblocks destroy friendship in the following ways:

1. They diminish our feelings of self-worth.
2. They make us feel defensive, resistant, and resentful.
3. They lead to withdrawal and feelings of defeat.
4. They block real solutions to our problems.
5. They block feelings.

Michael's Day

A look at one day in Michael's life will illustrate the effect of roadblocks. Try to imagine how you'd feel if you'd been in Michael's place.

Michael was still lying in bed five minutes after his alarm went off. His mother yelled, "Michael, you lazybones, get down here before I send your father to get you!"

He got up and headed for the bathroom to wash his face and comb his hair. His older sister was locked inside. She shouted, "Go away! I got here first!"

At breakfast he faced cold oatmeal porridge. "It's your own fault!" his mom said. "Come when you're called if you don't want gummy porridge."

He ran to catch the bus, but had to go back for his lunch. "I do believe you'd forget your head if it weren't attached!" his mother scolded.

"Oh, Mom! Cut it out!" Michael yelled as he ran to the road. The bus had gone without him. He had to walk to school.

He went to the office for a tardy slip, and the principal remarked, "Young man, you've got to be on time for appointments if you want to succeed in life!"

In reading class he stumbled over a new word. The class laughed. Embarrassed, he lost his place. "Michael, pay attention to what you're doing!" his teacher ordered. "What's wrong? Stay up late watching TV?"

Michael slammed his book shut, his face turning red in anger. He closed his eyes to keep the tears from coming.

"Stay in at recess," his teacher ordered.

At recess Michael complained, "It's not fair. Everybody picks on me. I didn't do anything to anybody."

Having no idea about all the roadblocks Michael had already faced that day, she put up another: "Michael, I really think you're overreacting. Go get a drink and some fresh air. You'll feel better when you cool down."

Try to find these roadblocks in the story: reassuring, distracting, ordering, naming, shaming, blaming, criticizing, threatening, and diagnosing.

IF ANYONE IS NEVER AT FAULT IN WHAT HE SAYS, HE IS A PERFECT MAN. JAMES 3:2, NIV.

KEEPING FRIENDS

Avoid roadblocks if you want to keep your friends! None of us is perfect, but we can do better with God's help.

Verbal Villains

APR. 29

THE LIPS OF THE RIGHTEOUS KNOW WHAT IS FITTING, BUT THE MOUTH OF THE WICKED ONLY WHAT IS PERVERSE. PROVERBS 10:32, NIV.

KEEPING FRIENDS

Which five use judging roadblocks? Which four use sending solutions roadblocks? Which three use avoiding the others' concerns roadblocks?

Verbal villains are people who use words in perverse ways to hurt others and destroy friendships. Check them out. Do you know any verbal villains? Have you ever been one yourself?

1. *Sign Painter.* Sign painters have to label everything and everyone. They name and shame.

2. *Prosecutor.* Prosecutors want to fix the blame onto someone. Once they know whose fault something is, they're ready to punish that person.

3. *Detective.* Detectives monopolize all the conversation, trying to get the facts and details of what happened. They blame.

4. *Lawyer.* Lawyers feel they're always right. They argue their points.

5. *Doctor.* Doctors think they can read minds. They know exactly why everyone does what they do. They diagnose.

6. *Magician.* Magicians try to make you think that your problem isn't there or that things aren't as bad as they seem. Everything will be better after a good night's rest! They divert, distract, and reassure.

7. *Preacher.* Preachers like to tell you what is the right thing to do. They tell you what you should and shouldn't do. They often threaten you with what will happen if you don't do as they suggest.

8. *Drill Sergeant.* Drill sergeants expect to be obeyed. They like to give orders. They command and demand.

9. *Editor.* Editors criticize everything you say and do. They're ready to change what you say to make it the way they think it ought to be. You can never be right with editors.

10. *Prophet.* Prophets always know exactly what's going to happen to you. They make their predictions and then sit back smugly to watch it take place.

11. *Florist.* Florists want everything to be lovely. They have flowery things to say to try to make you think that things are better than they are. They don't want to face your pain.

12. *Clown.* Clowns think everything is funny. They want to avoid unpleasant situations, so they try to make jokes to get you to forget your troubles.

Roadblocks Checkup

ow often do you use the following roadblocks to communication? *Always* is bad news; *never* is good news. In which areas do you need God's help?

1. I'm critical of other people and their actions.

Always   Usually   Sometimes   Never

2. I label people and call them names.

Always   Usually   Sometimes   Never

3. I blame someone else when things go wrong.

Always   Usually   Sometimes   Never

4. I like to figure out why people do things. I tell them why I think they acted as they did.

Always   Usually   Sometimes   Never

5. I'm quick to give unsolicited advice to people. I think I'm helping by offering solutions.

Always   Usually   Sometimes   Never

6. I feel that it's my duty to inform my friends what's right and wrong—what they should and shouldn't do.

Always   Usually   Sometimes   Never

7. I try to avoid others' pain by diverting their attention to something that happened to me or someone else.

Always   Usually   Sometimes   Never

8. I try through reassurance to get my friends to stop focusing on their pain.

Always   Usually   Sometimes   Never

9. I argue with my friends.

Always   Usually   Sometimes   Never

10. I feel envious when my friends get something better than I have or accomplish more than I do.

Always   Usually   Sometimes   Never

11. I don't want my friend to be friendly with others. I'm possessive in my relationships.

Always   Usually   Sometimes   Never

12. I complain a lot if things don't go my way.

Always   Usually   Sometimes   Never

13. I unfairly expect everyone to look at me as being the greatest. I expect my friends to praise me and admire me.

Always   Usually   Sometimes   Never

14. I blame God when things go wrong in my life.

Always   Usually   Sometimes   Never

MAY MY SPOKEN WORDS AND UNSPOKEN THOUGHTS BE PLEASING EVEN TO YOU, O LORD MY ROCK AND MY REDEEMER. PSALM 19:14, TLB.

127

Friends Forgive

BEAR WITH EACH OTHER AND FORGIVE WHATEVER GRIEVANCES YOU MAY HAVE AGAINST ONE ANOTHER.
COLOSSIANS 3:13, NIV.

KEEPING FRIENDS

Forgiving each other is part of what friends do to help keep their relationship close.

It was a warm spring afternoon in Washington, D.C., just the kind of day to give students spring fever. Since the junior high school had no air-conditioning, the windows were wide open.

The music teacher was called out of class for a few minutes, and the students took advantage of his absence. Bill stood with his friend, John, at the window looking across campus.

"I'm bored!" John exclaimed. "Let's have a little excitement around here!" He picked up the nearest pile of books and dropped them out the window.

"Hey! Those are mine!" Bill yelled as he watched them sail the three floors to the sidewalk below. Then he joined John in laughing since he didn't want to look like a spoilsport.

"Here! Let's dump some more!" Bill said between chuckles as he handed another pile to John.

John grabbed the books and tossed them automatically, then gasped as he realized they were his books this time! For a moment he was speechless, and then he bent over laughing again. "I guess I had that coming to me!" he said.

Such a prank could have caused a fight between the two, but they were friends and wanted to stay that way. Each had sensed a moment of anger that his friend would do that to him. Just as quickly each let go of his anger and decided to laugh instead and enjoy the joke, even if it was on him.

Bill and John considered their friendship more important to them than their feelings of anger over having a trick played on them. That's what forgiveness is—letting go of anger and deciding not to let something stand in the way of the relationship. Sometimes it's easy, as in the case of Bill and John. Other times it's incredibly hard to forgive.

This month we'll learn about forgiving friends as well as enemies. We'll discover that forgiveness is important to all of our relationships in life: family, school, church, community, and world.

The Bargain

ourteen-year-old Dan Ripley stood talking to the tall stranger who had just awakened him from his sleep under a tree.

It was July 7, 1863, just after the Battle of Gettysburg during the American Civil War.

"Are you going to war?" Dan asked. "I am."

"Does your father know?" the tall man asked.

"I reckon he does now," Dan answered darkly. "He killed my dog yesterday without my knowin', so I left without *his* knowin'. I'll never forgive him for that, never!"

"Why did he kill your pet?"

"'Cause my dog killed some sheep. But I'll never forgive him!"

"I agree with you," the stranger nodded. "Never forgive him . . . and never forget it—under one condition."

"What's that?"

"That you also never forget all the good and kind things your father has done for you. But then I suppose he's done a lot of mean things to cancel all the good ones off. Right?"

"No," Dan frowned.

"Since you've been honest with me, I'll be honest with you," the stranger said. "They say I'm the commander in chief of the army, and I've got a decision to make. I've been up all night trying to decide whether I should have 24 deserters shot, or whether I should forgive them. You've helped me decide, Dan."

"To shoot them?"

"No, not to," he said. "Here you are punishing your father because he did just one bad thing after so many years of good things. Seems a shame. It's like that with these 24 men. After all the brave deeds they have done for our country, why should I shoot them for just once falling asleep on duty? Doesn't seem right. I'll make a bargain with you, Dan. If you will go home and forgive your father, I'll forgive the 24 deserters."

"It's hard to forgive," Dan said. "But, I'll try."

"Good! Here's my card if you ever need me," the tall man said. Daniel could hardly believe his eyes. It said "A. Lincoln."

FORGIVE US OUR DEBTS, AS WE ALSO HAVE FORGIVEN OUR DEBTORS.
MATTHEW 6:12, NIV.

KEEPING FRIENDS

It's hard to forgive, but it's the best way to go with family as well as with friends.

One for Dan

MAY 3

BLESSED ARE THE
MERCIFUL, FOR
THEY WILL BE
SHOWN MERCY.
MATTHEW 5:7,
NIV.

KEEPING FRIENDS

The way of mercy and forgiveness is the way of friendship.

Dan Ripley ran all the way home, so anxious was he to tell his parents that he'd talked with the president of the United States. He was surprised to find his mother and father on the front porch, weeping before a uniformed officer. The soldier was saying, "I'm sorry. The president will not see him. More pardons are not to be expected."

His mother turned then to Dan, and drew him close. "You're our only son now," she sobbed.

"Will was found sleeping on duty, Dan," his father continued. "All we can do now is pray for Will."

"You pray, and I'll run," Dan said, breaking away from his mother's embrace.

"Where are you going?" his mother sounded alarmed.

"To the White House to see the president. He'll see me; I know he will. We have a bargain!" Then Dan told his story and showed them the card bearing Abraham Lincoln's name.

"Take my horse and carriage," the messenger offered.

"Take Mother with you," Mr. Ripley ordered.

It didn't take them long to cover the few miles to the White House. At the door Dan showed the card that said "Please admit Daniel Ripley on demand. A. Lincoln."

Within minutes Dan and Mrs. Ripley stood before the president. "Did you keep your part of the bargain?" he asked.

"Yes, and it would have killed my folks if I'd not gone home," Dan spoke quickly. "Because, you see, Will, that's my older brother, has been found sleeping on duty, and he's to be shot. I told my mother you'd help. You wouldn't let him be shot, if you knew."

"I agreed for 24 lives," the president smiled, "but I don't mind throwing in an extra one for you, Dan."

"Oh, thank you! Thank you!" Mrs. Ripley cried.

"Thank Dan," said Lincoln. "If he had not let the warmth of forgiveness soften his heart, Will Ripley and 24 others might well have died." To the boy he said, "Goodbye, Dan. We shall remember today with an easy conscience."

Leo Finds God

eo D'Arcangelo paced his cell like a caged lion. Back and forth, back and forth he walked, angry that he was in prison again, arrested this time for jumping bail.

Before that he'd been in jail for picking pockets and for drug possession. He'd been mainlining heroine since he was 16 and stealing since he was 11. His first job was to steal a lady's handbag on a crowded trolley car. His first arrest had been for shoplifting in a Philadelphia department store.

What have I got to show for my life? Leo thought as he paced. *Nothing but a lousy past and a worse future. What's the use of living? This is the worst place I've been in yet!* Leo looked around at the bleak cell. The bed was about to fall apart, and the walls were filthy, covered with graffiti scribbled there by previous occupants.

Leo stopped pacing to read a poem crudely written on one wall. It said:

"When you come to the end of your
    journey,
And this trouble is racked in your
    mind,
And there seems no other way out
    than by just mourning,
Turn to Jesus, for it is Him that you
    must find."

Yep! I've made a mess of my life, and this is the end of my journey, Leo mused. *Jesus, I need Your help. There's nothing I can do about my past except to ask You to forgive it. If You can change my life, please do it. Help me make tomorrow different.*

Leo lay down on his cot and stared at the ceiling. The feeling of despair was gone. He felt strangely at peace, loved, and forgiven.

After serving his time, Leo studied for his high school diploma and then went on to study for the ministry. Today Leo D'Arcangelo is a popular speaker. He loves to tell how he became God's friend in a prison cell.

WE HAVE FORGIVENESS OF SINS BECAUSE OF GOD'S RICH GRACE. EPHESIANS 1:7, ICB.

KEEPING FRIENDS

Friendship with God is based upon His marvelous grace and forgiveness. You don't have to wait until you come to the end of the journey to ask for it. He wants to be your friend today.

The Foot Washing

As I HAVE LOVED YOU, SO YOU MUST LOVE ONE ANOTHER. JOHN 13:34, NIV.

It was on a Friday that Tim Sharpe begged to drive his dad's car. "Please, Dad! I'll be careful!" But he wasn't careful enough. While turning around in a parking lot, he'd managed to put a big dent in the fender. His dad was boiling mad.

"I almost never let you drive my car, and when I do you wreck it!" Mr. Sharpe stormed. "Don't ask for it again!"

For the next two weeks Tim and his dad avoided speaking to each other—Dad because he was so angry, and Tim because he figured anything he'd say would only make matters worse.

Now it was Communion Sabbath, and Dad, known to everyone else as Pastor Sharpe, was having a hard time with his sermon. He was preaching about the attitude of the disciples at the Last Supper. He said, "True Christian love will lay aside differences, and each will serve the other. Even if you have a reason to be upset with others, you have to let it go. Jesus forgave us; we can do no less for those who have wronged us. Foot washing is a time to wash those feelings away."

Pastor Sharpe was feeling miserable inside. He cut his sermon short, dismissing the people for the foot washing. At the door of the men's room he caught Tim's eye. "Do you have anyone to serve you yet?" he asked.

Tim shook his head.

While Dad was on his knees washing his son's feet, he was praying silently, *Lord, please help me release my anger toward Tim. It's destroying my relationship with him and with You.*

Then as the two stood, the anger was suddenly gone, and Pastor Sharpe felt only love welling up in his heart for his son. "I'm sorry, son," he said. "You're more important to me than any stupid car. I love you, Tim."

"I'm sorry, too, Dad, I . . ." Then the two were in each other's arms, hugging.

KEEPING FRIENDS

Love shows itself in forgiveness. Only Jesus can help us release our anger so that we are able to forgive.

Welcome Home

Fifteen-year-old Isaiah Moody had run away from home soon after the death of his father. Months had gone by with no word.

"Dwight, go to the post office and see if there's a letter from your brother," Mrs. Moody said one day as usual.

"It's no use," Dwight complained. "There won't be a letter. There never is. Why bother?"

"But today might be the day!" she spoke cheerfully. "My firstborn has not forgotten me. Run along now."

Dwight took his time coming home. He hated having to tell her that once again there was no letter from Isaiah.

"He's coming home soon," she said. "I'd better trim the lamp and put it in the window. Maybe he'll come tonight."

"What makes you so sure?" Dwight questioned.

"God hears a mother's prayers," Mrs. Moody answered. "He'll bring my wandering boy home. I know He will."

Dwight couldn't argue with his mother's faith. On stormy nights he could hear her voice crying out to God above the howl of the wind, "Lord Jesus, look after my boy tonight. Keep him safe from harm and danger. Bring him back home!"

On Thanksgiving Day she always put an extra chair at the table for Isaiah, "Just in case he should come."

The months turned into years. Then one day as she sat at the door of her house, Mrs. Moody saw a stranger coming along the road. *I wonder who that could be?* she asked herself. He had a long flowing beard and looked like no one she knew.

He stopped at the door of the house, folded his arms, and began to cry. When she saw those tears, she exclaimed, "Oh, it's my lost boy! Come in, son, come in!"

"No, Mother," he spoke through his sobs. "I will not come in until you say you have forgiven me."

She rushed to him, threw her arms around him, and said, "Of course I forgive you! Welcome home!"

CAN A MOTHER . . . NOT HAVE LOVE FOR HER OWN SON? YET EVEN IF THAT SHOULD BE, I WILL NOT FORGET YOU. ISAIAH 49:15, TLB.

KEEPING FRIENDS

God loves you even more than your mother loves you. Nothing you ever do can cause Him to forget you. He's always willing to welcome you home.

133

The Broken Balloon

SHOULDN'T YOU HAVE MERCY ON OTHERS, JUST AS I HAD MERCY ON YOU? MATTHEW 18:33, TLB.

KEEPING FRIENDS

God has shown mercy on us. After He's forgiven us for all the bad things we have ever done, shouldn't we be willing to have mercy on those who do bad things to us?

Albert White picked up some stones and began tossing them at a row of starlings on a telephone wire. He tried to be careful not to hit Mrs. Hamilton's window not far behind the wire. His aim was poor, and the starlings still sat there.

The more Albert tried, the more determined he got. He picked up a larger stone and threw it with all his might. It missed the starlings, but crashed through Mrs. Hamilton's window. She came running outside.

"Albert White! Now look what you've done!" she scolded.

"I'm sorry," Albert apologized. "I'll pay for it. How much will it cost?"

"At least $40," she said.

"But all I have is $8!" he exclaimed.

"Well, then you won't have to pay for it," Mrs. Hamilton said. "I'll forgive you this time, and pay for it myself."

"Thank you!" Albert was all smiles.

Albert went home then and discovered his little sister, Ruth, playing with his balloon. Just as he walked in, it popped.

"Now look what you've done!" Albert shouted. "You'll have to pay for it—25 cents!"

Ruth began to whimper. "I have only 10 cents."

"Give me the 10 cents," Albert growled. "But you'll still owe me 15 cents!"

Ruth ran to her room and got her 10 pennies, and then she went outside bawling. Mrs. Hamilton was in her yard cleaning up the glass from her broken window. "What's wrong, Ruth?" Mrs. Hamilton asked.

"I broke Albert's balloon, and he took all my pennies," she sobbed.

Mrs. Hamilton was very angry. She marched over to Albert's house and told him, "Young man, I've changed my mind about that $40 it will cost to fix my window. You must pay for it. I can't believe that after I was willing to forgive you the $40, you weren't able to forgive Ruth a quarter! You don't deserve to be forgiven."

Act As If

've been hurt really bad," Tammy told me. "I know in my head that I should forgive this person, but I don't feel like it in my heart."

"Do it anyway," I urged.

"But wouldn't I be a hypocrite?"

"There are two parts to forgiveness," I explained. "One part has to do with your will. It's a decision you make. This is the action part of forgiveness, being merciful in action. You don't have to feel merciful to be merciful. You can act as if you were merciful. It isn't being a hypocrite if this is a choice you've made."

"OK. I can act as if," Tammy replied, "but what about the feeling?"

"That's God's part!" I replied. "If we do our part and choose to forgive, then God will do His part and supply the feeling of forgiveness."

"I think I'm beginning to understand," Tammy said.

"Do you remember the story of when the Israelites were being defeated in battle, and the Lord told them to go out singing the song of victory? They must have felt stupid acting like they were victorious when everyone could see they were being defeated. However, when they demonstrated the actions of victory, God supplied the victory, and the feelings followed their actions."

"Have you tried it?" Tammy wanted to know.

"Yes. Once a woman criticized me severely. I was hurt and angry and cried about it for days. The more I cried, the more I hated her for what she'd done. Then I sensed the Lord speaking to me: 'Dorothy, you've got to forgive her.'

"'How, Lord?' I asked.

"'Act as if she's your best friend,' He seemed to whisper to me.

"So I did. I sent her notes. I gave her a little gift. I met her with a smile and a hug. I performed the actions, and sure enough, God supplied the feelings. We became good friends."

[BE] MERCIFUL IN ACTION, KINDLY IN HEART. COLOSSIANS 3:12, PHILLIPS.

KEEPING FRIENDS

When you don't feel like forgiving, make a conscious choice to forgive anyway. Perform the actions of forgiveness, and God will supply the feeling.

135

Nettie's Essay

MAY 9

IF HE IS SORRY, FORGIVE HIM. LUKE 17:3, PHILLIPS.

KEEPING FRIENDS

It's a real struggle to forgive someone who has hurt us, but we can do it with Christ's help.

"Is your essay finished?" 11-year-old Amy asked.

"All done!" 12-year-old Nettie beamed.

"Please help me, Nettie," Amy begged. "You're so much better at writing than I am."

Nettie shook her head. "Mr. Mason said we weren't to get any help at all. It would be wrong to help you."

"Please! Just a little bit," Amy persisted. "No one will ever know!"

Still Nettie refused. "It's wrong. I can't do it."

"If you won't help me get a prize, then you won't get one either!" Amy grabbed Nettie's essay and tossed it into the fireplace.

"Oh, Amy!" Nettie ran to rescue her paper, but it was too late. Both girls stood there and watched it go up in flames.

Too upset for words, Nettie ran to her bedroom, locked the door, and cried her heart out. She had spent days on that essay. She'd never get another done in time for tomorrow's deadline.

I'll never speak to Amy again! Nettie resolved. *She had no right to burn my paper. I'll never forgive her, never!*

But as she lay on her bed, a new thought entered her mind. *I was baptized just last month. I've become a Christian, and Jesus wants us to forgive everyone. I should forgive Amy, but I can't!*

At last Nettie got tired of crying. She knelt beside her bed and told Jesus all about her problem. "Please, dear Jesus, help me forgive Amy. I want You to forgive me, so help me forgive her. It's so hard, but please help me to do it."

Later when Amy apologized, Nettie said, "Of course, I forgive you."

The next day a very surprising thing happened at school. When Mr. Mason gave out the prizes, he called up both Nettie and Amy.

"I'm giving a prize to Amy for her honesty in telling me what happened to Nettie's essay. And I think Nettie deserves a prize for the way she's forgiven the one who wronged her."

Making Up

From Ilene Miller's vantage point on the hill she could see the blue minivan that belonged to her sociology teacher. She watched as he helped carry Maria's suitcases and boxes to the van. Maria, an 18-year-old exchange student from Mexico, was going to live with a different family.

Tears streamed down Ilene's face as she remembered the fun she and Maria had had during the past month.

"The Millers are too strict," Maria had told the teacher.

It's not fair! Maria thought. *I don't think my folks are too strict. Sure they say "No" sometimes, but that's only to protect us. I'm glad they care about when we come in and what we do.*

Ilene stopped crying. She clenched her fists and spoke into the October wind, "How could she do this to me? We loved her, and she's treated us like dirt! I don't ever want to see her again!"

Ilene struggled with feelings of hurt, anger, and hate. *I feel like quitting school! What will the other kids think? This is awful! I hate her!*

After they were gone, Ilene went back to the house. She went to her bedroom, turned on a cassette, and flopped onto her bed. The song was about Jesus being a friend. *I guess if anyone can make sense of this whole mess, Jesus can.*

Ilene closed her eyes and prayed silently. She shared the whole rotten situation with Jesus. *Lord, please give me strength to get through this. Help me love Maria, when I feel like hating her. Help me know what to do, what to say.*

The next morning, Ilene sat in a corner near her locker. The hall was full of kids when Maria arrived. Ilene's heart skipped a beat. Then to her own surprise, she got up and put an arm around Maria. "Hi!" she said. "What you up to?"

It was as though yesterday had never happened. Both girls started laughing and crying together. They were friends again.

BE RECONCILED TO THY BROTHER.
MATTHEW 5:24.

KEEPING FRIENDS

If we talk over our relationships with God, He'll help us know what to do and what to say.

Reuben's Pardon

YOU ARE A GOD OF FORGIVENESS, ALWAYS READY TO PARDON. NEHEMIAH 9:17, TLB.

KEEPING FRIENDS

God offers you a pardon today for all the sins and mistakes of your past. Will you accept His forgiveness?

It was a bleak December day when the governor paid a visit to the state prison. Reuben Johnson, along with hundreds of fellow prisoners, marched silently to the chapel to hear him speak. "It's customary to give gifts at this holiday season," the governor said. "I hold in my hands some gifts—pardons for several of you sitting here."

The men sat up, now alert. They hadn't been expecting this! Who'd be the lucky prisoners?

"I'll read the names," the governor said. "When your name is called, please come forward so that I may have the pleasure of personally giving you this very special Christmas gift!"

It won't be me, Reuben was thinking. *No, not after all I've done.*

"Reuben Johnson!" the governor declared, his eyes scanning the audience for the fortunate man.

No one stirred. Deep in his own miserable thoughts, Reuben sat staring at the floor. A seatmate nudged him with his elbow, "Johnson, it's you!"

"Where's Reuben Johnson?" the governor asked.

Reuben didn't move, didn't even look up.

The warden stood, located Reuben, and commanded, "Reuben! It's you! Come on up now and get your pardon!"

Slowly Reuben responded, shuffling past the others sitting in his row, walking hesitatingly toward the front. Smiling, the governor held out the pardon.

"Thank you," Reuben whispered as he accepted the pardon and went back to his seat.

When the ceremony was over, the pardoned men remained behind as the unlucky ones filed out of the chapel. All that is, except Reuben. Automatically he took his place in line and headed back to his cell.

"Reuben! Get out of line!" the warden said. "You don't have to go back. You're a free man!"

At last the reality of his pardon dawned on Reuben. He smiled and straightened his shoulders as he stepped out of line.

Randy's Revenge

R andy was so furious that he ran all the way home after school. Out of breath, he stopped inside the kitchen door where his older sister, Cynthia, was already seated at the table doing her homework.

"I could kill that stupid jerk!" Randy said, his fists raised.

"Whoa!" Cynthia held up both hands. "Who?"

"Brian North! Who else?"

"What happened?"

Randy sat down opposite his sister. "Mr. Matthews offered a prize to the person who could do a really hard math problem the fastest. Five of us were willing to try. We all took our places at the board. Brian took a place next to me. I was ahead, when the door opened. I turned around to see who had gone out. It was the school secretary with a notice for the teacher. When I turned back to finish my problem, it was gone—erased. I know Brian did it! I had to start over, and of course he won! I'm going to get even! I want my revenge!" Randy pounded the table.

"I know a glorious revenge," Cynthia said.

"Like what?"

"How about trying to do what the Bible says? 'Overcome evil with good'" (Romans 12:21, NIV).

"No way!" Randy said, but he thought about her suggestion all evening and by morning had decided to try it. That afternoon he invited Brian to come home with him to see his collection of model cars. After playing with them for a while, Randy picked up a bright-yellow racer.

"I want you to have this one, Brian. It's your favorite."

"You've got to be kidding!" Brian exclaimed. "After what I did to you?"

"Sure," Randy said. "I want you to have it."

"I feel awful," Brian said.

"Don't," Randy commented. "Now, let's forget it and be friends. OK?"

Later Randy told his sister. "It worked! You should have seen the misery on Brian's face when I gave him that racer! He promised he'd never do that again, and better yet we're still friends."

DO NOT BE OVERCOME BY EVIL, BUT OVERCOME EVIL WITH GOOD. ROMANS 12:21, NIV.

KEEPING FRIENDS

Revenge is a sure way to destroy friendship. Returning good for evil is a much better route to take.

The Grudge

DO NOT SEEK REVENGE OR BEAR A GRUDGE. LEVITICUS 19:18, NIV.

KEEPING FRIENDS

If we're going to get rid of grudges, we'll need to do the "outrageously impossible thing" and forgive. Forgiving is tough, but with God's help we can do it!

rudge (gruj) *n.* A strong, continued feeling of hostility or ill will against someone over a real or fancied grievance" *(Webster's New World Dictionary)*.

Lewis Smedes had a grudge, all right. After the way Leo Sedman, the football coach, had treated him, Lewis figured he had every right to feel hostile.

It happened at the end of gym period. The boys all took a shower, except for Lewis. After they were inside the shower room, he quickly undressed and wrapped a towel around his waist. He hung around the shower room door for a couple minutes. When he figured it was safe, he went back to his locker and began to get dressed. The problem was that he looked like a skinny runt beside the other boys, and he figured they'd laugh if they saw him naked. Relieved that he'd succeeded in avoiding embarrassment, he was dressing when Mr. Sedman walked in. He gave Lewis the once-over and noticed the still-dry towel.

"I've been watching you, Smedes," he yelled. "You'd better believe me, buddy boy, that you'll not get away with disobeying the rules. I'll teach you to cheat on the shower! Off with your clothes! Now! Into that shower!"

By now the other boys were finished. They gathered around Lewis to gawk. His neck turned pink. He dropped his pants and bolted for the shower, mortified to be made a spectacle of in front of the whole class.

Writing about his feelings many years later, Lewis said: "He knew what he was doing and I can't excuse him. You were guilty, Leo Sedman, and I hated you. Boy, did I hate you!"

After carrying that grudge for many years, Lewis finally decided that the only person he was hurting was himself. He chose to forgive, one of the hardest things he'd ever done.

In his book *Forgive and Forget,* Lewis calls this act of forgiving his coach the "outrageously impossible thing."

How to Forgive

What if Paul had said, "I'll capture the snake and keep it in my pocket! Then I can remember what hurt me." What would you think of Paul? Top story missing? Not all there? Foolish?

Yet that's what some people do with the vipers in their lives. Instead of destroying them, they keep them so that they can hurt some more. Here are three steps to help you get rid of the vipers that may be bothering you.

1. *Write it down.* Write down the name of a person who has hurt you. Then list all the hurtful things he or she did or said.

2. *Burn it.* Say "I choose to let go of these bad feelings. I choose to forgive this person for the things written here." Throw the paper into the fire; watch it turn to ashes.

3. *Pray about it.* Say "Dear Lord, I've demonstrated what I want to happen in this relationship. Please come into my heart and burn out the bad feelings I have. Make the acted forgiveness become real."

A speaker suggested this simple process at a weekend retreat I attended at Camp Hope, British Columbia. I wrote down the name of a woman who had said some cruel, untrue things about me. For many weeks I cried every time I thought about what she'd done. The anger I felt toward her was keeping me awake at night and making me most unhappy. I wanted to expose her and make her suffer. Even though these feelings were like the poison of a viper, I found it hard to shake them off into the fire of forgiveness.

For a long time I held that list of my hurts in my hand, refusing to throw it in the fire, refusing to forgive. I went to my room and asked God to give me strength. At last I went to the fireplace and threw in the crumpled paper. It felt so good to get rid of the poison. It felt so good to forgive!

BUT PAUL SHOOK THE SNAKE OFF INTO THE FIRE AND SUFFERED NO ILL EFFECTS. ACTS 28:5, NIV.

KEEPING FRIENDS

Hanging on to hurts is foolish. Forgiveness is the only way to "feel no ill effects."

Short Circuit

Something was short-circuiting Barbara Mandrell's prayers. She tried to pray, but she felt as if something was blocking the flow. She wasn't getting through to God.

"What is it, Lord?" she asked. "Something is wrong, but I don't know what it is. Please show me." She stayed there on her knees in the semidarkness of her bedroom and waited for the Lord to show her the trouble.

The picture of a woman came to Barbara's mind. (We'll call her Nancy, though that isn't her real name.) Barbara and Nancy had been friends until Nancy had gossiped about her. The nasty comments had been repeated to Barbara, and she was angry and hurt. Barbara resented Nancy and wished someone would hurt her as much as she had hurt others. Never would be too soon to see this woman who had once been her friend.

"Yes, Lord," Barbara whispered. "There's trouble with Nancy, that's for sure! So my bitterness with her has blocked my communication with You! Is that what You're trying to tell me?"

The words of Mark 11:25 came then to Barbara's mind. "But when you are praying, first forgive anyone you are holding a grudge against" (TLB).

"Of course, Lord," Barbara continued. "Please forgive me for holding this grudge against Nancy. Please take away my anger and bitterness. I no longer want her to hurt as she's hurt me. Please bless Nancy, and bring her happiness."

For the first time in many days, Barbara felt at peace as she got up off her knees. She knew this time that God had heard her prayer and that He'd answer.

A few days later Barbara saw Nancy again. Without a thought she ran up to her and hugged her. Nancy warmly hugged her back.

About the restoration of her relationship with Nancy, Barbara writes: "I had forgiven her, and she somehow sensed this change in me. The power of forgiveness is mystifying but real!"

WHEN YOU ARE PRAYING, AND YOU REMEMBER THAT YOU ARE ANGRY WITH ANOTHER PERSON ABOUT SOMETHING, THEN FORGIVE HIM. MARK 11:25, ICB.

KEEPING FRIENDS

A break in our relationships with people often causes a break in our relationship with God. Forgiveness is the way to set both relationships right.

Second Chance

he tracheotomy was finished. An emergency room nurse sat by the bedside of her 6-year-old patient and watched his rhythmic breathing through the tube that the doctor had inserted in his windpipe.

He'd been gasping for breath when his mother had brought him in. The doctor on duty had diagnosed diphtheria and had begun to operate at once to save his life. The nurse had assisted.

How exciting to be part of saving a child's life, she mused as she settled back for the long night's vigil. The doctor had told her to sit up with the boy to make sure that the tube remained clear.

"Wake me if there's a problem," he had said.

The nurse was tired too, and had to pinch herself more than once to keep awake. Sometime after midnight she fell asleep and awoke later to silence. The tube was blocked. She cleared it, but there was no response. She felt for the boy's pulse. Nothing. Frantic, she ran down the hall and pounded on the doctor's door.

"He's dead!" she sobbed. "I tried so hard to keep awake. Really I did, Doctor. You've got to believe me!"

He rushed to the room, but there was nothing he could do. "Come to my office!" he said curtly. Fearfully, she followed him down the silent hall.

"Your mistake has cost a life," he scolded. "I'll see that you're fired!"

She watched as he picked up a pen and wrote furiously, then he handed her his report. It showed no mercy or compassion.

"Well, do you have anything to say?" he asked coldly.

Turning her tear-stained face toward the doctor, she said, "Please, sir, give me another chance."

No way! the doctor thought. To her he said, "You may leave."

But the doctor couldn't sleep. He thought of how many opportunities God had given him. The next morning he took the report from his desk and tore it up.

The nurse made good on her second chance. Eventually she became the head of a famous children's hospital in England.

SHOW MERCY AND COMPASSION TO ONE ANOTHER. ZECHARIAH 7:9, NIV.

KEEPING FRIENDS

Do you know someone who needs a second chance?

Forgiving Yourself

MAY 17

DON'T KEEP LOOKING AT MY SINS—ERASE THEM FROM YOUR SIGHT. PSALM 51:9, TLB.

KEEPING FRIENDS

Don't keep reviewing your mistakes. Use your eraser. Press the delete button. Forgive yourself as God has already forgiven you.

Cami Dale took another tissue from the box on Richard Hammond's desk and blew her nose. "I'm facing this problem," she sobbed, "and there's no way I can surmount it! It's more than I can handle."

Elder Hammond listened patiently as Cami related the circumstances that had led to her problem.

"There's no one else to blame but me," she admitted at last. "If I'd only acted differently, I wouldn't be in this predicament! It's my own fault!" More sobs, more tissues.

"My pencil has a well-used eraser," Pastor Hammond smiled at the distraught student. "Don't worry about what you might have done. Let's look for a way out."

"My pencil has a well-used eraser." I'd like Richard Hammond for a friend, wouldn't you? We'd all like someone who's willing to wipe out blame.

God has a pencil with a well-used eraser too! He's promised that if we confess our sins, He'll blot them out, eradicate them, erase them, remove them from us.

The delete button on God's computer is used every time we confess our sins. Zap! Just like that those sins are gone from our records in heaven! You can't find them in any backup file. Once erased, they're gone for good!

Call them what you will—sins, mistakes, transgressions, bloopers, errors, iniquities, misconduct, misdemeanors, crimes, felonies, wrongdoings, or misdeeds. God's eraser can remove them.

In fact, Psalm 103:12 declares that our sins are removed from us as far away as "the east is from the west." And Micah 7:19 informs us that God has buried our sins in the depths of the ocean.

If God is so willing to forgive us, then why not forgive ourselves? The next time you're tempted to blame yourself for all the things you've done wrong, remember Elder Hammond's advice, "Don't worry about what you might have done. Let's find a way out."

Jack, the Broom Seller

It happened on Kid Street in the slums of Nottingham, England, 150 years ago. Seventeen-year-old William Booth stood on a chair in front of the shack of Besom Jack, the broom seller.

Everyone knew that Jack was a drunk, cruel to his family, and a problem in the neighborhood. A crowd gathered to see why a teenager was standing on a chair in front of his house.

William began to preach. "Friends, I want to put a few straight questions to your souls. Are your wives sitting now in dark houses waiting for you to come home with money?"

Jack threw open the door to his hovel and staggered toward William. The teenager kept on preaching. "Are you going away from here to the tavern to spend on drink money that your wives need for food and your children for shoes?"

"My wife is no concern of yours!" Jack shouted. "Go away!"

William stayed on the chair. "Jack," he said, "God loves your wife, and so did you, once. Can you remember how much you loved and cherished her when first you met? Well, God loves you with a love far greater than that."

"Me?" Jack spoke softly.

"Yes, Jack, God loves *you*." William jumped down from the chair and took Jack's arm. "Come, Jack, just kneel down here, and tell the Lord you love Him too."

Jack fell to his knees and began to cry. The crowd pressed in closer to hear his prayer. "Lord, I'm just a miserable drunk. I don't deserve Your love. Please forgive me for the way I've treated my wife and children. Help me, Lord, to get sober and stay sober. Help me to do what's right."

The amazing thing was that Besom Jack did change. He quit drinking and began to treat his wife with kindness. He stopped causing trouble in Nottingham. He was a new person, changed by God's forgiving love.

MAY 18

YOU ARE FORGIVING AND GOOD, O LORD, ABOUNDING IN LOVE TO ALL WHO CALL TO YOU. PSALM 86:5, NIV.

KEEPING FRIENDS

God loves you no matter what you've done. He offers you forgiveness and power to live a changed life. He's the best friend you'll ever have.

145

Saving an Enemy

Two hundred years ago a pastor named Peter Miller lived in Pennsylvania. In the same area lived a man who hated the pastor and made life miserable for him.

It so happened that this troublemaker was found guilty of treason and was sentenced to be hanged. When the news reached Peter Miller, he set off walking to find General George Washington.

After 60 miles of trudging through the wilderness, he found the general. "Please, sir, spare the life of this man. I'll vouch for him. Grant him a pardon for my sake."

"That isn't possible," General Washington said. "Your friend is a traitor to our country."

"My friend?" Peter Miller exclaimed. "Oh, no! He's my worst enemy. He's mocked me and abused me, but I still would beg for his life."

Now it was Washington's turn to be shocked. "What? You've walked 60 miles to save the life of your enemy? This puts the matter in an entirely different light. I'll grant the pardon."

General Washington made out the pardon document and handed it to Peter Miller. Without taking time to rest, Pastor Miller began the 60-mile walk home again. He arrived in the village square just as the traitor was being led to the scaffold.

"Why, there's old Peter Miller!" the traitor shouted when he saw the pastor hurrying up to join the crowd. "He's come today to rejoice over his revenge in seeing me hanged!"

"Wait! Wait!" Peter called to the executioner as he pushed his way through the crowd and held up the pardon for all to see. "I have here a pardon signed by General Washington. The man goes free."

There was no hanging that day. No sermon Peter Miller ever preached could have been as powerful as what he did that day for an enemy. He gave a demonstration of God's love for a sinner.

BUT GOD DEMONSTRATES HIS OWN LOVE FOR US IN THIS: WHILE WE WERE STILL SINNERS, CHRIST DIED FOR US. ROMANS 5:8, NIV.

KEEPING FRIENDS

Even if you feel that God is your enemy, He still loves you and will forgive you freely. Shouldn't you be willing to do the same for your enemies?

Helping an Enemy

At recess Alice Brown sneaked back into the classroom and drew a funny picture on the board. She labeled it, "Teacher."

When the bell rang, the other children were surprised to see the picture on the board. So was the teacher.

"That wasn't a nice thing to do," the teacher said. "We shouldn't make fun of people. Does anyone know who drew this picture?"

Alice's hand shot up. "It was Patty," she said.

Patty's mouth dropped open. Her face grew red. She just shook her head.

"Patty, you'll stay after school!" the teacher ordered. As a result, Patty had to sit for 20 minutes after the others had left. When she went outside, she noticed a crowd gathered around Alice and her bicycle. Patty could see that the tire was flat.

"What am I going to do?" Alice wailed. "I have a newspaper route. Now I'll be late, and I might lose the job!" She started to cry.

Serves the little sneak right! Patty thought. She started to walk away. Then she had another thought: *Jesus says we should do good things for our enemies. I guess I should help Alice.*

"You can use my bike, Alice," Patty said, surprised that she felt so good saying it. "Just be careful with it, and bring it back when you're finished."

Alice was speechless for a moment. "Really? Are you sure?"

"Really. Please, take it. I can walk home."

Alice did a lot of thinking on her newspaper route that evening. The next day she went to the teacher and told the true story of what had happened.

Would you be surprised to learn that Alice and Patty became good friends? And better than that, Alice became a friend of Jesus because of Patty's unselfish actions.

IF YOUR ENEMY IS HUNGRY, FEED HIM; IF HE IS THIRSTY, GIVE HIM SOMETHING TO DRINK. IN DOING THIS, YOU WILL HEAP BURNING COALS ON HIS HEAD. ROMANS 12:20, NIV.

KEEPING FRIENDS

Forgiveness has a way of turning our enemies into our friends. As hard as it may be, it's what Jesus would have you do.

Bianca's Secret

GET RID OF ALL BITTERNESS . . . AND ANGER. EPHESIANS 4:31, NIV.

KEEPING FRIENDS

Sooner or later we're all tempted to become bitter because of the unjust treatment we receive. At such times our choices are between hate and love; bitterness or forgiveness.

eenager Bianca Rothschild had every reason to be bitter. In 1939, just before her sixteenth birthday, war broke out in Poland. Six years later she was the only one of a family of 43 who was still living; all the others had died in concentration camps.

Today Bianca wears a brace because of the beatings she received at the hands of her captors. A Nazi guard stomped on her with his heavy boots, breaking ribs and damaging her back. He broke her wrist and mangled one leg. The pain was excruciating.

"Oh, God, please let me die!" she prayed that night. "Please let them drop a bomb to take me out of my misery." When Bianca found herself alive the next morning, she did some serious thinking. She realized that she had two choices. She could spend the rest of her life feeling sorry for herself, hating her enemies, and becoming bitter, or she could choose the way of love and forgiveness, looking away from herself to the needs of others.

That day she turned her back on bitterness and hate. She prayed, "Dear God, help me through this terrible ordeal, and I vow to give myself in true and loving service to bless others."

After the war she immigrated to the United States and ended up living in a condo in San Diego. There she found a very special way to love.

Most of the residents are old people who often need a little bit of sunshine. Whenever anyone is in the hospital, she sends a cheery get-well card. Each one she signs "The Sunshine Lady." Through the years she has sent hundreds of cards.

A neighbor commented, "There's something wrong with Bianca's back, but it never seems to affect her cheerful spirit."

They don't know about her battle with bitterness, hate, and anger that day in the concentration camp. They know only the results of her choice to love and forgive.

Forgiveness Is a Gift

On February 3, 1945, James Harris joined 1,799 other prisoners of war in a death march that lasted 91 days. From the day they left their prison in western Poland until they were liberated by the American forces, the men never changed clothes. Hunger, filth, pain, and disease stalked them.

They hiked from 10 to 15 miles a day through ice, snow, sleet, hail, and mud. At night they slept on barn floors, which caused their hair to become matted and fouled with animal dung. The men became infested with body lice. On a diet of two potatoes a day the men soon became weak. Dysentery raged through the ranks.

One morning when James was too weak to rise from the barn floor, two of his buddies carried him to the "meat wagon," where he rode for three days with dead bodies piled around him. On the third day a soldier ordered him off the wagon.

"I was so weak, so emaciated, and yet I felt strength—strength beyond my human power or emotion, strength I believe that came from God," says Harris.

At one point someone gave him a handful of weevil-infested flour. He knocked the manure out of an old tin can lying in the barnyard and gathered some dry manure for a fire to cook the gruel. His wet matches wouldn't light, and he stood there weeping from frustration. That day the liberating forces arrived.

Looking back on his ordeal, Harris says, "I think the greatest blessing is that I came away from that death march, from the imprisonment, with no hate. Not the slightest bit of hate. I think that was God's greatest gift of all. The love."

James Harris is right. Love is a gift. There's no way we can forgive on our own.

What would life be without love? Of what use are showers that cleanse the outside if bitterness contaminates the heart? Liberation is pointless if we're still bound by hate. What is a mansion if suspicion walks the halls? Yet poverty and persecution can be endured if love is there.

**LOVE COMES FROM GOD.
1 JOHN 4:7, NIV.**

KEEPING FRIENDS

We know we have the gift of love when we're able to forgive our enemies.

149

Corrie's Struggle

BE KIND AND COMPASSIONATE TO ONE ANOTHER, FORGIVING EACH OTHER, JUST AS IN CHRIST GOD FORGAVE YOU. EPHESIANS 4:32, NIV.

KEEPING FRIENDS

Ask God to give you enough love to forgive those who have been mean to you. If you do the actions, He'll supply the feeling.

I hate that man! Corrie ten Boom's face hardened as she watched the former guard at Ravensbruck walk toward her after a church service in Munich. *That's the one in the shower room. I'll never forget his face!*

Corrie's knees felt weak as the scene came back to her—the pile of clothes, shivering naked women walking before the mocking guards, her shame as she brushed past this particular guard. She wanted to run, but there was no time. Already he was before her, stretching out his hand.

"A fine message, Fraulein! How good it is to know, as you say, that all our sins are at the bottom of the sea!"

She fumbled in her pocketbook rather than take the outstretched hand. She was face-to-face with one of her captors, and her blood ran cold.

"You mentioned Ravensbruk in your talk. I was a guard there," the man admitted. "However, I don't remember you. There were so many. I have become a Christian. I know God has forgiven me for the cruel things I did there, but I'd like to hear it from your lips. Fraulein, will you forgive me?"

Suddenly Corrie realized she had no control of the hate, bitterness, and anger in her heart. She couldn't forgive him. The horrid memories were too strong.

For what seemed forever she wrestled with her feelings. The words of Matthew 6:15 came to mind: "If you do not forgive men their sins, your Father will not forgive your sins" (NIV).

Love this man, her enemy? *Forgive* him? How could she?

Jesus help me! she prayed. *I can lift my hand. I can do that much. You'll have to supply the feeling.*

Woodenly, mechanically, she thrust her hand into the one stretched out to her. And as she did, something incredible happened. She said: "The current started in my shoulder, raced down my arm, sprang into our joined hands. And then this healing warmth seemed to flood my whole being, bringing tears to my eyes."

"I forgive you, brother!" she cried. "With all my heart I forgive you."

Bless Your Enemies

This story happened about 40 years ago in South America. In this particular country the people didn't have freedom to worship God. Anyone who joined the Adventist Church was in great peril. Seventeen-year-old Christobob knew that his life was in danger, but he determined to remain true to Jesus.

Christobob arrived home from work one afternoon to find a police officer waiting for him. The officer led him, along with six other Adventist men, at gunpoint into the woods.

Christobob's mother and sisters stood weeping as the Christians were led away. He called out to them, "Don't worry! They may persecute me, but I'll never give up my faith! If necessary, I'll be faithful unto death!"

The women dropped to their knees and began to pray. "Please, dear God, deliver Christobob if it is Your will." After their prayer they cautiously entered the jungle in the direction the men had gone.

Suddenly a shot rang through the forest, then another, and another. One. Two. Three. Four. Five. Six. Seven. Then all was silent. By now the sun had set, and the women were afraid to go deeper into the woods in the dark.

Early the next morning they discovered the seven men. Six were dead, but Christobob was still alive. They fixed a stretcher and carried him to the hospital.

Christobob slept for a while. When he awoke he scooted over to the edge of his cot and slid off onto his knees. He began to pray. For whom do you suppose he prayed?

His prayer went something like this: "Dear Lord, please bless the police officer who led me into the woods. Bless his helpers. Forgive them for what they've done. Help them find Your truth in the Bible. Help them turn from their sins so that I might see them in heaven! Then bless my mother and my sisters. Help them be faithful!" Then he died.

PEOPLE CURSE US, BUT WE BLESS THEM.
1 CORINTHIANS 4:12, ICB.

KEEPING FRIENDS

The God who gave Christobob the love to bless his enemies is still alive. He'll help us pray for those who don't treat us very nicely.

151

A Forgiving Friend

THE LORD, THE
COMPASSIONATE
AND GRACIOUS
GOD, . . .
FORGIVING
WICKEDNESS,
REBELLION AND
SIN. EXODUS
34:6, 7, NIV.

KEEPING FRIENDS

Do you feel guilty for things you've done in the past? Do you fear exposure of your deeds done in secret? Jesus offers you pardon and freedom from condemnation and guilt. He wants to be your Friend.

When he was 17 William Herschel joined the Hanoverian Guards in Hanover, Germany. However, William didn't enjoy his life with his rough companions in the army. He was interested in music and astronomy and the finer things of life. So he deserted the guards and escaped to England, where he lived in constant fear of discovery and punishment. Should he be caught, the penalty would be death.

After several years of successfully dodging the guards, he received a summons to Windsor Castle to present himself before King George III.

Oh, no! I've been found out! the now successful astronomer thought. *I'll surely be exposed and thrown into prison to await execution!* To run away now was out of the question. He'd have to face the music!

It was with a racing heart that William, a deserter of the king's guards, walked into Windsor Castle to meet the king. *There's nothing to do but admit my fault and take my punishment,* William decided. He fearfully walked toward the king.

The king smiled as William approached. He left his throne and greeted the scientist. He said, "Before we discuss science, there is a little matter of business that we must attend to." With that he handed William a document with the royal seal signed by King George himself.

With trembling hands William opened the document. It was a pardon for his desertion, written in the king's own hand! Tears came to his eyes as a tremendous load of guilt was lifted from his shoulders. He no longer had to hide. He no longer faced death for his crime.

During his time of hiding from justice, William had accepted Jesus as his personal Saviour. He saw in this experience of the king's pardon an illustration of what Jesus had done for him by forgiving all his sins.

Toyohiko Forgives

Toyohiko felt uneasy as he followed a fellow student across the campus of the Japanese college toward the athletic field. *Why would anyone want to see me on the field at this hour of the day?* he wondered.

Toyohiko knew that most of the students were against him because he didn't believe in war. He thought that Christians today should follow the example of Jesus in not resisting evil persons.

He was almost to the sports field when a group of students leaped from the bushes yelling, "Traitor! Coward!" They beat, scratched, kicked, and punched him.

Blood ran down Toyohiko's face and mingled with the dirt on the ground. Oh, how it hurt! Unbelievable pain tore through his body! He felt angry and humiliated.

Weren't my ancestors the samurai, who never forgave anyone? I'm strong. I could show them a thing or two about fighting bravely! Then he thought of Jesus, the leader he'd chosen to follow. Jesus was the forgiving Saviour. *I must be like Jesus,* Toyohiko decided. *I must do what Jesus would do if He were here in my place, feeling my pain and humiliation.*

His attackers stood back as Toyohiko tried to stand. He was shaking from his beating. He struggled to steady himself. Then clasping his hands together, he looked toward heaven and prayed, "Father, forgive them. They know not what they do."

One by one his attackers left the sports field. When he opened his eyes, he stood alone.

This wasn't Toyohiko's last opportunity to imitate Jesus. In the years to come his attackers drew knives, shot into his home, smashed his dishes and cooking pots, and took the very clothes off his back. Once an attacker knocked out his four front teeth. Not once did he fight back. He faced them all with a smile, and when that didn't work, he ran away. But always he prayed, "Father, forgive them. They know not what they do."

FATHER, FORGIVE THEM, FOR THEY DO NOT KNOW WHAT THEY ARE DOING. LUKE 23:34, NIV.

KEEPING FRIENDS

Try praying Toyohiko's prayer the next time someone hurts you. It will be the bravest thing you ever did.

Carrie and the Thief

I WILL FORGIVE
THEIR WICKED-
NESS AND WILL
REMEMBER THEIR
SINS NO MORE.
JEREMIAH 31:34,
NIV.

KEEPING FRIENDS

Jesus needs your
example of
forgiveness to
help someone
learn of His
love today.

Twelve-year-old Carrie Whittenburg sat with her parents in their living room as they discussed the events of the day. While she'd been in school, a thief had broken into their house. Alerted by someone, the police had caught him before he'd left the house. Nothing was missing except $25 from Carrie's bedroom.

"How do you feel about what happened today?" Mr. Whittenburg asked.

"I feel uneasy and a bit vulnerable," his wife, Diane, admitted.

It was Carrie's turn. "Daddy, remember that story you told in a sermon once about Harry Orchard, and how the wife of the man he murdered gave him a Bible? Why don't we do that for this man?"

"Good idea!" her parents agreed.

"And let's put his name on it!" Carrie suggested.

So that's what they did. A couple of weeks later Elder Leroy Albers visited Rufus in prison and gave him the Bible from Carrie.

When Rufus saw his name on the Bible, he began to cry. He'd already had a letter from Carrie. It said, "I don't know what it's like to be in prison, because I've never been. But I do know what it's like to be forgiven, because I've been baptized. And I'd like to offer you forgiveness for what you did to us."

Rufus answered her. "I read your letter and got the Bible. I saved that letter, and each time I read it, I can't help but cry. To think that a person like me could do what I did to you, someone so undeserving, and yet have that same person tell me she loved me! I don't know what to say."

Several months later he wrote, "It was love and forgiveness, accompanied by deeds of providing for my spiritual needs that opened my eyes to God's care and concern for me. I hope that one day we'll meet and be able to pray together and thank God for all He's done for us."

Today Rufus knows the meaning of God's love, because one 12-year-old was willing to forgive.

False Forgiveness

For 30 years an old farmer had been fighting with his neighbor over the placement of a fence. On his deathbed the old man decided to make things right. Calling his wife, he said, "Please tell Abner that I'm dying and wish to speak to him."

Before long she was back with Abner. The old man trembled as he spoke. "Abner, you and me has been feudin' about the fence line nigh unto 30 years. I've said some pretty hard things about you, and I want to tell you I'm mighty sorry. I'd just like to be friends with you before I die. Will you forgive me?"

"Of course," Abner said, his eyes moist. "I reckon I've said some pretty hard things about you in the past 30 years as well. Yep, it's time to be friends."

After a solemn handshake, the sick man shook a finger at Abner and said, "But mind you, Abner, if I get well you can fergit all that I just said! I'm right about that fence!"

Mickey had a similar experience. He'd picked a fight with Chris on the playground. They'd been bickering over something for the past two weeks. A teacher marched the two boys into the principal's office.

"You're not leaving this office until you apologize to Chris and ask his forgiveness," the principal declared. "You've got to forgive each other, and you'll sit here until you can do it."

Stubborn Mickey sat there until nearly time for the afternoon recess. Afraid he'd miss the ball game, he decided it was time to put on a show of forgiveness. In front of the principal he told Chris, "I'm sorry for picking a fight. Please forgive me." He looked very sincere.

"Sure," Chris agreed. He didn't want to miss the ball game either!

Once out of earshot of the principal Mickey said, "I'll get you on the bus after school!"

FORGIVE US THE SINS WE HAVE DONE, BECAUSE WE FORGIVE EVERY PERSON WHO HAS DONE WRONG TO US. LUKE 11:4, ICB.

KEEPING FRIENDS

Forgiveness is false if it isn't meant from the heart. Forgiveness that's forced by fear of punishment isn't forgiveness at all.

Taught by a Lame Man

"THEN NEITHER DO I CONDEMN YOU," JESUS DECLARED. "GO NOW AND LEAVE YOUR LIFE OF SIN."
JOHN 8:11, NIV.

KEEPING FRIENDS

Forgiveness is choosing not to hold a sin against someone. It's treating him or her as though the hurt had never happened.

The practical application of Jesus' words is illustrated in the following encounter between a train conductor and a lame man.

A man with a cane in one hand and a suitcase in another slowly approached the door of a train car. It was time for the train to leave, but the old man seemed in no hurry to get aboard.

The conductor, a young man in a smart uniform, watched him with contempt. At last he called, "Hey, Limpy! Better get on board, or the train will leave without you!"

Later when the conductor asked for his ticket, the old man replied, "I don't pay."

"Who do you think you are? Of course you'll pay," the conductor said as he held out his hand.

"No, sir."

"Then you're off at the next station!" the conductor spoke roughly. "No free rides on this train!"

Scowling, the conductor continued down the aisle taking tickets. One of the passengers asked, "Do you know who that lame man is?"

"No, and I don't care."

"Well, I *would* care if I were you," the passenger replied. "That's Peter Warburton, the president of the road."

The conductor turned pale. "Are you sure?"

"I know him personally. That's Peter Warburton."

After finishing his task of taking tickets, the red-faced conductor approached the old man again. He handed over his account books and the tickets. "I resign, sir," he said.

"Sit down, son," Mr. Warburton ordered gently.

The president continued, "There's no need for you to resign. I have no desire for revenge. You were rude. I could fire you, but I won't. In the future be polite to everyone who rides this train. Here are your books and the tickets. Just remember that everyone, no matter their appearance, is worthy of your respect."

"Yes, sir! Thank you, sir!" the astonished conductor responded.

Forgiveness Is Not . . .

 f we understand what forgiveness is *not*, we should be better able to understand what forgiveness *is*. This month's stories have taught us the following principles about forgiveness. One example is given for each principle. See if you can remember others.

1. *Forgiveness is* not *easy*. In fact, it's one of the most difficult friendship skills to learn. "It's hard to forgive," Dan Ripley said ("The Bargain," May 2).

2. *Forgiveness is* not *feeling good about the bad thing someone has done to you*. According to Lewis B. Smedes, there are four stages: hurt, hate, healing, and coming together. To acknowledge your hurt is to take the first step toward forgiveness ("Nettie's Essay," May 9).

3. *Forgiveness is* not *denying your feelings of anger and hate*. Rather it's facing those feelings, then choosing not to act on them ("Making Up," May 10).

4. *Forgiveness is* not *making excuses for someone*. We can excuse people when we understand they aren't to blame. But forgiveness is necessary even when we can rightfully blame someone for what happened. Forgiveness is holding a person accountable, but then clearing the record by a conscious choice ("The Grudge," May 13).

5. *Forgiveness is* not *forgetting*. We forget little hurts that are too trivial to even remember. It's because you haven't forgotten a hurt that you need to forgive. Remembered hurts are like stored-up pain. Forgiveness is the way we get rid of the pain ("How to Forgive," May 14).

6. *Forgiveness is* not *a feeling*. Forgiveness is a choice we make to treat a person as a friend even though we don't feel like doing it. It's a choice we make not to hold a hurt to another person's account. It's erasing the record of their sin ("Helping an Enemy," May 20).

7. *Forgiveness is* not *something you can manufacture*. Forgiveness is a gift from God. It's the "outrageously impossible act." It's something we cannot do without God's power ("Forgiveness Is a Gift," May 22).

MAY 30

DO NOT JUDGE, AND YOU WILL NOT BE JUDGED. DO NOT CONDEMN, AND YOU WILL NOT BE CONDEMNED. FORGIVE, AND YOU WILL BE FORGIVEN. LUKE 6:37, NIV.

KEEPING FRIENDS

Forgiveness is a choice we make to treat people with mercy as God has treated us with mercy. It's choosing to release our judgment of another person.

157

Forgiveness Checkup

Rate yourself on the following areas; then ask God to help you to be a more forgiving person.

1. I'm able to forgive my parents for hurts they have caused.

Never   Sometimes   Usually   Always

2. I'm able to forgive my brothers and sisters for the bad things they've done to me.

Never   Sometimes   Usually   Always

3. I'm able to forgive my friends for hurts they cause me.

Never   Sometimes   Usually   Always

4. I'm able to forgive adults (teachers, pastors, church members, neighbors) for things they've done.

Never   Sometimes   Usually   Always

5 I'm able to forgive myself for mistakes I have made, sins I've committed.

Never   Sometimes   Usually   Always

6. I put the "act-as-if" principle to work in my relationships, choosing to act as if someone is my friend, even though he or she has hurt me.

Never   Sometimes   Usually   Always

7. I make a conscious choice to forgive people in spite of what they've done.

Never   Sometimes   Usually   Always

8. I try to return good for evil in my relationships.

Never   Sometimes   Usually   Always

9. I refuse to store up my hurts, hold grudges, because I realize that an unforgiving attitude hurts me, not the other person.

Never   Sometimes   Usually   Always

10. I experience an intimate relationship with God because I have no unforgiving spirit that blocks communication.

Never   Sometimes   Usually   Always

11. I give people who have wronged me a second chance.

Never   Sometimes   Usually   Always

12. I bless my enemies, praying for their happiness.

Never   Sometimes   Usually   Always

13. I try to follow the example of Jesus in all my relationships.

Never   Sometimes   Usually   Always

Live at Peace

During World War II, shortly after the Allied invasion of Italy, Italian families were required to house the invading soldiers. So it happened that an American soldier was assigned to the home of an Italian farmer.

The farmer was poorer than anyone the American had ever known. The house was a far cry from his own comfortable one back in the United States. It had no carpet on the rough floor. The only furnishings were a rustic table and benches. There was no bright tablecloth or ruffled curtains.

Neither was there a radio, CD player, or TV for entertainment! He spent evenings with family and friends just talking, sharing stories of the present and the past.

One evening the American sat with his hosts in the yard under the grapevines. They were watching a crescent moon rise over Mount Vesuvius. A tall column of smoke arose from the volcano, and a stream of molten red lava flowed down its dark sides.

How majestic! How beautiful! the soldier mused. The others must have been thinking similar thoughts, for all were quiet. At last the soldier spoke: "It's so peaceful here tonight! You'd never know a war was going on."

"It's a senseless war," someone else commented. "Too much hate, too much killing."

"War turns decent people into monsters," another said. "Brother is fighting against brother. It's such a waste!"

Again the group fell silent, thinking their own thoughts, enjoying the tranquillity of the moment. Suddenly the silence of the night was broken by the roar of 50 American planes streaking across the sky on their way to a mission of destruction.

After the sound had died away, the old Italian father spoke softly, "We've learned to swim like the fish under the sea, we've learned to fly like the birds in the air, but we haven't yet learned to walk the earth in peace with our fellow men."

LIVE AT PEACE WITH EVERYONE. ROMANS 12:18, NIV.

KEEPING FRIENDS

This month we'll learn how to live at peace with one another. If we want to keep our friends, we must learn how to handle conflict.

159

Three Choices

I WILL GO IN TO SEE THE KING; AND IF I PERISH, I PERISH. ESTHER 4:16, TLB.

We can select three different ways to handle conflict: fight, flight, or focus. We can fight about a problem, run away from it, or we can focus on solving it. The story of Queen Esther beautifully illustrates these three ways to handle conflict.

Fight. Haman decided to fight Mordecai. He chose aggression to meet the difficult person in his life. He built a gallows on which to hang the man he hated. And as so often happens in a fight, he was harmed more than the one he sought to harm.

Flight. Haman's relationship with King Ahasuerus is an example of flight. When the king sent him to lead Mordecai through the streets, Haman meekly submitted to the king's wish, all the time hating what he had to do. He avoided conflict. By submitting, he was running away from the problem.

Focus. Esther was willing to face the problem. She focused on finding a solution. She confronted the king. She asserted herself. She said, "King Ahasuerus, when you make a law to kill all the Jews, I feel threatened, because I also am a Jew. The Jews are my people."

By using the right technique, Esther solved the problem. Notice the three parts to the message she gave the king.

1. "When you make a law to kill all the Jews." She stated the specific behavior that was causing her a problem. She did it without blaming anyone or putting anyone down. She simply stated the fact.

2. "I feel threatened." She expressed exactly how she felt as a result of that behavior.

3. "I also am a Jew." She told the specific effect that the king's decree would have upon her. Because she was a Jew, she also would die with her people.

Taking the focus approach to conflict requires that you do three things: (1) give a nonjudgmental description of the problem that's bothering you; (2) tell how that behavior makes you feel; and (3) show the concrete and tangible effect that the behavior has upon you.

KEEPING FRIENDS

Not fight, not flight, but focus is the best way to handle conflict.

Archie's Problem

JUNE 3

Archie Shipowick had a problem, and like Jacob, he was afraid to face it. He chose flight, pretending to submit while he tried to figure out some way to handle the conflict without facing his father. The conflict came to a head the evening Samuel sent his son to the tavern to buy a bottle of vodka.

Archie accepted the money from his father and went out the door. Instead of going directly to the liquor store, he headed in the opposite direction while he tried to figure out what to do.

I wish Papa wouldn't drink so much, Archie thought. *We need the money for other things. The house needs a new roof. We all need clothing. I'm the oldest boy in the family, and I should do something about this problem.*

Archie decided to avoid buying the vodka. He took the long way around to the tavern. By the time he got there, it was closed. He went home without the liquor and with the money safely in his pocket.

By avoiding a confrontation, he made the conflict worse. As soon as he stepped inside the door he knew he was in for trouble. His father stood beside the table, hands on hips, jaw thrust forward, and chest heaving. "Archie, where in the name of all the saints have you been?"

"I went to the tavern, Papa, but it was closed," Archie looked straight into his father's flashing blue eyes.

"You could have been there and back three times," Mr. Shipowick stormed. "I'll teach you not to pull tricks on me!"

Archie's father took a leather strap from a hook on the wall and beat him unmercifully. When his dad's anger was spent, Archie left home to stay with his grandmother. For two years the conflict between Archie and his father remained unresolved. For the second time Archie chose flight rather than deal with the conflict. It wasn't until he chose to return home and face his father that the relationship was restored.

"WHY DID YOU RUN OFF SECRETLY AND DECEIVE ME?" . . . JACOB ANSWERED LABAN, "I WAS AFRAID." GENESIS 31:27-31, NIV.

KEEPING FRIENDS

Fear causes us to want to avoid facing a friend or family member over a disagreement, but running away from a problem doesn't solve the problem.

Turpentine Reminder

EVERYTHING THAT IS HIDDEN WILL BECOME CLEAR. EVERY SECRET THING WILL BE MADE KNOWN. LUKE 8:17, ICB.

KEEPING FRIENDS

Facing a problem is the best way to get a solution. Avoiding conflict only postpones the solution.

Guglielmo Marconi, inventor of the wireless telegraph, was always getting himself into some kind of trouble when he was a child growing up in Italy.

On one occasion his cousin Daisy was painting a picture. She'd just laid her palette of colors on a chair while she stepped back to admire what she'd painted. Just then Guglielmo bounced into the room and sat down on the chair.

He shot back off that chair with a shriek. His white flannel pants were patterned with the colors of the rainbow. "Now look what you've done!" the boy whined. "My nice white pants are all spoiled. Mother will be angry with me! Why don't you watch where you put things?"

"Well, why don't you look before you sit?" Daisy responded, giggling at her small cousin's predicament.

"Don't just stand there laughing at me!" Guglielmo wailed. "Do something!"

"What can I do?" Daisy looked around the room for a solution. "I know! The turpentine!" Frantically she rubbed away at the trousers with a rag dipped in turpentine.

"Not so hard!" complained Guglielmo, reaching for his backside. "You'll rub a hole right in the pants!"

"Stand still, will you?" Daisy demanded. However, when the lunch bell rang, she was still rubbing. She dropped the rag, and both ran to wash their hands, because being late for meals wasn't allowed in the Marconi household.

Guglielmo managed to enter the dining room and take his seat without anyone seeing the design on the bottom of his trousers. The smell of turpentine was still strong, but no one seemed to notice.

Just after the blessing, the boy began to squirm. The turpentine had soaked through to his skin, and it burned painfully. He wriggled from side to side, trying to avoid facing his mother with the problem.

"Guglielmo, sit still!" his father ordered. All eyes were on him now. Daisy giggled. Embarrassed, Guglielmo whispered an explanation to his mother. She excused him from the table to change his pants.

The Silent Treatment

"What's wrong, Penny?" Mrs. Greene asked her fifth-grade student. "You seem worried."

"It's Judy," Penny said. "She won't speak to me. We've been best friends since first grade, and now she avoids me. I phone, and she hangs up. I speak to her, and she walks away. I've written her notes, but she won't answer them."

"I can tell it's really bothering you," Mrs. Greene sympathized. "You aren't able to concentrate on your lessons. You seem very tired, too."

Penny nodded. "I guess that's because I can't get to sleep at night. I lie there thinking about what I've done to deserve this silent treatment from Judy. I've always tried to please her, to do whatever she wants to do."

"Maybe if I talk to Judy, it will help. Do you mind if I try?"

Penny shook her head.

That afternoon Mrs. Greene talked with Judy. The girl was ready to talk. "Penny acts too smart all the time," Judy said. "She thinks she's better than I am. She's always telling me what to do."

"Can you give me an example?" Mrs. Greene asked.

"Sure. The last time she was over at my house she said, 'Don't wear that dumb sweater anymore, Judy. It doesn't look good on you.' Well, my folks don't have lots of money like hers do. I can't just ask my mom for a new sweater because Penny doesn't like it."

"Why don't you talk to Penny and tell her what you've told me?" her teacher asked. "Avoiding the issue is causing a break in your friendship."

"I don't care!" Judy said. "I don't want to talk to her about it. I don't need her friendship."

If Judy had been willing to face Penny, their relationship could have been restored. Then Penny would have understood that what she'd been doing bothered Judy. By talking the issue out, Judy might have discovered that Penny didn't feel superior at all.

That friendship never was restored because Judy chose flight from the conflict rather than focus on the problem.

BUT WHEN I WAS SILENT . . . , MY ANGUISH INCREASED. PSALM 39:2, NIV.

KEEPING FRIENDS

There's no behavior more destructive to a relationship than the silent treatment.

Uprooting Bitterness

WATCH OUT THAT NO BITTERNESS TAKES ROOT AMONG YOU. HEBREWS 12:15, TLB.

KEEPING FRIENDS

Denying problems exist or fighting over the problem causes bitterness to grow. Facing each other and honestly discussing the problem is a good way to uproot it.

Ted Engstrom met Bob Pierce at a Youth for Christ conference. They became instant friends. They visited each other's homes, talking, laughing, praying, and working together on several projects.

After more than 15 years of friendship, Bob, the president of World Vision, asked Ted to become the vice president. Ted agreed, but that's when their troubles began.

One of Ted's jobs was to do something about the money problems that World Vision was having. They had almost a half million dollars in debts, and it was Ted's job to get rid of the debt.

"The radio program has to go," Ted decided. "Every month it's causing us to go another $30,000 in debt. We can't keep it up!"

The board of directors agreed, but Bob was angry. "I didn't bring you into World Vision to take me off the air!" he told Ted. "Fine friend you are!"

For the next five years Bob and Ted were at loggerheads over many issues. It was no longer fun to be together. Bob became so bitter about Ted's part in the loss of the radio program, that he resigned from World Vision.

Another five years went by while the root of bitterness grew in Bob's heart. He knew it was destroying not only his friendship with Ted, but his friendship with God. He cabled Ted, who was in Africa at the time, "We need to talk."

As soon as Ted got home he made an appointment to meet Bob at the Derby Restaurant one day at noon. The two men talked until 5:00 p.m. For the first time they weren't running away from the problem; they weren't fighting about it; they were facing it squarely, focusing on a solution.

They each shared their hurts and disappointments. They each listened to how the other person saw things, how he felt. They asked God to help them resolve their differences and help them to be friends once more. God answered that prayer.

Matt and the Cat

att, our golden retriever, was in constant conflict with Sammy, the Siamese cat next door. If Matt was inside when Sammy came onto our property, he begged to go outside and defend his home. Barking furiously, Matt would launch his attack.

When this happened, Sammy took off in panic, climbing the first tree in sight. From a safe limb she raised her fur and spat out her argument in cat language. Matt stood on hind feet, fighting right back in dog language.

While I watched one afternoon, there was a most unusual turn of events. Matt had chased Sammy through the front yard. For some reason Sammy decided not to run anymore. At the base of a fir tree she turn around to face the charging dog.

Caught off guard, Matt slid to a halt just inches away from the cat, which was now hunching her back and spitting at him. He took a step backward and lay down, head between his paws, to study this amazing creature who faced him. For several minutes Sammy stared Matt down, spitting and growling. Matt was silent.

Matt must have understood he was to leave Sammy alone. She turned around and walked quietly through the woods to her home while he lay there watching her go. I thought, *What a perfect example of the power of facing your antagonist!*

By confronting Matt, Sammy took control. I believe this is what Jesus is trying to teach in the Sermon on the Mount. I believe Jesus is saying, "Don't fight when you come into a conflict with difficult people. Neither should you meekly submit to injustice. Stand and face the person. Confront him or her with your need to control your own life."

That's exactly what you're doing when you say, "OK, if you want me to go one mile, I'll make the decision here. I'll go two miles. Do you want my coat? I can do better than that. I'll give you my cloak as well. I'm in charge of this encounter!"

IF SOMEONE FORCES YOU TO GO ONE MILE, GO WITH HIM TWO MILES. MATTHEW 5:41, NIV.

KEEPING FRIENDS

The Christian way of dealing with conflict isn't fight. It isn't flight. It's confrontation and focus.

Hiding From God

Tommy was different. When everyone else wore their hair clipped short, he wore his shoulder length, sometimes tying it in a ponytail. His nails were dirty; his shirts rumpled.

Tommy made it plain that he didn't believe in God. Although he was attending a Christian college, he made fun of those who expressed faith. He sat in the back row of John Powell's Bible class and smirked.

On the last day of class Tommy swaggered to the teacher's desk with his exam. He asked, "Well, Prof, do you think I'll ever find God?"

"No!" Mr. Powell responded.

"Oh, I thought that's the product you're pushing!"

Just as Tommy reached the door, Mr. Powell called after him, "No, I don't think you'll ever find God, but I'm absolutely certain that He'll find you!"

Tommy shrugged slightly and walked on.

Several years later Tommy visited his former Bible teacher. He was terribly thin, his head bald from chemotherapy.

"Good to see you, Tommy," Mr. Powell said. "I heard you were sick."

"I'm very sick," the young man admitted. "I've got cancer in both lungs. The doctors say I've only a few weeks left."

"I'm sorry, Tommy."

"Could be worse," the 24-year-old youth said. "Remember when I asked you if I'd ever find God? Well, I thought about your answer a lot. After they discovered my cancer I tried to find Him. I beat against the doors of heaven with my prayers, but He didn't come out, so I gave up.

"I decided to go visit my folks. I told Dad how much I loved him. He did two things he'd never done before. He hugged me, and he cried. We talked all night.

"Then one day I turned around and God was there. He had found me. You were right. He found me even after I stopped looking for Him. Now I'm ready to go."

John Powell said nothing. He couldn't. The lump in his throat was too big. He just let the tears flow.

CAN ANYONE HIDE FROM ME? AM I NOT EVERYWHERE IN ALL OF HEAVEN AND EARTH? JEREMIAH 23:24, TLB.

KEEPING FRIENDS

You can't run away from God's presence. He will find you. He wants to be your friend.

Stop Quarreling

It had been raining hard all day. By lunchtime Kevin and Dirk Hanson were quarrelling.

"It's your turn to wash," Kevin said, grabbing a towel.

Dirk took the other end and pulled. "It is not! I washed last time."

"Did not!"

"Did too!"

"Stop your arguing!" Mother said. "Kevin washes. Dirk dries."

The boys worked in sullen silence. The next argument was over the trucks. "The big truck is mine!" Dirk said. "You play with the little truck."

"You played with the big truck all morning. Now, it's my turn," Kevin whined. "Mom, make Dirk share his truck!"

"Dirk, share your truck," Mother ordered.

Scowling, Dirk pushed the big truck toward his little brother. "Take it and play over in the corner. I've got this spot by the fireplace."

"But I want to play by the fireplace."

Finally, Mother could stand their quarreling no longer. "If you boys don't stop your bickering, both of you are going to your bedrooms to spend the rest of the afternoon."

There was silence as the boys thought about the possibility of playing alone for the rest of the rainy day.

"OK," Dirk said, "you can play here by the fireplace if you want to. I'll go play in the corner."

"No, you were at the fireplace first," Kevin insisted. "It's only fair that I go to the corner."

"No, come on. I had the fireplace spot all morning," Dirk argued. "You should have it now."

Suddenly both boys burst out laughing. "First we quarreled about both wanting to play by the fire," Kevin said. "Now we're quarreling because we want the other person to have that spot."

"I guess our problem wasn't about the spot before the fireplace," Dirk commented. "I think we just felt quarrelsome."

"I think you're right," Mother chuckled. "Quarrelsome hearts will fuss over anything."

REMIND THEM . . . TO AVOID QUARRELING. TITUS 3:2, NRSV.

KEEPING FRIENDS

People with quarrelsome hearts will pick an argument over anything. They'll soon be short of friends.

Charles's Funeral

DO YOU KNOW WHERE YOUR FIGHTS AND ARGUMENTS COME FROM? THEY COME FROM THE SELFISH DESIRES THAT MAKE WAR INSIDE YOU. JAMES 4:1, ICB.

KEEPING FRIENDS

We can choose not to allow the selfish desires of our hearts to cause us to fight.

Eight-year-old Lauritz of Copenhagen, Denmark, didn't get along with his cousin Charles. The two fought daily. Invariably Lauritz got beaten soundly.

Wait until next year! Lauritz told himself. *I'll be older and stronger. Then I'll beat him up.* But of course, by the next year Charles was also bigger, and Lauritz still got his daily beatings.

Then Charles got very sick. Each day he got weaker. *Hallelujah!* Lauritz thought. *I hope he stays sick long enough for me to catch up to him.*

Just about the time Lauritz figured he could finally beat his cousin in a fight, Charles died. Lauritz felt cheated out of the chance to beat up his cousin.

At the funeral Lauritz heard the priest say that Charles was in heaven. *The priest doesn't know what he's talking about,* Lauritz thought. *He was a rascal and a scoundrel. He can't have gone to heaven!* While Lauritz was trying to imagine his cousin in heaven, the priest announced that Charles was at that moment with them in the church. Lauritz tried to see where Charles was sitting, but couldn't see him.

Oh, well, wherever he is, Charles is probably sitting there making faces at me, the 9-year-old reasoned. *The priest said he could see us, so I'd better make some faces back at him!* Lauritz proceeded to make faces all around, sure to catch his cousin somewhere. He'd covered only half the audience with his faces, when his mother gave him a pinch hard enough to put an end to his face-making.

She should have let me finish my round! Lauritz thought. *This is my last chance to get even with cousin Charles!*

Lauritz grew up to become a Seventh-day Adventist minister and was known as Elder M. L. Andreasen. He taught in the Theological Seminary, wrote 15 books, and made a host of friends. Fortunately, by the time he grew up he'd learned that fighting isn't the way to win friends and influence people.

Battle in the Office

ouise Majors had just been hired as an accounting clerk at the California Institute of Technology. Everyone welcomed her except Hildur.

"We don't need an accounting clerk!" Hildur said as she slammed her ledger shut. "I don't know why they hired you!"

Hildur had made up her mind to be Louise's enemy. At noon when the other women invited Hildur to go to lunch with them, she asked, "Is Louise going? If so, I'm not!"

Weeks passed, and the tension between the women got worse. Hildur refused to speak to Louise. Louise tried to be friendly. She kept greeting her each day, but there was no response. Hildur ignored every move of friendship. It came out later that Hildur was jealous of Louise and was afraid she'd been hired to replace her in the accounting department.

"Lord, how long must I keep on trying to turn her into my friend?" Louise prayed one morning. The words of a Bible verse came to mind, "Unto seventy times seven."

"Well, God, I'm nowhere near that number!" Louise smiled. "I'll keep trying!"

Two months later, on a stormy March day, Louise was driving home after work in her old green Pontiac. She noticed Hildur huddled under an umbrella at the bus stop. She pulled up to the curb, opened the door on the passenger side, and said, "Come on, Hildur. Get in, quick!"

Hildur got in. She was soaked through already. Louise turned up the heater and said, "Tell me how to get to your place."

They didn't talk all the way there, except for Hildur telling Louise when to turn. "Thank you very much," Hildur said when she got out. Her voice sounded softer than usual.

The next morning was a beautiful, sunny day. Louise greeted Hildur as she walked into the office: "Good morning, Hildur!"

"Good morning, Louise!" Hildur answered cheerily. It was as though someone had let the sunshine and singing birds into the office. The battle was over.

LORD, HOW OFT SHALL MY BROTHER SIN AGAINST ME, AND I FORGIVE HIM? . . . JESUS SAITH UNTO HIM, . . . UNTIL SEVENTY TIMES SEVEN. MATTHEW 18:21, 22.

KEEPING FRIENDS

No matter how long it takes for focusing on friendship to work, it's still better than fighting with the person or ignoring the problem.

Treaty of Friendship

IF YOU LOVE THOSE WHO LOVE YOU, WHAT REWARD WILL YOU GET? MATTHEW 5:46, NIV.

KEEPING FRIENDS

Fight and flight are unnecessary in the presence of love. Love can face people with differences and find a way to be friends.

Many White settlers avoided the Indians out of fear. Others came with guns and cannon-balls, but for years they were no match for the brave warriors of the forest. William Penn and the Quaker settlers chose a different way. They approached the Native Americans as equals, seeking their friendship and understanding.

A handsome Indian chief and his warriors sat under a large elm tree on the banks of the Delaware River that fall day in 1682. With them sat William Penn, leader of a group of White settlers. After the peace pipe had been passed around, the chief invited William Penn to speak.

"My people and your people look different, but we're all children of the Great Spirit who wants us to dwell together in peace," Penn began. "We have come to meet you without guns or swords, with only good will and love in our hearts. I've come to offer you a 'Treaty of Friendship.'"

This agreement proposed that the Indians and the settlers should live together as friends. All paths of the forest should be open and free to all. The White people's doors would be open to the Indians, and their lodges would be open to the Whites. It proposed that they wouldn't believe false reports about the other, but that they should make careful inquiry to see if those accusations were true. No one was to take revenge for a wrong done. Rather they'd promise to bring their complaint to a counsel of 12 honest men, who would declare justice. All wrongs were then to be buried in a pit that had no bottom.

The chief stepped forward and took William Penn's hand. Thus the "Treaty of Friendship" was ratified under the elm tree that day in the presence of witnesses from both groups of people. For many years after that the Quaker settlers and the Indians lived together in peace.

Is a treaty of friendship needed in your school? Your church? Your community?

Surprised Hoodlums

Mary Slessor walked down the narrow street of a slum in Dundee, Scotland. The teenager was slight of build and had strawberry blond hair cut short. Happiness sparkled in her blue eyes as she thought about the stories she'd be telling the children that day at Sunday school.

Farther along the street a group of dirty, ragged boys hid in the shadows of a building. "Here she comes!" a lookout warned.

"Wait until she passes, then we strike!" the leader commanded.

"Hello, lads!" Mary greeted them as she passed. "Coming to Sunday school today?"

"No!" the boys shouted as they formed a circle about her. "We don't want any of your goody-goody teachings! You'd better stop that Bible class!"

The leader began swinging a lead weight on a string in circles that came closer and closer to her head. She could feel the wind as it passed. "Leave us alone if you don't want to get hurt!" he threatened.

Mary stood absolutely still. Even when the lead came within a fraction of an inch of her forehead, she never flinched. *Be strong and courageous, Mary,* she told herself. *Don't be afraid for you are doing God's work, and He's with you. He'll strengthen you.*

The leader's hand dropped, and the lead clattered to the pavement. "She's game!" he nodded to his cohorts. "We can't frighten Mary Slessor!" The boys moved back and made a way for her to pass. Some of the toughs slunk away, but others followed her to the Bible class.

A few years later Mary went alone to be a missionary in Africa. There, too, she refused to take the easy way out by running away from trouble. She didn't waste her time fighting, either. She courageously faced tribes governed by witchcraft, where torture by poisoning and boiling oil were accepted practices. She won their respect, because she was brave enough to reason with chiefs face-to-face.

JUNE 13

BE STRONG AND COURAGEOUS. DO NOT BE TERRIFIED; . . . FOR THE LORD YOUR GOD WILL BE WITH YOU WHEREVER YOU GO. JOSHUA 1:9, NIV.

KEEPING FRIENDS

Fight and flight make conflict worse. Facing a problem brings conflict into focus. It allows the other person freedom to help resolve the conflict.

171

Facing Mildred

[LOVE] BELIEVES
ALL THINGS,
HOPES ALL
THINGS, ENDURES
ALL THINGS.
LOVE NEVER
FAILS.
1 CORINTHIANS
13:7, 8, NKJV.

KEEPING FRIENDS

Love doesn't run away from a problem. Love doesn't fight about a problem. Love finds a way to solve the problem and be friends.

Mildred was the most despicable girl Marion Bond had ever met. The girl had no friends, but lots of enemies. From the first day of school Marion became the target of Mildred's meanness.

Mildred would sneak up behind Marion, slap her, then run away. She walked behind her and stepped on her heels, causing her shoes to slip off. Mildred tormented her on the way home at night and on the way to school in the morning.

"I don't want to go to school anymore," first grader Marion cried one evening after another day of torture by Mildred.

"What's wrong?" Mother asked.

Marion didn't want to tell. When Mother insisted, she sobbed out the story of what Mildred had done. "You can't do anything about it, Mama!" she said. "If you tell my teacher, all the kids will call me a tattletale!"

A couple mornings later at breakfast Mother said, "I'm walking you to school this morning. We need to talk to Mildred."

"No, Mama! Please don't do that! It will make things worse," Marion begged.

"We'll see" was all Mama would say.

About halfway to school they met Mildred. "Hello, Mildred," Mother began. Mildred stopped. Mother knelt down and took Mildred's hands in hers. "Mildred, I need your help. Marion doesn't have any brothers or sisters. She needs a special friend to look after her, to walk home with her after school. I think you'd make a fine friend for Marion. Would you be Marion's friend?"

Mildred blinked as she stared at Mrs. Bond. Then she nodded her head and smiled a tiny smile.

"Oh, thank you!" Mother said, giving Mildred a warm hug.

Mildred kept her promise. Every morning and evening she walked with Marion. At school she became Marion's special bodyguard, going with her everywhere. Soon they were laughing, talking, and playing together. On Valentine's Day Mildred sent Marion a huge card that was signed "From your best friend."

Fighting God

Sophia Hawthorne, wife of the famous American author Nathaniel Hawthorne, was worried. Her daughter, Una, had a very high fever. She had tried everything she knew, but nothing helped. Una lost consciousness and became delirious.

"It's malaria," Dr. Franco said. "A very bad kind. Unless her fever goes down before morning, she'll die."

"It's hopeless," Una's father said after the doctor left. "We're going to lose our girl."

"No!" Mrs. Hawthorne wept. "She must not die!"

"Tell that to God!" her husband suggested.

That's exactly what Mrs. Hawthorne did that dark February evening in 1860. She sat beside Una's bed and struggled with God.

"Why, God, why?" she whispered. "Why our daughter? How can You do this to us? It isn't fair! It's cruel to take someone so young! She has such promise! Why are You doing this to us, God?"

God was silent. The pain Mrs. Hawthorne felt for her daughter was awful. She looked closely at Una, who lay there as still as death. She couldn't bear the sight, so she got up and went to the window to look outside. There was no moonlight. The sky was dark, silent, and heavy with clouds. *All is dark and heavy, just like my heart,* she thought. *I cannot bear this loss!*

Then suddenly a new thought came to her. *Why should I doubt the goodness of God? He knows best. I'll give Una to Him.*

Turning back to Una's bedside, she whispered, "Here she is, Lord. I give her to You. I won't fight against You anymore. Do as You see best."

She turned again to the window, feeling this time a sense of joy and happiness instead of darkness and dread. Going back to Una, she felt the girl's forehead. It was cool and moist. Her pulse was slow and regular. Rushing to the next room, Sophia exclaimed, "Nathaniel, God has given us a miracle! Come and see!"

LET US NOT FIGHT AGAINST GOD. ACTS 23:9.

KEEPING FRIENDS

Fighting isn't the answer when dealing with people or with God. Often God waits until we stop fighting Him before He supplies the solution to our problem.

173

Learn to Compromise

SETTLE MATTERS QUICKLY WITH YOUR ADVERSARY. MATTHEW 5:25, NIV.

KEEPING FRIENDS

Those who want to keep their friends need to learn how to compromise and cooperate instead of arguing.

There are three ways to settle an argument.

1. Do it your way. Your opponent loses everything; you win.

2. Do it his or her way. You give up everything; he or she wins.

3. Compromise. You give up a little; he or she gives up a little; and you both win!

Teenager Andrew Carnegie chose compromise. The argument was among Davy, Bob, and Andy, the three messenger boys of the Eastern Telegraph Line in Pittsburgh. The problem concerned the 10 cents that they were permitted to charge for messages delivered beyond a certain limit. These were called "dime messages."

Each of the three wanted his fair share of dime messages. It was understood that these bonus messages should be taken in turn. However, that didn't always work. It might be Bob's turn to take a dime message, but he and Andy were both gone on other messages. So Davy took the message.

"You had the last message!" Bob complained. "You should give that dime to me since it was my turn!"

"It's not my fault you weren't here to take it!" Davy argued. "I was here. I did it. I get the dime!"

"But that isn't fair at all!" Bob countered. "How are you going to feel when you lose a turn, and you couldn't help it?"

"That'll just be my luck, I guess," Davy shrugged.

"I've got a better idea," Andy suggested. "Why don't we pool the dimes from these special messages? We'll save up the dimes for one week and then divide them equally among the three of us."

"Great!" Davy and Bob agreed. "You be the treasurer."

The plan worked to the satisfaction of all three boys. The arguments about whose turn it was stopped. The boys were back to being friends again.

Andrew Carnegie's lesson in compromise and cooperation was one he never forgot. He later became a very wealthy man. He believed that he could attribute a good deal of his success to the fact that he'd learned how to get along with people.

Fighting Words

George and Allen, facing their mother, stood in the backyard. "What's the problem?" she asked.

"George wrecked my bike," Allen said.

"I couldn't help it. I ran over a tack. I'll fix the tire," George answered. "It will be as good as new."

"No, it won't!" Allen argued. "He has to get me a new one." Turning to George, he said, "I hate you! You old bike-wrecker!"

"Do you realize that you've just murdered your brother?" Mother asked.

"What? I haven't touched him. You told us not to fight, so I didn't. You told us not to run away, so I didn't. I faced him and told him exactly what I thought of him. He's an old bike-wrecker, and I hate him! That's all I did. I talked to him. I didn't murder him!"

"But you felt like it," Mother insisted. "The Bible says that if we want to do a bad thing, in God's sight it's the same as doing it. You didn't fight with your fists, but you fought with your words. Fighting words don't solve anything. I think Jesus feels very sad about what you said just now."

Allen was so shocked at what Mother had said that he didn't know what to do, so he ran off crying. That evening he didn't feel much like eating supper. He was still mad at his brother, plus he knew that the way he'd handled his conflict was wrong.

Later Father sat on his bed and talked to him, "Allen, what should you do when you've done something wrong?"

"Ask God to forgive me?"

"Yes, and that's not all. What else?"

"Tell George I'm sorry?"

"Sounds right to me," Father said. "Let's get started." He knelt down beside the bed. Allen got out and joined him. After asking God's forgiveness, he ran to his brother's room. "I'm sorry I got mad at you and said all those things."

"It's OK," George said.

All of a sudden Allen felt better.

ANYONE WHO IS ANGRY WITH HIS BROTHER WILL BE SUBJECT TO JUDGMENT.
MATTHEW 5:22, NIV.

KEEPING FRIENDS

Fighting with words is as bad as fighting with fists. It isn't the way Christians should handle conflict.

Monica's Secret

BE PATIENT AND STAND FIRM. JAMES 5:8, NIV.

KEEPING FRIENDS

Patience is needed when dealing with angry people. Let them spout off, then patiently give your focus message. Describe the behavior without judging the person. Describe your feelings. Tell how it affects you.

One thousand six hundred years ago there lived in a little village near Carthage, Africa, a Christian woman named Monica. She was married to Patricius, a pagan. Their son Augustine became a great Christian leader.

All was not well in Augustine's home. His dad was an irritable man, becoming angry very quickly. Augustine learned to hide when his dad was mad, but his mother endured his anger without argument or complaint.

"How can you get along with such a man?" a friend asked. "I'd have sent him packing long ago! What's your secret?"

"When he's angry, I hold my peace," she replied. "I've learned that an angry husband shouldn't be resisted, neither in deed, nor even in word. So I just keep quiet."

"But you shouldn't let him get away with such behavior!" her friend protested.

"Ah, but I don't!" Monica returned. "I wait until his anger is spent. When his rage is over and he's calm, I quietly tell him my feelings and opinions."

"And does he listen?" the friend asked.

"Yes," Monica answered. "He doesn't always agree, but at least I've expressed myself. He knows how I feel about things. It takes time, but he slowly comes around."

Monica's patience with her pagan husband paid off. He gave his heart to Jesus and became a different man. He became a Christian because of her patience.

No books on friendship and communication skills were available for Monica to study in the fourth century. She attended no seminars on how to deal with conflict, yet by following the principles of the Bible she did the correct thing.

Monica avoided fighting language. She didn't judge Patricius or call him names. She didn't blame him. Rather she simply described his behavior. Then she told how she felt about what he had done. She disclosed her feelings. She told how his actions affected her.

The Shopping Trip

t was Sunday, just before lunch, when the phone rang. Vickie answered. "Hi! This is Vickie!"

"Hi! This is Chantel! There's a half-price sale on at the mall today. Let's go!"

Oh, no! Vickie thought. *I promised Mom I'd do the laundry and vacuum the house, and I've got to study for the French test tomorrow. But I don't want Chantel to be mad at me. I wonder what's the best way to handle it.*

Here are three choices she has. Which should she do?

1. *Blame Chantel.* "Oh, Chantel, how come you always wait until I have a million things to do before asking me to go with you somewhere? You could have said something before this! Now I've promised to help Mom. You're so inconsiderate. Sometimes I wonder why I bother being your friend!"

2. *Don't make waves.* "Sure, Chantel. No problem. When do you want to go? I'll be ready."

3. *Express feelings. Explain problem.* "I'd love to, Chantel, but I don't see how I can. I promised Mom I'd do a couple loads of washing and vacuum the house. Then I have to study for my French test tomorrow. There just won't be time for me to go. I'm sorry."

Which is the response that has the best chance of resolving the conflict while still keeping the friendship?

Number 2? No, because it is the flight response. By saying nothing about the conflict, the frustration is increased. All afternoon Vickie will be worried about how she'll get everything else done. She may have to stay up until midnight, and then she'll be mad at herself and Chantel, feeling persecuted. Hard feelings will lead to a quarrel sooner or later.

Number 1? Who needs a friend who's always picking a fight and blaming you for all her frustrations? Wrong choice.

Number 3 is the best option, because it focuses on the problem. Vicki states her situation and her feelings without judging anyone. It opens the way for a solution.

If you were Chantel, how could you help solve the problem?

IT IS HARD TO STOP A QUARREL ONCE IT STARTS, SO DON'T LET IT BEGIN.
PROVERBS 17:14, TLB.

KEEPING FRIENDS

Fight and flight responses are good ways to start a quarrel that separates friends.

Conflict Commandments

KEEPING FRIENDS

We may not be able to prevent conflict from happening, but we can choose how we'll handle that conflict. The purpose of learning how to handle conflict is so that we might live at peace with everyone.

178

What has your week been like? Has everything gone right for you? Have you never once felt annoyed, irritated, frustrated, or angry? Has your life been completely devoid of conflict?

No? Then welcome to the human race! Parents can upset us, and teachers do annoy us. Friends may disturb us, and enemies persecute us. Inevitably we find ourselves in conflict with people.

Think of one conflict you've experienced during the past few days. Close your eyes for a moment and relive the scene. Was your approach fight, flight, or focus? Did you erupt into angry words that you later regretted? Or did you keep all the frustrations deep inside, hoping the conflict would disappear? Or did you face the problem squarely and deal with it?

Which of the following commandments for dealing with conflict did you keep? Which did you break?

Conflict Commandments

1. Thou shalt not fight with fists or with words.

2. Thou shalt not run away from the conflict or pretend that it doesn't exist.

3. Thou shalt not blame the conflict on someone else or judge his or her motives.

4. Thou shalt not use absolutes such as "always" and "never" in describing the person's behavior.

5. Thou shalt focus on the problem, not on the person.

6. Thou shalt briefly describe the specific behavior that's bothering you.

7. Thou shalt accurately describe how that behavior makes you feel. Don't say it makes you furious when you're only annoyed.

8. Thou shalt tell the specific effect that the behavior has upon your life. Don't confront someone just because your tastes are different.

9. Thou shalt refrain from telling the other person what he or she must do to help you solve the problem.

10. Thou shalt deal with only one conflict at a time. Don't confuse the issue by recalling all the mistakes the person has made in the past.

Mayling's Reason

When the Communists took over China, the Chinese leader they conquered was General Chiang Kai-shek, who took his government to Formosa, which is now Taiwan. His wife, Madame Chiang Kai-shek, a great spokesperson for peace, was once a little girl in China. Her name back then was Mayling.

Mayling's name meant "beautiful life," but as a child she didn't always act beautifully.

One day Mrs. Ainsworth came upon Mayling having a hot argument with a friend. "Mayling," she said, "aren't you ashamed to be carrying on like this?"

"No, Mrs. Ainsworth," Mayling said innocently.

"Why are you fighting?" the woman asked.

"I don't know," Mayling shrugged her shoulders.

Why do people fight with each other? Why do families have feuds and nations go to war? Below are a few reasons conflicts happen. Which ones are important? Which are foolish?

1. *Injustice.* Archie Shipowick (June 3) felt that his father was unfair in spending money for liquor when the family was in need.

2. *Accidents.* Guglielmo Marconi (June 4) found himself in a conflict with his parents, because he accidentally got paint on his white flannel trousers.

3. *Roadblocks.* Judy and Penny (June 5) were in conflict because of some judging roadblocks.

4. *Differences.* Ted and Bob (June 6) were in conflict over differences in how World Vision should be run.

5. *Jealousy.* Hildur thought Louise (June 11) was going to take her job away. This caused a power struggle in the office.

6. *Religion.* The hoodlums in Dundee, Scotland, (June 13) were fighting a mini-religious war.

7. *Personal problems.* Mildred (June 14) had no friends and didn't know how to make any.

8. *Money.* The three messengers (June 16) had a conflict over money.

9. *Property.* Allen's (June 17) problem was anger about his damaged bike.

10. *Time.* Vickie (June 19) didn't have time to do all the things she wanted to do.

DON'T HAVE ANYTHING TO DO WITH FOOL-ISH AND STUPID ARGUMENTS, BECAUSE YOU KNOW THEY PRODUCE QUAR-RELS. AND THE LORD'S SERVANT MUST NOT QUARREL. 2 TIMOTHY 2:23, 24, NIV.

KEEPING FRIENDS

Some matters aren't worth arguing about. Others are important and need to be dealt with.

179

Bathroom Prayer

**HE WHO IS
SLOW TO ANGER
IS BETTER THAN
THE MIGHTY,
AND HE WHO
RULES HIS SPIRIT
THAN HE WHO
TAKES A CITY.
PROVERBS
16:32, RSV.**

KEEPING FRIENDS

God can do for
us what we can't
do for ourselves.
He can help
us handle
our conflicts.

Fourteen-year-old Ben Carson sat on the edge of the bathtub and stared at the wall. His heart raced wildly as he realized how close he'd come to murdering a neighborhood boy.

The other fellow had been tormenting Ben. Flashing his camping knife, Ben had lunged fiercely at the boy's stomach. His aim was poor; he'd hit the boy's heavy belt buckle instead, breaking the steel blade of his knife.

I might have killed him, Ben thought. *I'm out of control. I've got to do something before I get into real trouble.*

Then words from Proverbs came to mind: "He who is slow to anger is better than the mighty, and he who rules his spirit than he who takes a city" (Prov. 16:32, RSV).

Yeah, those words are for me, Ben mused. *If I don't get control, I'll end up in jail . . . or dead. I guess it's time to ask the Lord for help, like Mother has been telling me to do.*

Ben dropped to his knees on the bathroom floor. "Oh, Lord," he prayed, "take away my temper. I know You can. I believe You will."

Writing about that experience later, Ben said: "The Lord took away my temper, just like that. Whenever I'd feel it begin to boil, it would somehow simmer down as if someone had turned off the burner. I was in awe at what had happened to me."

When Ben grew up he became a neurosurgeon at Johns Hopkins University and Hospital in Baltimore, Maryland. The same hand that had almost killed his antagonist when he was 14 was now used to save lives with his surgeon's scalpel.

His colleagues describe the Ben they know as someone who is unusually calm. Ben knows that it wasn't always that way. Before his bathroom conversion he says: "I would just fly off the handle at the slightest provocation. I would throw rocks and take hammers after people."

What a difference that prayer in the bathroom made!

Donna's Canary

What are you so sad about?" Mrs. Morton asked when her daughter Donna came home for lunch. "I've noticed you've not been yourself for several days."

"Nothing. It doesn't matter," Donna replied.

"Of course it matters," Mother prodded. "Now tell me what's wrong! Have you had problems at school?"

"It's Alice Barnes. We've always been friends, and now she's mad at me. She runs away from me at recess, and she never calls me anymore."

"Did you do something to upset her?"

"Not that I can remember."

"Well, why don't you ask her why she's mad at you?" Mother suggested. "I'm sure a little talk will straighten matters out."

"No!" Donna snapped. "It's her fault. She should come to me."

"Could it be that pride is keeping you apart?" Mother asked. "When all we can think about is ourselves and our own hurt feelings, then sometimes we imagine things that aren't so. If you want Alice's friendship, then you should forget your pride and go to her. It could be you've made some false assumptions."

Donna didn't answer, but in her heart she knew that Mother was right. After school she caught up to Alice. "Why are you mad at me?" she demanded.

"You're the one who's mad at me," Alice said coldly. "I'd like to know why you said all those mean and awful things about me."

Donna shook her head in disbelief. "I haven't said anything mean about you."

"Yes, you did. I heard you with my own two ears," Alice insisted. "I heard you tell Betty Porter that I was the most mischievous little thing you ever saw! So there!"

Donna burst out laughing. "Alice, yes, I said that, but I was not talking about you; I was talking about my canary. Don't you remember that I named it Alice after you?"

"So that's what you were talking about!" Alice joined in Donna's laughter. "How silly of me to get upset!"

THE PRIDE OF YOUR HEART HAS DECEIVED YOU. OBADIAH 3, NIV.

KEEPING FRIENDS

Pride leads to faulty thinking and wrong assumptions. Wrong assumptions lead to misunderstanding and conflict.

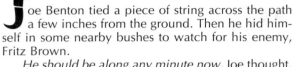

Getting Even

Do not try to punish others when they wrong you. Romans 12:19, ICB.

Keeping Friends

It takes two to fight. Getting even is a sure way to make enemies, not friends.

Joe Benton tied a piece of string across the path a few inches from the ground. Then he hid himself in some nearby bushes to watch for his enemy, Fritz Brown.

He should be along any minute now, Joe thought. *I can't wait to see him flat on his face with all the eggs in his basket scrambled in the dirt!*

Hearing footsteps, Joe peeked out to see Cousin Herb approaching. Joe released the string, hoping he wouldn't be noticed.

"What's going on?" Herb said, pushing aside the bushes.

"I'm waiting for Fritz Brown," Joe said. "He wrecked my toy sailboat. I plan to trip him as he comes by. That will teach him to leave my things alone!"

"That's an old trick," Herb said. "I know a better one."

"Tell me!"

"Put some hot coals on his head!"

Joe looked puzzled. "But how?"

"'If thine enemy be hungry, give him bread to eat; and if he be thirsty, give him water to drink: For thou shalt heap coals of fire upon his head,'" Herb quoted.

"That's no punishment!"

"Oh, but it works! Treat Fritz as a friend and see what happens. What do you have that Fritz might really enjoy? Share with him. You'll be amazed."

Cousin Herb left Joe to mull over what he might do. By the time Fritz came along Joe had a plan.

"Hi, Fritz," he said. "I was waiting for you. Come over to my place after you deliver the eggs. I have a neat book on travel that I think you'd enjoy. I'd be glad to loan it to you. I'd ask you to help sail my boat today, but someone ripped its sails."

Fritz hung his head. "I did it . . . and I'm really sorry." Without another word he rushed off down the road. Later Joe found that Fritz had repaired the damaged sailboat, making it almost as good as new. After they became friends, Joe was glad he'd listened to Herb.

Redhead

It was the first day of school, and Edward dreaded it. They'd just moved to town because of his father's job, and he had no friends. He walked slowly onto the playground before school started, hoping he'd escape notice.

Some boys in a group were talking near the basketball hoop. One of them said something and pointed at Edward. The others looked, began to laugh, and walked in his direction.

"Hey, Redhead!" one called out. "Where are you going?"

"Where do you think, stupid!" Edward shot back. "And don't call me a redhead."

"Try to stop us!" the tallest boy challenged.

"Redhead! Readhead!" the others joined in. "Redhead wants to fight!"

"If you don't stop, I'll hit you!" Edward said.

"Go ahead, Redhead!" the tallest boy laughed.

"OK, boys! Break it up!" ordered the teacher on duty. "It's time for the bell. Go line up."

Edward was miserable all morning. The boys kept showing him their fists, and the girls stared and giggled. He was the only boy in the school with red hair and freckles, and he wished he could fall through the floor and disappear.

I don't want to fight with anyone, Edward thought during math class. *I want to be a friend, but I don't like being called Redhead. They didn't give me a chance.*

Just then Edward remembered something his Sabbath school teacher had said. "It's easy to start a fight, but it's just as easy to keep from fighting. We can choose to be kind when people are rude. We can choose to use gentle words instead of fighting words."

I'll try it, Edward decided. At recess he got his chance.

"Redhead! Redhead!" one of the same boys began to tease again.

Edward smiled and said, "Just be glad it's not green or purple!"

The other boy laughed. "That *would* be weird! Want to play ball with us?"

"Sure!" Edward said.

A GENTLE ANSWER TURNS AWAY WRATH, BUT A HARSH WORD STIRS UP ANGER. PROVERBS 15:1, NIV.

KEEPING FRIENDS

If you can take teasing with humor, you'll find that others will soon warm up to you. You can choose to use friendly words instead of fighting words.

183

Putting Out Anger

KEEPING FRIENDS

Angry answers add fuel to the fire and prolong the fight. Gentle words are the best way to snuff out anger.

Anger is like a fire. It's hot. It burns. It destroys. But it can't burn unless it has fuel and air. We can put out the fire of another person's anger by choosing not to add fuel or air to keep it burning. Speaking kind, gentle words to someone who's angry is like throwing sand on a campfire.

Carole Mayhall had this experience while visiting at her mother's home. She answered the phone one night, but the angry man on the other end thought it was her mother. Carole soon figured out that it was the neighbor whose dog had jumped the fence and attacked her mother's tiny pomeranian.

After taking her pet to the veterinarian for surgery, her mother had called the neighbor to tell him what had happened. He denied it was his dog. Then his dog jumped the fence a second time, and her mother had called the police. The police had told him to make his fence higher.

The neighbor was now furious. He'd called several times already to berate her mother. His curses were so loud that Carole had to hold the phone away from her ear.

"It's a lie!" the man screamed into the phone. "My dog wouldn't hurt a flea! You're just trying to get me into trouble with the police!"

Carole listened as the man ranted and raved, cursed and swore a blue streak. The more he talked, the madder Carole got. However, she bit her tongue and decided she wouldn't add one bit of fuel to his fire. After a while he sputtered to a stop.

Then, softly she replied, "I'm so sorry you feel that way. It must have been a very disturbing experience for you. Is there anything else you wanted to tell me?"

The man on the other end said not another word. He just slammed down the phone and never called again. Carole's patient answer had put out his fire.

Don't Pop Your Top

Devon, Curt, Jeff, Mark, and Steve were five teenagers with nothing much to do on a Sunday afternoon. They climbed into Devon's beat-up Chevy and cruised around town looking for excitement. They stopped at a 7-Eleven store to pick up some pop and pretzels.

Curt sat in the front with Devon. Mark was scrunched in the middle of the back seat between Jeff and Steve as they drove around, all windows open. It was a great day, and they honked at pedestrians and waved. They laughed as Devon swerved around a corner, sending Jeff and Mark crashing against Steve.

Steve good naturedly pushed back, and the three began to tussle in fun. Without a thought Jeff turned his pop can upside down, pouring cold root beer into Steve's lap.

"Steve needs a restroom!" Mark yelled. He and Jeff were laughing hysterically, trying to prevent Steve from dumping the rest of his can on Jeff. Mark grabbed the can and hurled it out the window.

By now everyone was cracking up, and Steve joined in. He didn't feel very comfortable with his soggy pants. He wanted to get even, but he couldn't think of anything to do just then.

By the time they reached Steve's house they had all calmed down somewhat, but started laughing again as he sloshed up the steps to his house.

"You should see what you look like!" Curt yelled as the Chevy drove away.

I guess I do look pretty funny, Steve admitted to himself when they were gone. He chuckled at how he must look from the rear. *I guess I've done my share of stupid things. No use to pop my top over a dumb prank. My friends are more important to me than a wet pair of pants.*

Steve's decision to not get upset over a friendly joke even though he didn't like it, was a practical application of Proverbs 10:12.

JUNE 27

HATRED STIRS UP DISSENSION, BUT LOVE COVERS OVER ALL WRONGS. PROVERBS 10:12, NIV.

KEEPING FRIENDS

If you'd like to keep your friends, then you need to be slow to pop your top over trivial matters. Learn to overlook faults. Some things aren't worth confronting.

185

Polar Bear's Enemy

KEEPING FRIENDS

Whether someone will be your friend or your enemy is a choice only you have the power to make.

Polar Bear was a 12-year-old fluffy, all-white cat with green eyes. He belonged to Cleveland Amory in New York City. That cat ruled Mr. Amory's apartment and was quite pleased with his little kingdom.

Then came a day when Mr. Amory found a stray Old English sheepdog in Central Park. He made a leash for the dog out of his belt and walked around the park looking for the owner. When none was found, he decided to take the dog back to his apartment.

Wrong decision. The Old English sheepdog made a beeline for the kitchen, where he slurped up all Polar Bear's water and gulped down his dish of niblets. Polar Bear sprang after the intruder, ready to claw him to pieces, but he was caught midair by Mr. Amory.

The Old English sheepdog, satisfied that he wasn't in danger from the cat, went over to the fireplace in the living room. He made a couple of circles and settled down for a snooze by the fire.

Mr. Amory decided to take Polar Bear to the bedroom. Once inside, Mr. Amory lay down on the bed to rest, but Polar Bear was nervous. On the other side of that door was his enemy, and he wanted out. When Mr. Amory opened the door to check on the dog, Polar Bear made a dash for freedom. Once out he charged toward his enemy.

As the cat streaked across the carpet, the dog opened one eye and lifted a playful paw. The cat skidded to a stop. The dog gave a long sigh and closed his eye. The cat sighed, curled up with his back against the dog, and closed his eyes. He began to purr.

I can't believe what I'm seeing! Mr. Amory thought. *How wonderful that Polar Bear should decide to turn his doggy enemy into a friend! What a better world we'd have if all of us could do the same thing.*

Tim's Helper

On the way home from school Tim tripped over a root he hadn't seen and fell flat on his face.

"Good show, man!" Lesley said, starting to laugh. He threw back his head and laughed until the tears rolled down his cheeks.

A crowd gathered.

"What ya tryin' to do, kiss the sidewalk?" Lesley joked.

The crowd laughed.

"It ain't funny!" Tim said, pulling himself up and clinching his fists. He swung at Lesley and missed. Lesley punched back. The fight was on. Tim fought like a wildcat, so angry was he at what his friend had done.

Just then, a gray-haired woman was walking down the street past the school. She stopped when she saw that one of the boys on the ground was her grandson, Tim. "Timothy!" she spoke sternly, "stop it this minute!"

The two boys broke apart. Timothy stood facing his grandmother. His shirt was torn, his pants muddy.

"What's the meaning of this?" she asked.

"He laughed at me!" Tim shouted.

"I didn't mean nothin'," Lesley growled. "You didn't have to get so mad about it."

"You'd better go home, Tim," Grandmother said.

After Tim got cleaned up, they had a talk.

"I didn't know you had such a temper, Tim," Grandmother said.

"I can't help it, Grandma," Tim admitted. "When someone makes me mad, I have to fight. I just can't seem to control myself. I wish I had a big brother or somebody to stick up for me, somebody to keep me out of fights."

"But, you do have help," Grandma said. She reached for her Bible and read John 14:16: "'He will give you this Helper to be with you forever.' God has promised to send His Holy Spirit to be with you when you need help. He can help you control your temper. He can help you not fight."

"That's neat, Grandma," Tim said. "After this I'm going to ask Jesus to send me His Helper."

HE WILL GIVE YOU THIS HELPER TO BE WITH YOU FOREVER. JOHN 14:16, ICB.

KEEPING FRIENDS

God cares about your relationships. He can help you keep your temper as well as your friends.

Conflict Checkup

TURN AWAY FROM EVIL AND DO GOOD. TRY TO LIVE IN PEACE EVEN IF YOU MUST RUN AFTER IT TO CATCH AND HOLD IT! 1 PETER 3:11, TLB.

How well do you do at facing conflict and handling it peacefully?

1. When confronted with a problem, I try to face the problem and find a peaceful solution.

Never   Sometimes   Usually   Always

2. I try to discuss disagreements openly with people so that a root of bitterness does not grow.

Never   Sometimes   Usually   Always

3. When someone does evil to me, I try to return good to them, blessing them and praying for them.

Never   Sometimes   Usually   Always

4. I believe that love can always face differences and find a way to be friends.

Never   Sometimes   Usually   Always

5. I'm willing to compromise in a conflict situation so that both of us can be winners.

Never   Sometimes   Usually   Always

6. I have patience when I'm dealing with angry people. I listen quietly and use only gentle words in response.

Never   Sometimes   Usually   Always

7. I'm able to state a problem that bothers me without judging or putting down the other person.

Never   Sometimes   Usually   Always

8. I'm able to express my feelings clearly about a problem, not minimizing or exaggerating how I feel.

Never   Sometimes   Usually   Always

9. I refrain from telling others what they must do.

Never   Sometimes   Usually   Always

10. I don't confuse the issue by recalling mistakes a person has made in the past. I deal with only one conflict at a time.

Never   Sometimes   Usually   Always

11. I can take teasing in good humor.

Never   Sometimes   Usually   Always

12. I know that wrong assumptions lead to conflict, so I avoid jumping to conclusions.

Never   Sometimes   Usually   Always

13. In my relationship with God I may not always understand why things happen, but I choose not to run away or fight Him, but to face Him honestly as a friend.

Never   Sometimes   Usually   Always

BEING
FRIENDS

Charlie Brown's Job

GOD WILL USE YOU, TO BLESS ALL PEOPLE ON EARTH. GALATIANS 3:8, ICB.

BEING FRIENDS

Being a friend means focusing on the happiness of our friend, not our own needs. It's thinking of ways to make our friend feel good.

In a Peanuts cartoon Lucy asks Charlie Brown, "Why do you think we're put here on earth?"

"To make others happy," says Charlie Brown.

She replies, "I don't think I'm making anyone very happy, but of course nobody's making me very happy either."

She hauls off and hits the unsuspecting Charlie Brown, sending him spinning. She yells, "Somebody's not doing his job!"

Through this cartoon, Charles Schulz expresses the truth of Galatians 3:8. Although Paul here quotes God's words to Abraham, we all have a job to do on earth—to make other people happy. There are a lot of unhappy, miserable, discouraged people so somebody isn't doing his or her job!

Too often we have the self-focus of Lucy, "Why isn't somebody making *me* happy?" The secret of being a friend isn't in waiting to see what our friend will do to make us happy, but rather to look for ways to make our friend happy.

Sally understood this principle of being a friend. She proved her friendship to Laura the day of the contest in fourth grade. The girls had decided to vote on who was the nicest girl in the room. Twelve girls voted. Six voted for Sally; six voted for Laura. The girls decided they'd have to vote again.

Just before they voted, Sally whispered something to Jessica. Jessica nodded. The vote was taken. This time there were five votes for Sally and seven for Laura.

"I'm glad you won," Sally told Laura on the way home from school.

"But I won only because you asked Jessica to vote for me," Laura commented.

"That's OK, because I think you should have won. After all, I like you better than I like me!"

This month we're going to think about how to make other people happy. We'll learn that we can make others happy with compliments, words of appreciation, notes, phone calls, a touch, a smile, a prayer, a look, our presence, and our gifts.

Spreading Happiness

n New York City Art Buchwald was riding with a friend in a taxi. When they got out, the friend spoke to the taxi driver. "Thank you for the ride. You did an excellent job."

"Are you a wise guy or something?" the cabby asked.

"No," Art's friend replied, "I mean it. I admire the way you keep your cool in this New York traffic."

The driver mumbled something and drove away.

"What was that all about?" Art asked.

"I'm trying to bring love back to New York," his friend replied.

A little while later the two men walked past workers eating their lunch at a construction site. Art's friend stopped to comment, "That's a magnificent job you have done."

The workers continued eating quietly, but looked at him as though to say, "What do you want from us?"

"That's very impressive," Art's friend added before walking on. "You must all be very proud."

After they were out of earshot, Art's friend said, "Those workers will be a little happier for what I've said. And somehow the city will benefit from their happiness."

Ellen White counsels: "Never lose an opportunity to say a word to encourage and inspire hope" (*Testimonies,* vol. 5, p. 613).

"We should be self-forgetful, ever looking out for opportunities, even in little things, to show gratitude for the favors we have received of others, and watching for opportunities to cheer others and lighten and relieve their sorrows and burdens by acts of tender kindness and little deeds of love" (*Testimonies,* vol. 3, pp. 539, 540).

Think of the domino effect of a kind word. Suppose that two of those whom Art's friend affirmed were motivated to speak kind words to two other people the next day. If this process continued, by the seventh day more than 120 people would have received a kind word. By day 14, more than 16,000 lives would have been touched by love. After three weeks more than 2 million lives would have been blessed.

LET YOUR SPEECH AT ALL TIMES BE GRACIOUS (PLEASANT AND WINSOME).
COLOSSIANS 4:6, AMPLIFIED.

BEING FRIENDS

Being a friend means appreciating others, watching for opportunities to cheer them and lighten their burdens with little acts of tenderness and little deeds of love.

The Barnabas Committee

JULY 3

THEY SENT BARNABAS TO ANTIOCH. WHEN HE ARRIVED . . . HE . . . ENCOURAGED THEM ALL.
ACTS 11:22, 23, NIV.

BEING FRIENDS

You can join the Barnabas Committee. Is there someone you could encourage today through a secret act of kindness?

The bell rang for the first-period class to begin. The Bible teacher, a recent graduate from the seminary, stood nervously at the front of the college class.

"I want to ask your understanding and forgiveness for the poor job I've been doing on preparation for this class," the teacher began. "I had no idea teaching a college Bible class would be so difficult. I feel overwhelmed by my class load. I stay up late at night to prepare, but there's never enough time. I need your prayers."

Jeanne Doering watched his hands shake as he put on his glasses and began the lecture. She thought of the times she'd walked home from the library late at night and had seen him sitting in his office, head bent over his books.

The poor man is working too hard, Jeanne thought. *I think he needs more than just our prayers. He needs our encouragement. I wonder what we could do.* By the time Bible class was over, Jeanne had an idea of something she could do.

During the next few days Jeanne shared her idea with some of her friends, and they organized what they called the Barnabas Committee. It was named after Barnabas, the disciple sent to Antioch to encourage the new believers. His name actually means "son of encouragement."

The Barnabas Committee agreed to pray for their Bible teacher and their other professors as well. But more than this, they decided to think of ways to encourage them through secret acts of kindness.

Little notes of encouragement began showing up on teachers' desks. Sometimes they were silly rhymes, and sometimes they had a small gift attached, such as animal crackers, a candy bar, or an apple. The notes were always signed "The Barnabas Committee."

Jeanne noticed that the mood on campus turned positive. Teachers smiled more. The Bible teacher began to do a better job. There was a spirit of love and excitement brought on by the secret acts of the Barnabas Committee.

Edward's Shame

Edward walked slowly along the shady Boston street, his head down. In his hand he clutched his first report card, and it wasn't good.

What's Mother going to say? Edward worried. He opened the card again and looked at his grades. He noticed the place where it said "class rank." In a class of 15, he was ninth. *She'll surely scold me for not coming first!* Edward thought.

He put off the fateful moment as long as possible, but at last he reached home, and there was his mother waiting for him at the door. "Well, Edward, how did you do?" Mother asked brightly, reaching for the report card.

Edward sighed and handed over the disappointing report.

His mother studied the report card for a moment, noting his class rank. "Never mind, Edward," she said quietly. "You'll likely do better next time. Besides, there's something about this report that makes me very happy. I notice that while you stand ninth in your studies, you're first for good behavior. That means far more to me, son, than if you were at the head of your class but had a poor standing for conduct."

Edward lifted his eyes to his mother's smiling face. He straightened his shoulders. Her encouraging words made him determine to do better. "I'll come first, Mama!" he said with determination. "Just you wait and see!"

It wasn't long before Edward Everett Hale did stand first in his class both in studies and in conduct. He grew up to be a minister and an author of many books. His most famous story is called "The Man Without a Country."

He became chaplain of the United States Senate. He also led out in the Lend-A-Hand Society that looked for ways to encourage new immigrants. Its motto was one of encouragement: "Look up and not down, look forward and not back, look out and not in, lend a hand."

JULY 4

YOU ALONE CAN LIFT MY HEAD, NOW BOWED IN SHAME. PSALM 3:3, TLB.

BEING FRIENDS

By speaking encouraging words to friends you can motivate them to do better. Your words can give them courage to be all that they're capable of being.

The Druggist

THE WAY YOU GIVE TO OTHERS IS THE WAY GOD WILL GIVE TO YOU. MARK 4:24, ICB.

BEING FRIENDS

A compliment is a wonderful way to affirm a friend. There's a certain magic in a compliment that encourages people to be their best. No one can be a true friend without giving affirmation.

Frieda Davis had just moved to a small Midwestern town. She complained to her neighbor Esther Jones, "What this town needs is another drugstore. I've never had such poor service as I got yesterday. The pharmacist here is so slow and inefficient! I've a good mind to drive to the next town after this to get my prescription filled."

"Oh?" Esther said. "I hadn't noticed."

"Next time you go, watch how he works," Frieda suggested. "And I don't mind at all if you tell him what I said. He needs to smarten up if he wants my business."

Sometime later, Frieda had another prescription to fill and decided to give the local druggist one more chance.

"Good morning, Mrs. Davis!" the pharmacist greeted her with a big smile. "I hope you've settled in nicely and everything is going well for you. If there's anything I can do to help, just let me know!"

Surprised at his friendliness, she remarked, "Today I just need this prescription filled."

"No problem!" he said. "We'll have it for you in a jiffy. If you want to wait, I can have it in five minutes."

That afternoon she reported to Esther. "He was very friendly and efficient today. You must have told him what I said about his service last time."

"Well, not exactly," Esther replied with a sly smile. "I told him you were amazed at the way he'd built up this small-town drugstore. I told him you thought it was one of the best-run drugstores you'd ever seen."

"I can't believe you'd praise him after the service he gave me the first time," Frieda exclaimed.

"Well, it worked, didn't it?" Esther laughed. "I just know that compliments get a lot better results than criticism. 'Honey attracts better than vinegar,' as my mother used to say. I try to affirm people whenever I get the chance."

Saying Grace

Seventeen children gathered around the plain wooden table in a small house in Boston. "Let us pray," Josiah Franklin said.

Benjamin, the youngest son of the 17 children, wiggled on his chair as his father prayed. "Our Father which art in heaven, we have bowed here today to acknowledge Your goodness to the children of men. We know that every good gift and every perfect gift comes from You. You own the cattle on a thousand hills. It is You who enables us to plant and tend and reap a bountiful harvest of food," Father droned on and on as fathers often did in the eighteenth century.

Benjamin could smell the vegetable stew and bread, and his stomach grumbled. *Hurry up, Father, and finish saying grace,* the small boy thought. *The soup is getting cold.*

"We thank Thee, Lord, for Thy goodness to us, for supplying all our needs, for giving us freedom in this land to worship You, for giving us life and health and strength for this day. Make us truly thankful for Your bountiful goodness. Bless this food, and bless the hands that have prepared it. Amen."

"Amen," 17 children chorused, each one reaching for a spoon.

"Father, the grace was too long," little Benjamin said.

The other children's spoons stopped in midair. How dare little Benjamin speak up to their father! He wasn't a man to allow disrespect.

"Why, Benjamin?" Father asked.

"Because it's a waste of time to go on saying grace every day before every meal," the boy answered. "You always say the same thing, and our soup gets cold."

"What do you think we ought to do?" Josiah asked.

"Bless all the food in the whole house," Benjamin suggested. "Then it would be over and done with, and we wouldn't have to do it each time."

"Not a bad idea," Mr. Franklin laughed. "But I doubt God gets tired of hearing us thank Him for His blessings."

GIVE THANKS TO THE LORD, FOR HE IS GOOD. PSALM 118:1, NIV.

BEING FRIENDS

See if you can think of one blessing that begins with each letter of your name. Then take a moment to thank God for those blessings.

The Visitor

**GENTLE WORDS
CAUSE LIFE
AND HEALTH;
GRIPING BRINGS
DISCOURAGEMENT.
PROVERBS 15:4,
TLB.**

BEING
FRIENDS

Positive words of
affirmation will
do more than
anything else
to help a
friend succeed.

One day a man was walking along a road in Northern Ireland, when through an open window of a schoolhouse he heard the sound of children's voices. The man smiled as he heard them chant the multiplication tables. It made him think of his own school days. *I think I'll go in and have a look around,* the man thought.

Standing in the open doorway, he noticed that all was the same as when he was a child—the dusty blackboard, the rows of desks, and a boy standing in the dunce's corner.

The teacher approached the visitor. "May I help you, sir?"

"Hearing the lads recite their tables brings back memories of my own school days," the man said. "May I watch for a moment?"

"Make yourself at home," the teacher replied.

"What about the lad in the corner?" asked the visitor.

"That's Adam Clarke, the dumbest boy in the school," the teacher explained. "Either he cannot or he will not learn his times tables. I doubt he'll ever amount to anything."

The visitor noticed the boy's chin quiver at the teacher's cutting words. The man felt sorry for him and at his first chance, went over to speak to him. He laid a hand on the boy's shoulder and said, "It cannot be true that you're no good at your lessons. Keep on trying, and you'll succeed. I think you're a bright boy and will learn your lessons if you don't give up."

Adam Clarke smiled as the old man squeezed his shoulder. He stood a little straighter and tried again to memorize the nine times table. It wasn't easy, but he kept at it until he succeeded.

"When I was tempted to give up, I remembered the words of that old man," Adam said many years later when he was Dr. Adam Clarke, the author of a Bible commentary. "That was the kindest thing anyone had ever said to me, and it made me want to succeed."

Flattery or Praise?

wo incidents in the life of Pablo Casals, the famous cellist, illustrate the difference between flattery and praise.

One day a young cellist, Gregor Piatigorsky, was asked to play a Beethoven sonata before the famous musician. He was nervous and played badly.

"Bravo! Wonderful! Tremendous!" Casals applauded. He was trying to encourage Gregor, but ended up discouraging him. Why? Because Gregor felt the praise was undeserved. It sounded insincere to him; he dismissed it as flattery. He went away embarrassed.

Several years later the two cellists were together again for an evening. Now experienced, Gregor was not afraid to tell Casals how he had felt about the flattery of the earlier encounter.

"No! No!" Casals became angry. Rushing to the cello, he played a bit of the sonata Gregor had played that evening. "Didn't you use this fingering?"

"Yes, I did," Gregor agreed.

"That was a new fingering to me," Casals said. "I thought your use of that fingering was excellent, one I'd never tried before. I liked it."

Casals then played another passage from the sonata. "And didn't you attack it with an up-bow like this?"

Gregor nodded.

"That also was particularly pleasing to me. It showed a very strong ability you have to interpret the music in a creative way. I was really greatly impressed by your talent."

"But my mistakes. I played poorly."

"True, but I wasn't paying attention to your mistakes, but to your interpretation and your fingering technique. You did both of those things very well. That's why I applauded you that night."

Gregor said later, "I left with the feeling of having been with a great artist and a friend."

What made the difference in the two encounters? The first time, Casals used words that evaluated, such as "wonderful" and "tremendous." The second time, Casals used descriptive words that explained exactly what he was praising about the performance.

JULY 8

IN THE END, PEOPLE APPRECIATE FRANKNESS MORE THAN FLATTERY. PROVERBS 28:23, TLB.

BEING FRIENDS

Avoid evaluating a friend when you offer praise. Rather describe the behavior that you appreciate, and tell why you like it. Focus on the behavior rather than the person.

197

Jackson Sunshine Lady

**PLEASANT SIGHTS AND GOOD REPORTS GIVE HAPPINESS AND HEALTH.
PROVERBS 15:30, TLB.**

Do you remember the story of the "Sunshine Lady" in San Diego, California ("Bianca's Secret," May 21)? This week I heard about a Sunshine Lady in Jackson, Ohio. I can't tell you her name, although I know what it is. That would spoil her fun, so we'll call her Tracey.

Tracey read the story of the San Diego Sunshine Lady in my book *The Best You Can Be.* She'd been asking God to show her what really special thing she could do to help in her church in Jackson, Ohio. She decided that God wanted her to be another Sunshine Lady.

Each Sabbath she writes down all the names of members not attending. That week she sends them a little note telling them she misses them. She signs each one "The Sunshine Lady."

Tracey writes: "You wouldn't believe the response that I have gotten! Five people whom I have written to have started attending Sabbath school regularly again!"

The Jackson, Ohio, Seventh-day Adventist Church is just a small church. Most of the members are past retirement age. Tracey, a young person, has got the whole church buzzing. Everyone is asking everyone else, "Are you the Sunshine Lady?" Tracey is probably the last person they would suspect.

Tracey writes: "When I started this project I never dreamed it would have such an effect. Some weeks I send as many as 10 letters. One lady who has to live with a sick husband who is ill most of the time gets a letter from me every other week. Now all she can talk about at church is how the Sunshine Lady has helped her. I think every church should have a Sunshine Lady."

Isn't that exciting? Tracey has discovered a way to be a blessing to everyone in her little church. She's having so much fun encouraging people that she can't stop! She can't wait to get to church on Sabbath morning to catch the excitement from those who have received her letters during the week.

BEING FRIENDS

The beautiful thing about encouragement is that it makes the person giving it just as happy as the one receiving it.

One Thousand Percent

Words have tremendous power. A word spoken at the right time can change the whole course of a person's life.

Take, for instance, the case of Larry Crabb. During ninth grade he had to repeat a pledge before the whole school. Once on the platform, his knees knocked, his hands sweated, his mouth went dry, and he began to stutter. "I, L-L-L-L-Larry C-C-C-Crabb, do hereby p-p-p-promise . . ."

"I died a thousand deaths," said Larry. "I decided right then and there public speaking was not for me." He determined that he'd never make a fool of himself in public ever again.

Shortly after that experience he was called upon to offer prayer during the worship service in his church. Under pressure, he decided to give public speaking one more try. He soon realized he'd made a mistake. He not only stuttered, but his theology became confused.

"I remember thanking the Father for hanging on the cross," says Larry, "and praising Christ for bringing the Spirit from the grave."

Finally, Larry managed to say amen, and sat down. He knew he'd made a fool of himself, and he vowed to never again pray in public or speak before an audience.

As soon as the meeting was finished, Larry darted for the door, but he wasn't fast enough. One of the elders, Jim Dunbar, intercepted his flight.

Larry gulped. *Oh, no! Here it comes!*

Jim put his arm on Larry's shoulder and cleared his throat. "Larry, there's one thing I want you to know. Whatever you do for the Lord, I'm behind you 1,000 percent."

Today Larry is a college professor who has a wide public ministry. He often tells the story of Jim's encouragement, but he never tells it without choking up, so powerful was the impact of those few encouraging words.

JULY 10

LET US ENCOURAGE ONE ANOTHER. HEBREWS 10:25, NIV.

BEING FRIENDS

Encouragement is backing a friend 1,000 percent. It's believing in your friend and letting him or her know you care. You have the power to speak words that will put hope in your friend's heart and a spring in his or her step.

199

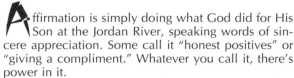

Love Affirms

**THIS IS MY
BELOVED SON, IN
WHOM I AM
WELL PLEASED.
MATTHEW 3:17.**

BEING
FRIENDS

How often have
you withheld
affirmation from
a friend who
needed kind,
caring words?
Whom can you
appreciate today?

ffirmation is simply doing what God did for His
Son at the Jordan River, speaking words of sincere appreciation. Some call it "honest positives" or
"giving a compliment." Whatever you call it, there's
power in it.

People who receive a compliment feel good.
Their self-respect grows, and miracles can happen.
One such miracle was Charlie Blake.

Charlie was known as the "sickest man in Britain."
He did nothing all day except sit in a chair. He seldom
moved and never talked. An orderly labeled him "Mr.
Zero." He hadn't said a word in 30 years.

At this point Dr. Irene Kassorla decided to try the
power of affirmation. Every day she visited him and
rewarded any movement or sound with a positive
word of appreciation. She said things such as "Good,
Mr. Blake" or "I like that sound you're making." After
31 days Charlie was talking, reading the newspaper,
and answering questions.

Many times Dr. Kassorla has used the power of affirmation to make positive changes in the lives of
schizophrenics and autistic children. She insists that
"honest positives" are her most valuable tool.

About her use of appreciation she says: "The results have been so remarkable that an untrained ob-
server might have wondered if I were administering a
potent new drug. But my 'drug' was often little more
than presenting warm, caring words."

Warm, caring words. We need not have a doctor-
ate in order to use them. Anyone can learn to speak
words of affirmation.

If someone's smile warms your heart, tell him or
her so. If you're blessed by the pastor's sermon, say
so. If a friend is helpful, voice your appreciation. If
someone sings or plays well, write a note to express
your delight.

Ellen White puts it this way: "Kind words, looks of
sympathy, expressions of appreciation, would be to
many a struggling and lonely one as the cup of cold
water to a thirsty soul" *(Thoughts From the Mount of
Blessing,* p. 23).

Look for the Good

It was a hot, muggy day, and practice for the Green Bay Packers wasn't going well. Coach Vince Lombardi decided the fault lay with one of the guards, Jerry Kramer.

"Jerry, you're one lousy football player. You're not blocking, you're not tackling, you're not doing your job! As a matter of fact, you're finished. Go take a shower," Lombardi ordered. "I'm not having anyone on this team who doesn't put out."

An hour later when Lombardi walked into the dressing room he saw Jerry sitting in front of his locker, his uniform still on. He was bent over, his head in his hands. He was crying quietly.

Lombardi walked over to Jerry and put an arm around his shoulders. Jerry braced himself for another lecture. "I told you the truth out there," the coach said. "You're a lousy football player. You weren't blocking, you weren't tackling, you weren't doing your job. However, I need to tell you the rest of the story."

Jerry looked up at his coach, wondering what was coming next. He saw a big grin on Lombardi's face, and he relaxed.

The coach continued, "Inside of you, Jerry, there's a great football player, and I'm going to stick with you until the great football player inside of you has a chance to come out and show us what he can do!"

"Thanks, Coach," Jerry said. "I'll do my job!"

Jerry Kramer went on to become one of the all-time greats in football. It wasn't long before he was voted the all-time best guard in the first 50 years of professional football.

Vince Lombardi produced some great football players, because he saw the good in his players and helped them develop their potential abilities.

None of us is yet the best we can be. We all have wonderful capabilities hidden away inside of us. What we all need is a friend to recognize and affirm those excellent qualities.

WHATEVER IS ADMIRABLE—IF ANYTHING IS EXCELLENT OR PRAISEWORTHY—THINK ABOUT SUCH THINGS. PHILIPPIANS 4:8, NIV.

BEING FRIENDS

If you'd be a friend, look for the excellent qualities in other people. Affirm them; let them know the praiseworthy characteristics you see.

Praise the Lord

**I WILL PRAISE YOU AS LONG AS I LIVE.
PSALM 63:4, NIV.**

BEING FRIENDS

Being God's friend means to praise Him in all the circumstances of life, good or bad.

It was July 1967 when 17-year-old Joni Eareckson went swimming and recklessly dived into shallow water. Her head smashed against the bottom, breaking her neck and paralyzing her from the neck down.

For weeks she lay in a Stryker frame in the hospital, looking forward to a life without the use of hands or legs. Life seemed pretty hopeless in those days. Joni cried out in anger to God, "This isn't fair! I can't stand to go on living like this!"

One night alone in the darkness of the hospital room, Joni lay motionless on her Stryker frame and hit rock bottom in her life. For several days she'd begged friends to help her commit suicide. But they had refused. She lay there feeling so utterly helpless, unable even to take her own life.

That night in the numb blackness of her despair she cried out to God, "God, if I can't die, show me how to live, please!"

Writing about this experience, Joni says: "Things didn't change overnight, but with that simple prayer my outlook began to change. I realized that 'growing up' was just something I was going to have to learn how to do. I would have to learn how to do the impossible—handle life in a wheelchair."

It's been 29 years since Joni's accident. She's now an accomplished artist, drawing pictures with a pen in her teeth. She's a well-known speaker and a best-selling author. In a TV appearance she shared her faith that God has brought good from her being in a wheelchair. She said, "I want Him to be glorified through me."

At the bottom of every drawing she writes the initials P.T.L. She's delighted when people ask what they stand for. They stand for "Praise the Lord!" That gives her an opportunity to tell them why she wants to praise the Lord. "He's what life is all about," she says. How Joni learned to praise is another story.

Joni's Struggle

Joni couldn't understand how a good God could permit something as terrible as her accident to happen to one of His children. She was depressed, resentful, and angry.

During those months of frustration a friend, Steve Estes, often spent time with her. He'd bring her pizza or donuts and read to her from the Bible. Joni listened because she liked his company, but she wasn't much interested in the words he read.

Then came the day when he read 1 Thessalonians 5:18: "Give thanks in all circumstances" (NIV).

He closed his Bible and said, "Well, Joni, don't you think it's about time you got around to thanking God for that wheelchair of yours?"

"No way!" Joni responded. "I'm not thankful, and I won't say it. I won't give thanks when I don't feel like it."

"Whoa!" Steve responded. "Look at that verse again. It doesn't say you have to *feel* thankful. It says to give thanks in all circumstances, good and bad, whether you feel like it or not."

"But how can I thank God when I can't understand why all this has happened to me?" Joni whined.

"We'll never understand the ways of God," Steve went on. "You don't need to know why; you need to be thankful that God is in your life, leading and helping you."

So Joni gritted her teeth and through her tears prayed, "OK, Lord, I thank You for this hospital bed. I would really rather have pizza, but if You want me to have cafeteria oatmeal, that's fine. And Lord, I thank You that physical therapy is helping me. Lord, I'm grateful that when I practiced writing the alphabet today with that pencil between my teeth it didn't look like chicken scratches."

It didn't happen overnight, but eventually Joni changed. She writes: "Thankful feelings began to well up. It was as though God rewarded me with the feeling of gratitude for having obeyed and given thanks."

GIVE THANKS IN ALL CIRCUMSTANCES, FOR THIS IS GOD'S WILL FOR YOU IN CHRIST JESUS. 1 THESSALONIANS 5:18, NIV.

BEING FRIENDS

Being friends with God means thanking Him for all the circumstances of your life, good and bad, whether you feel like it or not.

Affirming God

**I LOVE THE
LORD, FOR
HE HEARD
MY VOICE.
PSALM 116:1,
NIV.**

BEING
FRIENDS

If we truly love
God, we'll want
to affirm Him
through praise
and thanksgiving.

What if Melissa were in love with Nathan and wrote him a letter that went like this:

Dear Nathan,

I need your help with my math assignment. Please change the tire on my car, and while you're at it you might even wash my car. I need someone to drill me in French. Can you do it tonight? I need a couple books from the library. Please pick them up for me.

With love,
Melissa

My guess is that the relationship wouldn't last too long. Nathan wants someone who not only wants help but also someone who admires him, appreciates him, and affirms him. We love those who encourage us and make us feel good about ourselves.

What about our relationship with God? Does God need encouragement? Does He want affirmation, appreciation, and words of affection? How do we affirm God?

We affirm God by our praise and words of love and adoration. We appreciate Him when we thank Him for His blessings. Too often my prayers have been unbalanced, filled with "gimmes." God wants us to ask for His help, but He also wants that to be balanced with words of praise and appreciation.

Here's a guide to help you write a love letter to God or to develop a balanced prayer of love. To do it use the letters of the word ACTS as an acrostic.

Adoration. Write a paragraph of praise and adoration. Tell Him why you love Him. Tell Him what you appreciate about Him.

Confession. Write a paragraph of confession. Be specific rather than general. Tell exactly what acts you did that were wrong. Describe the thoughts you had that were sinful. Ask God to forgive you.

Thanksgiving. Write a paragraph of thanksgiving. Express your gratitude for specific things.

Supplication. Write a paragraph about your needs. What is it that you need Him to do for you and your friends? Be specific.

Love Remembers

The stock market had plunged. Banks had failed. Unemployment was high. Many were hungry and homeless. The threat of war loomed in Europe. And Thanksgiving was just around the corner. This was the focus of the after-dinner conversation.

"I don't see much to be thankful for," one man commented.

"Don't be so negative!" someone responded. "There's always something to be thankful for."

"Like what?" the man replied.

"Mrs. Wendt," Bill Stidger spoke up. "She was my high school English teacher 30 years ago. She introduced me to Tennyson, and I've been grateful to her ever since. A marvelous teacher!"

"Does she know how you feel?" someone asked.

"No," Bill admitted.

"Then why don't you write her a note?" a friend suggested.

"All right, I will," Bill agreed. That night he wrote his letter to Mrs. Wendt.

After some time he got a reply in shaky handwriting that said in part, "You will be interested to know, Willie, that I taught school for 50 years, and in all that time, yours is the first note of appreciation I've ever received. It came on a blue, cold morning, and it cheered my lonely old heart as nothing has cheered me in many years."

"I wept when I read that letter," Bill Stidger says. "That letter was so successful that I made a list of 50 people I wanted to thank for some contribution they had made to my life."

All but two people replied. Those two had died, but their relatives sent letters of thanks.

That was the beginning of Dr. William Stidger's lifelong habit of writing letters of gratitude to those who had touched his life. Through the years he has collected more than 500 replies from people who were overwhelmed by his remembrance.

Typical of these letters was one that said, "You will never know how much your letter has warmed my spirit. I have been walking about in the glow of it all day long."

I HAVE REMEMBRANCE OF THEE. 2 TIMOTHY 1:3.

BEING FRIENDS

Writing letters is one way to express our appreciation of our friends. A note is special because it can be read over and over again.

205

Christine's Note

I HAVE WRITTEN YOU ONLY A SHORT LETTER. HEBREWS 13:22, NIV.

BEING FRIENDS

Friends are careful to write thank-you notes to those who have done something special for them. A written note puts a special glow in the heart of a friend.

Most of the New Testament is a collection of letters Paul wrote to his friends in different cities. Paul has given us a good example of how to be a real friend.

Christine was skipping home from school when a reporter from the small-town newspaper called out, "Hi, Christine! I need your help. Come pose for me in front of this pussy willow tree. I'll put your photo in the newspaper. It will remind people that spring is here. Is that OK with you?"

"Sure!" Christine said, following the reporter to the pussy willows. She held a pussy willow branch in her hands and stroked the soft gray fur of the new buds. She smiled her special smile, and the reporter snapped the picture.

A few days later Christine saw her photo on the front page of the newspaper. Then in the mail came an envelope addressed to Christine. Inside was a big glossy print of the photograph for her to keep.

"That was really thoughtful of the reporter to give you a copy of the picture," Christine's Aunt Jeanne observed. "Why don't you write her a note to say thank you?"

Christine ran to get a writing pad, colored felt-tipped pens, and a pencil. Aunt Jeanne helped Christine with ideas and spelling and soon the note was complete. At the bottom Christine drew a pretty flower. She folded the letter and put it in the envelope. She ran over to the newspaper office and left the letter for the reporter.

A few days later Christine's letter was printed in the newspaper. "Christine's letter made my day!" the reporter commented.

Written thank-you notes are very meaningful to those who receive them. Get into the habit of writing notes to people who have done nice things for you, such as inviting you for a meal, giving you a gift, or helping you with a project. You'll be glad you did.

Who Needs It?

This letter was written more than 100 years ago by George Mueller, the man who founded orphanages in Bristol, England. He prayed to God daily about the needs of the thousands of orphans he looked after, and God supplied their needs in miraculous ways.

> Dear Brother Taylor,
>
> An older brother who has known the Lord for 44 years writes this, saying for your encouragement, that He has never failed him. In the greatest difficulties, in the heaviest trials, in the deepest poverty and necessities, He has never failed me. I was enabled by His grace to trust in Him. He has always appeared for my help. I delight in speaking well of His name.
>
> Sincerely yours,
> George Mueller

The receiver of that note was Hudson Taylor, the founder of the China Inland Mission. He dressed as a Chinese, even shaving his head and wearing his hair in a long black pigtail. He trusted completely in God to supply the needs of his missionary work in China.

Can you imagine what a boost that letter was to Hudson Taylor when it arrived after months on a ship? It must have set his heart to singing and kept him joyful for many days.

Missionaries are one group of people who need letters of encouragement. Think hard. Is there someone working in a foreign land who'd enjoy a note or card from you?

Pastors seldom get words of encouragement about the work they're doing. Why not encourage someone who works for God in His church?

Teachers are another group who all too often feel unappreciated. Is there one who has been really nice to you? Why not surprise that teacher with a note of appreciation?

Parents are often taken for granted by us. They do many kind, unselfish things for us every day. Why not write a note and tape it to your parents' bathroom mirror? It will make their day!

HE [JOSIAH] . . . ENCOURAGED THEM IN THE SERVICE OF THE LORD'S TEMPLE. 2 CHRONICLES 35:2, NIV.

BEING FRIENDS

One way we can show our friendship is by writing a letter of appreciation to someone who seldom hears such pleasant words.

Gifts That Encourage

WE SHOULD CONTINUE TO REMEMBER THE POOR. GALATIANS 2:10, NIV.

BEING FRIENDS

Do you love your friends enough to help them out when they have a real need?

orraine had a toothache, a bad one. She went to a dentist, only to discover that the tooth was abscessed. She needed a root canal, a cap, and a crown.

"How long will it take? How much will it cost?" Lorraine asked.

"A couple months and $500," the dentist replied.

"Oh! I don't see how I can manage that!" Lorraine exclaimed. "Will you take payments?"

"I will," the dentist agreed, "but there's a second dentist involved. You'll have to ask him."

The second dentist insisted he must have his bill paid in full in cash within 90 days. The amount was $305, an impossibility for Lorraine, who was a college student earning her own way through school. Her mother was widowed and had no money to help.

Lorraine was worried. She had to have the dental work done. She started the treatments, having no idea how she would pay. At a weekend prayer retreat she shared her concern with her prayer group, asking them to pray for her and her problem.

Later a member of the prayer group handed her a folded piece of paper. Inside was a $5 bill.

A few days later a friend brought her $102 that his Bible study group had collected for her. She was able to make her first payment to the dentist.

"We thought you had no money," the receptionist said.

"I don't," Lorraine replied, "but I have a special Friend who cares about me."

The next day she found an envelope in her campus mailbox. In it was $200. She never found out who sent that money. She started to cry, she was so relieved. God had used friends to supply her need.

When she paid the dental bill in full, she told the dentist, "I believe God takes care of us, and one of the ways He does that is through people who believe in Him."

The dentist said, "Boy, your friends really love you!"

Yes, Lorraine thought as she walked out of his office, *my friends really do love me!*

Silent Encouragement

Solzhenitsyn, a great Russian writer, was in a prison in which no one was allowed to speak. There were no books to read, no TV programs to watch, no music to brighten their spirits.

In such depressing circumstances Solzhenitsyn felt very much alone and without hope. *I'll never get out of here,* he thought. *Perhaps I should find a way to kill myself, but how would I do it? Maybe the best way is to try to escape. The guards will shoot me and that will be the end of my misery.*

However, something kept Solzhenitsyn from doing anything that night. The next morning he was taken out to work. Later in the morning the prisoners were given a break, and Solzhenitsyn sat down with his back against a tree. He actually had one hand behind his back, ready to spring away and make a dash for freedom and the shot he hoped would end his life.

Another prisoner walked silently over to the tree and sat down on the grass beside Solzhenitsyn. It was a new man who had recently been brought to the prison camp. The new man said not a word. He simply looked at Solzhenitsyn and smiled.

"I saw something I had never seen in any face in prison before," Solzhenitsyn later said. "I saw a message of love and concern."

The new man picked up a stick, took a step forward, and drew a cross on the ground with his stick.

Solzhenitsyn's heart began to beat rapidly. He drew in his breath and smiled. He thought, *Jesus does love me. He's in command. It isn't hopeless!*

Three days later Solzhenitsyn was released from prison. It was then that he learned that many people around the world had been praying for him. God had answered those prayers by sending someone into his life at his moment of deepest despair to give him encouragement and hope.

FOR WE ARE SAVED BY HOPE. ROMANS 8:24.

BEING FRIENDS

Perhaps God has called you today to give hope to someone else. You can do it with words, a letter, or perhaps just a smile and a gesture of caring.

A Kind Word

FRIENDLINESS BEARS FRUIT FOR A MAN. PROVERBS 19:22, MOFFATT.

BEING FRIENDS

Often it takes only a kind word to turn a person's life around. You can do that for someone today.

Kindness is a seed that we plant in the heart of another person. We never know where it will take root, grow, and meet us again to fill our lives with unexpected joy.

John Morel, mayor of Darlington, England, was a friendly man who liked to walk the streets of his town and greet his friends and neighbors. On one of these expeditions about town he happened to meet a man who had just been released from jail for stealing funds from the company for which he'd worked.

"Hello, my friend!" Mr. Morel called in his usual friendly tone. "I'm glad to see you! How are you?"

Embarrassed, the man hurried on after the brief encounter. But the man didn't forget the kindness in Mr. Morel's voice.

Imagine that! The major himself spoke to me! the ex-convict thought as he walked down the street. *Perhaps there's hope for me after all. Perhaps I can start my life again and make a success of it so that I will be worthy of the mayor's kindness!*

It was several years later that Mr. Morel happened to meet this same person in another town. This time the man walked up to him, greeting him with friendliness. It was then Mr. Morel's turn to be surprised.

"I want to thank you for what you did for me when I came out of prison," the man said.

"What do you mean?" Mr. Morel responded. "I can't remember doing anything for you. You must be confusing me with someone else from Darlington."

"I remember you well, Mr. Morel," the man insisted. "Were you not the mayor of Darlington?"

"Yes, that's true," Mr. Morel admitted.

"I'd just been released from jail and was walking down the street feeling very sorry for myself," the man declared. "You spoke a kind word to me, and it changed my life. Thank you so much for giving me the courage to face the world again!"

The Kiss

Touch gives a stronger message of love than words can ever convey. Nothing expresses caring like a warm hug. A handshake makes people feel accepted. A pat on the back speaks encouragement. A touch on the cheek says "I love you!"

"Touch is the most important and yet the most neglected of our senses," says family counselor Helen Colton in her book *The Gift of Touch.* "We cannot survive without it."

No wonder Jesus touched people so often! There's miracle-working power in the touch of love. Make a list of the people Jesus touched. You'll be surprised at how often a touch accompanied a miracle.

Paulus Cassel, missionary to German Jews, is another example of the power in a touch of love. Paulus was brought up in a Jewish home, but his parents sent him to public school so that he would have a well-rounded education.

One Christmas the headmaster asked his students to memorize the Christmas story and recite it in class.

"Cassel, you're excused since you're a Jew," his teacher told him quietly.

"I don't mind learning it," Paulus replied. When his turn came to recite, he did it perfectly, with much feeling.

"Well done, Paulus!" his delighted teacher exclaimed. Then he did something surprising; he kissed the boy on the cheek!

"I'll never forget that kiss," Cassel said in later years. "The fact that a Christian should kiss a Jewish boy made a very deep impression on me."

From that time forward, Cassel had a soft spot in his heart for Christians and a very real interest in Christianity. After several years of careful study, Paulus Cassel accepted Jesus as his personal Saviour. From the moment of his conversion, Paulus became a zealous missionary, baptizing 262 Jews from his work in Berlin alone.

"Wherever there is an impulse of love and sympathy, wherever the heart reaches out to bless and uplift others, there is revealed the working of God's Holy Spirit" (*Christ's Object Lessons,* p. 385).

AND HE TOOK THEM UP IN HIS ARMS, PUT HIS HANDS UPON THEM, AND BLESSED THEM. MARK 10:16.

BEING FRIENDS

We can encourage others with a gentle touch that says we care. A brief touch will help us connect and be friends.

Healing Hands

GOD GAVE
MOST UNUSUAL
DEMONSTRATIONS
OF POWER
THROUGH PAUL'S
HANDS. ACTS
19:11, PHILLIPS.

BEING FRIENDS

When a friend is hurting and you don't know what to say, try a tender touch on the shoulder or a squeeze of the hand. God can work miracles through our hands.

God is still working miracles of healing through the touch of someone's hands. Take for instance the experience of Marta Korwin of Warsaw, Poland.

Nearly 60 years ago the Nazis invaded Poland and besieged the city of Warsaw. Thousands were wounded, and the hospitals were full to overflowing. Nurses were scarce, and volunteers from all walks of life were pressed into service. One nursing volunteer was Marta Korwin, a concert pianist.

She chose night duty, a time the sick and dying seemed especially in need of a friend. She walked up and down the wards trying to find small ways she could bring comfort to those in pain. Sometimes it was as simple as just being there to listen to the patient talk or holding a glass as he or she sipped water.

Late one night she was going through the wards when she noticed a soldier with his face buried in his pillow, sobbing. His cries were muffled, but his big shoulders shook with his grief.

Marta stopped at the foot of his bed and wondered what she could do. She looked down at her hands. *These hands can bring music out of a piano, causing the strings to vibrate in harmony,* she mused. *I wonder if these same hands could somehow quiet the turmoil of his soul and bring harmony and peace in the midst of his pain. Let me try.*

She walked nearer the soldier, taking his head in her hands, hoping that they might bring him some comfort and healing. He grabbed her hands quickly in his own, digging his nails into her palms.

Oh, Lord, please help some harmony to flow into his soul to alleviate his pain, Marta prayed silently.

The soldier's sobs gradually subsided. His hands relaxed their grip. Within moments he was asleep. His breathing was steady and peaceful. Marta knew that God had used her hands to bring the miracle of rest and relief from pain.

Helping Sandy

Tonya looked around the cafeteria for her friend Sandy. She was about to leave when she caught a glimpse of Sandy's blond hair bent over a table in the corner. Tonya made a beeline for the table and sat down opposite Sandy. Sandy looked up with blood-shot eyes.

"Things still pretty rough at home?" Tonya asked.

Sandy's eyes filled with tears. "It's pretty bad," she said. "Mom's a basket case, and I'm not much better myself."

"It's been months since your mom and dad split," Tonya said. "I know you miss him and it hurts and all that, but it's time you got on with your own life. Come to the basketball game with me tonight." Tonya reached out and squeezed her friend's hand.

Sandy sighed. "Oh, I don't know. I just don't feel like having fun, and I don't trust anybody anymore."

"Hey! You know you can trust me. Have I ever let you down? I'll be by at 6:00. No excuses allowed. And no games of hide-and-seek. OK?"

"OK," Sandy said, giving her friend a faint smile. "I'll go, but I don't promise to have any fun."

"That's fine with me," Tonya said. "Just come along."

That was the start of Sandy's recovery from her parents' divorce. It was slow, and sometimes she still felt awful, but with Tonya's help she started to learn to trust people again. She didn't cry as much at night, and occasionally she even laughed at Tonya's jokes. Sometimes she still tried to hide from people, but slowly she began to find new interests. She got a part-time job and joined the Outdoors Club. Life started to be good again.

"Thanks for sticking by me," Sandy told Tonya on a weekend backpacking trip. "You've been a real friend."

IF ONE FALLS DOWN, HIS FRIEND CAN HELP HIM UP. ECCLESIASTES 4:10, NIV.

BEING FRIENDS

If, like Humpty Dumpty, someone falls off the wall of life and feels broken into a thousand pieces, what that person needs is a friend to help put him or her back together again. You can be that kind of friend. You can help pick up the pieces.

213

Surprising Dad

**THIS IS MY SON
AND I LOVE HIM.
MATTHEW 17:5,
ICB.**

BEING FRIENDS

People in our
families need
to hear words
of love
and appreciation.

John Ritter was visiting his folks in Nashville, Tennessee. One day he and his dad went out for a drive alone. His dad, wearing an old cowboy hat and coat, was driving.

John looked over at the man at the wheel and thought, *I really love you a lot, Dad. You're a neat person. I'm glad you're my father. We've had a lot of good times together.* He smiled as he remembered some of those times.

Tell your father you love him, a small inner voice seemed to say. *Tell him how much you appreciate him.*

I couldn't do it, John thought. *We've never talked about things like that. He knows I love him. I know he loves me.*

Tell your father you love him, the inner voice prompted again. *Let him know how much you care.*

John took a deep breath. This would take a lot of nerve. "Dad," he began, "I just want to thank you for being my father. I think you're the greatest man I ever met, and I love you."

His dad smiled slowly as though he were searching for words to reply. At last he said, "Yes, son, that's nice."

"Dad, I'd like to hear you say it, too," John said.

"What?" his father asked.

"Do you like me, Dad?"

"Well, . . . I love you."

"I need to hear it, Dad."

"Son, I love you," Mr. Ritter repeated, somewhat embarrassed.

"Thanks, Dad," John said. "I love you, too."

Three weeks later Tex Ritter was dead. John was glad he'd listened to the inner voice urging him to tell his father how much he loved him.

Leo Buscaglia taught a university class in loving. One of the students' assignments was to go home, hug their dads, and say, "I love you, Dad." Almost everyone balked at doing it. However, when they did, they got a surprise.

"The common experience was that most fathers were overwhelmed by the experience, as well as very responsive to it," writes Buscaglia.

Eyes That Speak

George Butler, a world president of the Seventh-day Adventist Church, had a moving experience of seeing love in someone's eyes.

It happened near Waukon, Iowa. Twenty-two-year-old George was an infidel, doubting the truth of the Bible. Although his parents were Adventists, he'd been skeptical for several years.

Then one bitterly cold day George was riding home across the snow-blown prairie when he met Elder and Mrs. White on their return trip from Waukon, Iowa.

The two sleighs stopped. George got out and went over to greet the Whites. "Hello!" George reached out his hand to Ellen. "Good to see you, Brother and Sister White."

Ellen White shook his hand and smiled kindly at the young man. "And it's good to see you, George!" she said.

Despite the biting wind, George felt suddenly warm inside as he looked into Sister White's eyes. It was a kind and friendly look, a sort of motherly look of love and concern, which George would never forget.

Not long after that encounter George decided to read the Bible through to try and decide whether it was true or not. Finally, he got down on his knees and gave his heart to God.

When he later met Ellen White, he reminded her of that encounter on the frozen prairie. He shared how greatly he'd been encouraged to become a Christian because of the kind and friendly way she had looked at him. He told her, "I was very much struck with the kind of a motherly look you gave me at that time. I do not suppose you will remember all that, but I do."

I wonder if George would have ever become a Christian if Mrs. White had looked at him in disgust, perhaps warning him with a frown, "You'd better smarten up, young man, and give your heart to God." What do you think?

JULY 26

JESUS LOOKED AT HIM AND LOVED HIM. MARK 10:21, NIV.

BEING FRIENDS

Encouragement is communicated through more than the words we say, but also through our facial expression and the look in our eyes.

The Spider

So do not fear, for I am with you; . . . I will strengthen you and help you. Isaiah 41:10, NIV.

Being Friends

There's nowhere that we can go but that God can go with us. He'll strengthen us and encourage us in life's darkest moments because He's our friend.

Nien Cheng, a Christian, was imprisoned by the Red Guards during China's Cultural Revolution. She spent six and a half years in jail, alone yet not forsaken. On one occasion God sent a spider to encourage her.

One morning as Nien stared at the window, she saw a spider about as big as a pea. Slowly it climbed a rusty bar of the window. When it reached the top it swung away from the bar on a silver thread that it had spun.

Carefully the spider anchored the slender thread onto a lower bar, then climbed up the thread to the top. Again it swung out and spun another silvery thread, attaching it to another bar. The spider worked until the web was completed, filling the window with its lacy pattern.

Nien sat on her bed most of the day as she watched the spider. The setting sun glistened from the completed web, turning it into all the colors of the rainbow. *How beautiful!* Nien thought. *Thank you, little spider, for bringing beauty into my ugly cell.*

The next morning the spider was still there. It stayed for many days, like a companion sent by God to bring her hope in her lonely cell. Then one morning she awoke to find the web was no longer there. It had been destroyed by wind in the night.

"Oh, no!" Nien cried. "What will I do without my courageous little spider? It has been my messenger of hope sent by God, and now it's gone. How can I go on without hope?"

Then in that moment of darkness and despair she looked up again at the bare window. In a corner of the ceiling she saw the spider. "Ah, there you are!" she said. "You're back at work making a new web! How brave you are! Now I know God sent you to me. He's telling me, 'Nien, don't give up.'"

Nien Cheng survived because God encouraged her.

Kidnapping June

Christie and Kelly found June in her living room reading. She wore sweatpants and an old T-shirt. Her hair was a mess. The girls took positions on each side of their friend.

"Come with us! Right now!" ordered Christie.

"No way! I'm a mess. Give me an hour so I can shower and do my hair, OK?" the startled girl replied.

"No time!" Kelly tried to sound tough. "If I were you I'd get up and walk to the car peacefully. Otherwise we'll have to take drastic measures."

"Like what?" June laughed. "You don't scare me!"

"Like this!" Christie said. Both girls closed in on June, each grabbing an arm. "You leave us no choice. We'll just have to kidnap you!"

June kicked and struggled to get free from the girls' grip. They all fell in a heap to the floor as they laughed and tussled.

"Help!" Kelly yelled. "We need help!"

June's dad, who had been alerted about the kidnapping, entered the room and helped the girls carry June, kicking and screaming all the way, to the car.

"What's all this about?" June laughed when they were on their way. "Why am I being kidnapped?"

"It's your birthday!" Kelly said. "Had you forgotten? We've planned a surprise party for you! Sorry we had to get a little rough back there, but we couldn't let you spoil our fun!"

It was a glorious birthday celebration for June. The news of the kidnapping was the talk of the town for the rest of the week.

Don't you think that was a clever way to celebrate June's birthday? It certainly was a birthday that June would never forget. She'd been going through some discouraging times, and the surprise and laughter of the kidnapping was just what she needed to lift her spirits and make her feel happy again. Christie and Kelly had found a medicine that worked to cure the blues.

A CHEERFUL HEART IS GOOD MEDICINE. PROVERBS 17:22, NIV.

BEING FRIENDS

Good friends look for ways to give a dose of laughter to those they care about. Laughter is a wonderful way to encourage friends.

Encourage With Prayer

**O THAT ONE MIGHT PLEAD FOR A MAN WITH GOD.
JOB 16:21.**

BEING FRIENDS

Prayer is another way we can encourage our friends. Christian friends pray for each other.

Arthur Daniells was 10 years old when he gave his heart to God. He tried to be a good Christian, but often failed. *There's no use trying,* Arthur thought, *I might as well give up.* And that's what he did. He stopped reading his Bible. He stopped praying. He stopped standing up on Sabbath to give his testimony.

One Sabbath Arthur hurried out after the benediction before anyone got a chance to speak to him. He went around the corner of the church and hid in the shadows.

Just then an old white-haired elder turned the corner of the building and smiled when he saw Arthur. "Well! Well! There you are, Arthur. I've been looking for you."

Arthur wasn't happy to see the old man. His eyes darted around, looking for a way to escape, but he saw he was cornered.

"I'm interested in you, Arthur," the old man said. "I've noticed that you've missed speaking in the service for three weeks now. What's the trouble?"

"There's no help for me," Arthur mumbled, looking down at his shoes. "I'm not the kind of boy to be a Christian. I can't do it. I've tried and failed, so I've given up trying."

"You mustn't give up!" the elder declared. "I'll pray for you this week every day. Now, will you try? Will you join me in prayer every day this week?"

"Yes, sir, if you'll pray for me, then I'll try."

The old man put an arm around Arthur's shoulders and drew him close. He whispered, "Arthur, I'll pray for you every day. You pray too, and I know the Lord will help you."

Arthur kept his promise and greeted the old man with a smile the next Sabbath. "It worked!" he said. He had no trouble finding something to praise the Lord about that Sabbath.

Arthur grew up to be Elder A. G. Daniells, a minister, missionary, and a world president of Seventh-day Adventists.

The C Section

Bill Bair had flunked first grade and fourth grade. In his school the classes were divided into sections according to how well you did in your studies. Section A was for the best students; section D was for the worst. Bill was in the D section.

"Bill isn't doing well," his teacher told his mother. "He can't handle the work. I think he should be put back in grade three."

"Do whatever you think is best," Mrs. Bair said.

But before the switch occurred, a visitor came to fourth grade. It was the superintendent of schools, Mr. Smith. He arrived just before the children were to start a test. At the sight of him all knowledge Bill may have had disappeared.

The teacher began with question number one. Bill didn't know the answer. Usually, when he didn't know he just sat there. But this time he began writing furiously, because he was so scared that Mr. Smith would notice. He wrote anything that came into his head.

Mr. Smith stopped at his desk and picked up his paper, scanning the answers. Later Mr. Smith said to the teacher, "I think Bill Bair deserves a second chance to improve himself. Let's put him in the C section."

Surprised, the teacher said, "Bill move over to the seat in the second row behind Marion."

Bill couldn't believe his good fortune. Never in his life had he been higher than the D section. He rushed home after school to tell the good news. "Mom! Mr. Smith put me in the C section!"

"Why? You've never been in the C section," she said.

"He said I deserved a second chance."

"Well, if you're going out to play, change your clothes," his mother said. "I'll talk to your teacher about it later."

"I can't go out," Bill replied. "I've got too much homework."

Bill Bair never failed a grade again. Encouraged by the confidence placed in him by Mr. Smith, he worked hard and succeeded.

THEREFORE ENCOURAGE ONE ANOTHER AND BUILD EACH OTHER UP.
1 THESSALONIANS 5:11, NIV.

BEING FRIENDS

We encourage friends when we express our confidence that they can do a good job.

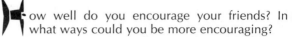

Encouragement Checkup

How well do you encourage your friends? In what ways could you be more encouraging?

1. I focus on the happiness of my friends, not my own needs.
Never   Sometimes   Usually   Always

2. I often voice my appreciation of my friends.
Never   Sometimes   Usually   Always

3. I do secret acts of kindness for people.
Never   Sometimes   Usually   Always

4. I affirm people by giving them compliments.
Never   Sometimes   Usually   Always

5. I try to praise a specific behavior a person does rather than give evaluative praise of the person himself.
Never   Sometimes   Usually   Always

6. I find happiness in bringing joy to others.
Never   Sometimes   Usually   Always

7. I believe in my friends and let them know that.
Never   Sometimes   Usually   Always

8. I look for the excellent qualities in other people, letting them know the praiseworthy characteristics I see.
Never   Sometimes   Usually   Always

9. I'm able to praise God in all circumstances.
Never   Sometimes   Usually   Always

10. I write notes to people to affirm them and express my appreciation to them.
Never   Sometimes   Usually   Always

11. I'm willing to help out my friends when they're in need, giving something concrete to meet their needs.
Never   Sometimes   Usually   Always

12. I use a tender touch to encourage people when they need it.
Never   Sometimes   Usually   Always

13. I offer words of encouragement and appreciation to members of my family.
Never   Sometimes   Usually   Always

14. I use prayer to encourage people.
Never   Sometimes   Usually   Always

Faithful Dog

"Lass, come!" rancher Phillip Keller called.

A handsome black border collie streaked across the field toward her master. She stopped when she reached him, looking up at him with love in her eyes as if to say, "Here I am. What do you want me to do?"

"Heel," Phillip said.

Lass fell in beside her master, walking with him several yards to an open gate where Phillip stopped.

"Sit," Mr. Keller commanded.

Lass sat.

"Stay," he ordered. "Don't let any of the sheep through this gate, or we're in for big trouble. It will take a lot of work to round them up again. Lass, stay!" Then he walked away.

Lass's eyes followed her master, but no matter how much she wanted to follow him, she stayed at her post of duty. She lay down, eyes and ears alert to any sheep that might want to pass through the gate.

A ewe approached the gate, intent on reaching the grass in the next pasture. Lass barked furiously. The sheep turned back.

A flock of crows flew toward Lass, cawing loudly as if to say, "Come on, Lass! Catch us if you can!" They swooped low over her with jeering caws, so close that Lass could hear the wind whistle through their wings.

Lass trembled with excitement. How she loved to chase crows! But she didn't follow the crows. She had a job to do. Her friend was counting on her.

"Good girl!" Phillip said when he returned. He knelt down and scratched Lass behind the ears. "What a loyal, faithful friend you are!"

Phillip says: "I am still stirred by the memories of the times when she proved so true to me. I can recall vividly how thrilled I was to come back and find that she had stuck to her post and played her part well."

Lass illustrates the meaning of loyalty. She was true to Phillip even when the crows teased. She was committed to her friend. She was there when he needed her.

BE LOYALLY FAITHFUL. REVELATION 2:10, AMPLIFIED.

BEING FRIENDS

Friends are loyal and faithful. They're committed. We know that we can count on loyal friends to be there when we need them.

221

Salute to Jesse

A FRIEND LOVES AT ALL TIMES, AND A BROTHER IS BORN FOR ADVERSITY. PROVERBS 17:17, NIV.

"Brrrr! It's sure cold out here!" Sixty-one-year-old Jesse Carpenter drew his tattered coat tighter around him to keep out the December wind. He tucked a blanket around the useless legs of his friend, John Lam, and adjusted the wheelchair so that the wind was at his back.

"You'd best go to the shelter tonight, Jesse." John shivered as he spoke.

"And leave you alone?" Jesse said. "No way! I'd gladly go if they'd let you in too, but they won't. So, I'm staying here with you. I'll be OK."

Jesse lay down on the frozen ground in the park across from the White House in Washington, D.C. He pulled a dirty blanket over his head and went to sleep.

Jesse Carpenter never woke up. He died at the feet of his friend, who was helpless because of Parkinson's disease. Someone called the police. A newspaper reporter showed up. The news of another homeless man frozen to death on the streets of Washington was in the paper that evening.

His ex-wife saw the account and thought he deserved a decent burial. She sent Jesse's Bronze Star to Washington. It was given to Jesse in World War II for carrying wounded comrades to safety while under enemy fire.

Jesse Carpenter, the wartime hero, was buried in Arlington National Cemetery with military honors and a 21-gun salute for his loyalty to comrades and country. There were some who felt that Jesse was just as much a hero for his loyalty to his homeless friend in the wheelchair.

Jesse was an alcoholic, a man who had turned to drink when he was unable to adjust to life after the war. He'd spent 22 years on the streets of Washington as a homeless nobody. The last two years of his life he'd spent pushing John Lam's wheelchair about the streets, sleeping in the park beside him at night because there was no place else for them to go.

BEING FRIENDS

Our loyalty to friends is tested in the really hard experiences of life. A friend in need is a friend indeed.

Don't Take My Bible!

She lived not long ago in an Asian country where the government was trying to destroy God's Word. She lived in fear of the day when the soldiers would search her home. *Where can I hide my precious Bible so that they'll never find it?* she wondered. *I know, I'll hide it under the cold ashes in my stove!*

Carefully she wrapped her treasured Bible in paper and placed it in the stove, covering it with ashes.

It wasn't long before the soldiers came to her door. Brushing her aside, they strode into the tiny house and began their search. They opened trunks and poked into mattresses. They looked in her cooking pots and in the bag of rice. Then one of them poked into the cold ashes of her fire.

The woman ran forward and grabbed the book from the soldier.

"Please, don't take my Bible!" she begged. "It's all I have to tell me about Jesus."

"It's nothing but a book of fables," the soldier said. "Give it to us, old woman!"

"No! I will not!" she protested.

Two soldiers clutched her arms and led her outside. There they took off her clothes and placed her naked on a platform. She curled up, holding her Bible close to her chest to cover herself. She closed her eyes and began praying.

A crowd gathered, laughing at her and spitting on her. After four hours a soldier came forward. "Now, old woman, are you willing to give up your Bible?" he asked.

"No!" she declared. "It's all I have to tell me about Jesus."

They dragged her off the platform and stretched her on the ground, with her hands above her head. They beat her hands with hammers until they were like mushy hamburger meat. They then took her Bible and let her go.

Her hands healed, but she was never again able to hold a book in those hands or even to dress or feed herself.

HOLD FAST TO THE SURE AND TRUSTWORTHY WORD OF GOD. TITUS 1:9, AMPLIFIED.

BEING FRIENDS

Being a friend of God means being loyal to His Word and His truth regardless of the consequences.

Armistice Day

**OBEY THOSE
OVER YOU, AND
GIVE HONOR
AND RESPECT TO
ALL THOSE TO
WHOM IT IS DUE.
ROMANS 13:7,
TLB.**

BEING
FRIENDS

Sometimes we
have a conflict
between being
loyal to friends
and being loyal
to what's right.
True friends will
respect us for
standing up for
our convictions.

It was November 11, 1918, Armistice Day. On that day people across the United States celebrated, because World War I had come to an end. Brothers, uncles, fathers, and friends would be coming home from battle.

"We should celebrate," students at Pacific Union College decided. "Let's suggest it to President Irwin." A group raced to the president's office on Howell Mountain.

"There will be no picnic today!" President Irwin announced. "Classes will go on as usual."

Once outside the building, the boys gathered around to discuss the situation. "People will be celebrating this day in every corner of the land," someone observed. "Why should we be the only ones left out?"

"It's not fair!" others agreed. "We should be allowed to celebrate!"

"Let's do it anyway," someone else said. "One of us could climb up to the roof of the administration building and ring the bell. We'll have a picnic, and no one will stop us."

"Yes! Yes!" the crowd agreed, all except Francis Nichol.

"I can't go on the picnic with you," Francis said firmly.

"What do you mean? Don't you want to be patriotic? The faculty isn't being fair! What's wrong with you?"

"The faculty is wrong," Francis said. "They should allow us a celebration. I *am* patriotic, and I want to celebrate as much as the rest of you. However, rules are rules. We all agreed to obey the rules when we came here. We agreed to respect the faculty. These are the principles of law and order, and I cannot go against them. That's why I won't be joining you."

The students had their picnic without Francis. Someone rang the bell, and several students got into big trouble. But none of his friends blamed Francis. Instead, they all respected him for being loyal to his convictions. In fact, they liked him even more because they knew he was a friend they could count on to do what was right.

The Errand Boy

"Do you have a moment?" Mr. Lang asked as he took the parcel from Jack, the errand boy.

Jack glanced at the clock. "Sure," he said. "I'm ahead of schedule with my deliveries." Jack followed Mr. Lang into his office.

"Have you ever thought of changing jobs?"

"Well, I think you should." Mr. Lang smiled at the puzzled youth. "I've been watching you for some time. You're honest, intelligent, and industrious—just the kind of boy I need to work for me. I'll pay you almost twice what Mr. Hill does. How about it?"

"I'm sorry," Jack said. "I really appreciate your offer. I could use the extra money, but I promised Mr. Hill I'd spend three years with him. I've still got two more years to go."

"Did you sign a contract?" Mr. Lang leaned forward and whispered the words. "If you didn't, then there's no problem."

"No, but I gave him my word," Jack answered. "I wouldn't want to break my promise. I don't think you'd want a boy who didn't keep his promises, would you?"

"You're right about that," Mr. Lang chuckled. "Come see me when the two years are up."

The next two years seemed to drag by. Jack worked faithfully for Mr. Hill. *As soon as my three years are finished, I'm going to switch over to Mr. Lang,* he thought.

When the time finally arrived, Jack went to see Mr. Hill. "Please, sir, my three years are up, and I'd like your recommendation so that I could get another job."

"With Mr. Lang?" his boss asked. "Did he offer you a job?"

"Yes, a couple years ago, but I turned him down."

"Why?"

"Because I'd given you my word. I stick by my word, sir."

"You're both honest and loyal. I like that," Mr. Hill said. "I've a place for you in the office at four times your present salary. Will you stay with me?"

"You bet I will!" Jack said with a grin.

YOU ARE A GOOD SERVANT. I SEE THAT I CAN TRUST YOU. LUKE 19:17, ICB.

BEING FRIENDS

Friends want to know they can depend on us to keep our word. Loyal friends are worth keeping.

Faithful Nalphi

WELL DONE, GOOD AND FAITHFUL SERVANT! MATTHEW 25:21, NIV.

BEING FRIENDS

Friends keep their commitments regardless of the sacrifices they may have to make.

In a little village in northern India lived a boy named Nalphi. Because his father was ill and couldn't work, Nalphi got a job to help support his family. His boss was Mr. Luwan, the owner of a large hemp plantation.

Nalphi's assignment was to dig irrigation ditches. For several weeks Nalphi worked hard digging ditches.

Then came the school registration day. *I sure wish I didn't have to work today,* Nalphi thought as he dug. *I wish I could go to school and learn how to read and write.*

The sun was hot and sweat poured down Nalphi's face and back. He stopped a moment to rest and watch his friends on their way to school. "Hi, Ladu!" he called out.

"Hi, Nalphi!" his friend answered. "Aren't you going to register for school?"

"I can't," Nalphi replied. "I have to work."

"Mr. Luwan will never know if you come away long enough to register," Ladu suggested.

No, I can't do that, Nalphi thought. *That would be cheating Mr. Luwan. I want to be a faithful worker like the men in the Bible story we heard about in Sabbath school. I want my boss to say "Well done!" to me.*

"I can't go," Nalphi insisted. Ladu went on without him. At the end of the day he met his boss near the warehouse.

"You're a good worker," Mr. Luwan told him. "You're also a faithful worker. You don't let anyone distract you from a job that needs to be done. I like that."

"How did you know?" Nalphi asked.

"I gave Ladu a ride to school this morning," Mr. Luwan said. "I talked to the teachers about you. Even though it's late, they're willing to register you in school. They said they could use a faithful boy to keep the buildings clean. They'll pay you. You can work for me a little after school as well. Would you like that?"

"Would I ever!" Nalphi said. "Thank you, Mr. Luwan!"

The Cost of Friendship

Jesus urged His disciples to sit down and figure the cost of being His friend. He said, "Anyone who does not give up everything cannot be My friend." A commitment to friendship is a decision to pay whatever price is necessary to remain friends.

Nelson Pendergrass and his wife made that commitment to David, a 16-year-old youth who was in trouble with the police. Shortly after he moved into their home, David stole a car. Nelson headed to the police station.

He was angry. *How dare David do this to us? We're trying so hard to give him a chance, and he goofs up again! He deserves to spend time in jail for what he's done. I feel like telling him to get out of my life!*

Then Nelson thought of a recent close call he'd had. He'd been in a bad accident. He was gasping for breath in the hospital. *It hurts too much!* he thought. *It'd be better to just stop breathing and be done with the pain forever!*

At that moment his nurse bent over his bed until her face was about six inches away. "Breathe! You've got to breathe!" she ordered.

Nelson breathed.

"Breathe! Breathe! Breathe!" she kept insisting. And each time he forced himself to obey. Because she hadn't given up on him, he was alive.

That's what I'm going to do for David, Nelson reasoned as he drove to the police station. *I won't let him destroy himself. I'll stick with him until he straightens out his life.*

Later Nelson sat beside David in his cell and said, "I'm not giving up on you, David, and I won't let you give up on yourself. We're not quitting. You're coming home. You and I and God are going to get through this together."

That commitment changed David's life. Today he's a responsible and productive person, because Nelson counted the cost of a commitment to friendship and decided he was willing to pay it.

AUG. 7

SUPPOSE ONE OF YOU WANTS TO BUILD A TOWER. WILL HE NOT FIRST SIT DOWN AND ESTIMATE THE COST? LUKE 14:28, NIV.

BEING FRIENDS

A commitment to friendship is costly. It means being friends in the tough times as well as the good times.

Defending Jeannie

**WHO WILL TAKE
A STAND FOR
ME AGAINST
EVILDOERS?
PSALM 94:16,
NIV.**

BEING FRIENDS

Friends stick up
for each other. A
friend stands up
for you against
thoughtless or
evil people.

Eleven-year-old Jeannie's shiny black hair hung loosely on her shoulders. Her slanted eyes danced with laughter as she walked beside her best friend, Radine.

Jeannie looked at her friend's blond hair, blue eyes, and pale skin and envied her. *Why did I have to be born Japanese?* she thought. *Life would be so much easier if I looked like Nadine.*

A girl on a bike rode up just then, stopping to watch the two walk down the street. She stared at the Asian girl, a look of disgust on her face.

Jeannie and Radine slowed down as they approached the girl on the bike. *I wish she wouldn't stare at me as though I were some kind of freak,* Jeannie thought. *I wish I had a magic wand I could wave to make myself invisible. Poof! And I'd disappear. I don't like being different from everyone else.*

As they walked past the staring girl on the bike, Radine growled at her, "What are *you* looking at? Haven't you ever see a Japanese person before? Anyway, she's an American citizen. She's got as much right as anybody else to walk around on the street!"

"Mind your own business!" the girl yelled as she peddled away.

"Thanks for sticking up for me," Jeannie said after they were out of earshot of the girl.

"Of course I stuck up for you!" Nadine squeezed her friend's hand. "After all, you're my friend!"

Jeannie sighed a happy little sigh. It felt good to have someone who took your side, someone who stood up to the evil people in your life. "Thanks," she said again. "Come on over to my house, and let's practice twirling our batons."

"OK, let's!" Nadine agreed. The two girls, one Asian and the other White, ran off down the street together laughing.

Things don't seem so bad when you've got a friend like Nadine, Jeannie thought as they ran. *I'm lucky to have such a friend!*

Brian's Friend

It was the end of the 1969 football season. Gale Sayers, running back for the Chicago Bears, was attending the Professional Football Writers' annual dinner in New York City with his wife. He should have been jubilant, since he was there to receive an award for being the most courageous player in pro football. Instead he felt sad.

Gale and his wife had planned to sit with friends Brian Piccolo and his wife for this event. But Brian was at home in bed, fighting a losing battle with cancer. Brian, a Chicago Bears teammate, hadn't played many games that season.

"I sure miss Brian," Gale whispered to his wife. She nodded and squeezed his hand.

He's the first White man I've ever had a close relationship with, Gale mused. *And I was the first Black person Brian had ever really known. We sure did hit it off! People are saying that ours is one of the best relationships in the history of sports.*

Gale thought of their two years playing football together. They'd been roommates on all the tours. Their interracial friendship often intrigued reporters.

Gale's wife nudged him. His name was being called. He stood to receive the George S. Halas Award as the most courageous player in pro football for the year 1969. Tears filled his eyes as he took the trophy.

He said, "You flatter me by giving me this award, but I tell you here and now that I accept it for Brian Piccolo. Brian Piccolo is the man of courage who should receive the George S. Halas Award. I love Brian Piccolo, and I'd like you to love him. Tonight, when you hit your knees, please ask God to love him too."

This story took place years ago when race riots were common, and Whites and Blacks in the United States distrusted each other. Gale Sayer was not ashamed to tell the world that he, a Black man, had a White Italian friend.

THIS IS . . . MY FRIEND. SONG OF SOLOMON 5:16, NIV.

BEING FRIENDS

True friends are loyal in public as well as in private. Friends aren't ashamed to acknowledge their friendship.

Daniel's Faith

ALL MEN WILL HATE YOU BECAUSE OF ME, BUT HE WHO STANDS FIRM TO THE END WILL BE SAVED. MATTHEW 10:22, NIV.

BEING FRIENDS

Being loyal to Jesus cost Daniel his two hands. What has your friendship with Jesus cost you? Would your faith sustain you in the face of death?

On Sunday morning, May 15, 1988, 23-year-old Daniel Segovia was at a watering hole on his father's farm in El Salvador. He and his older brother, Macario, had come there to get water for a sick cow.

"Daniel, your day has come!" someone shouted.

Daniel and Macario looked up to see four cousins running toward them waving machetes.

"We've given you until today to stop preaching the Adventist message in our community," they told him. "You haven't listened to us."

I'll give them the money I just got from selling a cow, Daniel thought. *That will distract them and allow us to escape.* Taking a large wad of money out of his pants pocket, he threw it at their feet and ran across the field toward home. His cousins followed close behind.

The cousins weren't after money; they were after blood. "Throw away your Bible, and we'll spare your life!" the leader said.

"No! I can't do that!" Daniel declared.

Two of the attackers held Daniel while they cut off the little finger of his right hand. "Now will you give up the Adventist faith?" they asked.

"I'll never do that!" Daniel affirmed.

At that, one of the cousins cut off Daniel's right hand. "Now will you give up your faith?"

"No, never!"

A cousin swung his machete and cut off Daniel's left hand. Weakened from the pain and loss of blood, Daniel fell to the ground. His cousins thought he was dead.

Meanwhile the other two cousins had attacked Macario and had left him for dead. Their work finished, the cousins fled.

Daniel's aunt had seen it all from the farmhouse on the hill. She ran to their aid and helped get them to a hospital. Both brothers survived. Later Hispanic Adventist churches in Los Angeles raised money for Daniel to get artificial arms and hands so that he could continue giving Bible studies.

"This tragedy has strengthened my faith in God," says Daniel.

No Grace, No Food

It was suppertime. Six-year-old Sarepta Myrenda Irish sat quietly waiting for someone to say the blessing as always happened at her home. She watched as the man of the house served food all around, then began to eat. Sarepta said nothing, but she didn't start to eat.

"Aren't you hungry, Sarepta?" the lady of the house asked.

"Yes," the little girl said, "but we didn't say grace."

"We don't say grace at our house," the man said.

"But why?"

"Because we aren't Christians," the man replied.

Oh, dear, now what will I do? Sarepta wondered. *Somebody has to say the blessing, and there's no one to do it but me. I never said a blessing before, but I could try.*

"I'll say grace," Sarepta said, sitting up straight and folding her hands. "Now everyone close your eyes and bow your heads while I pray."

Sarepta noticed that both the man and woman wiped their eyes after the blessing. Sarepta started to eat, but her host and hostess just sat there staring at their food. The man got up and left the table while Sarepta and the woman finished eating.

When it was bedtime Sarepta refused to get into bed without worship. "If you don't know how, then I'll show you," the little girl said. She read a few verses from the Bible and knelt down and said her bedtime prayer.

When Sarepta grew up she became Mrs. S.M.I. Henry, an evangelist for the Women's Christian Temperance Union and later a minister in the Seventh-day Adventist Church.

One day Mrs. Henry received a letter from the man at whose home she had said the blessing and conducted worship. He said: "The family altar you established in our home when you were 6 years old has never been broken up."

Sarepta understood that saying the blessing was one way to show her loyalty to Jesus, her best Friend.

I, THE MESSIAH, WILL PUBLICLY HONOR YOU IN THE PRESENCE OF GOD'S ANGELS IF YOU PUBLICLY ACKNOWLEDGE ME HERE ON EARTH AS YOUR FRIEND. LUKE 12:8, TLB.

BEING FRIENDS

When you go to a non-Christian's home to eat, do you say grace? Do you bow your head and pray before eating in a public restaurant?

Keeping Secrets

A GOSSIP BETRAYS A CONFIDENCE, BUT A TRUSTWORTHY MAN KEEPS A SECRET. PROVERBS 11:13, NIV.

BEING FRIENDS

Friends are able to keep secrets. They never betray the confidence of a friend.

Rochelle's phone rang. It was her best friend, Kathy Miller. "Hi, Rochelle! Guess what!"

"I can't imagine," Rochelle answered. "Tell me quick!"

"I'm pregnant!"

"You're what?"

"I'm expecting a baby!" Kathy almost shouted in her excitement. "After nine years Keith and I are finally going to have a baby! I can't believe it! I just found out, and I wanted you to be the first to know."

"Oh, that's wonderful!" Rochelle said. "I'm so happy for you."

"Promise me one thing," Kathy said before hanging up. "Promise that you'll not tell anyone yet. Mom and Dad are away on a trip, and I want them to know before I tell anyone else. Promise?"

"Sure, Kathy, I promise," Rochelle agreed.

But the news was just too good to keep. She told another good friend, who told another. Soon almost everyone knew that Kathy and Keith were going to have a baby. Within two days Kathy got four phone calls congratulating her. She was upset, and called Rochelle.

"I've had four phone calls from people who know I'm pregnant," she said. "You are the only person I told. I need an explanation."

"I couldn't help it," Rochelle apologized. "I know I shouldn't have, but I just told one other person, and she promised not to tell. I'm sorry, Kathy."

"Some friend you are!" Kathy said coolly as she hung up.

It was a long time before Kathy and Rochelle were friends again. It took a lot of apologies and many tears before the relationship was restored. Even after they became friends again, Kathy was careful what she shared with Rochelle. She didn't want her confidence betrayed a second time.

Someone has said that a person who has unhinged jaws has few friends. Friends must learn to keep their mouths shut tight when it comes to sharing the secrets of a friend. A friend must be able to trust in you and know that his or her secrets are safe in your keeping.

Telesomeone

My father often joked that the fastest way to get a message out was not by telephone or telegraph but by telewoman. To that I would like to add teleman, telefriend, and telesomeone. Even church members have been known to gossip.

Ann learned this the hard way. She was a new member of the church and hadn't made any close friends. Then a problem came up at work that was driving Ann bananas. *I've just got to talk to someone about this,* she thought. *I think I'll call Liz. She's been very friendly to me at church.*

Ann called Liz, who was happy to meet with Ann. Liz was an excellent listener. Liz did all the right things, so Ann knew she was really heard and understood.

"I'm so glad you let me share that," Ann said when the evening was finished. "I thought I might have a nervous breakdown, but talking to you has really helped. Keep praying for me. But please, please don't tell anyone else what I told you."

"Of course," Liz assured Ann. "I wouldn't think of sharing anything you've said."

Ann felt really good to have such a friend, until a couple weeks later someone she'd never met came up to her in the church foyer and handed her a book. "I thought this might help you," the woman said. It was a book about mental health.

What gave her the idea I have any problems with mental health? Ann wondered. Then someone else put her arms around her and said, "We're praying for you, Ann. Keep looking up!" *And what makes them think I need their prayers?* Ann was puzzled. *I need to talk to Liz about this.*

"Yes," Liz admitted. "I shared your problem in my prayer group. I didn't think you'd mind having people pray for you."

But Ann did mind. She felt betrayed, hurt, and angry. She never went back to that church. She never talked to Liz again.

DO NOT BETRAY ANOTHER MAN'S CONFIDENCE. PROVERBS 25:9, NIV.

BEING FRIENDS

Friends don't share what is told to them in confidence. Being loyal means learning how to keep your mouth shut.

In the Hole

JOAB SAID, ". . .
I WILL COME TO
RESCUE YOU."
2 SAMUEL
10:11, NIV.

BEING FRIENDS

A true friend is someone you can count on in times of difficulty.

Joab made this promise to Abishai in a time of great difficulty. He was saying, "When you get in a tough spot I'll be there for you." That's what loyal friends do for each other all the time. That's what Peter and Jerry did for their sister Lou Ann.

The three children were on their way to the meadow to pick daisies when Lou Ann remembered that they hadn't told Mother. "I'll run back and tell Mama where we're going," she said. "I'll catch up to you."

The boys hadn't gone far when they turned around and saw Lou Ann running toward them. A moment later they looked, and Lou Ann wasn't there.

"What happened to Lou Ann?" Peter asked.

"I don't know," Jerry said. "Maybe she's hiding, but I don't see any place to hide. Anyway, we'd better go back and find her."

After going a short way, Peter stopped. "Listen! I hear Lou Ann's voice."

"Peter! Jerry! Come and help me!" The voice sounded faint, yet very near at hand, almost under their feet.

"Where are you?" Jerry called back.

"I fell into the hole. Come, help me get out."

About two feet farther on they discovered the hole. It was round, and the iron top was lying nearby. Someone had opened it and forgotten to close it. The boys lay on their stomachs and peered into the darkness. They could see their sister standing in water at the bottom of the hole.

"I'll get Mama," Jerry said.

"Mama isn't home," Lou Ann said. "She went to the store. You'll have to find a way to get me out."

"I know what to do," Peter said. "Let's get Daddy's ladder."

The two boys ran off to the garage and dragged the ladder back to the hole. Carefully they put the ladder inside the hole. Lou Ann climbed out to safety.

Life is full of "holes" that we fall into from time to time. Difficulties cause us to look around for a loyal friend to help us out. Do you have such a friend?

Scout and Little Bit

Scout and Little Bit, two black Labrador retrievers, belonged to Mary Gladys Baker, an 84-year-old grandma living alone in Waurika, Oklahoma.

It was a freezing January night. Little Bit was inside, Scout outside. *I'd better change Scout's damp blanket for a dry one,* she thought. She put on some tennis shoes and stepped onto the patio. Just before reaching the dog's bed, she slipped.

"Oh, no! I can't move my legs!" Mrs. Baker said, trying to rise. "What will I do?"

Grandma Baker pulled herself along with her elbows across the rough, icy concrete. She got as far as the steps to the kitchen, but could go no farther.

"God, help me!" she cried out in despair.

Just then Scout got up from his bed and lay down against her back, protecting her from the bitter wind. Little Bit began to bark. He threw himself against the kitchen storm door again and again until the door flew open. Little Bit licked her face and laid his warm head against her cheek.

Scout got up from his place against her back. "Don't leave me, Scout," she whispered. "I'll freeze without you."

Scout went to his bed, took a corner of his blanket in his teeth, and pulled it across the patio to Grandma Baker. "Good boy! Thank you!" she said, spreading the blanket over her upper body and tucking it around her arms. Scout lay back down against her back again, stretching himself out. The warmth felt so good!

"Little Bit, come here," Grandma spoke to the younger dog. "Look at my legs. Lie down there by my left leg."

Little Bit stared at Grandma for a moment, then trotted over and lay down against her left leg. Grandma felt warm at last, cradled between the two shiny black dogs.

Early the next morning her daughter found her on the patio and rushed her to the hospital. Grandma Baker survived because of her three loyal friends—Scout, Little Bit, and God.

THE LORD HIMSELF . . . WILL BE WITH YOU; HE WILL NEVER LEAVE YOU NOR FORSAKE YOU. DEUTERONOMY 31:8, NIV.

BEING FRIENDS

God is a true friend who will never leave us nor forsake us. We can depend on Him.

The Thief

BEING FRIENDS

Have you ever been guilty of offering advice to a friend in difficulty? What a person in trouble needs isn't more advice, but a loyal friend who will come to his or her aid.

Once in a little village in Russia a thief crept into a farmer's house and emptied his storeroom.

"I've lost everything I owned," the poor farmer cried the next morning. He went to all his friends in the village and told them of his misfortune. "All my treasures are gone. All my tools are gone. All my seed is gone. I have nothing left!" he wailed.

"It's your own fault!" a neighbor remarked. "You shouldn't have boasted about how rich you are. Your boast was an invitation to the thieves."

"That's true," the farmer wept, "but now I need your help. Please help me."

"You should be more careful in the future to lock your storeroom. You need bars at your windows and locks on the doors," commented a second neighbor. "Be prepared when the thief comes again."

"Yes, yes, I must be prepared," the farmer sobbed. "But now I need your help to survive. Please help me."

A third friend spoke up, "If I were you, I'd get a good watchdog. Brave dogs would protect your property and run off the thieves."

"A good idea," the farmer moaned, "but where will I get the money to buy the dogs? I'm penniless. Please help me."

And according to the story this unfortunate farmer went home that night and wept. Dozens of his friends had given him advice, but not one was willing to offer any help. All claimed to be his friends, but none was willing to put talk into action. No one came to the aid of the poor farmer.

"I am of all human beings most miserable," the farmer said, "for not only do I have no possessions, but also I have discovered in my hour of need that I have no friends. Without friends, how is a person to survive in this evil world?"

Dora's Decision

"I have an announcement to make," Miss Warner, the teacher, said. "Our spring program is being postponed until Friday night."

Dora's heart skipped a beat, and she thought, *Now what am I going to do? I'm supposed to sing a solo in the program, but I can't do it on God's Sabbath day. I'll just have to tell her.*

"What's wrong, Dora?" Miss Warner asked as the solemn girl approached her desk.

"I can't come to the program on Friday night," she said. "That's the Sabbath."

"Oh, yes, that's right," Miss Warner said as she frowned. "I'll write a note to your mother. I'm sure she'll let you come anyway."

"I don't think it will do any good," Dora said. "My mother would never let me do it on the Sabbath."

As Dora left the room, William walked up to her. "Dora, I heard what you said to Miss Warner. You've got to come to the program. No one else can sing like you. The program will be spoiled without you there."

"I'm sorry," Dora said. "I'd like to be there, but I don't want to dishonor God on His holy day. He's my Friend, and I don't want to disappoint Him."

And Dora wasn't at the program. She was at home having sundown worship with her family.

Many years went by. One Sabbath morning a stranger came up to Dora in the church foyer. "You're Dora, aren't you?"

"Yes," she said, "but I don't think I know you."

"Do you remember when you refused to sing at the school program because it was on Friday night? Do you remember what you told me about not wanting to disappoint your Friend?" he asked.

"You must be William!" she exclaimed.

"I just wanted you to know that I was very impressed by your commitment to Jesus and the Sabbath. I decided that your kind of religion was what I wanted. Now my mother, my brother, my sister, and I are all Seventh-day Adventists."

REMEMBER THE SABBATH DAY, TO KEEP IT HOLY. EXODUS 20:8.

BEING FRIENDS

Loyalty to Jesus and His Word includes honoring the Sabbath as He's asked us to do.

Uncle Charles's Offer

**DO NOT LOVE
THE WORLD OR
ANYTHING IN
THE WORLD. IF
ANYONE LOVES
THE WORLD, THE
LOVE OF THE
FATHER IS NOT
IN HIM.
1 JOHN 2:15,
NIV.**

BEING FRIENDS

Loyalty to God
will often require
us to choose
between Him and
what the world
has to offer. We'll
never go wrong
by sticking by
God and
His truth.

John was mowing hay in the south pasture of his father's farm one warm September afternoon. He looked up and saw his Uncle Charles, the congressman, walking briskly across the field toward him. Dropping his scythe, John went to greet his uncle.

"Good to see you, Uncle Charles," John said. "I was needing a rest. Let's sit down over there in the shade of that apple tree."

"How old are you now, John?" his uncle asked.

"Seventeen."

"What are your plans for the future?" the older man wanted to know.

"I've decided to become a minister."

"I've heard rumors that you've started keeping Saturday as the Sabbath like the Jews," his uncle frowned. "Surely you aren't going to preach that nonsense!"

"I believe the Bible teaches that we should keep Saturday according to the commandment," John said. "Jesus didn't come to destroy the law, you know."

"Look, John, forget about preaching," his uncle said. "I've got better plans for you. With a mind like yours, you could do well at law. By the time I'm ready to retire, you could have my seat in Congress. I see a brilliant future for you, if you'll only forget this Sabbath business."

"My father's a poor man," John said. "I couldn't afford law school. Besides, he needs my help here on the farm."

"You needn't worry about money," his uncle declared. "I'll pay your way through any university you choose—Harvard, Dartmouth, Yale. It would be a pleasure to assist you."

"I'll give it some thought," John agreed. All afternoon John thought about the proposal. *This decision will change my whole life. I can't accept uncle's proposal because it would mean turning my back on God and His truth. I've committed my life to preaching His truth, and I won't turn back.*

John Nevins Andrews grew up to become the first Adventist foreign missionary. Andrews University is named after him.

The Chicken Farmers

AUG. 19

Rachel and Dave LeFever, with the help of 10-year-old Gwenda, 13-year-old Jeff, and 5-year-old Donovan, operated a chicken farm with 28,000 chickens that produced 17,000 eggs a day. That is, they did until the chickens got avian flu, a very contagious chicken disease.

Twenty-two birds died on Sunday, 44 on Monday, and 439 on Wednesday. Every day more and more chickens succumbed to the flu. On Saturday 1,806 died. Donovan and Jeff helped Dave load the dead chickens onto the truck and bury them in a long ditch Dave had dug. The rest of the chickens sat, not eating, not moving. It was only a matter of time until all died.

The U.S. Department of Agriculture sent inspectors, who put the remaining chickens to sleep to protect other chickens in the area. "The whole chicken house must be scrubbed clean and disinfected," the officials declared. "When you're finished call us again to inspect."

Cleaning up was no easy job. They had to blast the walls and floors with high-pressure hoses. They had to scrape 2,000 feet of conveyor chain and belt with putty knives, and scrub it with steel wool. Feeding troughs had to be scraped and scrubbed by hand. The cages and manure boards needed to be scoured until they were shiny clean. It would take weeks, maybe months, for five people to finish such a mammoth job.

Then their friends from church began arriving, more than 100 of them. They kept coming for days until the whole chicken house was squeaky clean. Other friends brought envelopes with "love gifts" of money to help them pay their bills. Within two weeks their farm passed inspection, and they were ready to get 28,000 new birds and begin again. It could never have happened without the help of loyal friends.

"When Dave and I stood in the dark the night those chickens arrived and listened to them clucking peacefully, my heart was so full it just wanted to burst," Rachel later wrote.

IF ANYONE HAS MATERIAL POSSESSIONS AND SEES HIS BROTHER IN NEED BUT HAS NO PITY ON HIM, HOW CAN THE LOVE OF GOD BE IN HIM?
1 JOHN 3:17, NIV.

BEING FRIENDS

Loyalty means sharing what we have to help a friend in need, doing what we can to ease his or her burdens.

Cemetery Adventure

WHEN YOU COME, BRING THE CLOAK THAT I LEFT WITH CARPUS AT TROAS. 2 TIMOTHY 4:13, NIV.

BEING FRIENDS

Loyalty includes faithfulness in doing for our friends what we can to help them out of a tight spot.

Paul was a prisoner when he wrote to his friend Timothy to do for him what he couldn't do for himself, bring his cloak from Troas. Teenager Lloyd of Philadelphia also had that kind of friend. He shared the following story with Joseph Bates.

While sleeping at a friend's house, they were awakened by the police, who had come to settle a fight. Afraid that they'd be arrested along with the troublemakers, Lloyd and his friend ran from the house, wearing nothing but their long nightshirts. They hid in the empty marketplace. After a while his friend said, "Stay here. I'll check things out and return with your clothes."

Shortly after his friend left, a gang of ruffians discovered Lloyd and forced him to go with them to the cemetery. There they lifted a stone slab from the vault of a rich woman who had been buried that day.

"Go down there and get her jewelry for us!" the gang leader ordered, giving Lloyd a push into the vault.

"I can't get the rings off her swollen fingers!" Lloyd said.

The gang leader handed him a knife, "Then cut off the fingers," he growled. Lloyd did as he was told and handed up the jewelry and knife. With that the gang lowered the stone slab, and Lloyd was trapped.

A few minutes later a rival gang showed up also with intent of robbing the grave. Lloyd was ready for them. As soon as the stone slab was pulled away, he jumped out of the vault in his long, white nightshirt.

Thinking it was the ghost of the dead woman, the gang members took off running, with Lloyd in his nightshirt close at their heels!

"Run, Patrick!" one of them called. "She's almost on us!"

Lloyd chased them through the marketplace, where he dropped behind and hid in the shadows. Within a short time his friend arrived with his pants and shirt.

"Am I ever glad to see you!" Lloyd exclaimed.

Love Endures

General Gilbert de Lafayette, hero of the American Revolution, took an active part in the French Revolution, which began in 1789. When he asked his troops to protect the king, they refused to obey. He was declared a traitor, fled the country, and was imprisoned in Austria.

Meanwhile the Reign of Terror began. The king and queen were sent to the guillotine along with approximately 18,000 other men and women. Among them were Lafayette's mother-in-law and sister-in-law. His wife, Adrienne, was imprisoned in Maison Delmas, where she lived in an unheated, vermin-infested garret room on the fifth floor, surviving on one meager meal a day.

In 1794 the radicals were overthrown and the remaining nobility were released, except for Adrienne de Lafayette. A committee from the new regime visited her in prison.

"Citeness, we'll release you provided you drop Lafayette's name," the spokesman said.

"It's the wise thing to do," added another. "Thousands of French women have dropped their married names and saved their lives."

"Besides, no one has heard from your husband in many months. No one knows for sure if he's dead or alive," put in a third.

"Most probably he's dead, Citeness."

"No! I refuse!" Adrienne spoke with conviction. "I believe my husband is alive, sirs. And if he isn't, then I'll bear his name all the more devotedly."

She was released a year later, an ill woman. Then began her search for Gilbert. She found him imprisoned in the fortress of Olmutz, Moravia. With much difficulty, she got permission from the emperor to share her husband's cell.

For the next two years she nursed Lafayette back to health, gladly sharing his lot as a prisoner. As a result of her hardships at Olmutz, Adrienne suffered the rest of her life from impaired breathing as well as swollen and painful arms and legs.

"I am willing to bear anything," she said, "for the joy of being with my husband."

AND NOW THESE THREE REMAIN: FAITH, HOPE AND LOVE. BUT THE GREATEST OF THESE IS LOVE. 1 CORINTHIANS 13:13, NIV.

BEING FRIENDS

Do you have a friend who doesn't know God? Are you tempted to give up? Love will keep hoping, praying, and believing for his or her salvation.

241

The Fugitive

Harriet Tubman scrambled up a rocky slope to the cemetery in Wilmington, Delaware. Exhausted, she fell among the tombstones and slept. She was awakened by a gentle tap on the shoulder.

"I'm a conductor, and I bring you a ticket for the railroad," said the Black man quietly. He was referring to the Underground Railroad, a network of people who helped fugitive slaves escape to northern states where they'd be free.

Behind some bushes Harriet dressed in the man's work clothes. She pushed her long hair up into the man's cap. She shouldered a rake and the two walked off down the road. At the bridge they passed guards who paid no attention to two Black men on their way to work.

The man took Harriet to the home of Thomas Garrett, a Quaker. He hid her in a secret room behind a bookcase in the wall.

"Thee must be very quiet," the man whispered. "My store is underneath. Patrols are looking for thee everywhere."

Two days later the Garretts gave Harriet new shoes, her washed and mended clothes, a silver dollar, and directions to the Pennsylvania border.

"When thou shalt pass the signposts, thee will be free," Thomas said.

Harriet ran along the path where he pointed. Soon she saw the signs. She passed the signs. She was free at last!

Harriet's journey had taken almost a week. She'd faced many dangers, but along the way many people, such as Thomas Garrett, risked their lives to help her escape.

Thomas Garrett cared for 2,500 runaway slaves before he was caught and brought to trial. All his property and possessions were taken from him.

"I hope you've learned your lesson," the sheriff told Thomas. "I hope never to see you caught at this again."

Thomas replied, "I haven't a dollar in the world, but if thee knows a fugitive anywhere on the face of the earth who needs a breakfast, send him to me."

JESUS CHRIST LAID DOWN HIS LIFE FOR US. AND WE OUGHT TO LAY DOWN OUR LIVES FOR OUR BROTHERS. 1 JOHN 3:16, NIV.

BEING FRIENDS

Would you be willing to risk your property, possessions, and even your life to help a friend? True friendship is willing to take risks.

The Japanese Farmer

Hirota-san was a Japanese farmer who lived on a peninsula that stuck out into the sea. Hirota-san had built his house on a hill overlooking the village down by the shore.

One evening after the rice was harvested, Hirota-san sat in front of his house as he looked down at the village. Suddenly the earth began to tremble and shake. Hirota-san didn't panic. He'd felt lots of earthquakes before. But this one shook more than usual and lasted longer than most. Then he noticed something strange about the water in the ocean.

The water backed up from the seashore for about two miles. He knew that soon it would come back in with terrible force, sending a wave 50 feet high that would destroy everyone in the village.

I must do something to warn my friends! Hirota-san thought. *What can I do? I don't have time to run down to the village. They can't hear me if I shout!* Then he thought of a plan.

Hirota-san ran to his house for matches. Quickly he set fire to his rice harvest. The dry stalks blazed quickly. Then he rang his fire gong.

When the people in the village heard his gong, they looked up on the hillside and saw his rice crop on fire. They rushed up the hill toward the fire. Everyone came—strong men, grandmas and grandpas, children, and mothers with tiny babies. All came to see the fire and do what they could to help.

Just before they reached Hirota-san's house, the people heard a mighty roaring sound. They turned around in time to see a large tidal wave rush into shore and sweep over their village, destroying every one of the houses.

Then they understood that Hirota-san had set the fire on purpose. He'd sacrificed his whole rice crop in order to save their lives. What a friend he was!

AUG. 23

DEAR FRIENDS, SINCE GOD SO LOVED US, WE ALSO OUGHT TO LOVE ONE ANOTHER. 1 JOHN 4:11, NIV.

BEING FRIENDS

True friends are much more interested in you than in their possessions. They're willing to sacrifice anything for you. Do you have that kind of friend? Are you that kind of friend?

243

Love Sacrifices

BEING FRIENDS

Loyalty includes
the idea of
sacrificing for a
friend. Watch for
opportunities to
show unselfish,
self-sacrificing
love to
someone today.

It was mealtime at Auschwitz. The men lined up to receive their meager portions of bread and gruel. They knew they'd need every ounce of energy they could get to carry stones that day.

Max Kolbe stood in line with the rest. He, too, had to haul rocks that day. But when his turn came, he quietly stepped aside and motioned for the others to take his portion.

After this happened several times, someone asked, "Max, why are you doing this? Why do you let us take your food?"

"Everyone has a purpose in life," Max answered. "Most of you want to return to your families. My goal is to give my life for others."

The other prisoners shook their heads in disbelief. *Could it have something to do with his religion?* they wondered. He was a Christian, they knew, because he'd been singled out for "special" treatment because of his witness. He'd been beaten senseless more than once as the guards tried to get him to deny his faith.

A few weeks later on July 30, 1941, five men were missing at line call. The rule was that for every man who escaped, two would die. The commandant announced 10 names, the last of whom was Francizek Gajowniczek.

"Oh, my God!" Francizek cried out. "I will never see my wife and children again!"

His fellow prisoners stood in awed silence, except for one. Prisoner 16670, Max Kolbe, marched up to the commandant. "Please, sir, may I take his place? I have no wife or children."

The men held their breath to see how the commandant would respond. He seemed for once to have lost his voice. He simply stood and stared at Max. At last he regained his composure, turned to the tenth prisoner, and said, "Return to your barracks."

Without another word Max took his place behind the other nine prisoners and walked off to cell block 13, where he faced death by starvation. Within moments songs of praise to God drifted through the camp from Max's cell.

The Attic Key

It was Sabbath morning in the Horn household. Siegfried, Elfriede, and Heinz were eating breakfast while Mrs. Horn was getting ready for Sabbath school.

"There are the police!" Heinz said.

"Quick! Follow me!" Siegfried ordered. They followed him to the back hall, where the cellar door and the attic door stood side by side. He snatched the key to the attic from the pegged board on the wall and unlocked the door.

"Upstairs!" Siegfried whispered. "And not a sound from either of you." He followed them and locked the door behind him.

Klara Horn let the policemen in. "We've come for the children to take them to school," Sergeant Schurtz announced.

The police began to search the house. The children weren't under the beds or in the closets. They weren't behind doors or in the wardrobes.

"Give us the key to the cellar!" Sergeant Schurtz said.

Klara took down the cellar key from the pegged board and gave it to him. There were no children in the cellar.

"Now, the key to the attic," he said, handing back the cellar key. Klara hung it up and looked for the attic key. It didn't seem to be there.

"Hurry! We've no time to waste!" the sergeant shouted.

She grabbed a key and handed it to him. But it didn't work. "Oh, well, they probably aren't up there anyway," the sergeant said. "Your fine is 30 marks for not sending your children to school on Saturday."

"I respect the government laws," Mrs. Horn said, "but I must first obey God's law."

As soon as they were gone, the three children emerged from the attic. Klara then realized that she'd given the police the wrong key by mistake.

Klara refused to pay the fine and was sent to jail. She had to appear in court to give her reasons for disobedience. She won the court case, which meant that children in Germany would never again have to be persecuted for keeping the Sabbath.

WE MUST OBEY GOD RATHER THAN MEN! ACTS 5:29, NIV.

BEING FRIENDS

Mrs. Horn was imprisoned for her loyalty to God and His commandments. Does your friendship with Jesus mean that much to you?

Adrift on a Raft

I LIVE BY FAITH IN THE SON OF GOD, WHO LOVED ME AND GAVE HIMSELF FOR ME. GALATIANS 2:20, NIV.

BEING FRIENDS

Because He loves us, Jesus gave His life and risked losing heaven Himself, in order to save you and me forever.

Melvin sat on the wooden raft and watched a bug crawl along one of the boards. After a while he got tired of watching it, and picked up his pole to move the raft.

"Oh, no!" Melvin cried. "The pole won't reach the bottom." While he'd been watching the bug, his raft had drifted far from shore. "Help! Help!" he shouted.

Just then his mother looked out the window of their cabin and saw Melvin's plight. She ran to the water's edge and called to him, "Melvin, come back!"

"I can't!" Melvin yelled. "The pole is too short."

Mother ran back inside and changed into her swimsuit. She jumped in and began swimming toward the raft. When she reached it, she hung on for a few minutes to rest, and then she began swimming back to shore with one hand as she held onto the raft with the other.

Melvin sat very still on the raft, watching his mother swim. It was a terrible struggle to go against the current. "Don't give up, Mother," Melvin said. "You'll make it!" After a long time she finally reached the shore.

That night at worship Mother said, "I'm glad I saw you in time. You were going farther and farther from shore. You could do nothing to help yourself. If I hadn't gone to help, you'd probably have drowned. I heard your cries for help, and I risked my life to save you."

"Thank you, Mother," Melvin said, giving her a hug. "I love you so much!"

"What I did for you is something like what Jesus has done for us," Mother continued. "We have all sinned, and because of this we were drifting further and further from God. Then Jesus came to this world to save us. He died on the cross to rescue us and bring us back to God. I love Him for saving me, don't you?"

"Yes, Mother," Melvin said. "Let's thank Him now."

I Will Find Her!

"Where's your home?" Mrs. Crowther, a missionary, asked a boy she met in the market.

"Yorubaland," the boy answered. "Portuguese men kidnapped me while I was playing with a turtle on the beach. I was released here in Freetown, Sierra Leone."

"Where's your mother?" the lady asked.

"Some people told me she left Yorubaland, but they don't know where she went. Someday I'll find her, and when I do she'll be proud of me. I'll learn to read, and I'll become someone important."

"I could help you," Mrs. Crowther offered. "If you'll help me in the house, then I'll teach you to read."

"OK," the boy agreed, and within six months he was able to read the Bible. His adoptive parents gave him a Christian name, Samuel Crowther.

He studied well and eventually became a minister. In 1864 he was ordained a bishop, the first African national bishop. He translated part of the Bible into Yoruba.

But not a day went by that he didn't think of his mother. *I wish I could find her. She'd be so happy to learn about Jesus.*

Wherever Samuel traveled, he looked at the women he met, hoping that one of them would be his mother. Years went by, and Samuel's hair began to turn gray. Then one day he arrived home to find a Yoruba woman waiting to see him.

"I want to be baptized," she said simply.

He looked at the old woman closely. Something about her made his heart beat a little faster. "Where were you born?" he asked. "Did you have a small son who was taken by the Portuguese slave traders while he sat on the beach playing with a turtle?"

"Yes," she nodded, and tears came to her eyes.

"I'm that boy," Samuel said. His dream had come true. He was able to baptize his mother. He gave her a Christian name, Hannah. "Because you're the mother of Samuel," he said.

MANY WATERS CANNOT QUENCH LOVE; RIVERS CANNOT WASH IT AWAY. SONG OF SOLOMON 8:7, NIV.

BEING FRIENDS

True love doesn't give up. It endures until the end. It hangs on to hope.

Jim's Sacrifice

LOVE OTHER PEOPLE JUST AS CHRIST LOVED US. CHRIST GAVE HIMSELF FOR US. EPHESIANS 5:2, ICB.

BEING FRIENDS

Fidelity—faithful devotion to duty, to a vow, or to a friend—is a special kind of loyalty that's seldom seen. Fidelity often requires sacrifice.

Jim crouched in the trenches as bullets flew across the wasteland dividing comrades from the enemy. He watched in horror as he saw his best friend running across the barren strip of land, dodging the bullets, trying to reach the safety of his own trenches.

"Come on, buddy! You can make it!" Jim shouted to his friend, but his words were drowned by another burst of enemy fire. His friend stumbled and fell sprawling in the mud.

Working his way over to his officer, Jim said, "My buddy just fell. May I go, sir, and bring him in?"

"No!" the officer barked. "No one can live out there. It would be suicide to try. We need you here."

"Please, sir. I'll be careful," Jim begged.

"This is war, Jim. Forget him. He's dead by now anyway."

I can't just stay here and let him die alone, Jim thought. *We've been soulmates all through this horrid war, best friends like David and Jonathan. He'll be expecting me. I've got to go.*

Disobeying the officer's orders, he climbed out of the trench and ran to his friend. He bent over him for a moment, cradling his buddy's head in his hands. Then lifting his friend to his shoulder, he staggered back to his trench. He was almost there when a bullet pierced his back. He managed the few steps to his trench and tumbled in with his friend's dead body.

"I told you not to go!" his officer scolded. "Now I've lost both of you!"

"It was worth it, sir," Jim whispered, gasping for breath.

"Worth it! How can you say that?" the officer responded. "He's dead, and you soon will be!"

"It was worth it, sir, because when I got to him, my buddy said, 'Jim, I knew you'd come.' I'm glad I didn't disappoint him, sir." With those words Jim's head fell onto his chest. He was dead.

Bail for a Friend

An old Jewish legend illustrates the truth of this verse as well as the uncommon loyalty of a true friend.

According to the story two boys grew up in the same village and were inseparable friends. But it so happened that when they were grown the two friends were separated, each living in a country hostile to the other.

"War cannot come between best friends," said one man who was a merchant. "I'll visit my friend." No sooner had he arrived in the capital city than news reached the king that a stranger was walking the streets.

"Bring him to me!" the king ordered.

So it was that the merchant was arrested and brought to trial in the king's court before he had reached his friend's home. The trial took but moments, and the king ordered, "Cut off his head!"

"Your Majesty," the merchant said, falling upon his knees, "please allow me to go home and settle my financial affairs so that my wife and children won't be destitute. I promise you that I'll return in 30 days."

"Am I a fool?" the king asked. "You'll never return."

"I have a friend in this country who will stand surety for me," the merchant said. The friend was brought to court. "I'm willing to stand as bail for this man," he said.

"If he doesn't return, you'll die," explained the king.

"I agree," the friend said.

Thirty days later the execution was scheduled for sunset. Just as the sun was setting and the friend had his head upon the chopping block, the merchant arrived. "I've come to take my punishment," he said.

Instead of being relieved, the friend declared, "No, I'll gladly take the punishment for you. Go back home!" The two argued for some time about who should be executed.

"Stop!" the king commanded at last. "I have never seen such loyalty, such friendship! You are both pardoned! I would be honored to have a friendship like yours!"

AUG. 29

HE IS DEVOID OF SENSE WHO GOES BAIL, WHO BECOMES SURETY FOR ANOTHER MAN. PROVERBS 17:18, MOFFATT.

BEING FRIENDS

Friendship counts the life and happiness of the friend to be of more importance than one's own.

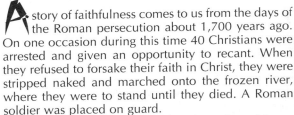

Forty Martyrs

THEY DID NOT LOVE THEIR LIVES BUT LAID THEM DOWN FOR HIM. REVELATION 12:11, TLB.

A story of faithfulness comes to us from the days of the Roman persecution about 1,700 years ago. On one occasion during this time 40 Christians were arrested and given an opportunity to recant. When they refused to forsake their faith in Christ, they were stripped naked and marched onto the frozen river, where they were to stand until they died. A Roman soldier was placed on guard.

The soldier drew his cloak tighter about him as the wintry winds whipped down from the mountains. On the ice 40 Christians huddled together, and within a short time one of their number dropped to the ice, dead.

At that moment the soldier heard the most beautiful music coming from the direction of the prisoners. Were *they* singing? Or was it angels?

"Forty martyrs and 40 crowns,
Be thou faithful unto death,
And I will give thee the crown of life."

Again and again a Christian succumbed to the biting cold and fell unconscious to the ice. And each time the soldier heard the haunting melody,

"Forty martyrs and 40 crowns,
Be thou faithful unto death,
And I will give thee the crown of life."

BEING FRIENDS

You may never face death by freezing because of your loyalty to Christ, but there will be a thousand tests of your faithfulness. Are you determined to be loyal?

One by one the Christians fell until only one remained. As he looked upon the frozen corpses of his 39 companions, he could take it no longer. He ran toward the soldier calling out, "I give up my faith. Spare my life."

All night long the soldier had stood amazed at the faithfulness of the Christians. He'd listened to the song of courage. He knew now what he'd do. Undressing, he gave his clothes to the pleading man. "Take my clothes," he said, "and I'll take your place on the ice."

He walked out to die, singing the melody he'd heard all night,

"Forty martyrs and 40 crowns,
Be thou faithful unto death,
And I will give thee the crown of life."

Loyalty Checkup

Measure your loyalty by answering the questions below. Ask God to help you be more faithful in the areas where you're weak. Loyalty is a conscious choice we make to be a better friend.

1. My friends can count on me to be there for them when they need a friend.
Never   Sometimes   Usually   Always

2. I respect people who are true to their convictions, even though I may not agree with them.
Never   Sometimes   Usually   Always

3. My friends can depend on me to keep my promises.
Never   Sometimes   Usually   Always

4. Once I've made a commitment, I stick with it regardless of the personal sacrifice involved.
Never   Sometimes   Usually   Always

5. I'm willing to be a friend in tough times.
Never   Sometimes   Usually   Always

6. I stand up for my friends against thoughtless or evil people.
Never   Sometimes   Usually   Always

7. I'm not ashamed to acknowledge my friendships. I'm a friend in public as well as in private.
Never   Sometimes   Usually   Always

8. I bow my head and say grace in a public restaurant.
Never   Sometimes   Usually   Always

9. I'm loyal to God and His truth regardless of the circumstances or the cost to me personally.
Never   Sometimes   Usually   Always

10. I can keep a secret shared by a friend.
Never   Sometimes   Usually   Always

11. I offer concrete help rather than advice.
Never   Sometimes   Usually   Always

12. I take risks for the sake of friendship.
Never   Sometimes   Usually   Always

13. I'm willing to sacrifice myself and my possessions for the sake of a friend.
Never   Sometimes   Usually   Always

14. I count the life and happiness of a friend of more importance than my own.
Never   Sometimes   Usually   Always

MOST OF ALL, LET LOVE GUIDE YOUR LIFE. COLOSSIANS 3:14, TLB.

Friends Are Trustworthy

SEPT. 1

A TRUSTWORTHY MAN IS A RARE FIND. PROVERBS 20:6, MOFFATT.

BEING FRIENDS

Six hundred people filled out questionnaires listing the qualities they look for in a friend. Eighty-five percent agreed that dependability is one of the most important qualities in a relationship.

When an ornithologist advertised in the local newspaper for help, Keith applied because he needed the money for college.

"Are you afraid of heights?" the scientist asked in the interview.

"Not really," Keith said. "Why?"

"I research the habits of birds," the man explained. "I study everything about them—what they eat, how they build their nests, and how they raise their young. Right now I'm studying an eagle that nests in the mountains near here. It's important that I get the eggs from one of these birds. I've found a nest. The only problem is that it's on a ledge under a large overhanging cliff. I need you to go over the cliff by rope and get the eggs for me. It's dangerous, but I'll pay you well. Will you do it?"

"Could I see the place first?" Keith asked.

"Sure thing," the scientist agreed. "Let's go there now."

After a long hike through the mountains, they came to a place where they could look up and see the nest on the side of the cliff. It was a drop of hundreds of feet from the cliff to solid ground. Keith pictured himself dangling over the edge of the cliff on a rope. Should the rope not hold, he'd be a goner! The prospects sent chills down his spine. Yet, he did want the job. He needed the money.

"I'll do it if my dad can hold the rope," Keith said. Of all the people Keith knew, his dad was the most reliable. He felt safe in trusting his life into the hands of his father.

To trust a friend is to rely on him or her, believe in him or her, depend on him or her, and count on him or her. Trust is knowing your friend will be there when you need him or her, year in and year out. Trust is having confidence in the dependability of a friend.

252

The Card Game

Ted Engstrom gave up poker when he became a Christian. He wasn't even tempted until one day on a long, slow train journey across the country.

"Want to join us for a game of poker?" two men across the aisle invited.

Ted hesitated a moment, arguing with his conscience. *I really shouldn't do it, but then what could be the harm of one game? I've nothing better to do, and besides, these men don't know who I am. They obviously don't think it's wrong.*

"Deal me in," Ted agreed. It wasn't nearly as much fun as he'd expected. Integrity was standing guard, making him uncomfortable. *I wish I hadn't started this game,* Ted thought, *but I might as well finish it now. I'm sure nobody on this train knows who I am, so it won't matter.*

A soldier in uniform came by just then, stopping for a moment to watch the game. He said nothing, but Ted was glad when he left.

"How about another game?" the men asked when that one was over.

"No, thanks," Ted said, paying heed to his conscience.

A few moments later the soldier came back down the aisle, stopping by Ted's seat. "Are you Ted Engstrom, who writes a column in the *Christian Digest*?"

Ted felt his neck and face grow hot. "Yes; have we met before?"

"No," the soldier admitted. "But I read your column every month. You've written some good stuff. However, I just want you to know that I've lost all respect for you."

Before Ted could think of something to say, the soldier turned and walked away. Ted closed his eyes and leaned back against the train seat. He felt overcome with pain and sadness. *I started that innocent little game to kill time,* Ted mused. *But the stakes were much higher than that. Why didn't I listen to my conscience telling me not to play that game? I've failed my Lord; I've failed myself.*

ASSIGN ME GODLINESS AND INTEGRITY AS MY BODYGUARDS, FOR I EXPECT YOU TO PROTECT ME. PSALM 25:21, TLB.

BEING FRIENDS

Integrity is the quality of being sincere, honest, and true to yourself and your principles. It's one of the qualities of a trustworthy friend.

The Bandits

SEPT. 3

Edith and Elizabeth were two women in China enjoying a leisurely trip to Chentu by boat. Suddenly the sailors began to talk excitedly.

"Something's wrong," Edith said. "Let's go find out what's happening."

The women found the captain and asked, "Is there some trouble?"

"Yes," the captain whispered. "Bandits are following us along the shore. They're just waiting for us to tie up at the next pier so that they can rob us."

"Don't worry," Elizabeth told the captain. "Our God will be with us. He'll show us what to do."

Soon they reached the pier. The sailors made the boat secure and pulled out their knives, ready to do battle.

"Put down the gangplank!" Edith ordered. "I'm going ashore."

"No, Madame! You must not! Those men are dangerous!" the captain protested, but Edith had already jumped to the dock.

The band of fierce-looking bandits rushed toward Edith. She bowed low to the leader, "Hello, honored gentlemen," she said.

Confused, the leader bowed in return.

"Thank you, gentlemen," Edith continued smiling at the astonished men. "Thank you so much for coming!"

Not sure what to do next, the men waited for their leader to speak. He, too, was speechless.

"We heard that there were terrible bandits in this country," Edith went on. "We've been so very frightened about what might happen. Now we're happy because you've come to protect us. We've nothing more to worry about. Thank you for coming!"

The leader smiled back at Elizabeth and nodded. "You're so right!" he said. "We are gentlemen as you've said. You needn't be afraid. We'll protect you from the bandits. You'll be safe in our care!"

All night the bandits squatted on the pier, guarding the two women. In the morning, they left bowing and smiling.

"I don't understand; I just don't understand," the captain said as he watched them go.

FOR OTHERS WILL TREAT YOU AS YOU TREAT THEM. MATTHEW 7:2, TLB.

BEING FRIENDS

It's a universal principle of psychology that people live up to our expectations of them. Trust inspires trust.

Annie Lou's Train Trip

Six-year-old Karen Shedd was having a wonderful time riding the fast streamlined train with her father. For a long time she sat with her nose squashed against the window, watching the countryside. Trees and houses seemed to whiz by.

A few seats away 4-year-old Annie Lou, dressing her dolls, sat with her grandmother. She climbed down from her seat, took a doll in each arm, and headed down the aisle toward Karen.

"Hi!" Annie Lou said. "What's your name?"

"Karen. What's yours?"

"Annie Lou. Want to play dolls with me?" The dark-haired girl handed one of the dolls to Karen.

"Where are you going?" Mr. Shedd asked.

"To my friend's house," Annie Lou replied.

"Where does your friend live?" he asked.

"I don't know," Annie Lou said as she tossed her brown curls.

"Then how are you going to know at which station to get off? How will you find your friend's house?" Mr. Shedd questioned.

"I don't have to know those things," she said with a big smile. "I'm with my grandma, and she knows."

"But what if your grandma took you to the wrong place?" Mr. Shedd asked.

The little girl frowned. "No! Grandma loves me. She wouldn't take me to the wrong place!"

There was no doubt about it, Annie Lou had found a friend she could trust—her grandma.

Life is like a train trip we've never taken before. We don't really know where we're going or what the future holds. It could be scary, but we don't have to be afraid. We just have to remember that we have a Friend named Jesus who is traveling with us. He knows the future. He'll show us what to do when the time comes. We can trust Him, because He loves us. With Him as our Friend we can face tomorrow with confidence.

**HE KNOWS THE WAY THAT I TAKE.
JOB 23:10, NIV.**

BEING FRIENDS

Jesus Christ is the one friend we can trust completely, for He's the only friend who will never, ever let us down. He's absolutely trustworthy, dependable, and reliable.

The Quaker Woman

The hot sun beat down on Harriet Tubman as she bent over to pick cotton. A friend caught up with her. Harriet would have liked to stop a moment to rest, but the overseer was watching. Harriet knew he'd not hesitate to use his whip on her back if she paused for but a moment.

"I've heard you're to be sold into the Deep South tonight!" her friend whispered.

Harriet's heart beat fiercely. *No, I won't let them march me off in a chain gang. I must leave tonight! From here in Maryland I've hope of reaching freedom. In the Deep South there will be no hope.*

Harriet's mind raced with plans for her trip on the Underground Railroad, the secret route slaves used to reach the North. Just a few days before, a Quaker woman had given her detailed directions and a note to deliver to the first "conductor" she'd meet.

It's incredible that White people would risk their own safety to help Black people like me, Harriet thought. *But I'm not sure I can trust any White person.*

Then she remembered what a friend had told her, "You can always trust the Quakers. They're almost as good as colored folk."

I'm going to have to trust them, Harriet reasoned to herself as she worked. *There are two things I have a right to—liberty or death. If I can't have one, I'll have the other.*

As soon as work was finished, Harriet threw some dry bread and meat into a ticking bag and grabbed a patchwork quilt she'd made. She set out in the moonlight, keeping to the shadows to avoid being seen. Her first stop was the Quaker woman's house, where she left the quilt on the doorstep. It was her way of saying thank you.

One week and many secret stops later, Harriet arrived safely in Pennsylvania. Her trust in the Quakers had been rewarded.

DO NOT TRUST A NEIGHBOR; PUT NO CONFIDENCE IN A FRIEND. MICAH 7:5, NIV.

BEING FRIENDS

Often people don't live up to our trust in them, but that doesn't mean that no one can be trusted. Ask God to help you find a trustworthy friend.

Captain Dad

James McConnell of Oklahoma City was fishing one day along the Missouri River. Suddenly he saw a barefoot boy of 9 or 10 run onto a homemade jetty not far away. He jumped up and down waving a red flag at a large steamboat coming down the river. Curious, James pulled in his line and walked over to the boy.

"That boat won't stop for you, sonny," James said.

"It'll stop, Mister," the boy answered, continuing to wave his red flag. "I know it'll stop."

"No one will see your flag," James insisted. "And even if someone did, the boat wouldn't pull over to this rickety wharf. I know these big boats. They have a schedule to keep. See, it isn't headed this way at all. It's headed on down river."

"I'm not worried," the boy grinned. "I know it'll stop."

Just then the steamboat whistle sounded twice, and its bow swerved toward the little homemade jetty. Slowly it approached the boy who had now stopped waving and stood there grinning from ear to ear. As it drew alongside the pier, someone let down the gangplank, and the boy ran up to board the boat.

"I told you, Mister," the boy called over the railing. "I knew it would stop! My dad's the captain of this boat!"

Do you have that kind of dad—one who would do almost anything to make his child happy? Can you depend on your dad as much as that boy relied on his father? If you can, then you have a picture of what your heavenly Father is like.

But maybe you aren't blessed with that kind of father. Some earthly fathers are too busy to be there for their kids. Others just aren't there because of death or divorce. It's tough not having a dad to rely on. But although your earthly father may fail you, your heavenly Father never will let you down.

AS A FATHER HAS COMPASSION ON HIS CHILDREN, SO THE LORD HAS COMPASSION ON THOSE WHO FEAR HIM. PSALM 103:13, NIV.

BEING FRIENDS

Have you made friends with your heavenly Father? He wants to see your red flag every day. He delights knowing that you're depending on Him for help.

The Man in White

"The next stop is yours, miss," the conductor said.

"Thank you," Mary responded. Gathering her belongings, she went to the door of the train to wait. The whistle blew, and the train chugged to a stop, its engine still puffing steam.

The conductor opened the door for her, and she stepped down onto the station platform. All was so dark! The station was closed for the night, and no one was waiting for her.

Now what am I going to do? Mary puzzled. Already the train was moving away from the station. *How will I find my way to the missionaries' house? I've no idea where to go.*

Mary knelt and did the only thing she could do—pray. "Dear God, I don't know what to do or where to go. But I remember that You've promised that 'the angel of the Lord encampeth round about them that fear him, and delivereth them.' You've also promised that You'd never leave me or forsake me. Lord, I need You now. Please help me!"

As she rose from her knees a man dressed in white walked up to her. "Follow me!" he ordered.

"Oh, I'm so glad you came for me!" Mary said. The road was dark, and strange noises came from the bushes on each side, but Mary could easily follow the man dressed in white.

The man in white stopped at a gate. Mary could see a light on in the window of a small house. She opened the gate, then turned to thank her guide. He was gone.

"How did you find your way out here in the middle of the night?" the missionaries asked when they opened the door and saw her standing there with her bags.

"The man you sent showed me the way," she replied.

"We didn't send anyone," they said. "We waited at the train station for three hours and decided you weren't coming today."

Then Mary knew God had sent an angel in answer to her prayer.

BLESSED BE THE LORD WHO HAS FULFILLED HIS PROMISE. 1 KINGS 8:56, TLB.

BEING FRIENDS

Jesus is our Friend. He'll keep His promises to us. We can always depend on His word.

Dad's Promise

Bill Gaither has composed more than 400 gospel songs. He's a member of the Bill Gaither Trio, which draws thousands of fans to concerts. He's also a man of integrity, one who keeps his word. He's a man you can count on to do what he says he'll do.

The phone rang at the Gaither home. Bill answered.

"Bill, do you have April 7 open?" the caller asked.

Bill looked at his calendar. April 7 had a big X marked through it. He knew this meant an at-home night with his family—wife Gloria and his children Suzanne, Amy, and Benjy.

"Sorry," Bill said. "That's my evening with the family."

"Maybe you'll want to cancel your evening at home when I tell you that the president is appearing in Grand Rapids, and they want you to do the music," the caller persisted. "What do you say, Bill? It's a chance in a lifetime!"

I'd love to do it! Bill thought. *But I've promised my kids I'd spend time with them on Monday night. I've just come home from a long trip, and I need to be with them. I've given them my word, and I think I should keep it.*

"No," Bill told his caller. "I've scheduled that night for my family. They're more important to me than the president."

To Bill Gaither family was more important than anything else. To him keeping a promise to your wife and kids was just as important as keeping it with a bank president or a recording studio.

Good relationships are based upon that kind of commitment. Good relationships are built on promises made and promises kept. What would it take to get you to break a promise to a friend? Would you do it for an opportunity to meet the president?

You might be interested in singing a song written by Bill Gaither, the dad who kept his promise. You will find one in the *Seventh-day Adventist Hymnal*, No. 526, "Because He Lives."

**GO AHEAD THEN, DO WHAT YOU PROMISED!
JEREMIAH 44:25, NIV.**

BEING FRIENDS

Friendship is founded on promises made and promises kept.

Livingstone's Word

THE JUST MAN WALKETH IN HIS INTEGRITY. PROVERBS 20:7.

BEING FRIENDS

It's very important to do what you say you'll do. Friends need to know they can depend on you come rain or shine, earthquake, or high water.

David Livingstone, the great missionary to Africa, sat talking to Sekeletu, an African chief. "I need to go on a long journey toward the setting of the sun," Livingstone told the chief. "It's more than 1,000 miles and will take many weeks. Will you give me young men to be my carriers?"

"The journey is too perilous," said one of the counselors.

"What will happen when you reach the great water?" another asked. "You'll probably get on a ship and leave our men to find their way back alone."

David Livingstone listened to their concerns. At last he said, "If you'll give me the 27 men for the journey, I promise to return with them and deliver them to their homes and families again. I pledge this to you with my life."

"Very good!" Chief Sekeletu nodded. "We know we can trust the word of David Livingstone. We've known him for years, and he's never once broken his promise to us."

"Yes! Yes!" the counselors all agreed. "We can depend on David Livingstone to keep his word."

Chief Sekeletu accompanied Livingstone and his carriers for several days' journey into the jungle to the west. At last he turned around, believing that David Livingstone would do all in his power to keep his word.

When Livingstone reached the West Coast, he found a British warship in the harbor. The commander of the vessel welcomed David Livingstone aboard.

"Why don't you go home to England for a rest?" the commander said. "All England is waiting to honor you. It would be my privilege to take you back to England."

"I'm sorry," David Livingstone replied, "but I've given my solemn pledge to Chief Sekeletu that I would personally return with my carriers and deliver them safely home again."

The ship returned to England without David Livingstone. Ever after Livingstone was referred to as "the man who kept his word."

Vince and the Car

Sixteen-year-old Vince wanted to drive the family's second car. His parents wanted him to get better grades. They thought that basing the privilege of driving on his scholastic improvement might help. They talked about it one evening.

"What do you think would be fair terms?" Dad asked. "What about straight A's, and you get to drive the car?"

"Give me a break, Dad!" Vince made a face. "Get real! Straight A's are impossible."

"You don't think you could make all A's?" Dad asked.

"I suppose I could if I wanted to, but who wants to? It's too much work."

"So tell me what you think is fair," Dad insisted.

"Straight B's?" Vince suggested. "That's pretty good since I've been getting C's and D's."

"Not good enough," said Dad.

"Then what if I make the honor roll? That would mean half A's and half B's. Would you let me drive then?"

Dad talked it over with Mom. "OK, we agree," he said. "Make the honor roll, and you can drive."

At the end of the semester Vince had two A's and four B's. "Now can I drive?" Vince asked. "I didn't quite make the honor roll, but I sure did improve!"

"We're glad you improved," Dad said, "but the bargain we made was that you make the honor roll; no honor roll means no car."

Vince wasn't very happy about it, but he admitted that it was fair to stick by their agreement. He showed he was learning the meaning of responsibility when he said, "It's OK. I haven't earned the car yet. But I will. I'm going to be on the honor roll. You'll see."

However, the next semester Vince didn't make the honor roll either. And he didn't get the car. His parents insisted that he live up to their agreement. Do you think they did the right thing?

SEPT. 10

A PERSON WHO IS TRUSTED WITH SOMETHING MUST SHOW THAT HE IS WORTHY OF THAT TRUST.
1 CORINTHIANS 4:2, ICB.

BEING FRIENDS

Friendship carries with it a certain amount of responsibility. If a relationship is to do well, each person must be able to count on the other person to live up to the agreements.

Late for Work

FOR THERE IS A
PROPER TIME
AND PROCEDURE
FOR EVERY
MATTER.
ECCLESIASTES
8:6, NIV.

BEING FRIENDS

Friends have a
right to expect us
to meet our
appointments.
Reliability is a
character trait
appreciated
by parents,
teachers, and
work supervisors
as well as
our friends.

After school Fred Mote headed home. He had no time to waste. He needed to change his clothes, get the address where his dad was working, and make it to the work site by 4:00.

"Fred, I expect you to be punctual," Mr. Mote lectured when he offered him the job. "Time wasted can never be regained. See that you're on time for work. Reliability is necessary in the workplace. I've no time to go looking for you. It's your responsibility to be on time for work. See that you are."

It was nearly 4:00 by the time Fred reached the railway overpass two blocks west of his home. He'd just crossed over the bridge when a schoolmate called out, "Hey, Fred, hear the train!"

Fred could hear the engine struggling up the hill before it came chugging into sight.

"We dare you to catch a ride on the caboose!" one of the boys said. "I'll bet you can't do it!"

"I'll bet I can!" Forgetting his work appointment, Fred accepted the challenge. Dropping his books, he ran down the embankment. A long line of rail cars thundered by, shaking the earth beneath his feet. As the caboose came into view, Fred ran for it, reaching out his hand to grab a handrail.

"Fred! Come here this minute!" Fred's arm froze in midair. The caboose rumbled by. The crowd of boys and girls gathered on the overpass began to laugh and jeer. Fred turned and ran up the bank to his father.

"You're late for work!" his father frowned.

"Sorry," Fred said. "They dared me to do it."

"It doesn't matter what they did," Mr. Mote replied. "You have a job, and I'm depending on you to be there. I'll teach you to try that stunt again." With that he hit Fred's backside with his carpenter's rule, breaking it into several pieces.

Fred never forgot his lesson in reliability.

John's Good Name

William scraped his porridge bowl and spread a slice of his mother's homemade bread with butter and jam. Outside an icy wind whipped around the corners of the farmhouse. It had been snowing all night; now sleet beat against the windows.

"I'm glad we don't have to go far in this weather!" Mother exclaimed as she stood a moment looking out at the stormy weather.

"Well, I guess we won't see anything of John Haws today," Father added. "He promised to pay me today for that masonry work I did, but I wouldn't blame him for not wanting to ride nine miles to our place in this weather."

"It's no weather to be out and about in," Mother agreed.

"Yippee! It's a snow day!" William put in.

The whole family stayed near the fire most of the morning while the storm raged outside. Then just about noon, someone pounded on the kitchen door. Father went to see who it was.

"Why, John Haws! Whatever are you doing out in this weather?" he exclaimed. "Come in and warm yourself by the fire. You must be nearly frozen. I didn't expect you on such a day."

"Didn't I give you my word that I'd come today?" Mr. Haws asked.

"Well, yes, you did," Father agreed. "But I could have waited until the storm was over. I wouldn't have minded at all."

"I gave my word to you," Mr. Haws replied. "I keep my promises regardless of the weather."

"But it was such a small amount," Father protested. "I could have waited a month for it without any harm."

"Ah, but I needed to keep my word," Mr. Haws said. "That's the issue. A man ought to do what he says he'll do."

"You certainly do have a reputation for keeping your word," Father said. "No one ever doubts the word of John Haws. We know you're a man who keeps his promises. We can depend on you."

A GOOD NAME IS MORE DESIRABLE THAN GREAT RICHES; TO BE ESTEEMED IS BETTER THAN SILVER OR GOLD. **PROVERBS 22:1, NIV.**

BEING FRIENDS

To be known by your friends as a dependable person, one who keeps promises, is indeed better than gold or silver.

263

Gerhardt the Shepherd

SEPT. 13

A FAITHFUL MAN WILL BE RICHLY BLESSED. PROVERBS 28:20, NIV.

BEING FRIENDS

Your faithfulness may not always be rewarded with fine gifts. More often the blessing of faithfulness is the gift of friendship.

In a lovely green valley in Germany lived a young shepherd boy named Gerhardt. One day as he watched his sheep graze near the edge of the forest, a hunter came out of the woods and asked, "How far to the closest village?"

"Six miles," the boy replied. He pointed to a path that was barely visible among the bushes. "Follow that sheep trail."

"I'm hungry and tired," the hunter sighed. "I'm already lost, and my guide has disappeared. Will you please guide me there?"

"No, sir, that isn't possible," the boy spoke politely. "I can't leave my sheep. They'll stray into the forest and may be killed by the wolves."

"But these aren't your sheep. Your boss won't miss one or two. Show me the way, and I'll pay you more money than you'll earn in a year of watching sheep."

"No," the shepherd declared. "My master has trusted me with his sheep. He pays me to stay with them. I've promised to watch over them carefully."

"At least be so kind as to let me watch your sheep while you go into the village and bring me a guide," the hunter begged.

"Again I must say no," the shepherd answered. "The sheep don't know your voice. They wouldn't listen to you. I must be faithful to the trust my boss has in me. I'll stay with the sheep."

"You're a faithful lad," the hunter said. "Show me the way, and I'll try to follow the path."

"Before you go, please share my lunch," the boy offered.

"I'll not forget you," the hunter said as he left.

The hunter happened to be a wealthy duke who owned all the land for as far as the eye could see. He was so impressed by the shepherd boy's faithfulness that he gave him a nice home and paid his expenses to attend the university. Gerhardt and the duke became friends because of Gerhardt's faithfulness.

Claiming God's Promises

"The pantry is nearly empty," the matron reported. "And need I remind you that the rent is due?"

"The Lord will provide," George Mueller said cheerfully. "He's promised to supply all our needs. He won't fail us now."

At that moment he had only 27 pence and a ha'penny to feed several hundred children.

Just then a letter arrived. George opened it and read, "Have you any present need for money? I know you have vowed to ask no one but the Lord to supply your needs. However, would it not be all right to answer when asked? How much money do you need?"

George Mueller shook his head. He took up a pen and wrote the following note. "I will not speak of the state of our funds. The main object of my work is to show that God is real and that He will keep His promises. Thus far we have told no one of our needs except God. We will not start now."

Having mailed the letter, George Mueller fell on his knees in his study. "Lord, we're in desperate straits. We have only 27 pence and a ha'penny. Please speak to this man Yourself and tell him to send us money."

When the man got George Mueller's letter, he felt impressed to send 100 pounds at once. When it arrived, there was not one penny in the Mueller household to buy bread for the next meal.

Once a friend asked George, "What would you do if God didn't send help in time?"

"I can't imagine that will ever happen," George replied. "God has promised to supply all our needs. God never tells a lie. He's dependable."

George Mueller took care of more than 10,000 orphans during the 63 years he trusted only in God to supply his needs. Not once did God fail to keep His promise.

HE WHO PROMISED IS FAITHFUL. HEBREWS 10:23, NIV.

BEING FRIENDS

God is a friend we can depend upon. He'll never let us down. He's given us more than 3,000 promises in the Bible. We can count on Him to keep His word.

Brother Bryan

BEING FRIENDS

Being a friend of God means keeping the promises we make to Him.

It was nearly midnight. The streets of Birmingham were empty except for James Bryan walking home after a visit with a friend. It was so quiet he could hear the crunch of his shoes on the sidewalk.

Crossing a dark alley, James thought he heard something else. He whirled around to check it out. He felt the barrel of a pistol in his stomach as the shadowy figure commanded, "Hands up! Don't move, or I'll shoot!"

James raised his hands and tried to peer into the face of his assailant to see if it was someone he knew. The robber emptied James's pockets. All he found was a handful of change and a cheap watch. He swore as he jammed them into his own coat pockets.

"Brother, let us pray!" James said.

Startled, the robber dropped his gun and stood there staring at the man with the beard who began praying, his hands still raised toward heaven.

"Lord, bless this man. I don't know his name, but he needs You, Lord. He needs to know You love him, so bless him. Lord, I know You're looking down upon the city of Birmingham tonight and see us and all Your children in this city. Bless everyone tonight, Lord. Bless those who are sick, the suffering, the hungry, the poor, and the afflicted, but especially bless my brother here whom I've just met. Amen."

The robber started fumbling in his pockets. In a moment he found the watch and handed it back to James. He found the coins and returned them. "You can go now," the robber said gruffly and disappeared into the shadows of the alley.

Pastor James Alexander Bryan walked on home, smiling to himself. He felt satisfied that he'd lived up to his promise to God that he'd pray with anyone who would let him. So impressed were the people of Birmingham with Pastor Bryan's prayers that they had a statue carved in his honor. It showed him on his knees praying for the people of Birmingham.

Chair for Sale

We were living in Bangalore, India, at the time. As we prepared to leave on an extended furlough, we decided to sell a number of items in our house. One of these was a black leather chair.

Our newspaper ad brought a steady stream of wealthy Indians to our home in search of bargains on foreign-made items. The black leather recliner was one of the first to go. A Muslim man paid our asking price, 700 rupees. We marked it "sold," and the buyer continued browsing through our other items.

A few minutes later a wealthy Hindu merchant approached me. "How much for that black leather reclining chair?" he asked.

"Sorry," I said. "It's already sold."

"How much did you get for it?" he asked.

"Seven hundred rupees," I replied.

"I want that chair very much," the merchant continued. "I'll give you 800 rupees for it. You can give the other man's money back to him. The chair is still here."

"No, it's already promised," I said.

"Then, I'll give you 1,000 rupees."

"Sorry."

"What about 1,500 rupees?"

"No."

"Two thousand rupees, and that's my final offer," the merchant said.

"My answer is still no," I replied.

"Why? I don't understand," he said, looking puzzled.

"The other man has given me money. I've given my word. It wouldn't be honest or right to go back on my word just for the sake of more money. My conscience wouldn't allow me to do that."

"Interesting," the merchant commented. "I've never met anyone who wouldn't change his mind if the price was high enough."

A few moments later the original buyer showed me a stack of money. "He gave me 2,000 rupees for the chair," he said. "He can have it." That man made 1,300 rupees profit before the chair left my house. It was extra money we could have had. Do you think we did the right thing?

A GOOD MAN IS GUIDED BY HIS HONESTY. PROVERBS 11:3, TLB.

BEING FRIENDS

Those who are friends of God will choose the way of honesty and integrity even if it means a loss to themselves.

The Man With a Lantern

SEPT. 17

HAVE YOU CONSIDERED MY SERVANT JOB? . . . HE IS BLAMELESS AND UPRIGHT. . . . AND HE STILL MAINTAINS HIS INTEGRITY.
JOB 2:3, NIV.

BEING FRIENDS

A healthy, lasting relationship is based on honesty and truth.

A barefoot old man in a long, flowing robe walked the streets of Athens, an ancient Greek city. He carried in his hand a lamp and appeared to be searching for something. This would have been a very ordinary sight had it occurred at night, but it was broad daylight, and the sun was shining brightly overhead.

People watched Diogenes, the old philosopher, with amusement. They pointed and laughed at him groping about the street as though it were midnight instead of noon. Some touched their heads as though to say, "Poor old man; he doesn't know daylight from darkness. Something must be missing upstairs!"

Curious as to what he could be searching for, a crowd began to follow him down the street. He stopped and held the lamp up close to the face of first one person and then another, studying their faces carefully.

"What are you looking for, Diogenes?" someone asked at last.

"An honest man," Diogenes replied, and walked on. According to the legend, Diogenes never did find what he was looking for.

Would Diogenes find an honest person were he to walk down the streets of your town, the halls of your school, the aisles of your church? If he found an honest person, what would that person be like?

The dictionary says that such a person would be held in respect, honorable, one who would not cheat, lie, or steal. That person would be known to be truthful and trustworthy, free from deceit. He or she would show fairness and sincerity. He or she would be what he or she seems to be—genuine, real. It would be a person of integrity, a person like God's friend Job.

A recent survey in the United States revealed that three out of every five people think lying is OK. It certainly isn't easy to be honest and truthful in a relationship at all times. Yet it's even more painful to trust someone and then to discover he or she has been lying.

Studies show that dishonesty is one of the main reasons relationships fail.

The Most Honest Man in Town

The train puffed into the station at Battle Creek, Michigan, early one morning in 1852. A 60-year-old man in a dark suit got down from the train and headed for the post office.

The Lord has someone He wants me to meet here, Joseph Bates reasoned as he walked along the streets of Battle Creek. *I was planning to meet some believers in Indiana, but I know the Lord has impressed me to come here instead.*

"Good morning!" Joseph Bates greeted the postmaster. "I'm looking for the most honest man in Battle Creek."

"David Hewitt is the man you want. He's a traveling salesman who always gives an honest deal. He lives on Van Buren Street, near Cass."

"I'm new to the town," Joseph Bates explained. "Just came in on the train this morning. Which way is Van Buren?"

"Cross the bridge over the Battle Creek River. Van Buren is just beyond it. Follow it to the west. Before you reach Cass you'll come to Hewitt's house."

Within a few minutes Joseph had found the house. He knocked on the door, and David Hewitt answered.

"I've been told you're the most honest man in town," Joseph began. "If this is true, I have some important truth to share with you."

"Come in," Mr. Hewitt invited. "Have you had breakfast?"

"No," Joseph admitted. "I was anxious to meet you."

"Then you must join us. We were just sitting down. After we've eaten we'll hear what you have to say."

After breakfast Joseph Bates hung up his prophetic charts and took out his Bible. He explained the prophecies of the soon return of Jesus. After lunch he gave them a Bible study on the seventh-day Sabbath truth. By 5:00 the most honest man in Battle Creek was convinced that Joseph Bates was telling the truth. He and his family kept the next Sabbath. They were the first Seventh-day Adventist family in Battle Creek.

SEPT. 18

BE BUSY WITH YOUR OWN AFFAIRS AND DO YOUR WORK YOURSELVES. . . . THEN THE WORLD OUTSIDE WILL RESPECT YOUR LIFE.
1 THESSALONIANS 4:11, 12, PHILLIPS.

BEING FRIENDS

David Hewitt's honesty helped him become a friend of Joseph Bates and a friend of God.

Cold Vegeburgers

**FOR WE ARE
TAKING PAINS TO
DO WHAT IS
RIGHT, NOT
ONLY IN THE
EYES OF THE
LORD BUT ALSO
IN THE EYES
OF MEN.
2 CORINTHIANS
8:21, NIV.**

BEING
FRIENDS

Integrity is the
quality of being
honest with
yourself, doing
what is right even
if no one would
ever find out.

Ten-year-old Gary placed the bag of hot vegeburgers on the kitchen table. His mom brought out the pickles and chips. They said the blessing and passed around the vegeburgers purchased from a local restaurant.

Gary took a bite of his vegeburger then put it down. Reaching his hand into his jeans pocket he brought out a handful of bills and change and shoved them across the table to his father. "Here's the change," he said.

Dad counted the change, then counted it again. "Is some of this money yours, son?" he asked.

"No," Gary said. "All I had was the $20 you gave me, why? Is something wrong?"

"Sure is," Dad said, getting up from the table. "We got too much change. They gave us a five when they should have given a one-dollar bill. We've got to take it back."

"Why, Dad? That's our luck, right?"

"Wrong. Vegeburgers don't come free to anyone. Someone has to pay for them," Dad replied.

"And we're the ones with the vegeburgers," Gary said.

"The ones who eat them should pay for them," Dad continued. "We've got to take the money back because it belongs to them, not to us. It simply isn't right to do anything else. To keep the money would be stealing."

When they reached the restaurant, Gary went inside and handed the clerk the $5 bill. "You gave us a five when we should have had a one," he said. "We owe you $4."

"Thank you so much!" the lady said, smiling at Gary as she punched a key on the cash register and handed him back a one-dollar bill. "I would have been short at the end of my shift, and I'd have had to make up the missing money. I'm sure glad you came back!"

"Me too," Gary smiled back. Inside he felt really good because he had done the right thing.

They went home then and ate their cold vegeburgers.

The Ball Moved

t was Tom Watson's first state golf tournament. At one of the greens he laid his putter down behind the ball. The ball moved slightly.

Oh, no! Tom thought, looking quickly around. *I'm sure no one saw that. Should I tell the officials? If I do, it will cost me a stroke, and I might lose the game. But if I don't tell, then I'll have to live with my own dishonesty.*

Tom walked over to the official. "My ball moved," he said.

"That will cost you a stroke, Tom," the official replied.

"That's OK," he said, walking back to pick up his club and finish his putt. Tom's honesty caused him to lose that hole. His personal integrity was more important to him than his desire to win. In spite of that hole, Tom won the match. He went back to win the state golf championship three times.

Those who knew Tom Watson considered him more than a golf champion; they considered him a champion in the game of life. His friends knew that Tom was someone they could depend on to always do the right thing, regardless of the personal cost.

What if you were in a tennis match with no linesmen or umpires? The ball is just inside the back line. Your opponent can't see where it landed, and you have to call the shot. Would you be tempted to call it out when you knew it was in? What would be the honest thing to do? What if you called it wrong in order to win? How might that affect your friendship with your opponent in the future?

What if you were in a hockey match, and you hit the puck toward the goal, hoping it would go in? You see a team member deflect it, directing it past the goalie to score. The announcer says you scored the goal. The crowd is roaring its approval. You know it belongs to your teammate, not to you. What would you do?

NOW WE PRAY TO GOD THAT YOU WILL NOT DO ANYTHING WRONG.
2 CORINTHIANS 13:7, NIV.

BEING FRIENDS

To be dishonest, even in little things, lays the foundation of distrust that will eventually destroy a relationship.

God Sent a Wind

**HE HAS GIVEN US HIS VERY GREAT AND PRECIOUS PROMISES.
2 PETER 1:4, NIV.**

While still in his teens, Hudson Taylor felt certain God wanted him to go to China as a missionary. Wanting to learn more about China, Hudson borrowed a book from a local minister.

"So you want to go to China?" The minister sounded skeptical. "And how do you propose to do that? Where will you get the money for your ticket and for your support?"

"I intend to trust God for all my needs."

"Ah, my boy, as you grow older you'll get wiser than that," the old minister said.

Hudson Taylor was not discouraged. He told the Lord, "If You want me to go to China, You'll have to provide the money for me to go. I'll trust You to do it."

By the time Hudson was 21 years old he was on the ship *Dumfries,* bound for China. At one point of the journey there was great excitement. "There is no wind and a strong current is carrying us toward a sunken reef," the captain told him. "The reef will rip the ship apart."

"That won't happen," Hudson assured him. "I've prayed, and God has assured me that we'll arrive safely in China."

"You're crazy!" an officer laughed, pointing to the blue cloudless sky. "No clouds, no wind. We're helpless. We'll die."

"Never mind," Hudson said. "God is going to send a wind to take us away from that island. You'd best let out the corners of the mainsail."

"It won't do any good," the officer protested.

"Already a wind is blowing."

"It won't last," the officer scoffed.

"Let down that mainsail!" Hudson kept at him. Finally the officer complied. Immediately a strong wind developed, taking them safely beyond the dreaded island.

"Jehovah-jireh," Hudson declared. "The Lord provides."

Later Hudson Taylor wrote: "From the beginning of my Christian life I was led to feel that the promises were very real, and that prayer was a sober matter-of-fact transacting of business with God."

BEING FRIENDS

Being a friend of God means to trust in Him, knowing that He'll keep His promises.

The Bulldogs' Trophy

Every member of the Rockdale Bulldogs, a basketball team from Conyers, Georgia, was excited. A gleaming trophy sat in the new glass trophy case outside the high school gymnasium. They were the winners of the Georgia boys' basketball tournament.

Coach Cleveland Stroud had called the team together to give them some bad news. "We've just discovered that one of you who was scholastically ineligible played 45 seconds in our first postseason game. We didn't know he was ineligible at the time, but that's our mistake. We should have been more careful."

"So what?" one of the players asked. "Did it make a difference in the scoring of the game?"

"No," Coach Stroud admitted. "But that's not the point. It's against the rules. By breaking the tournament rules we're disqualified to receive the trophy."

"Do the tournament officials know about it?" someone asked.

"No, but we've got to tell them," the coach said. "We've got to do what's honest and right and what the rules say. People will forget the scores of the basketball games; they won't ever forget what kind of stuff we're made of. We're going to be honest and report our mistake. I want you guys to know, and I want your support in doing what's right. The state is sure to demand that we send the trophy back. You'll all have to bring back the medallions you got for winning. I'm sorry, but right is right."

The team members nodded. "We're with you, Coach," the captain said. "Do what's right."

When the news became public, all 8,000 people of Conyers, Georgia, rallied around their team and coach. They were glad their school hadn't tried to cover up their mistake. The Bulldogs lost the state trophy and the medallions, but the newspaper put on a campaign to get them a new trophy and medallions to commemorate their winning season.

The Bulldogs are proud of their new trophy, for it's a tribute not only to their skill but also to their honesty.

LET US WALK HONESTLY, AS IN THE DAY. ROMANS 13:13.

BEING FRIENDS

It may be hard to tell the truth, but friends will appreciate us more for doing it.

273

The Casserole

BEING FRIENDS

Deception, even
when meant for
someone's good,
is still a lie, and
it destroys trust,
the foundation
of a good
relationship.

Tammy and Richard had been married only a few days when she tried out a new casserole recipe she'd clipped from a magazine. She set the table with a pink linen tablecloth, her prettiest plates, and wedding silver. She lit candles and called her new husband to supper.

"Mmmmm! It looks delicious!" he said, giving Tammy a hug. "And it smells wonderful, too."

After the blessing, Richard piled lots of the casserole onto his plate. He took a bite and nearly gagged. It tasted awful! *She's worked so hard on this meal,* he thought. *I hope she doesn't ask if I like it.*

But of course she did. "Honey, do you like my new casserole recipe? I made it just for you!" Her eyes were shining with love.

Richard took a deep breath and swallowed. *I just can't tell her the truth. It would hurt her too much,* he reasoned. After a drink of juice he said, "Oh, yes! I like the casserole very much. It's really good!"

Believing that he really liked it, Tammy made the casserole almost every week. And because she was new at cooking and unable to cut down the recipe, there was always lots of it left over. They ended up having it for several days in a row.

After a few weeks of struggling through his meals of a casserole he couldn't stand, Richard decided he could bear it no longer. In anger, he told Tammy the truth. "I hate your cooking. It makes me gag! I don't ever want to see this casserole as long as I live!"

Tammy burst into tears. "You lied to me!" she cried as she ran from the room. "I'll never believe you again!"

It was such a little lie. Richard thought he was doing it for a good reason. But by choosing to deceive he only made matters worse. That little deceit caused a rift in the relationship that was a long time in healing.

Honest Abe

The New Salem, Illinois, post office was closed in 1836. On the last day of business the postmaster sat down and figured his accounts. According to his calculations he owed the United States government $17.

Seventeen dollars may not seem like much today when a person can easily earn that much in a few hours. However, in 1836 that was approximately four months' wages for the postmaster, whose annual salary was $55.70.

The young postmaster had received word that he was to send the post office records to the postmaster general in Washington, D.C. He would check them over and send an agent to collect the money due the government. Therefore, the young man took the $17 and tied it in an old cotton rag and carefully stowed it away in a corner of an old trunk.

Several years went by, and no one came to settle the accounts of the New Salem post office. The ex-postmaster was now a struggling young lawyer who wasn't doing very well. He was often broke, but not once did he open the cloth rag where the $17 was kept.

Then one day a government agent walked into the law office of the former postmaster of New Salem. "We've checked the records," he said. "You owe the government $17. I've come to collect."

The lawyer nodded, crossing the room to an old trunk. He lifted out a yellowed rag tied with a string and placed it in the hands of the agent. Opening the packet, the man counted out $17.

"Do you mean to say this is the same money you took from the post office till the day it closed?" the astonished agent inquired.

"I never use any man's money but my own," he said.

The agent took the money and left. The young lawyer who watched him leave was Abraham Lincoln. Nearly 25 years later he became president of the United States.

How does the experience of Abraham Lincoln relate to Luke 16:10? Can you think of something from your own life that relates to this verse?

SEPT. 24

WHOEVER CAN BE TRUSTED WITH VERY LITTLE CAN ALSO BE TRUSTED WITH MUCH. LUKE 16:10, NIV.

BEING FRIENDS

Integrity is tested in the small interactions of everyday life.

Stolen Stones

**THOU SHALT
NOT STEAL.
EXODUS 20:15.**

BEING
FRIENDS

Being friends
with someone
doesn't mean that
you can help
yourself to what
belongs to him or
her. If you want
to remain friends,
you won't take
things without
permission.

The Franklin family was vacationing at the beach. One morning young Benjamin and his friends were having a great time catching fish left in the pools after the tide had gone out.

"I've got a good idea," Benjamin announced. "Why don't we build a stone dike so that we can catch the fish without getting our feet wet?"

"Splendid!" agreed his friends.

"But where will we get the stones?" asked one boy. "I don't see many stones on the beach."

Benjamin pointed to a house that was under construction not far away. "There's a whole pile of stones. Let's use them."

"Are you sure it's OK?" someone asked.

"That man is our friend," Benjamin said. "I don't think he'll mind at all. We aren't going to hurt the stones. We're only going to play with them."

The boys ran to the pile of rocks and began lugging them down to the beach. Before long they had built a fine dike and were enjoying themselves immensely.

In the midst of their fun. Josiah Franklin arrived on the beach and inspected the dike. "You've done a fine job," he commented. "But where did you get the stones?"

"Over there," Benjamin said, pointing toward the new house.

"Do the stones belong to you?"

"No, Father," Benjamin sighed.

"Did you ask for permission to use the stones?"

"No, Father."

"My son, you're a thief," his father said. "Do you know what the eighth commandment says?"

"Yes, Father. 'Thou shalt not steal.'" Benjamin was feeling ashamed now for what he'd done.

"You've broken that commandment," Mr. Franklin observed sadly. "My son is a thief."

Benjamin and his friends tore their dike apart and returned the stones to the owner of the new house. Ever afterward Benjamin Franklin was known for his honesty and trustworthiness. Because of his integrity, Benjamin Franklin made many friends not only for himself but for his country.

Facing Father

The Lord and Bob Brooks felt the same way about lying lips. Seven-year-old Charles knew that, but it didn't make it any easier to face his father. He'd told a lie, and his dad knew he'd done it. Still Charles refused to tell the truth, thinking up a new lie each time to cover up for what he'd said before.

Charles was miserable. *I wish I hadn't told that first lie. It just gets harder and harder to cover up. I wish Dad would just forget it.*

But Bob Brooks wasn't about to forget it. He hated lying more than any other sins. He himself was a man of his word. Businessmen said about him, "You can trust Bob Brooks. He keeps his word!" Bob wanted his 11 children to have the same reputation, so he wasn't about to let up on young Charles. He kept on his case for four days.

On the fourth day he said, "Charles, are you ready to tell me the truth now?"

Charles looked at his father and saw love and concern in his eyes. *I'm sick of this lying business,* Charles reasoned. *Dad's going to keep at me until I tell the truth, so I might as well confess and take my whipping.*

Bob Brooks listened to his young son's story. He smiled his approval. "That's what I wanted to hear," he said. "I hope you've learned your lesson."

I can't believe it! He didn't even whip me! Charles thought. *I almost wish he had. Anyway I've sure learned my lesson. After this I'll try to always tell the truth the first time around.*

Had Charles D. Brooks not learned his lesson, it's not likely he would have grown up to be an evangelist and speaker-director of the *Breath of Life* television series. Today Charles Brooks has friends around the world because he learned the lesson of trustworthiness.

> **THE LORD DETESTS LYING LIPS, BUT HE DELIGHTS IN MEN WHO ARE TRUTHFUL. PROVERBS 12:22, NIV.**

BEING FRIENDS

One falsehood leads to another until such a tangled web of lies is woven that it's hard to extricate oneself. It's better to tell the truth the first time around.

Long Division

EVEN A CHILD IS KNOWN BY HIS ACTIONS, BY WHETHER HIS CONDUCT IS PURE AND RIGHT. PROVERBS 20:11, NIV.

BEING FRIENDS

When we're dishonest, we disappoint not only our earthly friends, but our heavenly Friend as well. Honesty is still the best policy.

It was a sunny October afternoon, and Miriam could think of lots of things she'd rather be doing than 30 boring long division problems. Since no one was looking, Miriam found the answers to the problems in the back of her math book and copied them.

Since they were long division problems, she knew she'd have to show all her work. She hastily multiplied the numbers and wrote them below, not bothering to check if she'd done it correctly. It looked fine, and she knew the answers were right.

I'll get by with it, Miriam thought. *Why spend all afternoon doing long division when I could be out playing in the sunshine?*

"I'm done, Gammie," Miriam called to her grandmother as she ran out to play.

After supper Grandpap went to prayer meeting without checking Miriam's homework. She thought no more about her math assignment until the next morning when she was awakened very early by her grandfather.

Miriam rubbed her eyes and shivered in the coolness of the morning as Grandpap led her to the kitchen where he faced her with her crime. "What's the meaning of this?" he asked. "I checked all your work after returning from prayer meeting last night. You copied the answers, didn't you?"

Miriam began to sob. "Yes, Grandpap, I copied. I'm sorry."

"Sit right down here, and do every problem from beginning to end," Grandpap ordered. "I'm surprised that you'd disappoint Jesus by doing such a thing. I'm shocked that you'd even think of it, Miriam. Never forget that 'honesty is the best policy.'"

Miriam never forgot that lesson. It stuck with her through eight more years of school, four years of college, and then graduate work at the university. She was seldom tempted again.

You probably have heard of Miriam Wood. She's written many books and has written a regular column in the *Adventist Review,* answering people's questions about life.

Storm at Sea

It was Saturday morning on the *Spree*. Dwight L. Moody and his son were resting in their bunks, as were most of the ship's passengers. Suddenly they heard a splintering crash. His son jumped out of bed and rushed to the deck. In a few minutes he returned.

"Father, things are serious," he said. "The shaft has broken, and the vessel is sinking. You'd better dress and come up on deck."

Once there, Dwight stood silently with the 700 other passengers, feeling helpless as water continued to flood the ship. By noon the sailors had been able to stop water from entering the ship, but already the bow was high in the air, and the stern was sinking low in the water. The Atlantic Ocean was rough, rolling the ship from side to side.

They were still afloat as the sun went down. Dwight watched as the ship fired rockets into the dark night sky. No ship answered their SOS messages. All night the ship drifted. All day Sunday no help came.

That evening Dwight gathered the passengers for a prayer meeting. He read Psalm 91 and prayed, claiming the promise of verse 11: "He shall give his angels charge over thee, to keep thee in all thy ways."

He also read Psalm 107:20, 23, which says: "He sent his word . . . and delivered them from their destructions. . . . They that go down to the sea in ships, that do business in great waters."

"Is that really in the Bible?" a German passenger asked. "It seems written for this very experience we are having."

"Indeed it is. Come, see for yourself," Dwight said.

After the prayer meeting Dwight went to bed and slept peacefully, assured that God would keep His promises and deliver them. About 3:00 on Monday morning his son awakened him. "Come on deck, Father! A ship has spotted us and is on its way to rescue us."

The steamer *Lake Huron* attached cables to the sinking ship and towed it to Queenstown. All aboard were saved.

IT IS ONLY THE LORD'S MERCIES THAT HAVE KEPT US FROM COMPLETE DESTRUCTION. GREAT IS HIS FAITHFULNESS. LAMENTATIONS 3:22, 23, TLB.

BEING FRIENDS

Friends may fail us and disappoint. Jesus is a friend forever trustworthy, a friend who keeps His promises.

Playing Store

Six-year-old Dottie May was playing store on the front porch. Teddy Bear was the storekeeper.

I wish I had some real money to play with, Dottie May thought. Suddenly her face brightened. *Mrs. Behm has lots of money.* She ran across the road to the neighbor's house. She could hear the milking machines going in the barn. She knew that the Behms would both be busy with the cows.

Dottie May opened the kitchen door and walked in. Going straight to the cabinet where she'd seen Mrs. Behm put her money many times, Dottie May pulled open the drawer. There was a whole box of coins! She reached in and took a handful, putting it into her mother's big purse.

Carefully she closed the drawer then ran back home. She had a good time until Daddy came in from the garden. "Where did you get the money?" he asked.

Dottie May's face felt hot. She hadn't planned on getting caught. Quickly she invented a story. "I found the money under the rocks in the creek in front of the house," she lied.

Daddy picked Dottie May up and set her on his lap. "You aren't telling me the truth," he said. "Where did you really get the money?"

Dottie May began to cry. "Mrs. Behm's kitchen," she sobbed. "I'm sorry, Daddy."

"I'm sorry too," her father said, "and I know Someone else who feels disappointed. What do you think we should do now?"

"Ask Jesus to forgive me?"

"Good idea," Daddy replied, kneeling down and praying with Dottie May. "Now, you must take the money back," he said.

"Will you go with me?" Dottie May's chin trembled. Together they walked over to Mrs. Behm's house and gave back the money. Dottie May said she was sorry and promised never to do it again.

Dottie May kept her word, and she and Mrs. Behm were friends for many years, even after Dottie May grew up and got married.

BETTER BE POOR AND HONEST THAN RICH AND DISHONEST. PROVERBS 19:1, TLB.

BEING FRIENDS

How do you think the friendship of Dottie May and Mrs. Behm would have been affected if she hadn't made things right?

280

Trust Checkup

The administrators of the Medo-Persian empire investigated Daniel carefully and found that he was trustworthy. If others checked up on you, how would they rate your trustworthiness?

1. I'm a person of integrity. I'm true to my principles even when no one else is looking.

Never   Sometimes   Usually   Always

2. It's easy for me to trust other people.

Never   Sometimes   Usually   Always

3. My word can be trusted. I keep my promises.

Never   Sometimes   Usually   Always

4. My friends know they can count on me to do exactly what I say I'll do.

Never   Sometimes   Usually   Always

5. I take responsibility for my actions. I live up to my agreements.

Never   Sometimes   Usually   Always

6. I'm a reliable person. People can count on me to keep my appointments and to be on time.

Never   Sometimes   Usually   Always

7. I have a reputation for being honest.

Never   Sometimes   Usually   Always

8. I trust God completely. I believe His promises and know that He'll do exactly as He says.

Never   Sometimes   Usually   Always

9. I keep my promises to God.

Never   Sometimes   Usually   Always

10. I tell the truth in all circumstances of life.

Never   Sometimes   Usually   Always

11. I avoid even the smallest type of deception in my relationships with others.

Never   Sometimes   Usually   Always

12. My friends can depend on me to respect their property, never taking what belongs to them without their permission.

Never   Sometimes   Usually   Always

13. I don't become anxious when I face difficulties in life, because I know I can depend on God.

Never   Sometimes   Usually   Always

14. I can include myself with Job, Moses, Nehemiah, and Daniel as someone trustworthy.

Never   Sometimes   Usually   Always

[DANIEL] WAS TRUSTWORTHY. DANIEL 6:4, NIV.

CHOOSING
FRIENDS

Calamity Jane

YOU ARE LOOKING ONLY ON THE SURFACE OF THINGS.
2 CORINTHIANS 10:7, NIV.

CHOOSING FRIENDS

You can't tell the worth of an individual by outside appearances.

Bob was visiting a friend who lived on a large country estate in Australia. After lunch the two men took a walk through the gardens that surrounded the house. At the end of the yard they came to an old shed.

"What's in there?" Bob asked.

His friend led the way inside. "Nothing much," he said. "Just some old tools, garden equipment, and bits of this and that. This is where everything goes that we don't want any more."

Bob glanced around the dim interior at piles of junk covered with dust and cobwebs. His eye caught something of interest on a shelf. "What's that?" he inquired.

"Just an old golf club." His friend reached for the rusty putter. He blew off the dust and handed it to Bob.

Bob took a swing with the discarded club. "Yours?" he asked.

"Yes. That club brought me nothing but trouble, so I called it Calamity Jane. It's been about three years since I used it last. I had a bad day with my putting, and I blamed it on Calamity Jane. I brought it home, laid it on the shelf, and haven't used it since."

"Mind if I take it?" Bob asked.

"Not at all!" his friend said. "But I warn you, it's no good. Don't blame me if you lose your golf games trying to putt with that old iron."

Not long after that, Bob, known the world over as Bobby Jones, the champion golfer, made a putt with the unwanted club on the eighteenth green at St. Andrews. With that putt Bobby Jones won the open championship for Great Britain. That same year he won the United States national open championship with the same old discarded, rusty putter, Calamity Jane.

Are there some people whom you've put on the shelf? Have you ignored the possibility of friendship with the homeless, disabled, mentally handicapped, elderly, poor, or refugees? What about those of a different race, language, or culture? Our stories this month are about people who made some surprising friendships.

The Name on the Rafter

Jim was poor, dirt poor. His father died when Jim was 2 years old, and his mother struggled to feed and clothe her five children. As a teenager Jim did odd jobs to help support his family.

Every spring he looked for work as a farmhand. Trudging up and down the dusty Ohio roads, he came at last to the prosperous farm of Worthy Taylor.

"My name's Jim," the teenager said. "I need work."

Mr. Taylor studied the strong, athletic, blond youth. He noticed his shabby clothes, his tattered carpetbag, his work-worn hands, his warm, infectious smile. "Guess so," he said. "You can eat in the kitchen, but you'll have to sleep in the haymow."

"OK," Jim said. "I'm ready to start."

"Split some wood for the kitchen stove." Mr. Taylor pointed to a pile of logs by the barn. "After supper I'll show you around."

At supper Jim took notice that the Taylors had a teenage daughter. She smiled at him, and he knew at once that he was going to enjoy his summer's work. By summer's end he was in love with the farmer's daughter. He talked it over with Mr. Taylor.

"I love your daughter," Jim said simply. "I'd like your permission to court her, eventually to marry her once I'm established in life."

"You? Marry *my* daughter?" the farmer laughed. "No way! What do you have to offer her? You have no money, no name, and very poor prospects in life. I have higher hopes for my daughter than marriage to a farmhand!"

Jim was crushed. He put his belongings in his old carpetbag and disappeared.

Thirty-five years passed. Worthy Taylor pulled down his barn to make room for a larger one. On one of the rafters above the haymow where Jim had slept, he discovered his farmhand had carved his full name—James A. Garfield.

James A. Garfield was at that very moment president of the United States!

OCT. 2

JUDGES MUST ALWAYS BE JUST IN THEIR SENTENCES, NOT NOTICING WHETHER A PERSON IS POOR OR RICH. LEVITICUS 19:15, TLB.

CHOOSING FRIENDS

You can't always tell a book by its cover or a person by the clothes he or she wears. The potential of a person for friendship can't be measured by a bank account.

285

Leo's Gift

YOU ARE ALL BROTHERS. MATTHEW 23:8, NIV.

CHOOSING FRIENDS

Our choice of friends will be expanded as we grow to understand that we are kin to everyone. We are all brothers and sisters—linked by the invisible bond of our humanity.

Leo Tolstoy was a wealthy man who lived in Russia about 100 years ago. Unlike many rich people of his day, Leo found his friends among the poor peasants. He renounced his wealth and went to live, work, and write among the poor. He became famous for the books he wrote about life in Russia during the past century.

Once during a famine Leo passed an old beggar on a village street. The man was dirty, his hair unkempt, his clothes hanging in shreds. Leo looked at him and felt first pity, then love.

The poor, poor man, Leo thought. *I must do something to help him. He needs food so desperately. I'll gladly give him anything I have.* He searched through the pockets of his trousers and his jacket, but couldn't find even one kopek for the beggar. *Oh, no! I've given all my money away. There's nothing left for this poor starving man!*

Leo put his arms around the beggar and kissed him on his withered cheek. "Please forgive me," Leo whispered. "My brother, I've searched my pockets and have nothing left to give you."

Tears ran down the old man's face, but his eyes lit up with joy. A toothless smile wreathed his face. "But you called me brother—that's a great gift!"

All of us, deep within our hearts, want someone to look beyond the clothes we wear to see the human part of us on the inside that makes us all brothers and sisters. We all go through life wanting to find someone who'll look beneath the surface of our skin to see the beautiful person within.

After all, human beings are human beings, regardless of where they were born or how handicapped by the circumstances of life they may be. We all feel the same hungers, the same desires; the same longing to be loved and accepted, to find a friend.

Maung Maung

Albert Henderson, missionary doctor in Burma (now Myanmar) more than 60 years ago, was walking home along a jungle path. He noticed a man who appeared to be very ill lying at the base of a large banyan tree. He stank. Maggots crawled in his open sores.

Kneeling, Albert gave him water and a little rice from his own lunch. "What's your name? What happened?" the doctor asked.

"Maung Maung," the man whispered. "They brought me here to die."

"I won't let you die!" Albert said. "I'll get some help." He hurried to find a litter and some men to carry the sick man to the hospital.

But when the helpers arrived, they shrank at the sight of the repulsive, stinking body of the sick man. "No, honorable sir," they said, backing away. "Do not make us touch such a one!"

Albert bent down and tenderly lifted Maung Maung onto the stretcher. The helpers then picked up the bamboo poles and carried him to the hospital. For many weeks Albert tenderly cared for Maung Maung, until his sores healed and he was strong again.

A year later Albert was surprised to be greeted at a village clinic by a man running toward him shouting, "Praise God! You've come! Praise God!"

The man dropped to his knees in the dust in front of Albert and bowed his face to the ground.

"What's wrong?" Albert asked. "Are you not well, my friend? Stand up and tell me your problem."

As the man stood, Albert noticed a wide grin on his face. "Do I know you? I seem to recognize your face, but can't remember your name."

"I'm Maung Maung, the beggar you found under the banyan tree," he said. "You weren't afraid to touch me. You made me well and strong again. I'll never forget. I thank God for you every day. I'll always be your friend!"

I was only doing my duty, Albert thought. *Who would have thought that poor, stinking man would become my friend!*

HE WHO DESPISES HIS NEIGHBOR SINS, BUT BLESSED IS HE WHO IS KIND TO THE NEEDY. PROVERBS 14:21, NIV.

CHOOSING FRIENDS

Friendship is often the blessing we get when we help someone in need.

Love Never Fails

**LOVE NEVER
FAILS.
1 CORINTHIANS
13:8, NIV.**

CHOOSING FRIENDS

Love is full of
surprises. It can
turn the most
unpromising
person into
someone of
value. It can see
possibilities for
friendship in
the unlikeliest
people.

The courtroom was almost empty. The defendant, in his early teens, sat glumly listening.

His dad had come home drunk and beat his wife until she fell unconscious across the bed. He then staggered into the kitchen, where the boy sat at the table. The boy picked up a carving knife that lay beside his plate, held it in front of him, and let his dad walk into it. The man died instantly.

"Guilty," the boy admitted, then listened sullenly as the judge pronounced the sentence, "Life imprisonment."

From somewhere in the courtroom a voice called out, "Your Honor, may I address the court?"

The boy turned to see a man in a black robe and white clerical collar standing in the aisle. The man was Father Flanagan, founder of Boys' Town in Omaha, Nebraska.

"Yes, Father Flanagan?"

"I've come about the boy. I want you to let me have him."

"No use," the judge said as he shook his head. "There's nothing you can do for this kid."

"There's no such thing as a bad boy."

"You wouldn't want to turn a boy like this loose in Boys' Town," the judge continued. "He's a murderer."

"I've had them before," Flanagan said. "Murderers, bank robbers, car thieves, prostitutes, shoplifters, housebreakers, muggers—you name it, Judge. We've had it."

"But haven't you had trouble with them?"

"Oh, nothing serious," the priest answered. "Of the thousands of youngsters who've come to us, not one has since been in trouble with the law. A good number of them have finished their education and gotten good jobs. Some are professional men. Many are fathers now, respectable citizens. I believe we can help this boy."

"What's your secret?"

"No secret," the priest replied. "I just give the boys something they never had much of before."

"And what's that?" asked the skeptical judge.

"Love."

The Accident

oris Haines slammed her foot on the brakes. Following a sickening thud, she sat there for a moment, stunned. *I've just hit a woman!* she thought. *I'm in big trouble now.*

Doris opened the car door and walked around front. A middle-aged woman in a white nurse's uniform was just getting up, reaching for her purse and its scattered contents.

"No, let me do that!" Doris said. She quickly put the contents back in the purse and handed it to the woman. "I'm so sorry!" Doris began to sob. "Please sit down in my car, and I'll call an ambulance."

"You'll do no such thing!" the woman said with authority. "I'm perfectly OK."

"But the police. I've got to inform the police," Doris said.

"No need," the woman said as she reached out and squeezed Doris' hand. "You only grazed my leg, and I'm quite all right. God was with us. Everything is going to be OK."

"Then please let me drive you home," Doris insisted. When they reached the apartment building, she handed the woman a slip of paper with her insurance company's name and a phone number.

The woman tore up the paper. "I'm not going to get you in trouble just because of a little accident," she smiled. "I don't want to ruin your driving record. I'm worried about you, dear. Are you going to be all right? My name's Alma. Is there anything I can do to help you?"

Doris shook her head, then handed Alma another piece of paper. "My phone number—just in case something goes wrong," she said.

Later Alma phoned. "Just checking to see how you are. I'm praying for you. Remember that God is with you!"

I can't believe this! Doris thought. *I hit her, and she's concerned about me! This is amazing!*

Other phone calls and meetings followed. Doris and Alma became good friends. Better still, because of Alma, Doris also became a friend of God.

IN ALL THINGS GOD WORKS FOR THE GOOD OF THOSE WHO LOVE HIM. ROMANS 8:28, NIV.

CHOOSING FRIENDS

Do you think all accidents just happen? Or does God bring unusual people into our lives so that we might make a surprising new friend?

The World's Sun

ADAM NAMED HIS WIFE EVE, BECAUSE SHE WOULD BECOME THE MOTHER OF ALL THE LIVING. GENESIS 3:20, NIV.

CHOOSING FRIENDS

We're all one people, living on one planet, with one common origin. The same sun shines on us by day, the same moon by night. Why not be friends?

Sun Yat-sen, founder of the Chinese Republic, was visiting in the United States to raise money for the revolution he was leading against the Manchus.

While in Denver, Colorado, he stayed at the Brown Palace Hotel. That night he couldn't sleep. Just before dawn he got up and stood looking out his hotel window. Suddenly a great, round sun slid above the eastern horizon, setting the sky aglow.

Ah! How like China it is! he mused. *How often I've seen that sun come up in my homeland. It looks just the same!* A wave of homesickness washed over him. And then a sudden thought made him cry out, "That *is* China's sun!"

Then a new thought came to him, overwhelming the first. *That is not China's sun! That is the world's sun!*

Later Sun Yat-sen told a reporter, "It struck me with a sudden vision that the sun belongs to the whole world. It was not only China's sun—it was even Japan's sun. It was Russia's; South America's; it was Europe's sun. It was Turkey's sun. It was the whole world's sun!"

From that moment Sun Yat-sen began to think of himself as a citizen of the world, not just of China. For the first time he sensed his relation to every other person on the planet.

Yes, we're all related if we go back far enough. My ancestors came to New England about 300 years ago from England and Holland. If you and I could trace our lineage back thousands of years, at some point my family line and yours would merge. We'd become related.

If your family came from Europe, it wouldn't take as long to trace our common ancestors as it might if they were from the Maoris of New Zealand, the Nagas of North India, or the Mandarins of China. But eventually all our family lines would come together in Mother Eve.

A Friendly Heart

Helen LaMance was married to a serviceman stationed in Germany. They settled in a tiny cottage, and Helen tried to get used to living in a strange country where people spoke a different language, ate different foods, and had a different culture.

I'm so lonely, Helen thought one day as she sat watching her little girl play in the garden. *I wish I were back home where things are the same, where I could have friends.*

Across the street lived a young German woman about Helen's age. Helen watched as she hung out her washing on the shrubs to dry in the summer sun. The woman smiled at Helen; Helen smiled back.

Too bad she's German, Helen thought. *If she were English, we could be friends.* Day after lonely day followed. Sometimes the German woman sat in a chair on her lawn and knitted. Every day she smiled and waved.

Then one morning when Helen came outside to watch her daughter play, she noticed several pieces of wet laundry lying on the ground at her neighbor's house. She ran across the road and knocked on her neighbor's door.

"Your laundry," she spoke slowly and pointed. "It's all muddy! I'll help you pick it up." After helping pick up the dirty laundry, Helen went back home.

The next day the German lady knocked on Helen's door. "Please, come!" she motioned to her lawn. There she had set up a table for two. There were cups, a pitcher of cold milk, and fresh apple strudel. They had a wonderful time despite their differences in language and culture. After that they got together almost every day. What fun they had!

One day Helen reminded her friend of their first meeting when the laundry fell in the mud.

Her friend chuckled and said, "I put the laundry in the mud. I wanted so much to meet you. You looked like you had a friendly heart."

LIVE IN HARMONY WITH ONE ANOTHER. 1 PETER 3:8, NIV.

CHOOSING FRIENDS

A friendly heart is all you need to be friends with people of any culture. Are there people of a different culture living near you? Why not choose one for a friend?

The Sick Indian

**BLESSED IS HE
WHO HAS
REGARD FOR THE
WEAK; THE LORD
DELIVERS HIM
IN TIMES
OF TROUBLE.
PSALM 41:1,
NIV.**

CHOOSING
FRIENDS

Friendship often
has surprising
rewards! Acts of
kindness can turn
the worst enemy
into a friend.

ndians were on the warpath, burning settlers' cabins in revenge for wrongs done their tribe. Father rode immediately to Fort Bend for help, leaving teenagers Annie and Bud home alone.

It was early afternoon when a lone Indian staggered into the clearing of their cabin. "He's sick!" Annie said. "He needs help!"

"He's only pretending!" Bud warned. "Don't open the door!"

"No! That's not right! He's hurt, and I'm going to help him." Annie threw open the door. The man stumbled and fell in a heap on the floor. Annie bent over him, feeling his forehead. "Fever," she whispered. "I'll make tea from the fever bush. We have some dried in the loft."

While the tea steeped in a kettle, Annie made a bed of a patchwork quilt near where the Indian lay. Bud helped her ease him onto it. When the tea was ready, she sat by the sick man's side talking softly to him, coaxing him to drink. She watched as he began to breathe easier, the flush left his face, and he fell asleep.

It grew dark. Bud and Annie sat in the dim light from a crack in the kitchen stove and listened to the regular breathing of the sleeping Indian. Suddenly there was a bright glow through the window slats. Peeking out, they saw the clearing fill with yelling, whooping bareback riders with flaming torches. In the distance they could see their neighbor's house on fire.

"They've come!" Bud said. "We're next."

Just then the teenagers felt a draft of cold air. They turned to see the sick Indian, the patchwork quilt wrapped around his shoulders, leave the cabin.

"Now, they'll know we're here alone!" Bud groaned. "We're finished for sure!"

They watched as the sick Indian gestured wildly at the men on horseback and pointed toward the cabin. The whooping stopped. Someone lifted the sick man onto the back of his pony. The horsemen turned and rode away into the night.

"You did it, Annie," Bud whispered hoarsely. "Your kindness saved our lives!"

The Immigrant

Miriam Adeney, author, speaker, and university teacher, needed a baby-sitter for six weeks. A job placement service sent Ashraf, an Iranian woman, the mother of two children.

Ashraf's husband had promised to send her money, but after she arrived in the United States he discovered he couldn't get his funds out of Iran. Here she was, a woman who spoke little English, alone in a strange land with two children to support.

When the six weeks were passed, Miriam felt she just couldn't let Ashraf go without trying to help her get another job. Ashraf had started reading a Farsi Bible given her by her language tutor. "The story of Jesus is so beautiful," she told Miriam. Now it was Christmas, and Miriam felt compelled to help.

"Why do you bother?" friends asked. "It's really not your responsibility to get Ashraf a job."

"But I just can't push her out to starve," Miriam insisted. "I know I don't have time, but I have to do something to help."

Miriam got several newspapers and began looking at the "Baby-sitter Wanted" ads. Eventually she found a job for Ashraf.

Meanwhile Ashraf continued reading her Farsi Bible. As a result, she accepted Jesus as her Saviour. She phoned her husband in Iran to get permission to be baptized. He agreed.

Of course Miriam was present at her baptism. And so was her Christian language instructor. So were Christian friends who had invited her to their church and their homes.

In her testimony she said, "I'm being baptized today because of the love of Christians." She smiled at Miriam, her language teacher, and other Christian friends. "Through them I have discovered what a beautiful, loving person Jesus Christ is."

There are non-Christian immigrants in every Christian country. What might happen among these people if you and I would follow Miriam Adeney's example?

WE SHOULD LOVE ONE ANOTHER. 1 JOHN 3:11, NIV.

CHOOSING FRIENDS

Are there immigrants living in your community? Seek out one to be your friend. You might be surprised at how much fun it is to have a friend from another culture.

He Is Your Brother

AND THIS COMMANDMENT HAVE WE FROM HIM, THAT HE WHO LOVETH GOD LOVE HIS BROTHER ALSO. 1 JOHN 4:21.

CHOOSING FRIENDS

Is there any prejudice in your heart against someone who is your brother, your sister? Jesus can melt all hatred, suspicion, or fear with His love and bring you together as friends.

Festo Kivengere, a teacher in a Ugandan mission school, couldn't stand his boss. There was no reason, except that his boss was an English missionary.

I hate that man, Festo thought every time he saw him at a meeting. *I wish he'd go back to England where he belongs.*

One night while Festo was praying, he sensed that Christ was saying to him, "You hate that man, yet he's your brother!"

"Oh, no, Lord," Festo argued. "He isn't my brother! He's an Englishman. Only Africans are my brothers!"

"I love that man just as much as I love you," the Lord spoke to his heart. "I tell you, he's your brother. Now go to him."

"But Lord, what will I say?"

"Tell him you're sorry that you've hated him. Ask for his forgiveness," came the reply.

"Oh, but Lord, that will be hard for me to do."

"If you love Me, you'll love your brother," the words of Scripture burned in Festo's mind.

"All right, Lord, I'll go," Festo finally gave in.

Festo got on his bicycle and began the 50-mile journey through the mountains in the hot tropical sun to visit the man he hated. As he peddled along the dusty road a miracle happened.

In telling about the experience later, he said, "I felt as if my bicycle had an engine! My world had changed; now I had a brother in that house, not a lonely Englishman whom I hated. Such is the power of Christ." God's love had transformed Festo's hatred into love for a brother.

When Festo reached the missionary's house he walked in and embraced the man he had despised. "Jesus' love has shown me that you are my brother!" he exclaimed. "Please forgive me for hating you. I'm truly sorry."

Together the Black man and the White man wept in each other's arms and thanked God for the marvelous power of His love.

Chuma and Susi

Millions of visitors to London's Westminster Abbey have seen the simple stone honoring the great missionary to Africa, David Livingstone. Few have known of the amazing friendship between the famous missionary and two of his African helpers, Chuma and Susi.

At 4:00 on the morning of May 1, 1873, Chuma and Susi, with three other Africans, entered a small grass hut in Ilala to check on their friend. They found him on his knees, his head buried in his hands, dead.

Livingstone's two remarkable friends were determined to send his remains back to London for a burial in his own country 6,000 miles away. This seemed an almost impossible task, but so great was their love for the man who had given his life to tell them the story of Jesus that they were determined to try.

They took out Livingstone's heart and other internal organs, burying them in the Africa he loved. They filled his body with salt and brandy, leaving it in the sun for two weeks until it was dried out like a mummy.

They wrapped the embalmed remains in bark and sewed it into a canvas bag. Attaching poles to the precious bundle, Susi and Chuma lifted it to their shoulders and began the 1,500-mile walk to the ocean. The journey took them nine months and led them through swollen rivers, trackless deserts, torrid heat, and drenching tropical storms. They faced the terrors of wild animals, unfriendly tribes, and tropical fevers. They endured it all for the love of the man who had given his life for them and their people.

In February 1874 those two intrepid friends of Livingstone handed over his body, his journals, his instruments, and all his personal effects to the British consul.

"Amazing!" people said. "How can it be that these people have done such a great deed of love!"

Susi and Chuma accompanied Livingstone's remains to England, where they were given places of honor at Livingstone's funeral one month later on April 18, 1874.

OCT. 12

AND WE THANK HIM FOR THE WORK YOU HAVE DONE BECAUSE OF YOUR LOVE. 1 THESSALONIANS 1:3, ICB.

CHOOSING FRIENDS

The friendship of Susi, Chuma, and Livingstone is an example of the love that can exist between people of different races and cultures.

Oscar Was Afraid

AND I WAS WITH YOU IN WEAK-NESS, AND IN FEAR, AND IN MUCH TREMBLING.
1 CORINTHIANS 2:3.

CHOOSING FRIENDS

Love has the power to overcome the barriers of race, color, and culture. Give friendship a chance. You never know how surprising the results might be.

Paul, the author of these words, would have understood Oscar's feelings of fear the night he went to be with his friend Ernie.

Ernie's mother had died. Oscar, his friend for 30 years, wanted to go to the funeral home to sit with Ernie in his sorrow. He was determined to do it, but inwardly he trembled at the thought.

The problem was that Oscar was Black, and Ernie was White. Boston had been torn by racial strife in 1975 because of a decision that racial balance in all schools must be achieved through busing. Whites were attacking Blacks, and Blacks were retaliating. It wasn't safe for a Black man to go to a White neighborhood at night.

"I've got to go; Ernie's my friend," Oscar told his wife. "That's the least I can do."

It was almost dark when Oscar reached the funeral home. The parking lot was full. He had to go four blocks away to find a parking space. He then walked back in the gathering shadows through clusters of White teenagers who stared at him.

Will they attack? Oscar wondered, walking quickly and keeping alert for any sign of danger. He heard footsteps from behind. He walked faster. The footsteps came faster too. Oscar's heart was pounding. He felt trapped. What would he do if attacked?

The footsteps increased in speed. A teenager ran past him and across the street to join his friends. Oscar felt weak from his fear, but managed to make it into the funeral home.

Oscar was the only Black there. Ernie went to him immediately and threw his arms around him. Tears flowed down his cheeks as he said, "I prayed you'd come, Oscar."

The crowd looking on must have wondered about this friendship between men of two different races. They probably didn't understand all those two friends had gone through together. They probably didn't understand that friendship isn't a matter of race, color, or culture; it's a matter of the heart.

When Light Comes

An ancient Jewish story has something important to say to us about choosing friends.

"Exactly when is the moment of dawn?" an old rabbi asked his students. "How can we decide the precise moment when the night ends and the day begins?"

The students looked at one another, puzzled. What strange questions their old teacher asked!

"I'm serious," the rabbi insisted. "Exactly when does the night end and the day begin? Think!"

One of the boys gathered his courage and suggested, "When you can tell a dog and sheep apart from a distance."

"No," replied the teacher.

"Could it be when you can tell the difference between a fig tree and a grape vine?" asked another student.

"No," the rabbi shook his head. "Think again."

For a long while the boys sat in silence trying to imagine what their teacher was driving at. At last one spoke up, "Please tell us the answer. We give up."

"It's when you have enough light to look human beings in the face and recognize them as your brothers and sisters. Until then darkness is still with us."

By that standard there's a lot of darkness in the world today. How often we peer into the face of someone of another race and think, *He can't be my brother. He doesn't look anything like me. We're too different to be friends.* Or we may look into the eyes of a mentally retarded neighbor and think, *She doesn't have enough intelligence to be my friend.*

Or we visit an old people's home and see a shriveled, bent-over woman sitting vacant-eyed in front of a TV, and we think, *She's too old to be my sister. She isn't even aware of who comes and goes.* Or we avoid someone in a wheelchair and think, *There's no way we could be friends.* Or we make fun of someone who speaks our language with an accent or wears different clothes.

ANYONE WHO CLAIMS TO BE IN THE LIGHT BUT HATES HIS BROTHER IS STILL IN THE DARKNESS. 1 JOHN 2:9, NIV.

CHOOSING FRIENDS

We'll know we're truly people of the light when we can look in anyone's face, smile, and say, "This is my brother! This is my sister!"

The Light of Love

YOU ARE THE LIGHT OF THE WORLD. MATTHEW 5:14, NIV.

ove lights up people's lives. An old song titled "You Are My Sunshine" says that even during times of gray skies the person to whom the song is sung makes the singer happy.

Paul Brand did that for some friends of his who had leprosy. One day not long after his arrival at Vellore Christian Medical Hospital in India he came face-to-face with a need that was staggering—millions of leprosy patients with useless hands, theirs fingers curled tightly inward.

"What are you doing for claw hands like these?" he asked.

"Nothing" was the reply. "There's no treatment known."

Dr. Brand set about to find a solution, one patient at a time. He couldn't help millions, but he could help one.

"Send me a patient whose hands couldn't possibly be made worse," Dr. Brand said. "I'd like to see what I can do."

They sent him Krishnamurthy. Taking a muscle from the man's forearm, he withdrew it into the palm, and retunneled it into the fingers. After many months, several operations, and much therapy, the miracle happened.

"Look!" Krishnamurthy greeted Dr. Brand one day. He scooped up a ball of rice and curry and popped it into his mouth.

After one year in the hospital Krishnamurthy had more than new hands. He also had a new heart, because he'd found Christ.

That was the beginning of more than 3,000 hands that Dr. Brand operated on, one patient at a time.

About the results of Dr. Brand's work, Philip Yancey writes: "Many who arrived at the hospital barely looked human. Their shoulders slumped, they cringed when other people approached. Light had faded from their eyes. But months of compassionate treatment restored that light. . . . They became human again."

Such is the power of friendship to bring light into people's lives, sometimes the most surprising people!

CHOOSING FRIENDS

Is there someone in your school, in your neighborhood, who could use a little light and hope? You can choose to be his or her "sunshine," chasing away the gloom of life.

298

Beauty of the Heart

I t was Paul Scott's senior year in high school when he began fumbling the ball at football practice. Soon he couldn't tie his own shoelaces or cut up his food at meals.

Now the 18-year-old sat in the doctor's office waiting for the results of tests. At last the doctor called him into her office. "You have leprosy," she said.

Those three words put an end to his plans for university. He quit school and went to a leprosy hospital in Louisiana. His fingers drew inward in a clawlike shape. He got ugly welts on his face. Then the doctors discovered some wonderful medicine that could control the progression of leprosy.

After six years his leprosy was no longer active, but he was still disfigured and ugly in appearance. People moved away from him on trains. No one would give him a job. His old friends were embarrassed by his appearance and stopped calling.

He went out mostly at night so that people wouldn't notice him so much. One night he met a group of costumed children under a street lamp. They looked shocked at his appearance.

"Look at him!" someone said moving away. "He doesn't need a mask!" The others laughed and walked on.

Paul was devastated. *Am I so grotesque that people will always avoid me?* he wondered. Tears blinded him as he walked down the street, looking for a place to hide. He came to a church and went inside.

Seeking out the pastor, he said, "I'm coming to you because I have nowhere else to turn. I haven't a friend in the world."

"Well, now you have one," the pastor said. "Will you have dinner with me tomorrow evening?"

That was the beginning of an extraordinary friendship between the 24-year-old disfigured man and the aging pastor. "You'll never have many friends," the pastor told him, "but those you do have will be true friends."

After that Paul made several new friends—friends who didn't mind how he looked on the outside because they saw the fine person he was on the inside.

OCT. 16

CHARM IS DECEPTIVE, AND BEAUTY IS FLEETING; BUT A WOMAN WHO FEARS THE LORD IS TO BE PRAISED. PROVERBS 31:30, NIV.

CHOOSING FRIENDS

In choosing friends, beauty of heart is more important than beauty of face.

Florie's Party

WHEN YOU GIVE A BANQUET, INVITE THE POOR, THE CRIPPLED, THE LAME, THE BLIND, AND YOU WILL BE BLESSED.
LUKE 14:13, 14, NIV.

CHOOSING FRIENDS

The next time you have a party, why not invite someone who never gets invited to parties? You might be surprised at how much fun it can be! You might even make a new friend!

When Florie's birthday arrived, she helped Mother spread a white cloth on a table under a tree in her big backyard. She put out the finest china and silver and placed a little bouquet beside each plate.

Mother brought out a huge bowl of fresh strawberries and a large fluffy angel food cake. Florie added a plate of her favorite cookies.

At 3:00 the guests started arriving. First came an old woman, her back bent from years of toil, leaning on a cane. Her face was wrinkled, and her voice shook as she said, "Happy birthday, Florie." She was Mrs. Gray, who used to baby-sit for Florie when she was small.

Next came a man carrying on his back a boy with a physical disability. "Sure nice of you to invite Jamie," the man said. "He doesn't get out much."

Mary, who is visually impaired, was next. Florie ran to her and led her to her place at the table. "How lovely the flowers smell!" Mary exclaimed.

Amy, a very poor girl from Florie's Sabbath school class, was next. She wore a clean but faded old dress.

Tommy approached the table shyly, grinning at Florie. He tried to speak, but it sounded more like a grunt, because Tommy had been hearing-impaired since birth. He'd never been to such a fine party in all his life. Florie proudly led him to a place at the table.

"What an unusual group of guests!" Mother said after the party was over. "But they did seem to have a wonderful time!"

"And I did too," Florie said. "I asked them because my Sabbath school teacher said we weren't supposed to call our friends to our parties, but those who were in need, those who couldn't invite us back to their houses. I had no idea it would be so much fun to make them all happy."

Lisa's Summer Job

What 14-year-old Lisa Kerr wanted more than anything else was a friend. "Dear God, please send me someone to love, someone who cares about me," she prayed.

God answered Lisa's prayer, but in an unexpected way. It all started when her mother insisted she spend the first two weeks of summer working at a day camp for children with mental disabilities.

She got on the bus the first day and watched the children arrive. Someone thrust 6-year-old Robby into her arms. He was the size of a 2-year-old and couldn't talk. He babbled, and his head rolled uncontrollably on his shoulders.

The bus filled up with more children who acted strangely. A boy with a round, shaved head and green eyes kept winking at her and saying, "I'm going to marry you."

Charlie, the kissaholic, ran to her and covered her face with wet kisses. Brad followed her around all morning. Then there was Jeni, who was 13 but acted as if she were a 5-year-old. She was full of unending questions as she stuck close to Lisa. "What did you eat for breakfast? What's your middle name? What are you doing?"

By the end of the day Lisa wished she'd never agreed to take this job, but she was back on the bus the next morning. Charlie was there with his kisses, the green-eyed boy with his proposal, and once again she held helpless little Robby on her lap.

Jeni smiled when she saw her. "I missed you, Lisa."

Lisa suddenly felt all warm inside. "Thanks," she said. "Would you like to be my swimming buddy today?" Jeni's eyes lit up with joy.

Later Lisa put her arms around Jeni as they sang "That's What Friends Are For."

"Are you my friend?" Jeni asked.

"Of course I am," Lisa said.

"Do you love me?" Jeni persisted.

"Yes, I love you." Lisa replied, and she knew it was true. God had surprised her with a very special friend.

AND MY GOD WILL MEET ALL YOUR NEEDS. PHILIPPIANS 4:19, NIV.

CHOOSING FRIENDS

Do you know anyone who is mentally disabled? Perhaps God wants that person to be your friend.

Richard's Friends

FOR UNTO WHOMSOEVER MUCH IS GIVEN, OF HIM SHALL BE MUCH REQUIRED. LUKE 12:48.

CHOOSING FRIENDS

What excuses have you made lately for shutting certain people out of your life? If your heart is willing, you can find a thousand ways to be friends.

Richard wasn't the kind of person who attracted friends. Neither was he someone you'd expect to be a friend. Richard couldn't control his voluntary muscles. He grimaced when he talked, and his body jerked against his will. He's the sort of person people avoided if they could.

Richard had been on his back for 56 years. He was one of 5,000 who was cared for at Bethel in Bielefeld, Germany, a home for the mentally disabled, those with epilepsy, and others with disabilities.

Leo Bustad went there for a visit because he'd heard it was the "most remarkable place in the world." It was there that he met Richard and discovered the transforming power of love in action.

"Listening to him was difficult," Bustad says, "but one of the most important things we must do is to learn to listen to those who are hard to listen to, so I tried hard."

Richard quizzed Bustad, a veterinarian, about the treatment of birds with broken wings and all sorts of other animal problems. Then he asked a most unusual question, "Do you have any Indians working for you?"

"Yes," Bustad replied and moved on to other topics. After he'd left Richard's bedside, he asked his guide why Richard asked about Indians.

"Richard supports an orphaned child in India," the guide said.

"What?" Bustad asked. "Did you say Richard sends money to support a child in India?"

"That's right."

"But how?"

"Richard has control of his right foot, and some years ago he learned how to paint with that foot," the guide answered. "Using mirrors, he paints very beautiful pictures. We sell the pictures, and all the money goes to support his child in India."

"Richard is hard to forget," says Bustad. "His use of what little he had to help someone in need reminds me of the saying, 'Where the heart is willing it will find a thousand ways; where it is unwilling it will find a thousand excuses.'"

Strangers in California

Trankhi Trieuong was a stranger in a strange land. With no legs (they'd been shot off as he had tried to escape a prison camp in Vietnam) Trankhi had little hope of leaving the refugee camp in Thailand. Who'd sponsor a man who couldn't walk?

The answer was Nguyen Bao, pastor of a Vietnamese church in Westminster, California. "I don't care how many legs he has," Bao said. "If he needs help, we'll help him."

When Trankhi arrived at the Los Angeles airport, volunteers from Bao's church met him with a wheelchair. His new friends found him a place to live. They helped him apply for a Social Security card, and they taught him English. Today Trankhi drives a car and works full-time.

"I'm thankful to these people for taking in a stranger," Trankhi says. "They told me about the love of God, but I had already seen God's love at work in their care for me."

Trankhi is one of hundreds of refugees welcomed by Pastor Bao and his congregation. "We'll never refuse anybody," Bao says, "even if the number comes to the thousands, because that's the spirit of Jesus Christ."

When pressed about his motivation for his work with the refugees, Bao explains, "I was also a refugee. I escaped by boat with my 5-year-old son. Two hundred thousand people died at sea, but I survived. For what? For Christ. We live today for Jesus Christ and for our neighbor."

Ellen White wrote: "Our work in this world is to live for others' good, to bless others, to be hospitable; and frequently it may be only at some inconvenience that we can entertain those who really need our care" (*Testimonies*, vol. 2, p. 645).

If Jesus came as a stranger to your town, wouldn't you be happy to invite Him to your house to share whatever you have? Shouldn't we be just as willing to entertain the strangers who have fled to our country from war and persecution?

FOR I WAS HUNGRY AND YOU GAVE ME SOMETHING TO EAT, I WAS THIRSTY AND YOU GAVE ME SOMETHING TO DRINK, I WAS A STRANGER AND YOU INVITED ME IN. MATTHEW 25:35, NIV.

CHOOSING FRIENDS

There are thousands of refugees who need a friend. You could choose to be such a friend.

Christy's Friend

**I WAS EYES TO
THE BLIND AND
FEET TO
THE LAME.
JOB 29:15,
NIV.**

CHOOSING FRIENDS

Like Katriona, we
can choose to be
friends with
someone who
can't do anything
for us in return.
Do you know
someone for
whom you could
be eyes or legs?

Christy Brown had cerebral palsy because of brain damage at birth. At 5 years of age he was still as helpless as a newborn baby. His twisted arms and fingers twitched constantly, suddenly shooting out this way and that. His head lolled and sagged sideways. He drooled. He was a strange-looking, crooked little boy.

When he was 5 he learned how to hold a piece of chalk with the toes of his left foot, and was soon making words. Later he loved to lie on the floor and paint pictures with a brush held in his left foot.

One day his mother and constant companion was taken to the hospital. Eleven-year-old Christy lay all day on the sofa, not caring to write or paint. He was so lonely.

His father answered a knock at the door, and there stood a lovely teenager, Katriona Delahunt. "I came to see Christy," she said.

"Hello, Christy," Katriona began. "Your mother told me about you."

Christy grunted, and she sat down beside him on the sofa.

"I wanted to meet you," Katriona continued. "Your mother is worried about you. She told me how you paint pictures with your left foot. I thought maybe you'd write a little note to your mother. It would make her happy."

Christy nodded his head and grinned. His father lifted him to the table, and holding a pencil between his toes, Christy wrote, "Dear Mom. Don't worry. All OK. Lots of grub. Get well soon. Christy."

After that Katriona visited Christy often. She brought him brushes, paints, and drawing books as well as good news about his mother. She talked to him and watched him work. She helped him enter a drawing contest, which he won. She was his arms and legs, his link with the outside world. She encouraged him.

"She was my friend and a great inspiration to me in the years and struggles that lay before me," Christy wrote.

A Friend on the Bus

Barry got on the bus, the precious package under his arm. He'd just picked it up from the post office, a gift from his Uncle Mark.

Matthew sat nearby, looking out a window. *I should go wish him a happy holiday,* Barry thought. He frowned at the idea. He felt uncomfortable around Matthew. He always avoided him at school. He didn't want to be known as a friend of a kid with a mental disability.

Barry thought of the day Matthew had come up to him in the library with an article about a rocket. He'd asked him to read it, and Barry had nearly died. He did it, but kept looking up to see if anyone was watching.

Now there he was, Matthew, the mentally impaired boy. *Why bother?* Barry told himself. He got off at his stop without speaking to Matthew.

He was home before he realized he didn't have his package from Uncle Mark. *Oh, no!* he thought. *I left it on the bus! It's gone for good.*

The next morning the phone rang. It was a neighbor down the street. "There's a boy down at my house looking for you, Barry. His name is Matthew. He says he has a package that belongs to you. I'll drive him over if you like."

"Yes," Barry answered weakly. "Thank you."

All smiles, Matthew arrived a few moments later. "You left this on the bus," he said. "I found it under your seat. This morning I rode the bus to where you got off last night, and then I started knocking on doors, asking if anyone knew you. I'm glad I found you. I'm sure you wanted your package."

Barry stood there ashamed of himself, wanting to apologize for his actions but not knowing how to say it. "Thank you, Matthew," he mumbled. "Can you stay awhile?"

"I've got to go. My ride's waiting," Matthew said. He turned and flashed Barry a smile. "See you around!" he said.

Barry was suddenly proud that Matthew was his friend.

OCT. 22

WHEN PRIDE COMES, THEN COMES DISGRACE, BUT WITH HUMILITY COMES WISDOM. PROVERBS 11:2, NIV.

CHOOSING FRIENDS

A person's IQ isn't always a fair judge of his or her worth as a friend.

The Inheritance

**SHOW RESPECT
FOR THE ELDERLY.
LEVITICUS
19:32, NIV.**

There's an old Jewish story about a man who promised to give all 10 of his sons 100 gold coins on the day of his death. At the time it seemed an easy promise to keep, but bad times came to the land, and he lost part of his fortune.

Finally the old man called his children to gather round his bedside. One by one they knelt before their father, embraced him, and received 100 gold coins as he had promised.

When the youngest son stepped forward, the father motioned for the others to leave. When the door was shut, the old man said, "Son, I have only 20 left. I'm sorry!"

"It's not fair," cried the youngest. "Why didn't you divide it equally?"

"I wanted to keep my word to as many as possible," answered his father. Then with a slight twinkle in his eye he added, "But I've saved my greatest treasure for you—my 10 best friends. Their friendship is worth more to me than gold. Will you promise to treat them kindly?"

"Yes, Father, I promise," his son replied, trying to hide his disappointment.

Before long the father died. After the funeral the nine sons went away for a vacation, but the youngest had to stay home, for he didn't have enough money. After paying all his bills, he had only a little bit left.

I must honor my promise to Father, he thought. *Even if it takes all the money I have left I'll make a dinner and call my father's 10 best friends.*

After the meal, the 10 old men sat around and talked. Said one, "This is the only child who treats us with honor. Let's return his kindness."

The very next morning the 10 friends brought two cattle and a purse of money to their friend's son. They helped him breed the cattle and invest his money. Soon the younger son was much wealthier than his nine other brothers.

CHOOSING FRIENDS

Do you count any elderly people among your friends? Are you kind to the friends of your parents and grandparents?

Albert's New Friend

There comes that old Jew again!" someone yelled. Soon most of the boys of Günsbach, Germany, were running alongside the old man's donkey cart. They were shouting and jeering. Among them was young Albert Schweitzer, the preacher's son.

He watched how each boy pulled a bit of his shirt through his fist until it looked like a pig's ear. He made a pig's ear with his shirt, too, and laughed along with the others.

The old Jew said nothing, but turned and smiled at them, a patient, good-natured smile.

Albert looked at the old man's freckled face. He looked into his eyes and saw embarrassment and maybe a little bit of sadness. The man caught Albert's eyes and smiled again.

That smile was too much for Albert. He dropped his pig's ear and fell behind the other boys. *He's really a very nice old man,* Albert thought. *We've hurt his feelings with all our teasing. I won't ever do that again, no matter what my friends do.*

The next time the old Jew came riding into the village, Albert saw him first and ran ahead of the other boys to greet the old man with a smile and a handshake. He walked beside the donkey cart and talked with the man as an old friend, passing on news of the village.

The elderly Jew was relieved to have at least one friend in Günsbach when he came there on business. He looked forward to meeting his young friend. He knew he could always count on Albert to treat him with respect.

Albert Schweitzer never forgot that old man's smile and the hurt he'd seen in his eyes when the boys teased him. Albert vowed never again to hurt someone's feelings with his teasing. He discovered it was lots more fun to make people happy by treating them with kindness and honor.

**SHOW PROPER RESPECT TO EVERYONE.
1 PETER 2:17, NIV.**

CHOOSING FRIENDS

Try to find an older person in your neighborhood with whom you can visit this week. Ask him or her to tell you about life when he or she was growing up. You may make an unexpected new friend!

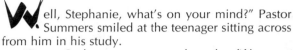

Parents Aren't Perfect

OCT. 25

**HONOR YOUR
FATHER AND
YOUR MOTHER.
EXODUS 20:12,
NIV.**

"Well, Stephanie, what's on your mind?" Pastor Summers smiled at the teenager sitting across from him in his study.

"Does God expect me to obey the fifth commandment?" she asked. "My father was a drunkard and made life hard for us when we were kids. He beat us and stuff like that. Then he just walked away and left us two years ago. Mom works all the time and she yells a lot. She makes me really mad, because she never has time to listen to me. I don't feel very good about either one of them right now."

"I see," Pastor Summers nodded. "But God doesn't add any qualifying statements such as 'if they're nice people' or 'if they don't make any mistakes.' God just says, 'Honor them.' It sounds to me like He wants you to do it anyway, regardless of how they've acted. It seems to me this is your duty as a Christian daughter. Do you see what I mean?"

"Yeah, I guess so," Stephanie sighed. "The problem is how do I do that when I don't like them very much."

"Honor means to give respect and esteem, that doesn't have to include friendship. However, I think if you ask God to help you forgive them and respect them in spite of how they've acted, you might find some surprising things happening!" Pastor Summers suggested.

"OK, give me some ideas," Stephanie said. "I'll try."

"Think of your parents as people with their own personalities and problems," he began. "How well do you really know your mom? What does she like and dislike? What activities does she enjoy? What are her hopes and ambitions? What makes her laugh and cry?

"How could you help your mom enjoy life more? Have you complimented her lately? Can you think of something fun you could do together? Could you sacrifice a little time or personal plans this week to do something to make her life easier? How long since you sat down and really listened to what she had to say?"

CHOOSING FRIENDS

What could you do to help build a better relationship with your mom or dad?

Impressing Parents

Brent sat down in a patio chair opposite his dad. "Something big's happening this week. Remember?"

"Hmmm!" Dad said from behind his paper. "The president is coming to town?"

"No, Dad! My birthday! Remember how old I'll be?"

Dad put down the paper and scratched his head. "Now, let's see . . . can't seem to remember . . . 14?"

"Da-a-a-d!" Brent laughed. "You know I'll be 16!"

"Really?"

"Really! And you know what that means!"

"Yeah!" Dad laughed. "Next year you'll be 17."

"Oh, Dad, you . . . you know what I mean. I'll get my license!"

"Watch out world! Brent's going to get his license to drive!" Dad faked horror.

Brent laughed. "We need a schedule for the car," he said. "I need wheels!"

"Hold on!" Dad replied. "I'm not even sure you're ready to drive! It's a big responsibility!"

What can Brent do to prove to his dad that he's mature enough to use the family car?

1. *Express appreciation.* Brent's dad doesn't owe him a car; its use is a privilege. The more he expresses appreciation, the better will be his relationship with his dad.

2. *Volunteer help.* He could offer to pay for the gas and part of the insurance. A display of generosity would leave Dad defenseless.

3. *Wash the car.* What dad could say no to a teenager with a rag in one hand and a bottle of polish in the other?

4. *Be on time.* When a teenager arrives home on time, parents see traces of maturity. It makes them feel warm all over.

5. *Recite the insurance oath.* "Teenagers who get too many tickets end up with insurance policies that won't fit in their glove compartment." Insurance is high for careless teen drivers.

6. *Say thank you and please.* Too many teens are unable to pronounce these words.

> **WHEN I BECAME A MAN, I STOPPED THOSE CHILDISH WAYS. 1 CORINTHIANS 13:11, ICB.**

CHOOSING FRIENDS

It really is possible to impress parents and to establish a friendship with them.

Friends Next Door

LET US THINK ABOUT EACH OTHER AND HELP EACH OTHER TO SHOW LOVE AND DO GOOD DEEDS. HEBREWS 10:24, ICB.

CHOOSING FRIENDS

Elderly people often make very good friends. They can even be lots of fun if you give them a chance.

"I'm bored," 9-year-old Philip said one hot afternoon.

"Me too," 10-year-old Connie agreed. "There's nothing much to do around here."

"Our friends are all on vacation," Philip added.

"Let's ask Mom," Connie suggested. "Maybe she'll have some ideas of where we could find some friends."

Connie and Philip found Mother inside. "We're bored," Connie explained. "We need some friends. Any ideas?"

"What about the Peters next door?" she offered.

"Oh, Mom! They're so old!" Philip said. "We want someone to play with!"

"Friends can be any age," Mom replied. "And you don't always have to play with friends. Friends help each other, too. Maybe you could become friends with Mr. and Mrs. Peters by helping them."

"Like how?" Connie was starting to get interested.

"They're both too old to work outdoors much, and they can't afford to have their grass cut very often," Mother replied. "I know Mrs. Peters loves flowers, but hers aren't growing very well because of the weeds."

"I could cut their grass!" Philip said, standing tall. "Dad says I do it as well as he does!"

"Pulling weeds isn't hard," Connie added. "I could do that. Why don't we get started right now!"

After checking to see if it was OK with the Peters, Connie and Philip got busy. Philip raced around the yard with his dad's power mower and had it trimmed in no time flat. Then he got busy and helped Connie finish pulling weeds from the beds of marigolds, zinnias, and petunias.

"It looks wonderful!" Mrs. Peters said, watching from the porch. "I've made some lemonade. Come sit awhile and cool off."

After the children had relaxed, sipping ice-cold lemonade, Mr. Peters hobbled out with a set of Chinese checkers.

"Think you can beat me?" he said with a twinkle in his eye.

The rest of the afternoon whizzed by as Connie and Philip had fun with their new friends.

It Takes Two

"Why's Dad always mad at me? Why me?" 15-year-old Vicky whined.

Her mom sat down on Vicky's unmade bed. Vicky plopped down beside her. "Your father wasn't angry. He made a reasonable request, and you refused to obey."

"But I didn't want to do what he said."

"That was evident," Mother smiled. "But even before you came to the table you were upset with your father. You just used that incident to make your unhappiness clear."

"He doesn't care about me," Vicky answered. "He doesn't spend any time with me."

"You're not being fair," Mother argued. "He's tried lots of times to talk to you, and you won't respond. It takes two people to have a conversation; it takes two to have a relationship. You want your dad to do everything, while you do nothing."

"Dad treats me like a child, but I'm grown up now!" Vicky wasn't going to give in easily.

"Vicky, a mature adult would never have acted the way you did this morning," Mother said. "Even though you're no longer a child, you owe your dad love and respect. The fifth commandment puts no time limit on honoring your father."

"So?"

"So why don't you stop obeying Dad just because of his authority? Instead, do it because you love him and want to make him happy."

"Like how?"

"Well, don't always wait for him to come to you for a talk. Show Dad you're interested in him, and you'll be surprised with the results."

"What should I do about this morning?"

"I think you can figure that out for yourself."

Vicky went to her desk, tore a page from her English notebook, and began to write: "Dear Dad, I'm sorry about this morning. Please forgive me. I truly love you and will try to do better. Love, Vicky."

That evening she found a note on her dresser. "Dearest Vicky, Thank you, sweetheart. I love you, too! Dad."

CHILDREN, OBEY YOUR PARENTS IN THE LORD, FOR THIS IS RIGHT. EPHESIANS 6:1, NIV.

CHOOSING FRIENDS

It takes two for friendship. Have you done your part to build a friendship with your parents?

Grandma Brown

CHOOSING FRIENDS

Have you
discovered how
special your
grandparents are?

A cheerful fire crackled in the wood stove. The circle of light from a lone kerosene lamp fell softly on Grandma Brown's wrinkled hands as she sat in her rocker while making a rag rug.

That very day Cindy had helped tear old dresses into one-inch strips, which grandma had sewn together and wound into large balls. Some of her own dresses had been in the pile of rags that were being recycled into an oval throw rug.

The room smelled of wood smoke, mint tea, cinnamon rolls, and eucalyptus oil, a unique blend of smells that made Cindy feel she was living in pioneer days. Her grandma was absolutely ancient! She remembered the American Civil War and the death of Abraham Lincoln. She could tell tales of homesteading in Kansas and raids by Indians. Grandma Brown was from another century when women wore sunbonnets and children wrote on slates in one-room country schools.

"Tell me about when you were young," 10-year-old Cindy spoke at last. "Tell me about the old days."

"Times were hard . . ." Grandma began. Cindy lay her head back against the velvet of the old chair. She closed her eyes and imagined what it must have been like to travel by ox cart . . . to watch out for mountain lions in the woods . . . to walk five miles along a forest trail to school . . . to take food to your father who worked in the coal mines.

Cindy loved these visits with Grandma Brown. It made her feel part of a family that had deep roots. It made her feel connected to her past. It gave her a wonderful sense of belonging.

But that wasn't the only reason Cindy loved to visit Grandma Brown. There were other things such as having someone with lots of time to listen, someone who made you feel special, someone who wasn't uptight about your bedroom or your homework, someone who never judged. Grandma Brown had lots of love, peace, patience, understanding, and faith.

I'd like to be like my grandma someday, Cindy thought.

Transformed Enemies

Clifford Goldstein joined a kibbutz in Israel to get away from Christians. He was angry because of the persecution Christians had waged against the Jews for centuries and for the difficulties his people still faced in many parts of the world.

"At least here there will be no Christians to harass me," he told himself. "It will be great to be among all Jews."

However, Clifford had not been in the kibbutz a week before 10 devout Christians from the United States moved in. He started arguing with them immediately, insulting them every chance he got. What right did they have to come to Jewish kibbutz? Why didn't they stay where they belonged? Why did they have to go around making life miserable for Jews?

Despite Clifford's abuse, the Christians didn't retaliate, complain, or condemn. Their only arguments were love and kindness. They tried hard to be friends. They went out of their way to be nice to Cliff.

"You make it hard for me to love you, Cliff," admitted Sue Norris, one of the group. "But I love you anyway."

They're really neat people, Cliff thought. *I want them to be my enemies, to hate me, but they won't cooperate. I guess I'll just have to let them be my friends.*

Cliff was amazed at the attitude of Asher, another one of the Christians, when he was unjustly fired.

"What are you going to do about it?" Cliff asked him.

"Nothing," Asher said. "Just forgive them."

As Cliff saw God's love reflected in the characters of Christians such as Sue and Asher, his prejudice melted. He could argue against doctrines and beliefs, but he couldn't argue against the way they treated people.

Once Cliff accepted the Christians as friends, he began to listen to what they had to say about Christ. He soon believed that Jesus must indeed be the Messiah. It wasn't long before he accepted Jesus and was baptized in the Jordan River.

OCT. 30

HE MAKES EVEN HIS ENEMIES LIVE AT PEACE WITH HIM. PROVERBS 16:7, NIV.

CHOOSING FRIENDS

Don't overlook the possibility of an enemy becoming a friend. Sometimes our worst enemies are transformed into our very best friends.

313

Choosing Friends Checkup

KEEP ON SOWING YOUR SEED, FOR YOU NEVER KNOW WHICH WILL GROW—PERHAPS IT ALL WILL. ECCLESIASTES 11:6, TLB.

Rate yourself on being able to cultivate friends from many different types of surprising people.

1. I don't judge people by outward appearances.

Never   Sometimes   Usually   Always

2. I accept each person as a possibility for friendship regardless of racial background.

Never   Sometimes   Usually   Always

3. I accept each person as a possibility for friendship regardless of language, culture, or nationality.

Never   Sometimes   Usually   Always

4. I accept each person as a possibility for friendship even though he or she may be poor.

Never   Sometimes   Usually   Always

5. I accept each person as a possibility for friendship even though he or she may be physically sick or disabled.

Never   Sometimes   Usually   Always

6. I accept each person as a possibility for friendship even though he or she may be mentally disabled.

Never   Sometimes   Usually   Always

7. I accept each person as a possibility for friendship even though he or she may be of another religion.

Never   Sometimes   Usually   Always

8. I accept each person as a possibility for friendship even though he or she may be ugly or deformed.

Never   Sometimes   Usually   Always

9. I accept each person as a possibility for friendship regardless of his or her age, even the elderly.

Never   Sometimes   Usually   Always

10. I work at trying to establish a friendship with my parents.

Never   Sometimes   Usually   Always

11. I work at trying to establish a friendship with my grandparents and other older relatives.

Never   Sometimes   Usually   Always

12. I'm willing to consider my enemies as possibilities for friendship, even though they may not be friendly to me.

Never   Sometimes   Usually   Always

Just Like a Snake

Watch out for Connie!" my husband said. "You're going to get hurt!"

"Oh, no!" I insisted. "Connie's my friend."

Connie was my pet python. I'd had her since she was a baby. She liked me to stroke her back. She wound herself loosely around my arm and unwound when I flicked her tail gently. Placed in the center of a room, she always sought me out. We were friends.

Others were afraid of her, so I locked her in the spare bathroom most of the time. One day I opened the bathroom door to find her missing! She was six feet long, with a diameter of five inches. There was no way she could have squeezed down the drain!

I found her inside the toilet water tank. The tank was near the ceiling, with a pipe that led down to the toilet bowl. She had climbed the pipe and gone inside to soak. I got her out and put a screen on top so she couldn't get back inside. Then she simply lay on top of the screen for two weeks.

One day I climbed onto the toilet seat where I could look Connie in the eye. I said, "Connie, you aren't much of a friend these days." Then I blew softly into her face.

Before I knew what had happened, Connie struck, biting me on the nose. The impact threw me off the toilet seat against the opposite wall. I carried the marks of her bite for several days.

Not long after that, Connie refused to unwind when I flicked her tail. She tightened her grip on my arm, cutting off the circulation. I panicked. "Connie, I'm your friend!" I cried.

She constricted tighter and tighter. My hand was white and numb. And oh, how it hurt! She had turned against me, just as Ron had warned. "Somebody help me!" I cried.

Ron rescued me and said, "Connie is no longer your friend. She's got to go."

THEY MAKE THEIR TONGUES AS SHARP AS A SERPENT'S. PSALM 140:3, NIV.

CHOOSING FRIENDS

Many times friends turn against us, just like a snake, hurting us deeply. What can we do? This month we'll find out.

315

Disappointed With God

THE LORD YOUR GOD GOES WITH YOU; HE WILL NEVER LEAVE YOU NOR FORSAKE YOU. DEUTERONOMY 31:6, NIV.

CHOOSING FRIENDS

Often we're disappointed with God when bad things happen to us. If we're patient, God will show us that He's a friend who is with us even in the bad times.

aymin Herschell was disappointed with God.

As a Jewish boy growing up in Strzelno, Poland, Haymin believed that all Jews were God's friends. However, something bothered Haymin. He thought, *If we're God's friends, then why does He allow bad things to happen to us?*

When Haymin was 15 he left home to study at Berlin University. He found no answers there. He traveled to London and Paris in search of peace. While in Paris he got word that his mother had died. He became very depressed, thinking, *If God is my friend, why did He let this happen? He must have forsaken me.*

But God hadn't forsaken Haymin. A few days later he was intrigued by words written on a paper that a merchant used to wrap something he'd bought in the market. He read the words again and again: "Blessed are they that mourn: for they shall be comforted" (Matt. 5:4). He didn't know that he was reading the Beatitudes, the words of Jesus spoken in the Sermon on the Mount. He just knew he wanted very much to read the book that spoke such comforting words.

Not long after that he visited in the house of a Christian friend. There he saw a copy of the New Testament. Curious, he opened the book to the very words he'd seen on the wrapper: "Blessed are they that mourn, for they shall be comforted."

He was shocked to find they were spoken by Jesus Christ, whom he'd been taught to ignore. He closed the book, disgusted. But he opened it again and read some more. His heart beat faster as he read the story about how Jesus had died for his sins.

It was all so exciting! Eventually he bowed his head and prayed, "Lord, I believe that Jesus Christ is the Messiah. I believe He died for my sins." How happy he felt to know that God was his friend after all!

Father's Suitcase

en-year-old Corrie ten Boom loved the times Father took her with him on the train. She loved the excitement, but most of all she loved the chance to be alone with her father. It gave her an opportunity to ask him hard questions. He usually had an answer.

One day after a particularly puzzling question, her father said nothing for a while. Finally he stood, lifted his suitcase from the rack over their heads, and set it on the floor. "Please carry this for me, Corrie," he said.

Corrie tried to lift the heavy bag. She tugged at it, but it refused to move. "It's too heavy," she said.

"Of course it is," Father replied, "and I don't expect you to carry such a load. It's the same way, Corrie, with knowledge. Some of it is too heavy for children to carry. When you're older and stronger you can bear it. Now you must trust me to carry it for you." Corrie sat back, content to let her father worry about all the hard questions of life.

Corrie remembered that incident 40 years later when she was being interrogated in a prisoner of war camp. Lieutenant Rahm threw her some hard questions.

"What I don't understand," he said, "is why God allows Christians to suffer. How can you believe in God now? What kind of God would have let your old father die in this prison?"

Corrie sighed. That was a hard question. Sometimes she wondered the same thing. She wondered, too, why God didn't protect her and her family when they were doing so much to be kind to the Jews. It just didn't seem right.

Then she smiled as she remembered her father's answer to her hard question as a child, "Some knowledge is too heavy. You can't bear it. I'll carry it for you until you're able." She knew that her heavenly Father would do the same for her now.

I HAVE MANY MORE THINGS TO SAY TO YOU, BUT THEY ARE TOO MUCH FOR YOU NOW.
JOHN 16:12, ICB.

CHOOSING FRIENDS

Because God is our loving Father, He knows we can't understand everything He does. He asks us to trust Him until He's able to make it plain to us.

317

When Friends Leave

Nov. 4

"You do not want to leave too, do you?" Jesus asked the Twelve. John 6:67, NIV.

Choosing Friends

It hurts when friends leave us alone. Do you agree with Mark or with Jennings? If Jesus had been there, what do you think He'd have said to the boys?

Jesus felt disappointed. Many of His friends had left Him. He was hoping they all wouldn't go away and leave Him alone. It's hard to be without a friend. Jesus would understand how Mark felt.

Mark had lived in an orphanage since he was a small child. No one visited him. No one came to adopt him. Other kids came, and he made friends with them, and then they went back home or were adopted. Then Jennings came to the orphanage. They became buddies.

Mark and Jennings sat together one afternoon, laughing. They'd had a good time playing all day. Now they sat and watched Butch wrestling with two bigger boys.

"Are they friends?" Jennings asked.

"No," Mark hung his head. "There are no friends here. Those boys just hang around Butch because he's tough. They want him to be on their side in a fight."

"What do you mean there are no friends in here?" Jennings was puzzled. "Aren't we friends?"

Mark didn't answer. He just sat there staring at the other kids playing. Jennings knew he didn't want to talk just then. That evening, when they were both brushing their teeth, Jennings tried again. "What did you mean this afternoon when you said there are no friends here?"

Mark frowned. "It's the rule," he said. "I don't mean a home rule, like when you go to bed and when you eat. It's a kids' rule, one you're supposed to learn on your own because nobody wants to talk about it. Know what I mean?"

Jennings shook his head.

"It's like this," Mark continued. "If you let someone be your friend, you're left alone when he goes away. If you keep on making friends and they keep going away, you feel worse than ever. It hurts." Mark ran from the bathroom and climbed into his bed.

That's weird! Jennings thought as he watched Mark go. *It seems to me a friend would make things easier.*

Jennings and Kevin

After a few months in the orphanage Jennings began to understand what Mark had said about the problem with making friends. Mark got sick and died. Jennings felt abandoned by his friend. Other friends got adopted. Some went back home. It was hard, just as Mark had said it would be.

Then Kevin came to stay. Kevin was younger and needed help. Jennings took him under his wing, being his friend as Mark had been to him when he first came. Then he got worried because Kevin followed him around everywhere, like a little puppy.

I really like this little kid, Jennings thought. *But I think maybe he's liking me too much. I'd better do something about it.*

"Come here, Kevin," Jennings said, leading his new friend to a place in the shade of the building. "You've got to start playing with other kids."

"Why?"

"It's the rules," Jennings said. "It's one of the rules that you've got to play with a different kid every day. Got it?"

Tears welled up in Kevin's eyes. He shook his head. "Don't you like me, Jennings?" he asked. "I want to play with *you.*"

"That's the problem," Jennings said.

"Why's that a problem?" Kevin pouted. "Don't you like me?"

"Of course! I like you a lot," Jennings said. "But if you like only me and nobody else, you're in for big trouble!"

"I don't want to play with anybody else," Kevin persisted. "I like you. How will that make trouble?"

"What happens if I leave?" Kevin said. "Then what are you going to do? You'll be all alone again and feel miserable."

"Are you leaving?" Kevin started to cry.

"Don't cry," Jennings put an arm around Kevin. "I'm not leaving, but you never know when I might. You got to have more friends, 'cause you always need a friend. Understand?"

Kevin nodded and dried his eyes. "I'll go play with someone else now."

NOV. 5

REMEMBER HOW SHORT MY TIME IS. PSALM 89:47.

CHOOSING FRIENDS

Friends leave us for one reason or another. It's a good idea to have several friends, then you've always got someone when one of them leaves.

The Snowball Fight

> I LIE AWAKE,
> LONELY AS A
> SOLITARY
> SPARROW ON
> THE ROOF.
> PSALM 102:7,
> TLB.

CHOOSING FRIENDS

Everyone has had an experience of losing a friend. Ask the other members of your family to share about a time a friend disappointed them. What did they do to remedy the situation?

"Let's have a snowball fight!" Ross suggested to the other neighborhood boys. "Come on over to my yard!"

Ross was one captain, and Chip was the other. They chose up teams, and Ross chose Jim, just as Jim expected he would. After all, they were best friends. It made Jim feel good to be on Ross's side. Ross was a year older, strong, and a good leader.

The teams were evenly matched. The fight started out friendly, but very competitive. Someone put a chunk of ice in his snowball, and it hurt. The game turned vicious.

Everyone packed the balls until they were extra hard. Chip's side seemed to be making the hardest balls. Before long some of Ross's team slipped away and joined Chip's side.

As it got dark, Jim noticed an awful lot of balls were aimed at him. "Help! Ross!" he called. "They're ganging up on me!" He looked around, but Ross wasn't there. He'd joined Chip's team too. Jim was inside the fence all alone.

"No fair!" Jim yelled. "You guys are cheating!"

At that the whole gang came over the wall and ran after Jim, pelting him with snowballs. He tried to defend himself, but couldn't keep up. Looking around frantically, he grabbed a small wooden chair and smashed it over the head of the nearest opponent.

The rest of the boys lit into Jim and gave him a good pounding before he yelled for mercy. They laughed at him as he ran home yelling, "It's not fair! It's not fair!"

That night as Jim lay in bed he felt really low. He'd lost whatever standing he had with the neighborhood boys. He'd lost his best friend. He hurt on the outside from the beating, but he hurt lots worse on the inside because he'd lost a friend.

Sometimes Love Hurts

Corrie adored Karel from the first time she saw him. She was 14, and he was 19 years old and a friend of her brother, Willem. During the next seven years Corrie and Karel became good friends. They talked a lot, sharing their dreams for the future. They went for walks together. They wrote long letters when they were apart. Corrie spent many hours dreaming of what life would be like as his wife.

Gradually the letters got shorter and further apart. "Why doesn't Karel write?" Corrie fretted.

"You surely don't think Karel is serious about you!" her brother asked. "Has he ever said he was?"

"No," Corrie admitted. "But I'd hoped."

"Well, forget it," Willem advised. "He'll never marry you. His mother has a girl from a rich family picked out for him."

I can't believe it! Corrie told herself. *I'll always love Karel, and I'm sure he'll always love me.*

Then one day she answered the doorbell, and there stood Karel with another girl. "This is my fiancé," he said. "I wanted her to meet you, Corrie."

Corrie wanted the floor to open up and swallow her. He visited a few minutes with her parents, then left. As soon as he was gone, Corrie ran to her room and began to sob.

After a long while Corrie's father came into her room and sat on the bed beside her. He spoke softly, "Love hurts a lot. It's the strongest thing in the world, and when it's blocked it causes pain."

Corrie nodded. The hurt was more than she could bear. Then Father continued, "You have two choices, Corrie. You can kill the love so that it stops hurting. But that will make you die a little inside. Or you can ask God to open up another route for that love to travel. God can show you the better way. He can take away the hurt."

Nov. 7

And now I will show you the most excellent way. 1 Corinthians 12:31, NIV.

Choosing Friends

It hurts a lot when friends let us down, but we don't have to let disappointment make us bitter. God can help us find other friends to love.

The Feud

NOW IT IS TIME TO FORGIVE HIM. 2 CORINTHIANS 2:7, TLB.

CHOOSING FRIENDS

Sometimes a sincere apology is all it takes to turn a friendship around. Someone has to take the first step.

Barry and Vicki had started out being friends, but something happened that turned him against her. He took every opportunity to make a nasty dig, and she would snap right back at him.

Then came the music contest. Vicki was playing a clarinet solo, a difficult number that she'd practiced for more than four months. As she walked onto the stage to play her piece, she saw Barry sitting on the front row. He made an ugly face at her.

Vicki tried to ignore him, but he kept it up, trying to distract her all through her number. Her fingers trembled on the keys, and it was hard to hold her lips firm on the mouthpiece because she felt like crying. Tears blurred her vision as she ran off the stage.

"He did that on purpose!" Vicki's friends said as they greeted her backstage. "He was trying to make you fail! Just wait until he plays his number! We'll show him what it feels like!"

"Two wrongs don't make a right," Vicki responded. "Forget it."

After that Vicki refused to speak to Barry. She simply looked daggers at him whenever they passed. The feud lasted all year. Bitterness ate away at Vicki until she could stand it no longer. She went to see her music teacher.

"Your feud has bothered me greatly," the teacher said. "I've talked to Barry. He feels bad, but he can't get up courage to come to you. Someone has to take the first step. Why don't you do it?"

Vicki arranged a meeting with Barry in the teacher's office. "I'm sorry, Barry, for all the mean things I've said and done to you in the past year," Vicki began. "Please forgive me. I want you to know I've already forgiven you for what you've said to me. Isn't one year long enough to be enemies?"

Barry turned away for a moment. When he turned back he was smiling. "Yeah," he said. "I'm sorry too. I'm ready to be friends."

Disappointing God

ave and Tony had become good friends during ninth grade when they roomed together at academy. They planned to room together the next year, too.

Dave got there first the next September. He hadn't seen Tony all summer, but someone said they'd heard he'd started to drink.

Oh, no! Dave thought. *I came here to get away from that. My dad's drunk all the time, and my brothers have started to drink. I don't need the temptation right under my nose. Dear Lord, help me know what to do.*

Dave wrestled with his decision as he waited for Tony to arrive, even hoping maybe he wouldn't come back. *Maybe I could help him stop drinking,* Dave reasoned to himself. *But then again, maybe he'd get me started. I don't want that.*

Tony arrived in high spirits. "Hi, mate!" he said slapping Dave on the arm. "Good to see you!"

Dave thought he smelled beer on Tony's breath. "So I hear you've started drinking," he said.

"Yeah, man! It's great! Only a beer now and again. Doesn't hurt you at all! Have you tried it?" he said, lifting his suitcase onto the empty bed.

"No, and I don't ever plan to," Dave said. "And I think it's best if you find a different roommate this year."

"Hey, man! You don't have to drink if you don't want to," Tony laughed. "I don't plan to bring any into the room."

"My mind's made up," Dave said. "I've seen all the drinking I want at home. I don't want to room with you."

"OK, OK!" Tony said. "You don't have to get so high and mighty about it. I'll find someone who's a bit more fun to be with!" He picked up his suitcase and left the room.

Dave felt really disappointed, because he liked Tony a lot. *But better to disappoint him than to disappoint God,* he thought.

Dave felt bad when Tony was kicked out of school. He heard later that Tony had become an alcoholic.

DON'T YOU KNOW THAT FRIENDSHIP WITH THE WORLD IS HATRED TOWARD GOD? JAMES 4:4, NIV.

CHOOSING FRIENDS

It's better to disappoint a friend than to disappoint Jesus Christ, your best Friend.

Inconsiderate Toni

LOVE FORGETS MISTAKES; NAGGING ABOUT THEM PARTS THE BEST OF FRIENDS. PROVERBS 17:9, TLB.

CHOOSING FRIENDS

If you were Sharon, which option would you choose? Why?

"I wonder where Toni is?" Sharon muttered as she carried a box of decorations into the church fellowship room. "She promised to be here to help me decorate for the party!"

Sharon plopped down on the stage floor to wait for Toni and began blowing up balloons. *I sure hope she at least gets here in time to help put them up!* she thought as she kept blowing and tying. Soon balloons covered the floor, but there was no sign of Toni.

The door opened. Eric and Brian had come to set up tables and chairs as they had promised. "Where's Toni?" Eric asked.

"Didn't show as usual!" Sharon grumbled. "I'm really mad this time. She promised!"

"Here, let me help you put up the balloons and streamers. You can't do this all alone."

"Thanks, Brian!" Sharon said. "You're a real friend. Wish I could say the same for Toni."

"She's always doing this to you," Eric said. "Why do you keep hanging out with her?"

"Oh, 'cause I can't help liking her," Sharon replied. "We have a lot of good times together. She makes me laugh a lot. She's really a good person, but her memory's pretty poor when it comes to work! In fact, sometimes she's downright inconsiderate. I guess I'm still upset."

"I wouldn't take it if I were you," Brian agreed.

Sharon was definitely disappointed in Toni. She had at least three options.

1. *Ignore the offense.* Every friendship has some irritations. We can't let every little disappointment break up a good relationship. She could learn to tolerate Toni's forgetfulness and skipping out on responsibilities.

2. *Confront her friend.* Sharon could face Toni with how her inconsiderate actions affect her. Criticism is hard to take, but sometimes it has to be given if a relationship is to be saved. It should be given with great tact and gentleness.

3. *Walk away.* Every relationship doesn't have to work out. Sharon could find someone who is more dependable and considerate.

The Promotion

Sometimes it happens between friends: one gets a promotion, and the other doesn't. One gets elected class president; the other doesn't. One gets first prize; the other gets second.

It happened to Jesus and John the Baptist. The crowds left John and flocked to Jesus. It happened to David and Jonathan. Jonathan was passed up; David was anointed king. It happened to Debbie and Laurie. Debbie was made supervisor; Laurie had to make way for Debbie.

Laurie found this hard to do. She and Debbie were good friends, and both were unit supervisors. The company boss decided to consolidate the units, putting them all under one main supervisor. He chose Debbie.

It's not fair, Laurie thought. *I've had more experience than Debbie. I love what I'm doing and want things to remain the same.*

One of the problems was that all the records, letters, and orders would now be handled from Debbie's office. If Laurie wanted anything for her unit, she'd have to clear it with Debbie.

At lunch one day Laurie decided to tell Debbie how she felt about the change. "I don't like this new arrangement," Laurie said. "I don't mind your getting the promotion; what I mind is all the changes that you're bringing in. I want to keep the letters and files in my unit. I want to keep making my own orders for what we need."

"It wasn't my idea," Debbie defended herself. "I didn't ask for the job; but if I didn't take it, someone else would. I didn't decide what changes would be made. I'm only following orders. Anyway, what difference does it make?"

"I'm not sure you'll be fair," Laurie said. "You'll probably favor your old unit."

"Ridiculous!" Debbie laughed. "You should know me better than that."

After that Debbie and Laurie drifted apart. Debbie was disappointed that Laurie hadn't trusted her to be fair. Laurie was disappointed that Debbie didn't seem to understand her feelings.

HE MUST BECOME GREATER; I MUST BECOME LESS. JOHN 3:30, NIV.

CHOOSING FRIENDS

The one who comes in second needs the attitude of John the Baptist. The one who comes in first needs the understanding of Jesus.

Tale of Two Monkeys

JEALOUSY IS CRUEL AS THE GRAVE. SONG OF SOLOMON 8:6.

CHOOSING FRIENDS

Jealousy results in a disappointing friendship. Jealousy separates friends. It's as cruel as death.

Bosco, our pet monkey, was 3 years old when another monkey dropped out of the tamarind tree and offered to be his friend. They chattered at each other. Bosco ran back and forth inside his cage, and the new monkey followed him back and forth on the outside.

For several days the new monkey talked to Bosco in monkey talk. One day they sat close together, with only the wire between them. Each reached through the wire and put his arms around the other. They sat this way for a long time, grooming each other and pulling each other's fur gently as though looking for fleas.

One morning we opened the cage door just a crack, and the new monkey ran inside to join Bosco. We closed the door behind him, and we had two monkeys. We called the new monkey Rama.

Rama and Bosco were very happy together. They climbed on the poles in their cage. They chased each other around in circles. They sat for hours grooming each other and slept together at night, their arms holding each other close.

Bosco and Rama were the picture of a perfect friendship until it came to feeding time. They scrapped over the food. Whatever one had, the other wanted. They screeched at each other and tried to get whatever the other had before it was swallowed.

One day I handed each of them a banana. Both tackled those bananas as though they'd not eaten for a week. But after the first bite Bosco looked up to see what Rama was doing. He saw Rama eating a banana, dropped his own, and went after Rama's treasure. After a tussle, Bosco won, grabbed Rama's banana, and headed for a far corner to finish it off.

If you observe people closely, you'll find that we aren't much different in our behavior than Bosco and Rama. How often good friends squabble because one is jealous of the other, or envious of what the other has, or unable to be happy because of something the other has that he or she wants!

The Lucifer Problem

Lucifer had a problem; it was an "I" problem. Read Lucifer's whole speech in Isaiah 14:12-14, and you'll find that every sentence begins with I. He says "I" five times in these two verses.

A Peanuts cartoon I have in my files shows how the "I" problem works among people. Charlie Brown says to Lucy, "You know, you talk about yourself all the time!"

Lucy stands there seeming not to comprehend.

He continues, "It's just 'I' this and 'I' that all the time! You may not realize it, but all you ever say is 'I . . . I . . . I . . . I . . . I!"

"I?" asks Lucy.

Charlie Brown rolls his eyes to the ceiling as though to say, "See what I mean!"

The big "I" is in the center of all sin—S-I-N. Selfishness in some form is behind all the problems among friends. Selfishness makes us inconsiderate of others. When we focus on ourselves, we don't see the needs of our friends.

A wise man once said, "A person wrapped up in himself makes a rather small package."

Try this experiment. Listen to people around you talk for a few minutes. Keep track of the times they use the word "I" in their conversation. Ask your mom or dad to keep track of how many times you use the word "I" for a specified length of time. To make it fair, they'll need to wait until you've forgotten about your request so that you're acting naturally. You may be surprised at how many times you use the big "I" yourself.

Selfishness is at the root of all friendship problems. It causes us to make friends for the wrong reasons. Selfish people choose friends for what those friends can do for them, not for the pleasure they can give their friends. Selfishness leads to exploitation, manipulation, and possessiveness in friendship.

Selfishness was Lucifer's problem. It doesn't have to be your problem. Jesus can help you to be unselfish, just as He was when He was your age.

Nov. 13

I WILL ASCEND ABOVE THE TOPS OF THE CLOUDS; I WILL MAKE MYSELF LIKE THE MOST HIGH. ISAIAH 14:14, NIV.

CHOOSING FRIENDS

Selfishness always leads to disappointment in friendship.

Breathing Room

CHOOSING FRIENDS

Friendships can be smothered by too much closeness. Allow breathing room. Respect a person's privacy.

Jesus knocks, but He doesn't break down the door! He offers you His friendship, but He never pushes it down your throat. He wants to be close to you, but He's willing to give you breathing room. How different from the way Monica treated her friends!

Monica was delighted when a new family moved next door. Before the movers had put one stick of furniture in Theresa's house, Monica walked through the open door with a basket of homemade cookies.

"Hi! I'm your next-door neighbor," she said. "I thought you'd be glad for some cookies and a friendly face!"

The next morning before breakfast Theresa took some boxes out to the curb for the garbage man. Monica was right there with a tray of cereal, fruit, sweet rolls, and milk. "I fixed your breakfast for you!" she chirped. "I thought probably you hadn't got to the store yet." She breezed into the kitchen ahead of Theresa and opened the cupboard doors looking for bowls to set the table.

Theresa was still in her pajamas. She'd planned to go back to bed after putting out the garbage. She was beat after the long drive with the moving van. Sleep is what she wanted, not food. She yawned, hoping Monica would take the hint.

"You must be tired," Monica said, sitting down at the table.

Oh, no! She's going to stay. I wish she'd leave so I can go back to bed. Theresa yawned again.

"What you need is a good breakfast to wake you up," Monica said, pushing a bowl toward Theresa. "I'll be glad to stay and help you unpack."

"No thanks," Theresa said rather curtly. "I'd rather do it alone."

"Well!" Monica huffed. "I was only trying to be friends."

What Monica didn't realize was that Theresa already felt smothered by her attention. Theresa needed breathing room. Friendship needs time and freedom to grow. It cannot be forced. Friendship knocks politely at the door of someone's heart; it doesn't go barging in.

Sometimes You Lose

The rich young ruler was disappointed in Jesus. He thought Jesus demanded too much. Jesus was disappointed because He loved the young man.

The truth is that you can't win them all. Everybody isn't going to be your friend, any more than everybody chooses to be God's friend. Someone rejecting your friendship doesn't mean that there's something wrong with you. The reason people choose to turn away is usually because of something within themselves.

Allison was excited about going to an Adventist academy. She was enthusiastic about the possibility of learning new things, making new friends.

Kate hated the thought of attending academy. She wanted to go to high school, but her dad insisted she had to go to a Christian school. She arrived on campus upset with the whole world, prepared to hate the academy experience.

Allison arrived to discover that her roommate was Kate. Kate was already there, sitting on a suitcase, frowning. She said, "Hi! My name's Allison. I guess we're roommates."

"Yeah? Well, I'm Kate. I hate this ratty little room. I can't figure out where to put all my stuff, much less your things."

"We'll figure something out. It's lunchtime. Want to come to the cafeteria with me?"

"No. I've got a hamburger from McDonald's. I know I'll hate the food here, all that phony baloney," Kate sneered.

"Suit yourself," Allison said. "See you later."

For several weeks Allison tried to be friends with Kate, but Kate always had something cutting to say, or she'd clam up and not talk at all. After a while Allison gave up. She made other friends and spent as little time as possible in her room. But she felt bad about it. What had she done to cause Kate to reject her?

The answer was nothing. Kate's put-downs had nothing to do with Allison personally. Kate rejected Allison because she rejected the whole school. Allison was the unlucky recipient of Kate's anger and resentment toward her father.

Nov. 15

WHEN THE YOUNG MAN HEARD THIS, HE WENT AWAY SAD. MATTHEW 19:22, NIV.

CHOOSING FRIENDS

There are many reasons a friend-ship doesn't fly. You can't win them all.

The Wedge

YOUR INIQUITIES HAVE SEPARATED YOU FROM YOUR GOD.
ISAIAH 59:2, NIV.

CHOOSING FRIENDS

When we sin, our guilt drives a wedge between us and God. The broken relationship can be restored through confession, restitution, and forgiveness.

Something was wrong with Ted's relationship with God, and he knew what it was. While an officer of his church's teen group, he had the responsibility of counting the offering. Every week he pocketed a quarter or two for himself.

I'm only borrowing it, Ted thought to himself. *One of these days I'll pay it back.*

Several years later Ted went forward during a call for commitment and gave himself fully to God for the first time in his life.

Ted decided it would be neat to be God's friend. There was only one problem. Every time Ted prayed, he felt uncomfortable, because God would remind him about those quarters he'd stolen from the church offering.

"That was a long time ago, God," Ted said.

"If you want to be My friend, you need to make that right," God kept speaking to Ted's conscience. "Your sin is separating you from Me."

Ted knew that God was disappointed that their friendship wasn't growing. He understood that even that little sin of his past was like a wedge separating him from his Friend.

The next time he was home, he spoke to Ralph Gibson, a church leader, about his problem. He was scared. Mr. Gibson was a tall, imposing man and could be very stern. "You probably won't believe this, but I stole money from the offering when I was president of the youth group here."

"Well, Ted, what are you going to do about it?"

"I'll pay it back. I don't have the money now, but I'll pay it back as best I can."

"Good!" Mr. Gibson said. "That's what you should do. Give it to me, and I'll put it in the offering. Only the three of us will ever know."

"Three?"

Mr. Gibson smiled. "You and I and God. Nobody else will ever know."

It took Ted all summer, but he turned in more money than he had stolen. He felt good to have made things right. Removing the wedge made a big difference in his relationship with God.

Cousin Hank

ousin Hank was older, bigger, and stronger than Lewis. He was friendly and fun to be around. But there was another side to Cousin Hank, a side that seemed to enjoy being mean.

The day after Lewis Smedes graduated from high school he went to stay with Uncle Klaas and work for him in the Smedes Iron Works. Cousin Hank took him under his wing.

As long as the two were alone, Cousin Hank was friendly. However, as soon as anyone came by, Cousin Hank showed his cruel side.

"Look at the mess you've made, Lew!" he'd yell. "Can't you do anything right?"

Or "Lew, you aren't worth two cents in this factory. You wouldn't have a chance if you weren't related!"

Or "I never saw such a poor excuse for a worker! Lew doesn't know the difference between a hammer and a curling iron!"

Lewis cringed inside, hating his cousin for making fun of him. Again and again it happened. Cousin Hank would spend time setting him up, then knock him flat in front of others.

I hate you! I hate you! Lewis thought, letting his anger smolder where no one could see it. *I hate you for taking me in as a friend, then kicking me around like a stray dog. I haven't done anything to deserve your insults, Hank. You make me so angry!*

But Lewis was smaller than Cousin Hank. He needed a friend, and Cousin Hank, mean as he was, was all he had at the time. So he spent time with him, hating him every minute they were together.

Even after Lewis left Detroit he couldn't leave the hurt behind. It was always there, making him angry.

Then Lewis did something really amazing. He decided to do for Hank what God had done for him, setting things right between them in his heart. He decided to forgive Cousin Hank, to let go of the hurt, to not allow it to fester inside him anymore. They never did become close friends, but at least the pain was gone.

WE WERE MADE RIGHT WITH GOD BY HIS GRACE.
TITUS 3:7, ICB.

CHOOSING FRIENDS

The best way to get over the hurt of a disappointing relationship is to forgive.

Picking Cherries

I WAS WOUNDED IN THE HOUSE OF MY FRIENDS. ZECHARIAH 13:6, NKJV.

CHOOSING FRIENDS

When a friend hurts you, decide how deep it is. Don't lose a friend over a shallow hurt.

Ten-year-old Lew was a town boy. He loved the three days they spent every summer on a farm 15 miles out of town.

Frank, the teenage son of the farmers, was Lew's idol. Lew followed Frank around, feeling very much a farmer himself. He sat with Frank for hours on the tractor. He went with Frank to bring home the cows for milking. He pitched hay with Frank. They discovered a nest of baby rabbits together. They picked cherries together.

But one day Lew picked cherries alone. He stood on a tall, rickety stepladder as he filled his bucket with the ripe, red fruit. A couple trees away, hidden from his view but not from his hearing, Frank picked cherries with a friend his own age.

Lew could hear them laughing. He paused to listen. Frank was talking about him!

"Lew is good for nothing," Frank said. "He's your typical city kid—wouldn't know enough to come in out of a storm if it was hailing coconuts!"

Tears stung Lew's eyes. *How can he talk about me like that? I thought we were friends!* It was as though he'd been punched in the stomach. He felt sick, hurt, and embarrassed.

Then a new thought came to him. *He's telling the truth. I am a city kid. I'm not much good as a farmer. He's not saying he doesn't like me, just that farming is not one of my good points. There's no use getting upset. He's not trying to hurt me. I'll just forget it.*

Lew had stumbled upon a very real truth about relationships. There are two kinds of hurts friends give us: shallow hurts and deep hurts.

Shallow hurts are things like annoyances, unintended slights, thoughtless remarks, and unmet expectations. Shallow hurts are like a slap in the face, but not worth quarreling over.

Deep hurts are things like disloyalty, malicious remarks intended to hurt, broken promises, betrayal, cruelty, and brutality. These hurts can't be excused. They have to be dealt with, confronted, and forgiven—or the friendship won't survive.

When Friends Fail

ail felt trapped. Her five older brothers and sisters refused to help. Worse than that, they tried to make her feel guilty about what she'd done.

Gail was the youngest of six children. The others had married and left home, but Gail had stayed behind to look after their aging, sick mother. Finally it got too much for her. Gail couldn't handle the problem alone, so she appealed to her brothers and sisters for help.

"I couldn't possibly do it," one said. "I have to work."

"Count us out," said another. "We have children. It would be too much for us."

"You have no children," another pointed out. "It's much easier for you than for us. You'll have to do it."

But Gail couldn't do it any longer. She was burned out, unable to cope. The only answer was to put her sick mother into a nursing home, where she could be cared for properly.

"How can you do such a thing," her siblings objected, "after all she's done for you!"

So Gail tried to hang on, struggling to manage.

"Why are you doing this?" a friend asked Gail. "It's the best thing to put your mother where she can get proper care."

"But my brothers and sisters will hate me!" Gail moaned.

"Do they love you now?" the friend asked. "They sure aren't acting like it. If they don't like your decision and want to be angry about it, that's their problem, not yours. Do what you know is best. Be nice to them, but if they don't want to be your friends, there's not much you can do about it."

It was hard for Gail. She wanted her brothers and sisters to love her, but life isn't a fairy tale. All relationships don't have a happy ending. Often there's very little we can do but accept it as a fact of life and go on.

MY KINSFOLK HAVE FAILED, AND MY FAMILIAR FRIENDS HAVE FORGOTTEN ME. JOB 19:14.

CHOOSING FRIENDS

Sometimes there's no perfect solution to the problem of a failing friendship. We have to do the best we can and then let go and not worry any more about it.

The Long View

**THESE TROUBLES AND SUFFERINGS OF OURS ARE, AFTER ALL, QUITE SMALL AND WON'T LAST VERY LONG.
2 CORINTHIANS 4:17, TLB.**

CHOOSING FRIENDS

Try looking at misunderstandings with your friends with the long view. Fifty years from now, what is it really going to matter? Is it worth ruining a friendship now?

Amy Carmichael sat with a friend in a fine restaurant in Glasgow, Scotland. It was a cozy little place with a reputation for excellent meals. A polite waiter took their order.

While they waited, the friends chatted about the dull, misty weather and the meeting they had just attended. The speaker had been as dull as the weather outside, but the message had been powerful. It had set Amy thinking about the grandness of eternity. It had given her a long view of life.

The waiter arrived with their orders. "This is the worst excuse for a meal I've ever seen!" the friend complained. "It's poorly cooked. There's no taste!"

Amy, her thoughts on heaven, hadn't even noticed her food. She looked up in surprise. She didn't say anything, but she thought, *In the light of eternity, whatever does it matter about today's dinner?*

Sometime later a friend criticized Amy for a talk she had given. The friend had misunderstood. It hurt. It was disappointing that her friend didn't seem to want to see her viewpoint. Then the thought came to her, *It won't matter 50 years from now, so what does it matter now? Nothing is important but that which is eternal.*

Whenever I take my dog Matt for a walk around Mill Lake, I like to pause for a moment at a certain bend in the trail. At that point I can see my house framed in the trees, a perfect picture. From that distance I can't see the crack in the sidewalk or the peeling paint on the windowsills. From the perspective of distance it's easy to forget small misunderstandings and to see only warmth and love shining from the windows. Fifty years from now, what difference is it going to make that Ron didn't pick up his socks or that my friend didn't remember my birthday?

Splitting Up

Paul and Barnabas had been best friends. They had traveled throughout Asia together. They had walked hundreds of miles together, shared their meals, their joys, and their sorrows. There were a lot of good memories. Then came the argument. I imagine it went something like this:

"Remember that young relative of mine, John Mark?" Barnabas brings up the subject one evening over supper.

"Yeah! Not very dependable as I remember!" Paul frowns.

"He's a good boy," Barnabas replies. "He's just young and has to learn, that's all. I'd like to take him along on our next missionary journey."

"No way!" Paul pounds his fist on the table. "When the going gets tough, then he'll take off again. I don't trust him. We've enough problems without worrying about him."

"I insist," Barnabas continues. "He's a good fellow, and he'll prove his worth. I'll see to it."

"I won't have him along," Paul says, rising from the table. "Let's hear no more about it."

"Then you'll have to find yourself another traveling companion," Barnabas says quietly. "The world is wide, and there's work enough for both of us."

"OK, if that's the way you want it," Paul answers. "I'll take Silas with me instead. No problem."

So the two friends agreed to disagree. They went their separate ways—Barnabas and John Mark to Cyprus, Paul and Silas to Syria and Cilicia.

The Paul and Barnabas friendship is an example of a disappointing relationship. Because of their different personalities, they saw things very differently. Paul was strong-willed, sure that his way was right, and unforgiving toward John Mark's mistakes. Barnabas was sensitive to John Mark's feelings as well as to his possibilities.

The best solution seemed to be to split, each going his separate way with a new friend and companion.

PAUL AND BARNABAS HAD A SERIOUS ARGUMENT ABOUT THIS. THEY SEPARATED AND WENT DIFFERENT WAYS. ACTS 15:39, ICB.

CHOOSING FRIENDS

Sometimes our best attempts at friendship fail. Sometimes we need to be honest and admit that we'd be better off to find a different friend with whom we're more compatible.

335

Tough Decision

DO WHAT IS RIGHT AND GOOD IN THE LORD'S SIGHT. DEUTERONOMY 6:18, NIV.

CHOOSING FRIENDS

When a friend disappoints us, we choose the attitude we'll take. We can choose to hate and be miserable, or we can choose to understand and forgive.

Don Hazell, a biology teacher at a state university, was good friends with James Bowers, basketball coach for the same university. Then came Don's tough decision.

After a disappointing basketball season, James recruited six-foot-eight Billy Collins, an all-American junior basketball player. He pinned all his hopes on Billy to help them win the next season.

Don faced a tough decision when he was making out his grades for first semester. Billy Collins had failed biology. Don thought about the consequences of failing James's star player.

If I flunk this guy, he won't be eligible to play basketball this season. Without him the team will lose the tournament, and James will probably lose his job. I hate to do that to James because he's my friend. But I've got to do what's right. I just hope he understands.

Don flunked Billy. James didn't understand. The next time the two old friends passed on the sidewalk, James turned his head away, refusing to acknowledge Don's greeting.

Don shrugged. *He'll get over it.*

But the next time Don headed his direction, James crossed over to the other side of the street, refusing to speak.

OK, be stubborn! Don thought. *If you don't want to speak to me, then I won't speak to you. If you want to avoid me, then I'll shun you, too!*

Months went by, and neither Don nor James spoke. It was as though they'd never met. Even their wives refused to be friends. This went on for two years.

Then one day the truth hit Don. *It's my own attitude that's making me miserable. I've been proud that I did what was right, but I've let myself be angry over James's response. I've treated him as badly as he's treated me. I'm going to ask his forgiveness.*

James responded with a warm hug. "Life's too short for hating," he said. "Let's forget it and be friends again."

The Great Disappointment

uring the early morning hours of October 23, 1844, William Farnsworth tossed in his bed, unable to sleep. Beside him his wife, Sally, sobbed softly. Tears ran down William's cheeks as he put an arm around his wife.

"Why didn't Jesus come?" William asked. "God's Word is true. I know it is. God cannot fail—then why this great disappointment?"

Sally nodded her head. The pain stuck in her throat and shook her body with sobs. That morning she'd cheerfully fixed breakfast, sure that Jesus would come before nightfall.

At breakfast William had gathered the children around the table and said, "This is our last meal on this earth. Tomorrow we'll eat with Jesus in heaven!"

They were all too excited to eat much. They could imagine how wonderful it would be to see Christ come in the clouds of heaven with all His angels. They could picture walking the streets of gold and eating from the tree of life.

Sally had hustled everyone to help with cleaning up after breakfast. They'd gone off then to the little white church to wait for the wonderful moment. It was a frosty morning, and a hot fire flickered in the stove. They stood around warming their hands, singing songs, and quoting Bible promises, such as the one in John 14:3: "I will come back" (NIV). Today was the day!

But the day dragged on. The children ran outside to play. The men put more wood on the fire. The sun went down, and someone lit the kerosene lamps. The smaller children fell asleep on the church benches. At midnight they blew out the lamps and went home to cold beds, where they cried and wondered why Jesus hadn't come.

William was disappointed Jesus hadn't come, but not disappointed in Jesus. At worship next morning he said, "We don't know why Jesus didn't come yesterday. But the Lord will send us light to understand. We have a God, and He'll hear us."

NOV. 23
I WILL COME BACK. JOHN 14:3, NIV.

CHOOSING FRIENDS

The disappointment happened because of a misunderstanding of a Bible prophecy.

The fault was theirs, not God's. Jesus will come again. We won't be disappointed.

337

Dad's Advice

A WISE SON HEEDS HIS FATHER'S INSTRUCTION. PROVERBS 13:1, NIV.

CHOOSING FRIENDS

Wise teens bring their friends home. They welcome a parent's opinions on something as important as friends.

Four-year-old Dottie May stood near the parrot's cage and admired the bird's red, blue, green, and gold feathers. Polly preened a wing while watching Dottie May out of one eye.

"Hello, Polly!" Dottie May called.

"Hello!" Polly croaked. "Polly wants a cracker!"

"Daddy, may I feed Polly?" Dottie May called to her father, who was sitting at the kitchen table.

"No, Dottie May. I've told you that before. Now come away from Polly's cage."

"Why?" she asked. "I like Polly. She's pretty."

"She might hurt you. Come away right now!"

Dottie May frowned and stuck out her lower lip. She walked away from the cage, thinking, *Daddy's being mean. Polly won't hurt me. She likes me. I know she does.*

As soon as Daddy went outside, Dottie May ran back to the cage. She crept closer and closer. Polly just sat there, watching little Dottie May.

"I like you, Polly," Dottie May said, poking a finger through the cage to touch Polly's wing. "Hello, Polly," she whispered.

"Hello," Polly rasped and grabbed Dottie May's finger in her beak.

"Daddy! Help! Polly's got my finger!"

Daddy ran back inside and freed Dottie May's finger. It was bleeding.

"Put it under the cold water," Mother said.

"It hurts!" Dottie May cried.

"Of course it does," Daddy answered. "Why didn't you listen when I told you to stay away?"

"I wanted Polly to be my friend."

"Well, maybe you'd better listen to Daddy after this when you're choosing your friends. It might save you a lot of trouble."

Now that Dottie May is grown up, she says, "I'm glad I learned to respect my dad's advice when it came to choosing friends. My friends were always welcome at our home, and more than once he steered me away from what could have been a disappointing friendship. I'm really thankful for my dad's advice."

Sundar's Sacrifice

Fifteen-year-old Sundar Singh watched as his uncle turned the lock and opened the family safe. He gasped at the stacks of jewels and gold coins, their family's fortune.

"It's yours one day," his uncle said, "but you must give up this foolish idea of being a Christian. Our family is proud of our Sikh religion. We want you to maintain our family honor. Please don't disgrace your family by being baptized a Christian."

Sundar shook his head sadly. "I'm sorry to hurt you, Uncle. I have no desire to disgrace my family, but if you offered me the whole world I couldn't turn my back on Jesus, who died for me."

His uncle slammed the safe door shut. "You'll be sorry!"

Shortly after that, his father prepared a family feast. "It's to say goodbye," his father said sadly. "I'm renouncing you as my son. I will have nothing more to do with you."

A few hours later Sundar began to feel strange. He made his way to the home of Christian friends, where he collapsed. "My father has kicked me out of the house, and I'm very sick. I think someone put poison in my food!"

Sundar's life was saved that night by the help of his Christian friends, and on his sixteenth birthday he was baptized in Simla, a town high in the Himalayan foothills.

During the next 25 years Sundar Singh wandered all across India, telling everyone who would listen about his Friend, Jesus Christ, who loved them and wanted to be their friend, too.

Not once did Sundar's new Friend let him down. The story of his life is full of incredible tales of deliverance from a leopard, from being sewn into a wet yakskin and being left to be crushed to death as it dried, from being tied into cloths laced with leeches and scorpions, and from being roped to a tree to be eaten by wild animals.

THOUGH MY FATHER AND MOTHER FORSAKE ME, THE LORD WILL RECEIVE ME. PSALM 27:10, NIV.

CHOOSING FRIENDS

Sometimes even parents may disappoint us, but when that happens we can turn to our heavenly Father, who will take us under His wings.

Happy-Time Friends

I WILL BE WITH HIM IN TROUBLE. PSALM 91:15, NIV.

CHOOSING FRIENDS

Friendships based on happy times often end in disappointment. True friends show their colors in times of adversity.

Doug and Mike were best friends. They rode skateboards together after school. They watched videos at Mike's house on rainy days, or shot baskets at Doug's house on good days. They went camping, boating, and fishing every summer.

One day Doug went over to see if Mike would go swimming. His mom answered the door. "Mike's sick," she said. "We're taking him to the hospital for some tests." She sounded worried.

A week or so later Mike shared the news with Doug. "I've got cancer," he said. "I have to have radiation treatments all summer. What a drag! The doc says I won't have much energy, so I can't go camping. So I don't suppose I'll see you much."

"Hey, man, what's a friend for?" Doug asked. "I'll come over to your place every day and do whatever you feel like doing."

Doug tried to keep his promise. He came every day for a while and tried to make Mike feel better. They watched TV and played a little Monopoly, but Mike was tired and had bad headaches. He wasn't much fun.

One day Doug breezed in for just a minute. "I've got to run," he said. "We're going on a five-day canoe trip, so I won't be around for a while."

Doug didn't show the next week, either. Mike called up and talked a few minutes. "When you coming over again?" he asked.

"Can't come tomorrow," he said. "I'm going on a church picnic, but I'll come over one of these days soon. I promise."

He never came back the rest of the summer. Other friends came, but not his best friend, Doug. Mike was disappointed. He asked his mom, "Why doesn't he come? Does he think he can catch what I've got?"

"I don't think so," she replied. "Some friendships can't stand the strain of adversity. Let Doug go. A real friend would stick with you in bad times as well as the happy times."

Poor Pussycat

Walking down the road one October afternoon I heard a weak meow above the noise of the traffic. I stopped a moment and listened.

"Meow!" There it was just a few feet ahead of me. Beside a pile of garbage I saw a tiny kitten lying on a large banana leaf. I knelt down and patted the kitten's matted fur.

Her eyes were sealed shut with pus, but at my touch I could feel her begin to purr. I picked her up. She weighed almost nothing and was so small she fit comfortably into the cup of one hand.

"Oh, you poor, poor thing!" I said. "Did someone throw you out here to die? I'll take you home with me."

At home I found a box and put in a soft pillow and a towel. I warmed some milk and fed it to her with a medicine dropper. She gratefully swallowed what I put into her mouth, but it was so little. I tried to get her to eat from a saucer, but she was too weak. I washed her wounds and talked to her. I kept her by my bed at night, getting up several times to feed her.

Despite my best efforts, the kitten died. When I realized that all my work had been for nothing, I flopped down onto the bed and sobbed for a long time. Then I found a shoe box and buried her in the back garden under the papaya tree.

"Poor, poor pussycat," I said as I covered the box with dirt. "I had you for only a few days to love, and I miss you so much already. I'll be glad when Jesus comes and we won't have to lose anyone ever again."

I thought of other friends and loved ones who had died: my father, Grandma Eaton, Grandma Brown, Aunt Nina, pet chicken Norman, and Frisky, my cocker spaniel. I cried some more.

HE WILL WIPE AWAY EVERY TEAR FROM THEIR EYES. THERE WILL BE NO MORE DEATH, SADNESS, CRYING, OR PAIN. REVELATION 21:4, ICB.

CHOOSING FRIENDS

Losing friends in death is painfully disappointing. Someday soon Jesus will come and wipe away all our tears and there will be no more death, crying, or disappointment.

Warning Signals

**GOD WILL GIVE
YOU WISDOM.
JAMES 1:5, ICB.**

CHOOSING
FRIENDS

God doesn't want
us to remain in a
poor relationship.
He has something
better in store for
us. He can give
us wisdom to
know what we
should do about
our friendships.

Sometimes relationships can be very compli-
cated. It's hard to know whether you have a
good friendship or a disappointing one. At such confusing times you can ask God to give you wisdom.

Below are some warning signals that will help
you know when you've formed a poor relationship.

1. *Irritability.* You feel restless and discontent
when with your friend. You feel a vague unease when
in his or her presence.

2. *Shame.* You feel guilty or unclean when with
that person.

3. *Watchfulness.* You're careful about what you
say and do because you never know what you might
do to offend your friend.

4. *Pressure.* You feel pressured to act in a certain way to be acceptable, even though you may not
think it right.

5. *Tempted.* You're tempted to do things you
would never do if you were left to your own choice.

6. *Drained.* The relationship drains away your
energy. An evening with your friend leaves you feeling exhausted.

7. *Put Down.* You feel verbally abused and put
down, even though it may be done in a joking manner.

8. *Sacrifice.* You find yourself sacrificing all
your own goals, dreams, and preferences to meet
the needs of another. You're living only for your
friend's happiness.

9. *Emptiness.* There's a certain emptiness in
your relationship because you don't share a common
love of Jesus and His message of truth.

10. *Dishonesty.* You find yourself hiding your
true thoughts and feelings in order to meet the expectations of your friend.

Any one of the above should flash a warning signal that something is definitely wrong in your relationship. Either the difficulty must be confronted and
a change occur, or the relationship should come to
an end. Breaking off a relationship can be very
painful to both you and your friend, but sometimes
that's the best way to go.

Dropping a Friend

"Have you got a minute?" asked 14-year-old Deena as she plopped down on the bed of Carmen, her older sister who was home from college.

"Sure. What's up?" Carmen laid aside her book.

"It's Jessie. Remember her?"

"Yeah! She's the bubbly one with short, curly blond hair." Carmen nodded. "What's wrong?"

Deena sighed. "I'm starting to feel annoyed with her. She always has to have her way. She's become very possessive and very controlling. She gets jealous if I spend time with anyone else. I'm beginning to feel like her slave."

"Sounds bad."

"But that's not all. I'm really uncomfortable about the kind of videos she watches. I've watched one or two, and I felt dirty afterward and wished I'd never seen them. I don't think Christians should be watching that kind of thing," Deena said.

"Have you talked to Jessie about your feelings?"

"I've tried," Deena replied, "but she laughs at my concerns or calls me an old fuddy-duddy or a stick-in-the-mud."

"I think it's time to split with Jessie."

"Any suggestions of how to do it? I don't want to hurt her."

Carmen thought a moment. "I can't guarantee she won't be hurt. You can't control her response. All you can do is try to control how you act. Here are four things you can do:

"*First, be certain.* If you act unsure, she'll persuade you that it doesn't matter. Make sure you really want to do this.

"*Second, be kind.* Try not to be harsh or cruel. Put her in the best light possible, even use a compliment or two. Let her know you'll always treasure her friendship, but think it best now to branch out and make other friends.

"*Third, be firm.* Don't hesitate or stammer. If your decision is made, then make it firm and final.

"And last, *wish her well.* Forgive her for whatever she's done and wish her happiness in the future. Treat her as you'd like to be treated if she was dumping you!"

DO TO OTHERS AS YOU WOULD HAVE THEM DO TO YOU. LUKE 6:31, NIV.

CHOOSING FRIENDS

Follow the golden rule when it comes to dropping a friend.

Disappointing Friends Checkup

Nov. 30

**I WILL NEVER
LEAVE YOU NOR
FORSAKE YOU.
JOSHUA 1:5,
NIV.**

Friends may disappoint us, but Jesus never will.

This month's quiz is different from the others so far. Instead of rating yourself, you'll simply answer Yes or No as it applies to you. A yes answer will indicate a disappointing relationship. What can you do about the disappointing ones?

1. I'm disappointed with God when bad things happen to me.
❏ Yes ❏ No

2. I have only one friend.
❏ Yes ❏ No

3. I still feel bitter and hurt about a friend who disappointed me a long time ago.
❏ Yes ❏ No

4. If there's a problem in my relationship, I expect the other person to make things right.
❏ Yes ❏ No

5. I've done things that disappointed God.
❏ Yes ❏ No

6. I'm jealous when a friend does better than I.
❏ Yes ❏ No

7. I choose friends for what they can do for me.
❏ Yes ❏ No

8. I force my attention on other people, smothering them with my love and concern.
❏ Yes ❏ No

9. I expect every relationship to be successful.
❏ Yes ❏ No

10. I hold grudges when someone does me wrong.
❏ Yes ❏ No

11. I hang on to a relationship even when I know it has failed and is hurting both of us.
❏ Yes ❏ No

12. When a friend hurts me, I make myself miserable with hate.
❏ Yes ❏ No

13. I see some of the following warning signals in my relationships: irritability, shame, watchfulness, pressure, put-downs, emptiness, possessiveness, and dishonesty.
❏ Yes ❏ No

Shingles or Sunsets?

Standing in a farmer's field, James sketched the glorious New England landscape spread out before him. Brush in hand, he concentrated on the emerging picture on his canvas. The sun was setting, casting a golden glow on the trees, seeming to set the land on fire.

In the foreground, silhouetted against the sunset, stood a ramshackle old barn. James squinted against the light as he painstakingly worked on capturing the intricate pattern of the shingles on the barn roof. Some were missing, and he wanted to make sure he got it just right.

For about 15 minutes William Hunt, his art teacher, observed James painting the roof of the old barn. All the while the western sky was ablaze. He watched as the colors changed from brilliant crimson to a breathtaking gold.

At last Mr. Hunt spoke quietly. "Son, if you spend too much time on the shingles, you'll never have time to paint the sunset, for it's rapidly changing. Soon it will be gone. You'll have to choose between the shingles and the sunset. What's your choice?"

James looked up from his easel. He gasped at the beauty spread before him. His face reflected the evening glow as he picked up his brush and said with sudden understanding, "The sunset, sir. I choose the sunset."

Your life spreads before you like a glorious picture. What will you paint? Where will you focus your attention? On barns or on sunsets? On things that really matter, or on the trivial? On the good, or on the evil? On heavenly things, or on earthly things?

The choices you make today are vitally important. The friends you choose will have a great deal to do with whether your life will be as glorious as a sunset or as drab as an old barn. Friends can lead you to concentrate on the earthly, or they can lead you closer to the heavenly. Every day you must choose between the barn or the sunset.

THEN CHOOSE FOR YOURSELVES THIS DAY WHOM YOU WILL SERVE. JOSHUA 24:15, NIV.

CHOOSING FRIENDS

Daily we have choices to make, powerful choices that may determine our happiness here and in the hereafter.

The Dare

"Did you know that if you're 17 you can join the Navy without getting your folks' OK?" Louie asked.

"Really?" Bill responded.

"Yeah! And I'm going to join. My folks want me to wait three months until I graduate, but a war's going on and I want to go now. In three months I could finish boot camp and be out on sea duty. I'm enlisting tomorrow."

"Wow!"

"Come with me, Bill. We'll win the war together. It'll be an adventure."

"I figured I'd wait until I was drafted after I'm 18," Bill replied.

"That's stupid!" Louie was getting angry. "Then you'll get garbage. If you enlist, you get your choice. I'm going on an aircraft carrier."

"Sounds exciting." Bill hesitated. "But I don't like the thought of not telling my folks, and besides, I'm not 17 until three more days."

"OK, then I'll wait the three days so you can join me," Louie conceded. "Or are you chicken?"

"I ain't scared!" Bill countered. "I can take a dare."

For three days Bill could think of nothing else but his coming enlistment. He thought, *I wish I'd said no. This is dumb. I don't want to go, and I let Louie bully me into this. I'm scared, but I'm not backing out now and have him laugh at me.*

Finally the moment came when the two friends walked up the steps of the post office and went to the room where the Navy was taking enlistments. They filled out some papers, then went for their physicals. Bill was taken first. Within a few minutes he stood before the petty officer and was sworn into the Navy. He waited for Louie.

Louie came out of the room, furious. "I flunked the physical," he said. "They won't take me!"

Within days Bill was gone. Many times during boot camp he felt like kicking himself for his foolish choice to accept Louie's dare.

I HAVE ACTED LIKE A FOOL AND HAVE ERRED GREATLY.
1 SAMUEL 26:21, NIV.

CHOOSING FRIENDS

A hasty choice can affect your life for many years to come. Look before you leap. Think before you follow a friend in a way you don't want to go.

Mohandas' Strength

One day at his school in India, Mohandas Gandhi and a friend were discussing the English, who ruled India at that time. "Why do you think the English are able to rule us?" Mohandas asked.

"Because they're stronger," his friend replied.

"What makes them stronger?" Mohandas wanted to know.

"Meat," his friend responded. "Englishmen eat meat, and Hindus are vegetarians."

"But you're strong, and you're a Hindu."

His friend laughed. "Don't tell anyone, but I eat meat secretly. Come to my house sometime and share my meat. Then you'll be strong too!"

Mohandas thought, *Maybe he has a point. He's tall, strong, and a fantastic runner. I'm short, skinny, and a poor runner. Maybe he's found the secret of strength.*

"I'll come with you tomorrow," Mohandas agreed. "You can give me some of your meat. I'll see if it makes me strong."

The next afternoon after school the two friends went to a quiet place by the river. The friend unwrapped a bundle from his school bag, and there were two hunks of curried mutton. Mohandas watched as his friend ripped off a piece and chewed it with relish.

"Come on, silly!" his friend laughed. "Do you want to stay weak and feeble all your life?"

Mohandas took a bite and chewed it as fast as he could. It didn't taste good at all to him, but he struggled to swallow it, all the time imagining how strong he'd soon be.

That night he felt as though the animal were kicking inside his stomach, preventing his sleep. His conscience bothered him too.

Before morning Mohandas resolved, *Never again. If the English will ever be conquered, it'll have to be some other way, because my conscience won't allow me to kill or to eat meat.*

Mohandas Gandhi grew up to be Mahatma Gandhi, the great teacher of nonviolence and the leader of a movement that brought about India's freedom from English rule. His strength came from following his conscience.

Dec. 3

So I strive always to keep my conscience clear before God and man. Acts 24:16, NIV.

Choosing Friends

We need to evaluate suggestions from friends in the light of what our conscience tells us is right.

Peer Pressure

THEY WERE AFRAID OF THE CROWD. MATTHEW 21:46, NIV.

CHOOSING FRIENDS

Have you ever done something foolish because you wanted to impress the crowd? Submitting to peer pressure is a choice, but often not the best one.

Have you noticed that we often act differently in a crowd? The group has an amazing ability to put pressure on the individual. If everyone thinks it's OK, then often we're tempted to go along. Sometimes we'd rather do something wrong than be laughed at by the crowd.

Everyone faces up to peer pressure sooner or later and has to make a decision. Twelve-year-old Horatio Nelson (who later became Admiral Nelson of Trafalgar fame) was no exception. It happened not long after he transferred to a new school in North Walsham, England. A group of boys sat talking.

"I'm starved," said one. "What I wouldn't give for a nice juicy pear!"

"I know where we can get some," another suggested. "There's a tree full of them in the schoolmaster's garden."

"Yeah! Why don't we go get some!" yet another said, smacking his lips. "Who's brave enough to go?"

Most shook their heads. One replied, "And get caned by the schoolmaster, or worse yet, expelled? Count me out."

"You're scared," someone taunted.

"Of course I'm scared," the other answered. "And so is everyone else."

"I'm not," Horatio announced, seeing a chance to prove his worth to the crowd. "There's nothing to it. You want pears? I'm your man!"

That night two of his friends made a rope from sheets and lowered Horatio out of his bedroom window. His heart raced. Stealthily he crept along in the shadows through the garden gate to the pear tree. He filled his shirt and pockets with pears, then was drawn back up into his room by his friends.

Everyone crowded around as he gave out the pears. Someone noticed he kept none for himself. "Don't you want any?" he asked.

"I did it only because you were all afraid," Horatio said. "I really don't want any." The truth was that Horatio was feeling a pang of conscience, knowing he'd done wrong.

The Wrong Path

A young social worker climbed the steps of the apartment house in the heart of the inner city and knocked on one of the doors. A drunken man stomped across the floor and jerked open the door. "What ya want?"

The young woman trembled a little at his rough greeting. "Mr. Czolgosz?" she asked.

"That's me. What ya want?"

"It's about your son, Leon. I'd like to invite him to a special program for children over at the church. We'll be having Bible stories and interesting things to do, and I think he'd enjoy it. Would you let him come?"

The man frowned. "Don't have no use for the Bible," he said. "My kid ain't going to no church." He slammed the door shut.

He didn't know it, but he'd made a decision about what path his son would take that day, a path that led away from God, a path that would lead to death.

Leon grew up in the streets and alleys of the inner city. His friends were a tough bunch who were always on the run from the police. When he grew up he joined a gang that wanted to cause trouble for the government.

On September 5, 1901, Leon joined a huge crowd that had gathered in Buffalo, New York, to hear a speech by William McKinley, president of the United States. Leon worked his way through the crowd until he was at the very front of the line waiting to shake hands with the president.

When it was his turn, he reached out with his left hand to take the president's hand. His right hand held a revolver covered with a handkerchief. He pulled the trigger, and the president slumped forward, fatally wounded by the assassin's bullet.

Leon's life could have ended so differently had his father chosen a different path many years before. At some point Leon also chose that path, and his friends helped keep him there.

DEC. 5

I HAVE SET BEFORE YOU LIFE AND DEATH. . . . NOW CHOOSE LIFE, SO THAT YOU AND YOUR CHILDREN MAY LIVE. DEUTERONOMY 30:19, NIV.

CHOOSING FRIENDS

Which path will you choose—the way of life or the way of death? Friends do make a difference in the success or failure of life.

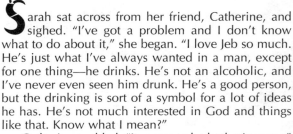

Love or Truth?

DEC. 6

**I HAVE CHOSEN
THE WAY
OF TRUTH.
PSALM 119:30,
NIV.**

CHOOSING
FRIENDS

God is a Friend
you can trust. If
you'll put your
future into His
hands, He'll
guide you to the
friends who are
best for you.

Sarah sat across from her friend, Catherine, and sighed. "I've got a problem and I don't know what to do about it," she began. "I love Jeb so much. He's just what I've always wanted in a man, except for one thing—he drinks. He's not an alcoholic, and I've never even seen him drunk. He's a good person, but the drinking is sort of a symbol for a lot of ideas he has. He's not much interested in God and things like that. Know what I mean?"

Catherine nodded. "It seems to be bothering you."

"It bothers me a lot," Sarah continued. "Sometimes I wonder if God's trying to tell me to give up Jeb."

"Could be," Catherine said. "What makes you think that?"

Tears glistened in Sarah's eyes. "I don't think I could hold on to my faith and Jeb, too. As much as I love Jeb, my relationship with God is even more precious. Thanks, Catherine. Talking to you has helped me see what I must do."

"And what's that?"

"I'm going to break the engagement. If God wants me to marry Jeb, He'll see that things change. If not, then He has someone else for me. It's going to be hard, but I've got to do it."

"Let's tell the Lord about your decision," Catherine suggested. They knelt together.

Tears running down her cheeks, Sarah prayed, "Lord, I'm putting my broken dreams and my unknown future into Your hands. I know I can trust You to do what's best for me."

Neither Jeb's drinking nor his ideas about God changed. Sarah broke the engagement as she had vowed. A year later Catherine received a happy letter from Sarah. "It nearly killed me to give up Jeb. Yet God knew that he wasn't the one for me. Recently I've met a wonderful Christian man. We're going to be married. I'm so thankful I trusted God. Thanks for your encouragement."

The Last Supper

An old legend illustrates the importance of choosing to follow Christ. The year was 1495. The city was Milan, Italy. Leonardo da Vinci stepped back from the mural of *The Last Supper* he was painting and sighed. It was complete except for the figures of Christ and Judas.

Where will I find a face so innocent and so sublime that it will truly represent Christ? he mused. *And how will I ever find a face so hardened by sin and deceit that it will represent Judas Iscariot?*

One morning in the choir of a tiny chapel he saw a young man with a face so innocent, so sublime, that he knew he'd found his model for Jesus. For several days the teenager sat for the great artist. When the figure of Christ was complete, the youth stared at the painting.

"It's awesome, isn't it!" he said. "I wish I could really be like Him."

"You can," Leonardo replied. "Just follow His example."

But the painting was not yet complete. There was still the missing figure of Judas. Leonardo walked the streets of the city, looking for a face lined with bitterness and remorse. No face was depraved enough to model Judas.

Months and years went by, but still the mural was unfinished. Then one evening in the year 1497 Leondardo was walking home when a beggar accosted him. As he looked at the face of the man in rags he saw intelligent eyes that were clouded with remorse, a brow lined by years of sin.

"You must come home with me," Leonardo said excitedly. "I'll give you food and a bed for the night. I must paint your picture tomorrow. I'll pay you well."

The next morning the rough, ragged beggar sat while Leonardo painted his face onto the form of Judas. When he was finished, the beggar stared at the completed painting. A tear rolled down his rough face.

"Don't you recognize me?" he cried. "I'm the same person who sat for your Christ so long ago. If only I had followed your advice."

CHRIST SUFFERED FOR YOU. HE GAVE YOU AN EXAMPLE TO FOLLOW. 1 PETER 2:21, ICB.

CHOOSING FRIENDS

Choose Christ as your friend today. You'll never regret that decision.

Friend Alcohol

CHOOSING FRIENDS

Alcohol is a poor
choice for a
friend. Those
who are wise will
leave it alone.

An old man hobbled along the San Francisco street, a bottle of cheap wine in his pocket.

"Hi, Al," an unshaven man slumped against a storefront waved to him with his bottle.

"Nice day," Al said as he shuffled by.

"Where you goin', old buddy?" the man on the sidewalk asked. "Come have a drink with me."

"Goin' home," Al said. "See you later."

The man on the sidewalk never saw Al again. Someone found him in his shack behind a waterfront store, an empty bottle of cheap wine beside him. The police came around to see if anyone knew Al's relatives.

"Don't know nothin' about him," the friend on the sidewalk said. "Don't even know his last name. Never saw no relatives. Sometimes I'd lend him money for a drink, and he always paid me back. Always spoke to me. I'll miss old Al. What'd he die of?"

"Cirrhosis of the liver," the policeman said. "Drank himself to death, I reckon."

"Poor old buddy." The drunk rubbed a tear from his cheek. "I'll miss old Al."

"His name was Alfred L. Beatie," the policeman continued. "He was once a lieutenant in the Army Air Corps, graduated from flying school in Texas, and was one of the most promising flyers in the nation."

"You don't say." The derelict looked shocked. "He never said nothin' about flyin'. Is that how he got crippled?"

"Yeah. He was in a crash soon after graduation, and no one has heard from him since. Looks like he came here to drown his troubles with alcohol."

The man on the sidewalk reached for his bottle. "Makes you feel better," he said. "Poor old Al. I'll miss him."

A Smelly Friendship

Trudy was thrilled that Julie and Lana wanted to be her friends. They seemed to be in the center of all the fun. They dressed really smart, and Trudy considered herself fortunate to find friends so easily after moving to a new town.

Then one day something happened that caused Trudy to reconsider their friendship. It happened one day in the mall while all three were Christmas shopping. They'd just come out of a crowded department store.

"Look, you guys, what I got!" Lana said, pulling a bright fuchsia silk scarf from her pocket.

"I didn't see you buy anything," Trudy said.

"I didn't, silly!" Lana laughed. "I took it when you and Julie were trying on hats. What a rush! It was great!"

"That's shoplifting!" Trudy gasped. "You could get put in jail for that!"

"Oh, don't be such a spoilsport," Julie said. "We do it all the time. Where do you think we get our neat clothes?"

"We're too smart to get caught," Lana continued. "We'll teach you how."

"No, thanks," Trudy said. "That's not my idea of fun. I'll see you guys around."

That evening she talked over with her mom what had happened. "I really like Julie and Lana, but I sure don't want to do what they're doing. I know it's wrong. Do you think I could change them if I worked on it?"

"I wouldn't try it if I were you," Mom replied. "It's easier to do wrong when several are doing it. Evil is like garlic—stay around it very long, and you begin to smell like it. I think I'd look for different friends."

"Yeah, I was thinking the same thing," Trudy admitted. "I'll speak to them and all that. I'll just not hang around with them. They probably won't want to after today, anyhow. Birds of a feather stick together, right, Mom?"

Mom chuckled as she repeated, "Birds of a feather stick together, so will pigs and swine. Rats and mice will have their choice, and so will I have mine."

DEC. 9

DO NOT IMITATE WHAT IS EVIL BUT WHAT IS GOOD. 3 JOHN 11, NIV.

CHOOSING FRIENDS

It's hard to break up a friendship, but sometimes that's the wisest route to follow.

Crawford's Proposal

YOU ARE NOT THE SAME AS THOSE WHO DO NOT BELIEVE. SO DO NOT JOIN YOURSELVES TO THEM. 2 CORINTHIANS 6:14, ICB.

CHOOSING FRIENDS

"Unless you would have a home where the shadows are never lifted, do not unite yourself with one who is an enemy of God" (Ellen G. White, *Messages to Young People*, p. 440).

ottie Moon, missionary to China, went to her room to be alone and to reread the letter from Crawford. A warm happiness filled her heart as she read, "I love you, Lottie. Come home. Marry me, and we can go as missionaries to Japan together."

Lottie and Crawford had been friends ever since she'd been his student in college. He'd admired her high spirit and gift with languages. He encouraged her to study Greek. They'd been writing since her arrival in China.

I'll do it, Lottie told herself. *I love him so much. Dear Lord, I'm first of all Yours. If this isn't right, then make Your way clear.*

A spring wedding was planned. She gave notice to the mission board that she was leaving China. She already had plans for a job at Harvard University, where Crawford was a professor. In due time they would go to Japan.

There was only one problem, and it kept intruding itself into Lottie's plans for the wedding. Crawford didn't believe in the inspiration of the Bible. He laughed at the idea that God made the world in six days and that the earth was only about 6,000 years old. He believed in the theory of evolution, which teaches that the earth evolved during millions of years and that humans came from apelike ancestors.

How can I live the rest of my life with someone who believes so differently? Lottie wondered. *I know he doesn't feel the call to mission service that I feel. Will that be a problem in the years to come? Will I end up breaking my covenant with God in order to keep my covenant with Crawford?*

After much prayer and struggle Lottie broke the engagement. Years later someone asked her if she regretted that decision. She said, "God had first claim on my life, and since the two conflicted, there could be no question about the result."

Weekly Visitor

The bell rang at Eastern High School. Doors opened and a flood of happy teenagers filled the halls. Bill Coleman headed for the gym.

A long hallway connected the main building to the gym. It was lined with pictures of famous athletes who had attended EHS. They were the sports stars of the past 40 years. Bill never paid much attention to them. There was no one there that he knew.

In his rush down the hall he nearly collided with a graying, stooped-shouldered old man. His clothes were old but clean and neat. A short, cold cigar dangled from his fingers. He stood there staring at the pictures on the wall.

"Excuse me," Bill said.

The man didn't seem to notice Bill or the throng of other students flowing around him like a river flows around a stone. He just stood there staring at the pictures.

After that, Bill noticed the old man with the cigar in the hallway about once a week. *Weird guy,* he thought. *Wonder why he comes here?*

"Have you seen that old man in the hallway?" Bill asked a teacher one day. "What's he doing here?"

"It's a sad story," the teacher replied. "He used to be a student here. In fact, he was a star athlete. He still holds a couple of track records. He was a good student and planned to go to college. Everyone thought he'd be a great success in life."

"Yeah? What happened?" Bill asked. It was obvious he wasn't much of a success now.

"On graduation night he joined a group of friends to celebrate with a few drinks. They piled into a car and headed for the open road. There was an accident. No one got hurt much except the guy who stands in the hall."

Then Bill knew why the old man came to stare at his picture on the wall. He was trying to remember what it was like before he went partying. He was thinking about the success he might have been.

DO NOT GET DRUNK ON WINE. EPHESIANS 5:18, NIV.

CHOOSING FRIENDS

Wise kids stay away from friends who include alcohol or drugs in their partying.

Freedom for Androcles

DEC. 12

CHRIST HAS SET US FREE.
GALATIANS 5:1, NIV.

CHOOSING FRIENDS

We too are slaves, bound to serve Satan. But Jesus Christ has freed us through the power of His love and friendship. What a terrific friend He is!

According to a very old legend, long ago in Rome a slave named Androcles ran away from his cruel master. Weary from running, he crawled into a cave, lay down, and fell fast asleep.

Suddenly a terrific roar echoed through the cave. Androcles awakened, terrified to see a lion at the cave entrance. But instead of crouching for the kill, the lion limped slowly toward him. Sensing the lion wanted help, he took the sore leg in his hand to see what was wrong. The lion rubbed his head against the slave's shoulder.

Androcles found a long thorn embedded in the paw and gingerly pulled it out with his fingers. The happy lion jumped about like a puppy and licked the hands and feet of his new friend. That night Androcles and the lion slept side by side in the cave.

The next day the lion brought home food for his new friend. The two lived together happily for some time. Then one day the soldiers discovered his hideaway and took him back to Rome.

Androcles was sentenced to fight a hungry lion, as was the custom in those days. Thousands of people came to the arena that day to see the fight. As the lion roared into the arena, the crowd cheered as a football crowd cheers for its home team.

Androcles, weak from fear, gave a sudden cry of recognition as the lion bounded toward him. The huge beast came to a sudden stop, then stood perfectly still as Androcles put an arm around his neck. Then it quietly lay down and licked the slave's feet.

The crowd became very quiet. What did all this mean? Androcles told the story of their friendship in the cave. A great shout went up from the throng, "Live and be free!"

So both Androcles and the lion were set free and lived together in Rome for many years—freed by the power of friendship.

Willing to Die

Ever since Solomon could remember, his father had built a special hut near the house each autumn. Its roof was covered with branches and was called a "sukkah."

"It is to remind us of the many years our Jewish ancestors spent living in the wilderness after our deliverance from Egypt," Father explained.

That special room was a gathering place for adult men for the nine-day celebration of the Feast of Tabernacles. When Solomon was 13 he was allowed to join the men in the sukkah to listen to them talk.

This is boring, Solomon thought. He picked up a book lying on the table. It fell open to Isaiah 53. He read: "He was wounded for our transgressions. . . . All we like sheep have gone astray; we have turned every one to his own way; and the Lord hath laid on him the iniquity of us all" (verses 5, 6).

I wonder who that is? Solomon thought.

He turned to his father. "Father," he whispered, "who is Isaiah writing about in chapter 53?"

Father looked startled, but said nothing.

"Who is it, Father? Who was hurt for our sins? Who bore our transgressions?"

Father again made no reply, but grabbed the book from Solomon's hands and slapped him in the face. Solomon felt hurt and humiliated, but he still wanted to know who it was.

Several years later Solomon was walking down Whitechapel Road in the Jewish section of London's East End. A man stopped him on the street. "Come hear God's message for Jews," the man invited. Solomon followed the man.

The preacher read Isaiah 53, the very chapter that Solomon had puzzled over when he was 13. Solomon learned that the man who had suffered for everyone's sins was the Messiah, Jesus Christ. He learned that Jesus had died on Calvary's cross for everyone in the world, even for him, Solomon Ginsberg.

Solomon gave his heart to Jesus that day. He spent the rest of his life telling others about his Friend Jesus who died that he might live forever.

JESUS DIED FOR US SO THAT WE CAN LIVE TOGETHER WITH HIM. 1 THESSALONIANS 5:10, ICB.

CHOOSING FRIENDS

Jesus died for your sins, too, because He wants you to live forever.

A Mother's Love

FOR GOD SO LOVED THE WORLD THAT HE GAVE HIS ONE AND ONLY SON, THAT WHOEVER BELIEVES IN HIM SHALL NOT PERISH BUT HAVE ETERNAL LIFE. JOHN 3:16, NIV.

CHOOSING FRIENDS

We can have no greater friend than Jesus Christ, who died so that we might live. We're saved by the powerful miracle of God's love.

It happened 50 years ago, during World War II. All night enemy planes flew over Liege, Belgium, dropping bombs that set the city ablaze. People huddled in basements and bomb shelters as they wondered if anyone would survive the worst air raid they'd experienced.

Morning light revealed hundreds of buildings in ruins, with who knew how many people dead or dying, trapped beneath the rubble. The cries of trapped people filled the silent streets, and soon scores of survivors were clawing at the stones, trying to help save someone whose moans they heard. The cries of distraught people looking for missing loved ones mingled with the pleas for help of those trapped.

The people of Liege worked for days trying to rescue any who were still alive. On the fourth day the rescuers began work on yet another building. As they began digging, they heard the cries of a child, "Please help me! I'm thirsty. I want water."

It was bitterly cold, and it took many hours to reach the place where he was trapped. They wondered if they'd find him still alive. They kept talking to him, hoping he'd stay alive until they reached him.

"Water," he cried. "I want water."

"How can anyone still be alive under such a pile of rubble?" someone asked, but they kept digging.

When the rescuers removed the last slab of stone, they found him still conscious, with hardly a scratch. "Water," he whimpered. "I want water."

"Amazing!" someone exclaimed. "How can it be?" Looking closer they understood. The little boy lay with his mother's body curved over and above him like an arch, protecting him from the weight of the rubble and the bitter winter cold.

In those last seconds before the building crumbled, that mother had deliberately enfolded him in her arms, knowing it was his only chance of survival. She died that he might live. He was saved by the powerful miracle of a mother's love.

The New Afrikaner

Robert Moffat was determined to take the gospel to the notorious Afrikaner, chief of Namaqualand. There was a price of $1,000 for his capture. People were terrified of him because this was the man who had killed White settlers, stolen from many others, and burned their property.

"Don't go!" farmers urged Moffat. "He'll use your skin for a drum and your skull for a drinking cup!"

"I'll go," Moffat insisted. "The gospel of Jesus Christ has the power to change Afrikaner into a child of God."

"Not Afrikaner," the farmers declared. "He's too bad. He'll not listen. There's no hope for Afrikaner."

Moffat went anyway, and he and Afrikaner became friends. Moffat built a house and church. Afrikaner often came to listen to the message from Moffat's black book. Eventually he accepted Christ as his Saviour and became a completely different person—kind, thoughtful, and loving.

Moffat convinced Afrikaner to accompany him on a journey to Cape Town to show the power of what God could do even with someone as notorious as he.

On the way Moffat stopped at a farmer's house, but left Afrikaner in the wagon. He wanted to break the news gradually about his new African friend. He knew that Afrikaner had once killed the uncle of this particular farmer.

"I can't believe my eyes!" the farmer exclaimed. "We thought you were dead, killed by Afrikaner!"

"Would you believe that Afrikaner is now a Christian?" Moffat asked.

"No! Not unless I saw him with my own eyes!"

"Come with me, then." Moffat's eyes twinkled in anticipation. As they approached the wagon, Afrikaner stood, removed his hat, and bowed politely.

"Oh, God, what a miracle of Thy power!" exclaimed the farmer. "What cannot Thy grace accomplish!"

Another Dutch farmer lifted his hands to heaven when he saw the transformed chief and declared, "This is the eighth wonder of the world! Great God, what a miracle of Thy power and grace!"

DEC. 15

IF ANYONE IS IN CHRIST, HE IS A NEW CREATION; THE OLD HAS GONE, THE NEW HAS COME! 2 CORINTHIANS 5:17, NIV.

CHOOSING FRIENDS

A friendship with Jesus Christ is the most powerful friendship there is, because it has power to completely change a person's life.

Picking Hazelnuts

**YOUR CHILDREN
I WILL SAVE.
ISAIAH 49:25,
NIV.**

CHOOSING
FRIENDS

Voice of Proph-
ecy speaker
Lonnie Mela-
shenko often tells
listeners about his
wonderful, pow-
erful Friend, Jesus.

"Everybody in the car!" Father ordered one morning. "Time to pick hazelnuts."

"Yippee!" shouted Lonnie. "This is going to be fun!"

Younger brothers Joedy, Dallas, Rudy, and
Eugene caught big brother's excitement and soon
were laughing and bouncing in the Melashenko family car. Mother climbed in too. Already that summer
they'd gone picking cherries, strawberries, and
Saskatoons with their parents. Each time was a great
family adventure.

"Hazelnuts will taste good in cookies this winter,"
Mother said. "With three of you big boys to help, we
should get a good supply today."

Father turned off the main road and onto a small
gravel road that led deep into the brush. Finding the
hazelnut trees, he parked the car on a slope in the road.

Rudy and Eugene, still toddlers of about 2 and 3
years old, were left to play in the back seat while the
rest of the family picked nuts. Tired of playing and
tired of waiting, the two babies went to sleep.

Meanwhile the car mysteriously began rolling
backward. It gathered speed and headed for a deep
ditch at the bottom of the slope. It bounced over
the edge and landed in a bed of cattails between
huge boulders.

"Oh, no! My poor babies!" Mother cried when
she saw what had happened.

Father scrambled down into the ditch and discovered that the babies were safely asleep on the back
seat. The rest of the family huddled around Mother,
praying that Father would be able to get the car out of
the ditch.

Father started up the engine and drove the car up
the steep embankment and out of the ditch without a
single scratch to show for it! Parking the car safely on
the road again, he climbed out and said, "Let's kneel
down and thank the Lord for saving the lives of Rudy
and Eugene."

The family knelt together in the gravel. The boys
saw tears flowing down their mother's and father's
cheeks as they thanked God for His marvelous pro-
tection.

Jan's Mother

Who here will promise to lead one person to Jesus this year?" Pastor May asked. "If this is what you want to do, then please stand to your feet."

Everyone just sat there as though they hadn't heard what he said. Then in the front row 7-year-old Jan jumped up and stood as tall as she could! Then everyone else stood up too.

At the end of the service Jan waited her turn to shake hands with Pastor May. "Did you see me stand?" she asked.

"I surely did," the pastor replied. "It was fabulous!"

"I think I did it wrong," she said.

"No, you looked fine to me," smiled Pastor May.

"But you said that we should stand if we wanted to lead one soul to Jesus, but I don't want to win one soul; I want to win two souls—my mother and my father. Is that OK?"

"That's better yet!" the pastor assured her. "I'll be praying for your parents, and I'll even come and visit them."

A few weeks later Pastor May did visit Jan's mom, and he asked her to come to church with her daughter.

"I don't need to," she said. "Jan comes home and preaches me the sermon every week."

"You're kidding!" Pastor May said.

"Oh, yes, she does!" her mother insisted. "I can tell you everything you preached last week." Then she started in and told him what Jan had told her. It was all there.

"Jan really wishes you'd come with her," Pastor May told her. "We'll be looking for you at church this next Sabbath."

Jan was so proud when the next Sabbath her mother walked in with her. After that her mother was always there, enjoying every minute of it.

"Now we've got to work on my dad," Jan reminded the pastor. And so he went to visit her dad, and the whole church began praying for Jan's father.

How do you suppose her father responded when the pastor visited? We'll find out tomorrow.

YOU WILL BE HIS WITNESS TO ALL PEOPLE. YOU WILL TELL THEM ABOUT THE THINGS YOU HAVE SEEN AND HEARD. ACTS 22:15, ICB.

CHOOSING FRIENDS

It's only natural to want to share such a wonderful friend as Jesus with those we love the most.

Jan's Father

JESUS LOOKED AT THEM AND SAID, "WITH MAN THIS IS IMPOSSIBLE, BUT WITH GOD ALL THINGS ARE POSSIBLE." MATTHEW 19:26, NIV.

CHOOSING FRIENDS

Jesus is the most powerful friend we'll ever have. He can do anything.

When Pastor May invited Marvin, Jan's father, to church, he leaned back in his chair and roared with laughter. "No way!" he said. "You'll never see me in church!"

Pastor May told the church members to pray for Marvin. "It's impossible to persuade him to come with Jan, but God can do anything."

One Sabbath when they sat down for lunch at home, Jan said, "Dad, we ought to pray before we eat. Can we do it?"

"No! I don't know how to pray. Forget it!"

"I don't mean you have to do it," Jan said. "I mean, can I do it? Will you let *me* pray?"

"Yeah, I guess it's OK if you want to," Marvin said. He kept his eyes open to see what Jan would do.

She stood up and bowed her head and closed her eyes. Then she thanked Jesus for the food, but she didn't stop. "Now, Lord, we've got a problem at this house, and it's my dad," Jan prayed. "He won't go to church, and he won't keep the Sabbath. He won't let the preacher talk to him, and he won't let You help him get rid of his bad habits."

Marvin gulped. He couldn't stand it. He got up and tiptoed to the bathroom and locked himself inside. He stood there and cried like a baby. When he got control of himself he went back to the table. Jan looked at him as if to say, "Boy, you are a tough case! You even leave the table during prayer."

The next Sabbath Marvin was in church, and then he disappeared. Jan and her mother got really worried when he didn't come home for several days.

On Friday morning Marvin showed up at Pastor May's house. "I went out and got drunk," he said. "I wanted to run away from God, but I can't. Please help me know how to become a Christian."

Jan's daddy went to church after that. He was baptized and was the head elder for many years.

Streetcar Encounter

Pastor F. B. Meyer got on a streetcar in north London and sat down in an empty seat. Opposite him sat a sad-faced elderly woman with a basket on her lap.

She's probably a cleaning woman on her way home from work, Pastor Meyer thought.

People began getting off. Soon he and the old woman were the only ones left. She spoke to him then. "Pastor Meyer?"

"Yes, may I help you?" he asked.

"I've been a widow for a long time," she began. "My only companion has been my crippled daughter. She was such a joy to me. Every day when I came home from work, she would welcome me. Every night in the darkness I could reach over and touch her. But she died, and I'm alone and miserable. I'm on my way home now, but it doesn't seem like home anymore, for she isn't there."

"The Lord will be there when you get home," Pastor Meyer said. "When you open the door, I want you to say out loud, 'Jesus, I'm home! I know You're here!' Then as you light the fire to fix supper, talk to Him about the happenings of the day. Talk to Him just as you used to talk to your daughter. Then at night in the darkness, reach out your hand and say, 'Jesus, I know You're here beside me.'"

The streetcar reached the end of the line, and the pastor and the widow got off, going different directions.

Several months later the pastor rode the same streetcar and was greeted cheerfully by a woman he didn't recognize.

"You don't remember me?" she asked. "I'm the woman who missed her crippled daughter so much. We talked in this same streetcar."

"Ah, yes!" he remembered. "And what happened?"

"I went home and said, 'Jesus, I know You're here!' and I kept saying it, and He's become my dear and constant companion. What a difference He's made in my life!"

THE LORD YOUR GOD IS GOING WITH YOU! DEUTERONOMY 20:4, TLB.

CHOOSING FRIENDS

Are you aware of Jesus' presence with you every moment of your day? Talk to Him. He's your Friend.

The Man With a Key

HE LIFTED ME OUT OF THE SLIMY PIT. PSALM 40:2, NIV.

CHOOSING FRIENDS

Jesus Christ, the powerful God of the universe, can help you with any problem you may face.

"Y ou must promise to stop preaching about Jesus," the chief Buddhist lama said sternly to the young man.

"I won't stop preaching to the people of Tibet," Sundar Singh declared.

"Throw him in the well!" the chief ordered.

His captors dragged him through the streets to a well with a heavy iron cover. They unlocked and removed the cover, pushing him over the edge. He landed on something slimy and soft. He heard the lid slide into place. He heard the turn of the key in the lock. He was in total darkness. The stench was unbearable. He felt around and realized that he was among the rotting bodies of dead men.

"Help me, God!" he screamed. "Don't let me die alone in this horrible place! But no matter what happens, I'll never turn my back on You!"

For two or three days Sundar lay in the slimy pit, often unconscious, overcome by hunger, thirst, and the stench of the rotting flesh.

Suddenly he was wide awake. Someone was putting a key in the lock. The person pulled away the lid, and fresh air rushed into the hole. Sundar could see stars shining brightly in the night sky. He could make out the form of a man.

"Hold fast to this rope," the man whispered.

Sundar grasped the rope and hung on tightly as the man pulled him slowly out of the well. When he reached the top, he sprawled on the cool ground, exhausted. When he finally was able to sit up, no one was there.

The lamas were amazed to find him preaching again in the marketplace. "Who set you free?" they asked.

"I don't know," Sundar answered. "I never saw his face."

"Someone must have stolen my key," the chief said. He lifted the ring of keys that hung on his belt. There hung the key to the well. He turned pale. "Your God is terrible and powerful," he said. "Go away lest harm come to us!"

The Mysterious Night Rider

The Buffalo Flyer, PG-16, raced along the rails through the mountains of eastern Pennsylvania. A full moon lit up the countryside almost as bright as day. Bill Henry, the engineer, had his hand on the throttle, and Hank, the fireman, was shoveling coal into the roaring fire.

Suddenly in the light of the moon Bill saw a man walk calmly up from the cowcatcher in front of the locomotive and swing up onto the steam boiler. With his left hand he held the handrail; with his right hand he gave the signal for a caution stop.

Bill noticed that the man was well-dressed in a light-gray suit and a soft fedora hat. "Hank," he said, "do you see that man in gray out there?"

"Yeah! I see him," he said. "Must be a bum catchin' a ride."

Bill watched as the man in gray stepped onto the running board that led from the front of the engine back to the cab. He turned his face then. Bill noticed he had a brown mustache. He also noticed that though the train was going at full speed, the man's clothes were not ruffled. The man took a step closer and signaled an emergency stop.

Bill released the throttle and put on the brakes, and the express train came to a grinding halt.

The flagmen jumped out. The man in front had gone only about 150 feet when he saw a gaping hole where the tracks should have been. "Cave-in!" he shouted.

The crew rushed to see the big hole. Suddenly Bill realized that they might all have died had it not been for the man in gray. He wanted to ask his name, but he was gone!

Though they tried to locate the man in gray, he was never found. The mysterious night signaler had disappeared as strangely as he had come.

Bill Henry had his own opinion about the man in gray. He figured that night he had a messenger from heaven riding on his train.

DEC. 21

FOR HE ORDERS HIS ANGELS TO PROTECT YOU WHEREVER YOU GO. PSALM 91:11, TLB.

CHOOSING FRIENDS

Can you relate an experience you have had when you felt pretty sure an angel was sent to help you?

The Unknown Horseman

CHOOSING FRIENDS

Our guardian angels are powerful friends sent from heaven to help us in time of need.

George Mathews had worked all summer selling books to earn money for school. At the end of the summer he borrowed a horse and wagon to make his deliveries.

All was going well, until it began to rain. It rained day and night for several days. Travel in the mud was treacherous. Then George came to what had been a trickling brook he could jump across. Now it was a raging, roaring river 100 feet across.

What am I going to do now? George pondered. *If I take the long way around over the nearest bridge, it will be 14 miles to the houses just across the river. I'll waste a whole day! I guess I'll drive through it.*

George urged the horses forward into the swirling waters. Halfway across they were caught in a strong current that swept them swiftly downstream. The horses fought to keep their noses above water.

"Lord, please save me!" George cried.

Suddenly the wagon came to a stop, caught on a large rock. The horses struggled to keep afloat. It began to rain again, and there seemed no way out.

"Help, Lord! We can't hold out much longer!" George prayed.

Just then someone shouted from the opposite bank, "Need some help?"

George opened his eyes to see a man on a gray horse with a rope coiled around the saddle horn.

"Yes! Please!"

George caught the end of the rope the man threw to him and fastened it around the wagon tongue. The horse on the bank pulled them free, and George was soon safe on the opposite shore.

"You saved my life!" George exclaimed. "Thank you so much."

"Glad to help," the man said and was gone.

At the first shelter George opened the boxes and found all the books dry, even though they'd been covered with water. At every house he told the story of his rescue, but no one knew the man on the gray horse.

Was I saved by an angel? George wondered.

Kata Ragoso

ou will do as I say!" the officer commanded.

"No, sir, I cannot," Kata Ragoso replied. "My religion and my conscience will not allow me to obey you."

The officer hit Kata Ragoso in the head with his revolver, beating him until he was unconscious. When he revived, the officer ordered him to stand against a tree. A firing squad took their places not far away, all guns pointed at the disobedient man. The soldiers had their fingers on their triggers.

"When I say three, all of you fire!" the officer barked. "Ready? One. Two . . ." Somehow he couldn't say the word three.

So he tried again. "One. Two . . ."

Frustrated, he tried a third time, but again couldn't get past two. As hard as he tried, his jaws seemed locked when he wanted to say the word three.

"Never mind," the officer said at last. "Lock him up!"

Hearing of Kata Ragoso's imprisonment, the Adventist believers in that area gathered for a prayer meeting just as the moon came up that night about 10:00. At about the same time a tall man carrying a bunch of keys strode to the prison gate and unlocked it. "Follow me," he said to Kata Ragoso.

Kata Ragoso followed the tall man along a path that led to the sea. At the edge of the beach the man spoke again. "There's a canoe. Take it and go home."

Kata Ragoso walked to the water's edge and found the canoe. He turned to thank the man with the keys. No one was there.

Kata Ragoso's disappearance caused great consternation among the prison officials. An investigation proved that the original bunch of keys had been on the peg in full sight of the sentry all night. The sentry had seen no one enter the prison or leave. Yet in the morning Kata Ragoso wasn't there.

The sentry had no explanation. They could have asked Kata Ragoso. He knew who it was.

I KNOW WITHOUT A DOUBT THAT THE LORD SENT HIS ANGEL AND RESCUED ME. ACTS 12:11, NIV.

CHOOSING FRIENDS

Did you know that God has appointed one of the powerful angels of heaven to be your constant companion and friend? Why not thank Him today for His gift of a guardian angel?

The Sabbath Potatoes

DEC. 24

CONTEND, O LORD, WITH THOSE WHO CONTEND WITH ME; FIGHT AGAINST THOSE WHO FIGHT AGAINST ME. PSALM 35:1, NIV.

CHOOSING FRIENDS

Some battles are too hard for us to fight. It's then we need to turn to our Friend Jesus to fight on our behalf.

The sun was just about to set on Friday evening. The children, freshly bathed, gathered around Annette at the piano. They began singing, "'Day is dying in the west; heaven is touching earth with rest; wait and worship . . .'"

"Get out to that potato field!" Joe's booming voice brought a halt to the singing. The children stared at their angry father, who stood in the doorway, hands on his hips, scowling. "Every one of you youngsters go right now and drop potatoes."

"Oh, please, Joe, they're all bathed and ready for Sabbath," Annette pleaded.

"That's your problem!" Joe snapped. "I never said they could stop work! Make it snappy, kids."

The children looked helplessly to their mother, then followed their father to the potato field.

Bitter tears ran down Annette's cheeks as she cried out in desperation to God, "Lord, curse those potatoes!"

A few weeks later it was celery-planting time. Again Joe interrupted evening worship to make the children plant celery. Again Annette prayed in frustration, "Lord, curse every row of celery the children are forced to plant on Sabbath. Show my children Your power!"

A few weeks later when her husband and children were gone to town, Annette went out to the potato field and checked the rows the children had been forced to plant on Sabbath. She probed around the roots of first one plant and then another. There were no potato balls! She tried other rows that hadn't been planted on Sabbath. There were plenty of potatoes. She could hardly wait to share the secret with her children!

As the celery matured, something strange began to happen. The children noticed. They ran in one day, shouting, "Mother, come look at the Sabbath celery! Every row we planted on Sabbath is turning yellow and withering, while the other rows are green and beautiful."

Annette smiled and looked to heaven. "Thank You, Lord!" she prayed. "What a powerful friend You are!"

Christmas Courage

It was Christmas Eve in Meath Park, Saskatchewan. Archie Shipowick sat with his father, Samuel, and younger brother, Roman, talking after supper. Suddenly Samuel stood. "Just remembered something," he said, disappearing into the bedroom. He came back with an unopened bottle of vodka.

He uncorked the bottle and filled three glasses. He pushed two across the table toward Roman and Archie. "It's Christmas," he said. "Let's have a drink!"

Archie made no move to pick up his glass. He swallowed twice then cleared his throat.

"Come on, boys, drink!" Samuel commanded, lifting his glass.

"I don't drink this stuff anymore," Archie said.

Samuel was angry. He'd offered a glass of liquor to his sons, as was the custom for Russian fathers to do on Christmas Eve, and Archie had refused. "Why not?" he asked.

Archie groped for words to explain his conversion experience and his new friendship with God.

"Archie has become a *Sabotnik* [Sabbath keeper]," Roman said.

"So you think you're better than the rest of us?" Samuel's face contorted in rage. "Sabotnik! Bah! You've disgraced the family!" He strode to the back porch and came back with an ax. He lunged at Archie. "You're no son of mine!"

"No, Papa!" Roman screamed, grabbing his father's arm; the ax fell to the floor.

"Get out of here! Both of you!" Samuel ordered.

Hurriedly Roman and Archie put on their boots and parkas and went out into the starlit night, leaving Samuel standing in the middle of the kitchen floor, the ax at his feet.

"You could have taken a sip or two to please Papa," Roman said after a few moments of silence. "Couldn't you have done that much on Christmas Eve to make the old man happy? What difference would it make?"

"Had I done that, I would have been hurting my heavenly Father," Archie explained. "I had to choose. I couldn't please them both. I love Papa, but I love God more."

ANYONE WHO LOVES HIS FATHER OR MOTHER MORE THAN ME IS NOT WORTHY OF ME. MATTHEW 10:37, NIV.

CHOOSING FRIENDS

If we love God, then we'll want to please Him more than we want to please any other friend.

Miracle River

EVERYTHING IS POSSIBLE FOR HIM WHO BELIEVES. MARK 9:23, NIV.

CHOOSING FRIENDS

We can never find a friend so mighty as Jesus Christ, who does exciting, marvelous things in answer to prayer.

A crowd gathered on the banks of the Vaipparru River in south India. Not that you could really call it a river, for there was simply a dry riverbed.

Here and there village women in their bright-colored saris squatted by stagnant pools of water, beating out their clothes on the rocks. A few goats roamed the riverbed looking for bits of grass. It hadn't rained for several months.

All night a group of Adventists had been praying for rain. Now it was morning, and no rain had come. Pastor Manual Mannasseh went outside and scanned the sky for some sign, but not a cloud was in sight. A slight breeze ruffled the tops of the palm trees and stirred up small whirlwinds of dust and dry leaves.

"Come, Paulraj and Meeran, you can help me find a place for the baptism," Pastor Mannasseh called to two boys playing nearby. "Get your shovels and come down to the riverbed. Perhaps we can deepen one of the stagnant pools enough for the baptism."

Seven-year-old Paulraj and 12-year-old Meeran ran off to get shovels. They joined Pastor Mannasseh at a small ankle-deep pool. They began to dig, but it didn't make much difference.

A crowd began gathering for the baptism. "Please, dear Lord, unless You do something, there will be no baptism today," Pastor Mannasseh prayed. "There isn't enough water here to immerse a small child, let alone all of these adults. Please, Jesus, I know You can do anything. I'm trusting in You."

Suddenly he heard a shout from the bank of the river. "Water! Run for your lives!"

Paulraj and Meeran looked up to see a large wall of water rushing toward them down the riverbed. Dropping their shovels, they ran for the safety of the bank. No sooner had they reached the bank than the water was upon them, flooding the river to the banks.

"It is a miracle!" the people said.

Night Guard

"Our chief is dead! Our chief is dead!" the mountain people wailed. "Who has killed our chief?"

"It must be that Christian teacher at Maibikee," the medicine man declared. "I'll put a spell on Faole and all the people in his village. We must go there tonight and kill everyone in the village and burn the church and school, or worse things may happen to our people."

That night 50 warriors took their spears and arrows and set out to destroy Faole and all the Christians in Maibikee, Papua New Guinea. One man who didn't agree with the plan ran many miles across the mountains to the coast, where a missionary lived. The missionary started out at once to see what he could do to help Faole. However, it would take him several days to get there.

Meanwhile in Maibikee, Faole felt uneasy. He sensed that something was going to happen that night. He gathered his family around him and opened his Bible to Psalm 34:7 and read: "'The angel of the Lord encampeth round about them that fear him, and delivereth them.'"

"We have nothing to fear," he said. "God will take care of us. Let's go to bed and sleep."

While the people of Maibikee slept, the 50 warriors arrived, but they were surprised to see a line of guards dressed in white, standing around the village. The warriors waited all night, and since they were far outnumbered by the guards, they went home.

When the missionary got there two days later, all was peaceful and Faole was alive and well. "There's been no problem," he said. "Whatever it was, the Lord has taken care of it."

The missionary then went to the village where the chief had died. "Did you go to Maibikee to kill Faole?" he asked.

"Yes," the headman answered, "but we couldn't do it."

"Why not?"

"You know very well," the headman said angrily. "You were there with an army of white-clad soldiers protecting the village."

IF GOD BE FOR US, WHO CAN BE AGAINST US? ROMANS 8:31.

CHOOSING FRIENDS

When we choose Jesus as our Friend, we have the whole army of heaven on our side!

The Tornado

He ALONE IS MY
REFUGE, MY
PLACE OF SAFETY.
PSALM 91:2,
TLB.

CHOOSING FRIENDS

Ask several
people you know
to relate an
experience when
God protected
them from danger.
Share your stories
for family wor-
ship. Discuss the
question: Does
God always
protect the
property of
Christians?

It had been a rather boring Sabbath afternoon. The Mutu family of New Zealand was stuck inside because of a storm.

"Time for worship," Father said at last. The family gathered around and knelt for prayer. All the while the storm gathered in intensity.

After prayer the boys jumped to their feet and ran to the window. Suddenly all boredom was gone. Not far away the roof of a building was going up and down. An open door banged on its hinges. A fierce wind whipped the trees.

"The building is going to explode," one of the boys shouted.

Dad's face turned pale. *If that building blows up, the wind will bring pieces of it toward our house!* he thought.

"Maybe the wind is getting in through the open door," one of the boys suggested. "Maybe if we shut it we could save the building."

"OK, come with me," he said, nodding to the two older boys. They fought their way against the gale force winds and managed to shut the door and make it back inside their house.

"There's the funnel!" someone yelled. They watched as it twirled down out of the gray sky and touched the building, exploding it into a million pieces. Large pieces headed straight for their house. Some hit the electric wires, sending up showers of sparks that lit up the whole yard. It was better than fireworks!

"Will our house blow up too?" someone asked.

"We'll just have to wait and trust the Lord," Father said. "There's nothing much we can do but pray."

Suddenly all was quiet. The storm had passed. The funnel was gone. The boys raced outside to see the mess it had made. Heaps of twisted metal lay around their house. Broken boards were scattered everywhere. A huge chunk of wall had landed three feet away from their house.

"Thank the Lord, none of us was hurt!" Father said.

That was one Sabbath the Mutu family wouldn't soon forget!

Invisible Friend

It was a warm spring day. Tulips and daffodils bloomed along the walks at Princeton Theological Seminary. Stanley Soltau breathed deeply the scent of new-mown grass and growing things. It was definitely not a day to be stuck inside a stuffy room, listening to a boring lecture.

At the steps to Miller Chapel he stopped and turned to his friend, Arch Campbell. "Arch," he said, "what do you say we skip the meeting tonight and go to my room and talk. We've not missed one of these Tuesday night meetings all year, so it won't hurt if we sit this one out."

"OK by me," Arch agreed. "I'm in no mood for a meeting myself."

They turned to go, but Stanley hesitated. It didn't seem right somehow. Something within him said, *Better not miss tonight. Why break your good record? Besides, you should set a good example to Arch. You're a senior, and he's a junior. Better go inside.*

"Wait a minute, Arch," Stanley said. "I've changed my mind. Perhaps we ought to go in after all, but let's sit in the back row so that we can leave if it gets boring."

By the time the two reached the chapel, the meeting had already started. The room was packed. They were standing for the opening song as the boys made their way up the aisle, searching for two seats. They found them at last, down near the front, under the eyes of Professor Warfield.

The professor nodded to the two boys, and Stanley knew they'd have no chance of escaping this meeting. He sighed and resigned himself to stay.

The speaker was a missionary from Korea. Suddenly, as the man spoke of the needs of people who didn't know Jesus Christ, Stanley knew the Lord was calling him to Korea.

He thought, *Wow! The Holy Spirit knew I needed to be in this meeting. That's why He brought me in, even when I wasn't planning to come. I'm glad I listened. I'm glad I came.*

THE TRUE CHILDREN OF GOD ARE THOSE WHO LET GOD'S SPIRIT LEAD THEM. ROMANS 8:14, ICB.

CHOOSING FRIENDS

The Holy Spirit is our friend too, speaking quietly to our hearts, nudging us in the way we should go.

Friends Forever

WE WHO ARE STILL ALIVE AND ARE LEFT WILL BE CAUGHT UP TOGETHER WITH THEM IN THE CLOUDS TO MEET THE LORD IN THE AIR. AND SO WE WILL BE WITH THE LORD FOREVER. 1 THESSALONIANS 4:17, NIV.

CHOOSING FRIENDS

Forever friends are the best kind! Can you name three forever friends you plan to meet in heaven?

Twenty-seven teenagers were on the bus headed down the steep mountain highway from Hog Pen Gap, Georgia. The driver pressed on the brakes to slow their descent. Nothing happened. He pressed harder. Nothing. There was no way to stop the speeding bus. It hurtled down the mountain faster and faster.

The tires screeched around the first curve. He tried to downshift. The gear wouldn't budge. Frantically he tried the hand brake. Nothing worked!

"Get down on the floor!" he yelled. Another curve was just ahead. He leaned into the wall of the cliff, hoping to slow the bus. It sent the bus spinning across the highway and crashing into the guardrail. It flew into the air, then rolled down the mountainside.

When the rescue workers arrived, they were amazed to find only one person dead, 14-year-old Angela Jones. Many were injured. One girl was unconscious, with a broken neck.

When the girl with the broken neck was released from the hospital, many of her friends were there to welcome her home. A reporter interviewed several of them. "Are the parents who lost their daughter in the accident here today?" she asked a young man on crutches.

"No," he said. "But I know them well. I don't think they'd say they've lost their daughter at all."

"What do you mean?" The reporter was puzzled.

"Angela isn't lost. They know where she is. They plan to see her again someday in heaven. You know, this is how we are all getting through this—knowing we'll definitely be with Angie again!"

One of the best things about having Christian friends is that you can have them forever!

Accidents happen. Death steals away good friends. But when Jesus comes we'll be reunited with those we love!

Friends move thousands of miles away. We may never get together again on this earth. But when Jesus comes, we can be together for eternity! What a party that will be!

Powerful Friendships Checkup

Rate yourself in forming friendships that will last for eternity.

1. I think carefully about suggestions my friends give to make sure I want to follow them.
Never   Sometimes   Usually   Always

2. I do what I believe to be right regardless of how my friends feel about it.
Never   Sometimes   Usually   Always

3. I'm able to handle peer pressure, refusing to allow it to influence my decisions.
Never   Sometimes   Usually   Always

4. I talk over my friendships with God, asking Him to guide me to the people who will be best for me.
Never   Sometimes   Usually   Always

5. I say no to friends who offer me alcohol, drugs, or tobacco.
Never   Sometimes   Usually   Always

6. I'm willing to break up a friendship if I find that it's wise to do so.
Never   Sometimes   Usually   Always

7. I appreciate the sacrifice Jesus made on the cross for me, and I want to be His friend.
Never   Sometimes   Usually   Always

8. I find it easy to talk to my friends about Jesus. I want to share what He has done for me.
Never   Sometimes   Usually   Always

9. I'm aware of the presence of Jesus with me. I often talk to Him about what's going on in my life.
Never   Sometimes   Usually   Always

10. I'm aware that my guardian angel is a powerful friend who is with me wherever I go.
Never   Sometimes   Usually   Always

11. I trust Jesus to fight my battles for me, believing that He will do what's best for me.
Never   Sometimes   Usually   Always

12. I listen to the voice of the Holy Spirit as He tries to lead me in the right path.
Never   Sometimes   Usually   Always

13. I look forward to heaven, where I'll be able to have a great reunion with all my forever friends.
Never   Sometimes   Usually   Always

DEC. 31

**TEST EVERYTHING. HOLD ON TO THE GOOD. AVOID EVERY KIND OF EVIL.
1 THESSALONIANS 5:21, 22, NIV.**

SCRIPTURE INDEX

SCRIPTURE INDEX

SCRIPTURE INDEX

SCRIPTURE INDEX

SCRIPTURE INDEX